GRAPEVINE

Anthony Rose is the wine correspondent of the *Independent*. He won the Glenfiddich Drink Writer of the Year Award in 1994, and the Wine Guild of the United Kingdom's Wine Columnist of the Year Award in 1988, 1989 and 1993 as well as its trophy in 1993. He has judged wine competitions in Australia, South Africa, France, New Zealand and the United States as well as the UK and contributes to *Decanter, Wine, Wine & Spirit* and *L'Officiel des Grands Vins*. He has also contributed to the *Oxford Companion to Wine*, the *Harrods Book of Wine* and sundry other publications.

A former deputy editor of *Wine* and editor of *Wine & Spirit*, **Tim Atkin** is the wine correspondent of the *Observer*. He also writes for *Wine, Wine & Spirit* and *Saveur*. He won the Glenfiddich Drink Writer of the Year Award in 1988, 1990 and 1993 and was the Wine Guild of the United Kingdom's Wine Columnist of the Year in 1991, 1992 and 1994. In 1994, he was the first recipient of the Wines of France Award. He has contributed to a number of.books on wine as well as publishing two of his own – *Chardonnay* and *Vin de Pays d'Oc*. He is a regular member of *Wine* magazine's tasting panels and has judged wine competitions in the UK, France and Australia.

Reviews of the 1995 Edition

'A great read, sound judgments and common sense clothed in racy language. Should please anyone interested enough in wine to read more than a newspaper article'
Which? Wine Monthly

'The most reliable and enjoyable buyers' guide to high street wines (including across the Channel)'
Sunday Times

'The best book of its type and certainly the most engagingly written'
Yorkshire Post

'*Superplonk* . . . is neither as reliable nor as helpful as *Grapevine*'
Sunday Express

'The best of where-to-buy-bargain booze guides'
Time Out

Reviews of the 1994 Edition

'Objective, contentious and helpful, Rose and Atkin give praise where it is due, but also dish out some pithily devastating criticisms'
Off-Licence News

'It's worth buying *Grapevine* just for the detailed critique of each store's buying policy and personnel, which leaves one or two well-aimed dents in immaculate reputations. Wonderfully judgmental'   *Scotland on Sunday*

'Articulate and opinionated'
Sunday Express

'The breadth of selection is impressive and the comments on each wine succinct'
Financial Times

'Accurate, up-to-the-minute, stylishly written and, though aimed at the consumer, makes useful and easy reading for people in the hospitality industry who wish to take the pulse of the market'   *Caterer & Hotelkeeper*

'A brilliant value book, this one is for the serious armchair shopping-spree planner. Study this, and your supermarket trolley need hardly touch the floor!'
Hampstead & Highgate Express

Grapevine

The Complete
Wine Buyer's Handbook
1996 Edition

Anthony Rose and Tim Atkin

HEADLINE

For George, Jane and Tom Entwistle, two of whom
already know that it's worth paying a little bit extra,
and one of whom will find out soon enough

First published in 1995 by
HEADLINE BOOK PUBLISHING

10 9 8 7 6 5 4 3 2

ISBN 0 7472 4722 6

Typeset by Avon Dataset Ltd, Bidford-on-Avon, B50 4JH

Printed and bound in Great Britain by
Cox & Wyman Ltd, Reading, Berks

HEADLINE BOOK PUBLISHING
A division of Hodder Headline PLC
338 Euston Road
London NW1 3BH

CONTENTS

ACKNOWLEDGEMENTS

Like its predecessors, this completely new edition of *Grapevine* could only have been written with the help of a large number of indulgent wine buyers and PRs, who organised extensive tailor-made tastings, checked the answers to our endless flow of questions and faxes and submitted themselves for the annual *Grapevine* inquisition.

Our thanks to the following people in Britain: at Asda: Nick Dymoke-Marr, Alistair Morrell, Illy Jaffar and Alan Crompton-Batt; at Budgens: Annie Todd and Tony Finnerty; at the Co-op: Master of Wine Arabella Woodrow and Paul Bastard; at Davisons: Michael Davies; at Fuller's: Roger Higgs and Sophie Knight; at Greenalls Cellars: Nader Haghighi, Kevin Wilson and David Vaughan; at Kwik Save: Master of Wine Angela Muir and Deborah Williams; at Majestic Wine Warehouses: Debbie Worton, Tony Mason and Sarah 'Icecube' Wykes; at Marks & Spencer: Jane Kay, Viv Jawett, Chris Murphy and Helen Long; at Morrison's: Stuart Purdie; at Oddbins: Katie MacAulay, Karen Wise and Steve Daniel; at Safeway: Master of Wine Liz Robertson and Nicki Dallison; at Sainsbury's: Diane Lamb, Master of Wine Claire Gordon Brown and Allan Cheesman; at Somerfield/Gateway: Angela Mount and Lewis Morton; at Spar: Liz Aked; at Tesco: Janet Lee, Anne-Marie Bostock and Trevor Dedman; at Thresher, Wine Rack and Bottoms Up: Kim Tidy, Julian Twaites, Jon Woodriffe, Lucy Warner, David Howse and David McDonnell; at Unwins: Bill Rolfe and Jim Wilson; at Victoria Wine: Nicola Harvey, Joanne Convert, Rosemary Neal, Mark Davies and Graham Maguire; and at Waitrose (John Lewis): Masters of Wine Julian Brind and Dee Blackstock, Evelyn Strouts and Paul Stacey.

And from the independent wine merchants: at Adnams: Simon Loftus, Bruce Kendrick and Alastair Marshall; at the Australian Wine Club: Masters of Strine Craig Smith, Phil Reedman and Mark Manson; at Averys: Michael Peace and Master of Wine John Avery; at Berry Brothers & Rudd: Nick Wright; at Bibendum: Willie 'Svensson' Lebus,

Simon Farr and Rosalia Vergera; at Eldridge Pope: Masters of Wine Robin Kinahan and Joe Naughalty, and Sue Longman; at Enotria Winecellars: Master of Wine David Gleave, Robin Davis and Monique Reedman; at Justerini & Brooks: Hew Blair and R. Williams; at Lay & Wheeler: Master of Wine Hugo 'That's R-O-S-E' Rose; at Lea & Sandeman: Charles Lea and Patrick Sandeman; at Tanners: James Tanner, Rebecca Trickey and Richard Tanner; at Thomas Peatling: Master of Wine Robin Crameri and Peter Limmer.

And for help with our cross-Channel chapter: at The Grape Shop: Katrina Thom; at La Maison du Vin: Master of Wine Richard Harvey; at The Wine Society: Julie Stock and Marcel Orford-Williams.

At Headline, our thanks to Ian Marshall, who once again edited the book at his characteristic canter, Nicky Grimbly, Claire Scott and Alan Brooke. Back in Colliers Wood, Lyn Parry once again pulled the book together in the last week and Susana Fernández stayed out all night at parties. Mary Ensor and Samuel Rose provided tea, coffee, badminton and printer paper. And lastly, a thank you to our agents Fiona Lindsay and Linda Shanks at Limelight Management.

It goes without saying that none of the above bears any responsibility for the opinions, comments and tasting notes which follow. Just as well, really.

HOW TO USE *GRAPEVINE*

Our marks need to be looked at in the context of their accompanying tasting note. It's also important to remember that wine changes and develops in bottle – for better or worse. Scores are not immutable or definitive. Every wine has its own intrinsic qualities and, by definition, our comments are subjective. With two palates to consider each wine, we hope to eliminate some of our individual prejudices. Nevertheless, just because we like something, it doesn't mean you have to, and vice versa. If tastes were uniform, we might as well pour a few samples into a computer, give you the print-out and go home.

Wines are divided into four price brackets in the UK:
Under £3
£3–5
£5–8
Over £8

and four in France:
Under 20 francs
20–30 francs
30–50 francs
Over 50 francs

Where a wine costs over £8 or 50 francs, we try to give a further indication of its price in the note. There is, after all, a big difference between something which retails at £8.49 and something which weighs in at £30.

We have made every effort to ensure that the wines we list are available, although some may be out of stock. By tasting in a concentrated three-month period, we aim to be as up-to-date as possible. Prices may also vary.

Grapevine's symbols

The symbols and numbers used in *Grapevine* work as follows:

QUALITY

20	Nirvana
19	The suburbs of Nirvana
18	Truly outstanding
17	World-class
16	Excellent
15	Very good
14	Good everyday drinking
13	Everyday drinking
12	Drinkable (occasionally with a peg over your nose)
11	Almost drinkable
10	Almost undrinkable

9 and below Faulty or plain disgusting

VALUE FOR MONEY

£££	Superb value
££	Good value
£	Fair value
0	Poor value

Unlike other guides, we score on quality as well as value for money. Hence it is perfectly possible for a wine to score 17 and £ or 14 and £££. Wines scoring 17 or more appear in bold for ease of reference. We also rate wines according to sweetness (for whites, sparkling wines and rosés) and weight (for reds and fortifieds), as well as drinkability:

SWEETNESS (WHITES AND ROSÉS):

1	Bone dry
2	Dry
3	Off-dry
4	Medium dry
5	Medium sweet
6	Sweet
7	Very sweet
8	Exceptionally sweet
9	Time to call the dentist

FB   Full-bodied
MB   Medium-bodied
LB   Light-bodied

DRINKABILITY

♪   Drink now
►   Drink now or keep
↑   Past it

STAR RATINGS:

Each of the chains in this guide is given a star rating out of five. These range from two stars, represented as **, to five, or *****. This year, only Oddbins Fine Wine shops achieved the full five-star rating. We have chosen not to give star ratings to the independent wine merchants, as they are already our selection of the best specialists.

HOW WE TASTE

We taste later and more thoroughly than any other guide. All the wines listed in this book were sampled between June and August 1995. At every outlet we ask to look at the top ten best-selling wines as well as a representative range from the chain's main list. In every case, this includes wines under £5, as well as more expensive fare.

We also visit and interview every retailer in person, whether it be in France or the UK. It goes without saying that we are both independent judges. We do not write for, work for, blend wines for or accept advertising or funding from retailers. Above all else, we are consumers and journalists.

Another special feature of *Grapevine* is that we include wines we don't like, as well as those we do. We believe that a critic's job is to criticise constructively, pointing out the bad as well as the good. Apart from providing a few laughs, this has a positive result: several wines that we trashed in last year's guide have not reappeared in 1996.

We try not to overdo it, though. Many of the poorest wines we tasted are not listed. We see it as our role to throw out some of the truly awful bottles. Where we've left them in, they tend to be popular wines, top ten best-sellers or things with an undeservedly inflated reputation.

We aim not to go over the top in our descriptions or become entangled in the wayward tendrils of the vine. We try to give you enough information to make the wine sound interesting – or not, on occasion. But more than that, we have no desire to dictate what you should enjoy. Happy drinking.

THE 1996 *GRAPEVINE* AWARDS

Wine Retailer of the Year: Bottoms Up
For enthusiastically extending and enhancing the quality of what the high street has to offer and proving that an off-licence chain can thrive without taking the downmarket route.

Most Improved Chain of the Year: Fuller's
For creating a wine range which matches the quality of its award-winning ales and demonstrating that a small, family-owned regional chain can compete with the biceps of the big boys.

Cross-Channel Wine Retailer of the Year: Tesco
For its audacious move in opening Europe's largest off-licence within the Cité de l'Europe complex and stocking not only the full Tesco range, but some well-selected additions too.

Independent Wine Merchant of the Year: Tanner's
For epitomising the best of what the traditional country wine merchant has to offer: good service, an extensive wine range at different price levels and an informative and well-written list.

Winemaker of the Year: Ignacio Recabarren
For raising the profile of Chile on the international market through a combination of dynamism, personality and winemaking talent.

GRAPEVINE'S WINES OF THE YEAR

This year, we have selected four cases of the year: red, white, and sparkling from the high street and cross-Channel stores, and one from the independent merchants. These are 48 wines that we think represent a variety of characterful, value-for-money drinking. There are plenty of other outstanding wines in the pages that follow, but we have picked these particular bottles for their combination of quality and availability. Stockists are listed after each wine.

Apart from the sparkling wines, most of our wines, independents excepted, cost less than £5. Most score 16 or more for quality and £££ for value for money. Where they score slightly less, it tends to be because they are inexpensive. A wine which gets 15 and £££ and sits on the shelf at £2.99 is arguably worthy of greater recognition than a £20 claret or red Burgundy.

WHITE WINES OF THE YEAR CASE

1994 Lenz Moser Grüner Veltliner

Crisp, inexpensive Austrian white, made from the widely planted native Grüner Veltliner grape by one of Central Europe's best known producers, and showing white pepper aromas and fresh, lemony fruitiness. Great value at around £3.50.

Stockists: Tesco, The Thresher Group (see pages 323 and 350).

1994 Bright Brothers Fernão Pires/Chardonnay, Ribatejo

The Fernão Pires grape variety is one of the most interesting of an impressive array of indigenous Portuguese grapes. Australia's Peter Bright has done a great deal to popularise this undervalued variety. Here he combines it nicely with the internationally acclaimed Chardonnay grape, adding a touch of oak to create an intensely flavoured dry white with a note of orange peel zest.

Stockists: Safeway, Victoria Wine (see pages 247 and 394).

1994 Muscaté Sec, Alasia, Vino da Tavola

Made by the original flying winemaker, Australian Martin Shaw working in Piemonte's Monferrato hills, this is an aromatic ginger and grapefruit-like dry white with excellent weight and length of flavour.

Stockist: The Thresher Group (see page 353).

1994 Rawsons Retreat Penfolds Bin 21 Semillon/Chardonnay

A good example of the new-style Penfolds whites. With its spicy vanilla oak, herby Semillon and Chardonnay richness, these two grapes combine harmoniously to produce a sundae of vanilla ice cream and lemony fruit.

Stockists: Asda, Fuller's, Greenalls Cellars, Morrison's, Oddbins, Somerfield, The Thresher Group, Victoria Wine (see pages 32, 90, 109, 189, 217, 296, 349 and 391).

1994 Caliterra Casablanca Chardonnay

Star winemaker Ignacio Recabarren has produced a brilliant value Chardonnay from Chile's most exciting white wine area, the Casablanca Valley, halfway between Santiago and the port of Valparaiso. Fresh, clean-cut, citrus-fruit flavours with a grapefruity tang and a touch of oak.

Stockists: Co-op, Fuller's, Oddbins, Tesco (see pages 62, 91, 218 and 324).

1994 Viognier Domaine de Mandeville, Vin de Pays d'Oc, Olivier de Mandeville

One of the best value Viogniers we've come across, this is a pungently aromatic, ripe, apricoty, unoaked dry white with masses of flavour, freshness and balance. Producers of Condrieu, look to your laurels.
Stockist: Marks & Spencer (see page 170).

1994 Canepa Oak Aged Semillon

One of winemaker Andres Ilabaca's most successful whites, this is a French oak-aged Semillon from Chile's Maipo Valley, showing oatmealy, full-bodied flavours of vanilla and lemon meringue. One of the best white wines we've tasted from Chile.
Stockist: Victoria Wine (see page 392).

1994 Vermentino di Sardegna, Sella & Mosca

Made by Italian Mario Consorte, this is a fresh, appealingly aromatic, delicately pine-scented Sardinian white, showing the benefits of new technology and stainless steel fermentation. With its crisp acidity and lemony tang, this is an outstanding example of Sardinia's near-native white Vermentino grape.
Stockist: Oddbins (see page 220).

1994 Viña Calera, Sauvignon Blanc, Rueda

A wine which proves that flying winemakers can produce more than basic styles, this is a beautifully fresh, lemon, gooseberry and melon scented Sauvignon Blanc made in Rueda, Spain, by Hugh Ryman in conjunction with Rioja's Marqués de Riscal.
Stockist: The Thresher Group (see page 354).

1994 Château Terres Douces, Cuvée Prestige

Made by the *négociant* house of Ginestet, this is a superb Graves-style white Bordeaux, with toasty new oak flavours, plenty of Semillon weight and waxiness, and a crisp, lingering aftertaste.
Stockists: Victoria Wine Cellars, Waitrose (see pages 396 and 420).

1993 Josephshöfer Riesling Kabinett, Von Kesselstatt

From Annegret Reh-Gartner's best vineyard in the Mosel Valley, this is a beautifully perfumed, violet-scented Riesling with typical Mosel green apple bite and spicy depth of fruit flavour. Von Kesselstatt is building a deservedly high reputation in this country for its outstanding Rieslings. *Stockist:* Oddbins (see page 223).

1994 Samuels Bay Riesling, South East Australia

After appearing at a ludicrously inflated price last year, Samuels Bay Riesling is now available at a more reasonable £6 a bottle. Not that there was ever anything wrong with the wine, as this follow-on vintage demonstrates. It's an aromatic, almost cassis-scented, refreshing style made from a blend of Coonawarra and Eden Valley grapes. *Stockists:* Bottoms Up, Wine Rack (see page 355).

RED WINES OF THE YEAR CASE

1994 Vintage Première, Cabernet Sauvignon, Iambol Region
An exuberant Bulgarian red with chunky, fresh, blackcurrant fruit
flavours unencumbered by the sort of drying oak that often mars the
more old-fashioned style of Eastern European red. Even better value than
the same company's Merlot.
Stockist: The Thresher Group (see page 361).

1994 Grenache, Peter Lehmann
Rich, alcoholic, vibrantly fruity Aussie red made by Barossa Valley
specialist Peter Lehmann. It's an unashamedly gluggable, strawberryish
red which shoves most Beaujolais into the nearest corked hat.
Stockists: Davison's, Fuller's, Greenalls Cellars (see pages 80, 97 and 116).

1994 Negroamaro del Salento, Kym Milne
A southern Italian red showing the aromatic spice and juicy Mediterranean
fruit of Puglia's Negroamaro grape. It's nice to see flying winemaker Kym
Milne making the most of a local, albeit under-appreciated variety.
Stockist: Majestic Wine Warehouses (see page 153).

1993 Chais Baumière Cabernet Sauvignon, Vin de Pays d'Oc
One of a number of successful reds from BRL-Hardy's French base at
Domaine de la Baume, showing grassy softness of fruit, good concentration
and backbone.
Stockist: Sainsbury's (see page 282).

1993 Château Haut d'Allard, Côtes de Bourg
With its rich savoury fruit, stylish oak handling and succulent texture,
this is a serious wine with backbone and complexity, which will repay
a year or two in the wine rack.
Stockist: Waitrose (see page 428).

1992 Fairview Merlot Reserve
One of the stars of Tesco's South African range, this fresh, minty,
succulent, strawberry-jam-like Merlot from Charles Back is almost
impossible to dislike. Go on, make our day!
Stockist: Tesco (see page 338).

1994 Torre del Falco, Rosso della Murgia, Vino da Tavola

A blend of Cabernet Sauvignon and the local Puglian Uva di Troia, which demonstrates that the heel of Italy can produce outstanding red wines at under £5. It's minty, dry and lightly oaked with the green pepper elegance of the Cabernet Sauvignon adding class to the Uva di Troia. It's handsomely packaged too.

Stockist: Oddbins (see page 230).

1993 Costières de Nîmes, Paul Blanc

Softly concentrated Provençal red made entirely from the Syrah grape. If it weren't for a touch of Mediterranean spiciness, this concentrated, deeply coloured wine could almost be mistaken for a top-flight Crozes-Hermitage, or better.

Stockist: Oddbins (see page 229).

1992 Palacio de la Vega Crianza, Navarra

A similar wine to the 1993 Cabernet/Tempranillo but with the benefit of a year's oak ageing. It's a sweetly succulent version in which the Cabernet Sauvignon character is nicely accentuated on the palate and the fruit enhanced by spicy vanilla oakiness.

Stockist: Oddbins (see page 230–31).

1991 Conde de Valdemar, Rioja Crianza, Martinez Bujanda

The best of the large number of Martinez Bujanda Riojas at Thresher, this is a modern, strawberry-fruity, elegantly oaked Spanish blend of mainly Tempranillo with 10 per cent of the rare Mazuelo grape. Well priced at around £5.50.

Stockist: The Thresher Group (see page 368).

1994 Valdivieso Pinot Noir, Lontue

This is a vibrant, weighty, spicily oaked, voluptuous Chilean Pinot Noir made from grapes previously destined for Valdivieso's sparkling wine production. But Australia-trained winemaker Luis Simian was given the opportunity to produce a limited amount of Chardonnay and Pinot Noir. This 1994 is an attractively made, worthy successor to the excellent first vintage.

Stockist: The Thresher Group, Adnams (see page 367 and 448).

1994 Chénas Domaine des Pierres, Trichard

One of the best Beaujolais we tasted in 1995, this is a lively, well-structured, immensely drinkable Beaujolais cru, showing the concentration which Gamay can attain in an *appellation* like Chénas. *Stockist:* Majestic Wine Warehouses (see page 155).

FIZZ OF THE YEAR CASE

1992 Croser Brut

Modestly named after the man who made it, Brian Croser's Adelaide Hills fizz is an intensely lemony, weighty blend of Pinot Noir and 30 per cent Chardonnay with an idiosyncratic, almost savoury, smoky bacon note. It's one of Australia's classiest sparkling wines – just as well Mr Croser didn't call it Brian.

Stockists: Bottoms Up, Oddbins, Victoria Wine Cellars, Wine Rack (see pages 237, 371 and 411).

Deutz Marlborough Cuvée

A fine, elegantly crafted blend of Pinot Noir and Chardonnay made in New Zealand using the southern hemisphere's only Coquard Champagne press. The result of a fruitful partnership between Champagne house Deutz and New Zealand's Montana, Marlborough Cuvée has established itself as a complex, dry fizz of considerable tangy complexity.

Stockists: Oddbins, The Thresher Group, Victoria Wine (see pages 238, 372 and 412).

Quartet Roederer Estate NV

Made by Frenchman Michel Salgues in northern California's ultra-cool Anderson Valley, this is a brilliant New World sparkling wine in which the company's French parentage shines through. A blend of 70 per cent Chardonnay and 30 per cent Pinot Noir, it's a vivid fizz with yeasty-toasty complexity, the faintest hint of oak, and a dry, lingering aftertaste.

Stockists: Greenalls Wine Cellar, Majestic Wine Warehouses (see pages 123 and 162).

Domaine de l'Aigle Tradition, Brut Chardonnay/Pinot Noir

With its barrel-fermented base wine, this Aude blend of Chardonnay and one-third Pinot Noir is a rich, concentrated fizz with toasty, cool climate crispness and a malty, savoury tang. Limoux's homage to Bollinger.

Stockist: La Maison du Vin, Cherbourg and St-Malo (see page 572).

Jean Louis Malard Champagne, Grand Cru, Bouzy

This Pinot-dominated fizz from the commune of Bouzy is big, rich and powerful with fine, richly flavoured bubbles and malty fruitiness. Another stunning grower's Champagne in the Bottoms Up line-up.
Stockist: Bottoms Up (see page 372).

Pol Roger White Foil Champagne, Extra Dry

An equal blend of Pinot Noir, Chardonnay and Pinot Meunier, Pol Roger's White Foil is consistently among the best non-vintage Champagnes. It's a soft, subtle, refreshingly elegant Champagne with delicate bubbles and biscuit and brioche notes. This was one of Winston Churchill's favourite Champagnes (Pol Roger have even named their top fizz after him), but that's no reason to raise two fingers to it.
Stockists: Widely available.

1985 Tesco Vintage Champagne

A first-rate successor to the 1982 Vintage Champagne, also from the Chouilly co-operative. In fact, we actually prefer this rich, toasty Pinot Noir dominated style from one of the smallest but best of Champagne's recent vintages. A wine which combines power with freshness.
Stockist: Tesco (see page 340).

Veuve de Medts, Premier Cru Brut, NV Champagne

From a co-operative situated in the heart of the Côte des Blancs, this is a Chardonnay-based blend largely from the excellent 1990 vintage. It's toasty, buttery and rich with commendable depth of flavour. Excellent value at around £13.
Stockist: Marks & Spencer (see page 182).

Joseph Perrier Brut Champagne, Cuvée Royale

A malty, traditional Champagne from the underrated Châlons-sur-Marne house of Joseph Perrier. It's a weighty, characterful, chocolatey style that's also excellent value for a Grande Marque Champagne at around £16.
Stockist: Fuller's (see page 104).

Michel Genet Grand Cru Blanc de Blancs Champagne, Chouilly

Still priced at under 100 francs, and still one of the best bargains in the Channel ports, this is a structured, complex, creamy grower's

Champagne made entirely from Chardonnay grown in the Côte des Blancs to the south of Epernay.
Stockist: The Grape Shop, Boulogne (see page 562).

Clos Cabrière, Cuvée Belle Rose

Clos Cabrière produces most of the Cape's best fizz. Made by the eccentric Achim von Arnim, a fellow who collects African elephant droppings and has twice been voted South Africa's worst-dressed man, this is a zippy, stylishly dry pink sparkling wine made exclusively from Pinot Noir grapes.
Stockist: Victoria Wine Cellars (see page 412).

1990 Green Point Rosé

A fizz that shows the benefits of using the classic Champagne grapes, Chardonnay and Pinot Noir. Moët et Chandon's Australian operation, based in the coolish climate of Victoria's Yarra Valley, is currently producing some of the best non-French sparkling wines of all. This delicate, onion skin-coloured rosé made by the multi-talented Dr Tony Jordan is a deliciously mature addition to the Green Point range.
Stockist: Victoria Wine Cellars (see page 411).

INDEPENDENT WINE MERCHANTS' CASE OF THE YEAR

Adnams
1992 Domaine des Aubuisières Cuvée Victor, Vouvray Sec, Bernard Fouquet
A brilliant Loire oddball from a mediocre vintage made by the youthful Bernard Fouquet from Domaine des Aubuisières. Dry Chenin Blanc can taste raspingly austere, but this aniseed and dry honey-like white shows the benefit of low yields in the vineyard and an experienced hand in the cellar.
(see page 445).

Australian Wine Club
1994 Tim Adams Clare Valley Riesling
Tim Adams thinks this is the best Clare Valley Riesling he's produced yet, and who are we to disagree? With its delightfully fresh, fragrant aromas, this is a toasty, herby, melon and lime flavoured Riesling with superb balance and a lingering dry aftertaste.
(see page 453).

Averys of Bristol
1992 Swanson Chardonnay, Carneros, Napa Valley
From former Averys owner Clarke Swanson's Napa Valley estate, this is a rich, powerful, but beautifully balanced California Chardonnay with well-judged oak, toffee-fudge fruit and piquant acidity, giving it the structure to age well. Even at £14 a bottle, this puts most village white Burgundy in the shade.
(see page 462).

Berry Brothers & Rudd
1989 Hermitage, M. Chapoutier
Packaged with a label made to look like a French country wine, this is in fact a concentrated, characterful red from one of France's best red wine *appellations*. Berrys' were able to bottle it themselves because of their long-standing relationship with the Chapoutier family in Hermitage. It's tannic, spicy and full of potential and blackberry Syrah fruitiness. It's

also pretty good value, especially by the arm-and-a-pin-striped-leg standards of St James's.
(see page 472).

Bibendum
1991 Katnook Cabernet Sauvignon, Coonawarra
Another wine for the long haul, this is a full-throated, attractively textured Cabernet with flavours of coffee bean, blackcurrant and green pepper, supported by fine-grained tannins. One of the best Australian reds we've seen this year.
(see page 480).

Eldridge Pope
1994 The Chairman's New World Sauvignon, Nelson
Via his messenger, wine buyer and Master of Wine Joe Naughalty, the chairman, Christopher Pope, has chosen well. This gooseberry-scented Sauvignon Blanc made at the Seifried family's Redwood Valley Estate in South Island's Nelson region is fresh, grapefruity, complex and attractively dry. The chairman should be happy with this one.
(see page 486).

Enotria Winecellars
1993 Rosso di Montalcino, Argiano
From the historic estate of Argiano in Montalcino, this is a soft, leafy Sangiovese with refreshing acidity and delicate, sweet fruit concentration. If the Rosso's this good, you can imagine what the Brunello must be like.
(see page 497).

Justerini & Brooks
1990 Chinon, Cuvée des Varennes du Grand Clos, Charles Joguet
Magnificent, concentrated, elegant Cabernet Franc from sculptor and star winemaker Charles Joguet, with pure, ripe cassis and blackberry sweetness and refreshing acidity. It would be hard to find a better expression of Cabernet Franc anywhere in the world.
(see page 504).

Lay & Wheeler
1991 Gabarinza, Heinrich
An exciting blend of the Central European Blaufränkisch, Zweigelt and Saint Laurent grapes made by Gernot Heinrich in his family winery at Gols in eastern Austria's Burgenland region. This is an oaky, yet elegant, plum and raspberry fruity red with spicy concentration and supple tannins. One of Austria's top red wines. It's good to see a wine merchant giving Austria's best producers the prominence they deserve.
(see page 511).

Lea & Sandeman
1992 Domaine du Deffends, Clos de la Truffière, Coteaux Varois
Made at a domaine owned by a Marseilles University law professor, this is an elegant blend of Syrah and Cabernet Sauvignon modelled on Domaine de Trévallon in the Côteaux des Baux de Provence. As the name suggests, it's truffley and aromatic with some black pepper Syrah notes to leaven the structured tannins of the Cabernet Sauvignon.
(see page 520).

Tanners
1993 Dolcetto d'Alba, Sandrone
Lively, exuberant Dolcetto from one of Piemonte's best exponents of the style with masses of damson and berry-fruit characters and considerable length of flavour. Why anyone would want to drink a Beaujolais cru when they can buy something as joyously juicy as this is a mystery to us.
(see page 530).

Thomas Peatling
1993 Mâcon-Viré, Domaine de Roally
Based in the village of Viré, Henri Goyard is one of the best producers in southern Burgundy, making intensely concentrated unfiltered Chardonnays from low-yielding vineyards. This is rich and extremely refreshing stuff, with beautifully judged weight and acidity.
(see page 537).

INTRODUCTION

Turn, turn, turn ...
Why do we do it? Why do we put ourselves through three months of
hard work, tasting thousands of wine samples and trying to find an
original way of describing the fifteenth Liebfraumilch we've had pushed
under our noses? The answer is that it's enormous fun. There's no better
place to be a wine consumer, or wine writer for that matter, than Britain.
We have the broadest selection of bottles, the canniest wine buyers and,
duty rates notwithstanding, the best-value wines.

We've made the point before, but it's worth repeating. Where else
can you walk into a supermarket or high street off-licence and be
confronted with a line-up which includes wines from Morocco, Croatia,
Argentina, Mexico and Slovakia as well as more familiar fare? The answer
is nowhere. The sheer diversity of wines available in this country is
awesome. Just when we thought further discoveries were impossible,
we've been introduced to new wines from Brazil, Uruguay, Japan and
Canada. They may not compare with the classics of Western Europe, but
they're worth considering for novelty value alone.

Grapevine is rewritten, not updated, each year. We taste an entirely
new set of wines. Indeed, the point of producing the book annually is
that vintages are different. In regions such as Bordeaux, Burgundy and
the Mosel, variations from one harvest to the next contribute to a wine's
character. With other wines, such as non-vintage Champagnes and
commercial Australian Chardonnays, producers aim to prove that,
despite vintage changes, house styles are consistent from year to year.

Nevertheless, however much the producer works at consistency, it's
not always easy to disguise a change of vintage. Wines from a particular
year also develop in bottle. Here, too, the differences may be more or
less marked. In a wine made for everyday drinking, a year can mean the
difference between fresh and fruity or tired and past it. In a fine wine, a
year in bottle, depending on storage conditions, may bring it closer to

its peak or begin the process of disintegration.

A year of improvement

This is the third edition of *Grapevine* and it's been by far the most pleasurable to write. The reason, apart from our enjoyment of each other's company, is the fine quality of the wines we've tasted this year. Almost everyone, from Budgens and Unwins to Bottoms Up and Waitrose, improved their range of wines in 1995.

In part, this is a reflection of how competitive the market has become. The days when a wine buyer could see a couple of suppliers over lunch and throw a list together in the afternoon are history. The wine trade has become a fast-moving business, sourcing wines from dozens of different countries. It's easy to forget how rapidly things have changed. Four years ago, Sainsbury's bought wine from 14 countries; today, it's 27.

This involves more travel than ever before for wine buyers. If you work in the wine department of a major supermarket or off-licence chain, you can expect to spend up to a quarter of the year abroad. As a consequence, the involvement of buyers in blending and sourcing the wines they sell back in Britain has increased dramatically. Projects such as Samuels Bay and the Winelands label at Bottoms Up, Safeway's Young Vatted Merlot and Tempranillo, Marks & Spencer's Il Caberno and Oddbins' The Catalyst are all instances of wine buyers getting their hands dirty.

The major chains also employ a growing number of flying wine-makers to produce tailor-made wines in Italy (Geoff Merrill and Sainsbury's, or Asda and Andres Ilabaca), Spain (Hugh Ryman and Bottoms Up), Brazil (John Worontschak and Tesco) and Hungary (Nick Butler and Safeway), to name but five prominent examples. Here too, the conclusion is unavoidable – retailers are cutting out the middle-men (importers and agents) and dealing directly with the people who make the wine.

Does cheaper mean better?

Before we're accused of being over optimistic, we must record our dismay at another of the year's dominant trends. The continuing spread of the £1.99 bottle is a cause for concern at *Grapevine*. Only a year ago, it looked as if the £2.99 bottle was an endangered species. A combination of small harvests, higher production costs and currency fluctuations had made it increasingly difficult to source bargain basement wine from Australia, Chile, France, Italy, Germany, Spain and the United States.

So what's happened? Well, a number of supermarkets have started to regard wine as what's known in the business as a 'loss leader'. In other words, something which makes no money but attracts customers. One smaller chain, Somerfield, has led the move downmarket. (At one point this year, it was offering a Vin de Pays de l'Hérault at £1.39 – barely enough to cover the cost of duty.) But it's been joined by Asda, Tesco, Sainsbury's and even Majestic. Of the Big Four supermarkets, only Safeway has been reluctant to follow the crowd.

Shoppers are extremely happy to drink such wines. Some of Somerfield's 'Price Check' wines have sold as many as 50,000 cases in a fortnight. That sounds like a lot, but it doesn't yield much in the way of profit. This, according to Angela Mount at Somerfield, is not the point of the exercise. 'We're offering wines at outrageous prices to increase activity and sales in our stores. Our approach is to drop the price of wines which are already on our list as a way of encouraging customers to try new things. And it's working. Even when we put the price back up, people continue to buy the wine.'

Some of Somerfield's competitors are slightly snooty about £1.39 promotions. Stephen Clarke of Tesco says that: 'In any market there will always be people who aren't doing that well. Some of them continue to believe that giving away wine is the best way to compensate for the performance of their business.' Ouch!

Nevertheless, this hasn't stopped Tesco selling bargain basement wine. 'We live in a real world,' adds Clarke, 'and it doesn't matter whether you sell wine, package holidays to Greece or Cartier jewellery. You have to remain competitive. Sometimes you have to remind customers that there's a commodity out there called wine.' Commodity, in our view, is the right word.

Nick Dymoke-Marr of Asda is another vociferous supporter of the £1.99 bottle. 'There are clearly people out there who will never spend more than £2 on a bottle of wine. We're not devaluing what we do by offering £1.99 wines. We're encouraging new people to come into the market.'

Is this true? Our feeling is that the £1.99 bottle is a dead end. It's hard to disagree with Simon Loftus of Adnams, who describes the whole thing as a 'catastrophe'. 'The wine trade as a whole – and that includes the supermarkets – has done a pretty good job over the last decade of introducing wine to a wider public as an enjoyable, good value drink. If we sell rubbish, we're going to endanger that achievement. The only way you can do it is if you don't care what the wine tastes like.'

Not only that. As Allan Cheesman of Sainsbury's rightly points out: 'The suppliers are the ones who get squeezed.' If the people who make the wines have no money to reinvest in vineyards and new cellar technology, eventually the quality of what we drink is going to suffer. It's about time wine retailers stopped chomping on the hand that feeds, especially given the fact that five supermarkets (Sainsbury's, Tesco, Asda, Safeway and Somerfield) sell close to 60 per cent of the wine we buy in this country and wield tremendous influence over consumer tastes.

The return of the Big Cheese

Still, you can be sure of one thing – if consumers go on buying £1.99 wines, supermarkets will be happy to go on selling them. Or will they? The return of Allan Cheesman, the man who almost single-handedly launched the supermarket wine revolution, to Sainsbury's booze department after a four-year spell at delicatessen and fresh produce appears to indicate otherwise.

In an exclusive interview, the Big Cheese told *Grapevine* that: 'We have to live with certain commercial pressures which result from our position as a leading supermarket, but in wine we will consciously try to avoid price-cutting. My view is that it's a pointless exercise.'

The return of Cheesman was one of the talking points of the year. Has he been passed over for promotion to the main board? Is he taking a backward step? Or will he again transform the supermarket wine sector? Cheesman himself is the first person to point out that he's 'not some guy who's going to charge down the corridor on a white horse'. But Cheesman wouldn't be Cheesman unless he had strong views about everything from cross-Channel shopping to flying winemakers. It will be interesting to see how the Sainsbury's range develops over the next year.

The high street fights back

Cheesman has seen a lot of changes in the time he's been away. One of the most striking is the extent to which 'the likes of Thresher and Victoria Wine have sharpened up their act'. They sure have. There's been a lot of rationalisation over the last few years – what with Victoria Wine buying Augustus Barnett and Thresher swallowing Peter Dominic – but those chains which are still standing have been transformed.

There has also been a welcome move upmarket in the high street since 1989, with the launch, or relaunch in one case, of Wine Rack, Victoria Wine Cellars and Bottoms Up. Oddbins, too, has continued to drive the whole sector forward, offering its characteristic blend of wacky, original and well-priced wines and, more recently, opening a series of Fine Wine stores.

This year has also seen marked improvements from smaller regional chains, such as Fuller's, Davisons and Unwins, as well as from Greenalls Cellars, the third-biggest off-licence group behind Thresher and Victoria Wine. Under new wine buyer Roger Higgs, Fuller's has developed a range of wines to match the quality of its award-winning beers; Davisons has joined forces with the excellent London wholesaler Mayor Sworder; Unwins has bought new wines and produced a smart T-shirt; and Greenalls Cellars is beginning to realise one or two of the extravagant plans of its managing director, Nader Haghighi, opening or converting existing stores into Berkeley Wines and Wine Cellar branches faster than you can say 'design consultancy'.

In one sense, the high street has been badly affected by supermarket price-cutting this year – the big off-licence chains still appear to be losing volume to the supermarkets. But our hunch is that they're performing rather better in the middle and upper reaches of the wine market – that is, above £4. One unsubstantiated statistic is that 20 per cent of all wine sold above £4 in this country is sold at Oddbins. And, according to Stats MR, the average price of a bottle of wine sold in supermarkets is £2.72, compared with £3.64 in a high street off-licence.

We certainly find the overall mood in the high street more optimistic than it was a year ago. Almost everyone we spoke to claimed to have improved their performance. In some cases this can be attributed to increased sales, in others it may simply be bluster. Nevertheless, the up-market arms of Oddbins, (Oddbins Fine Wine Stores), Thresher (Bottoms Up and Wine Rack), Victoria Wine (Victoria Wine Cellars) and Greenalls (Wine Cellar and Berkeley Wine) all appear to be outperforming the market and, as a result, creating confidence in the ability of the high street to fight back.

Load up your transit van?

Cross-Channel trade continues and now accounts for an estimated 1 in every 10 bottles of wine drunk in this country. This, as the trade magazine *Wine & Spirit* pointed out, is the equivalent of what Sainsbury's or Tesco sells in the UK. No wonder some of the smaller wine retailers in the south of England, not to mention the supermarkets and off-licence chains, are so frustrated by the whole thing.

For all that, as we point out in the introduction to our cross-Channel section on page 541–5, the French ports are less of an attraction than they were a year ago. French VAT has gone up, the pound is still weak against President Chirac's *franc fort*, and some of the deals being offered in the UK are difficult to match, even when you've subtracted the difference in duty.

This hasn't stopped Victoria Wine and Tesco following, and arguably bettering, the rather limp example of Sainsbury's by opening stores on the other side of the Channel. But our impression is that, failing a major devaluation of the franc, the cross-Channel tide is starting to turn.

The role of the independent wine merchant

This is welcome news for Britain's independent wine merchants, who have not had an easy time in recent years. Apart from cross-Channel buying excursions by some of their best customers, they've had to cope with the growth of the supermarkets and the renewed challenge of the high street.

Our conviction is that the independents offer something unique, which is why we've extended the scope of this year's *Grapevine* to include a dozen of them. From a purely personal point of view, we're glad we did. The wines submitted for our independent merchant tastings were some of the best we encountered this year. For more detail, have a look at our introduction on page 437–41 and subsequent tasting notes.

The airborne division

Independent wine merchants are often critical of the styles of wine produced by so-called flying winemakers. These are winemakers who are used as consultants in under-exploited viticultural regions. One wine merchant claimed recently that the airborne division was responsible for an 'ever-increasing move towards a homogeneous style of winemaking', with the result that people are 'drinking and being encouraged by the press to drink wines that have no regional differences and, although technically "squeaky-clean", lack individuality and character.'

We don't agree. For a start, the idea that flying winemakers are taking over the universe is incorrect. By our estimate, wines sold by the likes of Hugh Ryman, Jacques Lurton, Kym Milne, Nick Butler, Peter Bright, John Worontschak and Geoff Merrill add up to no more than 4.5 million cases, the equivalent of 7 per cent of the UK wine market.

It is true that flying winemakers make a lot of Chardonnay, Sauvignon Blanc and Cabernet Sauvignon, but this fashionable trio aren't the only grapes they use. Two of our wines of the year – a Negroamaro from Kym Milne and a Fernão Pires/Chardonnay blend from Peter Bright – prove that flying winemakers often work equally well with indigenous grapes. As Hugh Ryman argues: 'What we do is geared towards expressing the flavours contained in the grapes. That's why it's such nonsense to say that our wines all taste the same.'

The other thing that's easy to overlook is that flying winemakers generally make inexpensive, not fine, wines. In most cases, what they turn out is a massive improvement in the quality of the wines normally produced in that region by large volume co-operatives or *négociants*. The improvements in Eastern European wines, especially in Hungary, are almost entirely due to the efforts of the wing commanders.

Whither the New World?
The New World (convenient wine writing shorthand for Australia, New Zealand, the United States, Chile, South Africa, Argentina and even Mexico) continues to make progress on the UK market. Three Old World countries (France, Germany and Italy) still account for two-thirds of what we drink, but Australia, Chile and South Africa are out-performing the market.

Not all these countries are moving at the same pace, however. With around 7 per cent of the UK wine market, according to statistics in *Off-Licence News*, Australia is the dominant New World producer. But small vintages in 1994 and 1995 have led to shortages and, in our opinion, a drop in quality at the lower end of the market. Reds and whites from Down Under at £2.99 or less should generally be given the widest of all possible berths.

Where Australia scores is between £3.99 and £5.99, providing reliable, flavoursome reds and whites. Our view is that Australia has toned down the style of its more commercial wines, using less oak and more finesse in its Chardonnays, Cabernets and Shirazes. We've also noticed a growing awareness of the diversity Australia can offer – Semillons, Rieslings, Malbecs and Grenache/Mourvèdre blends. Provided it can satisfy our thirst for its wines, Australia, as they say in the Barossa Valley, should be right.

New Zealand, like Australia but on a much smaller scale, was also hit by reduced vintages in 1992 and 1993. Both years were also on the cool side, so we've seen the reappearance of green, vegetal Kiwi red wines. The whites are as good as ever, though – crisp, fresh and stylish. In terms of price, Kiwi bottles tend to be more expensive than other New World wines, but we reckon it's worth paying the extra to drink a Sauvignon Blanc from Palliser or a Chardonnay from Neudorf.

Mind you, New Zealand's position is under threat from Chile. The talk even five years ago was of Chile's reds, but the quality of its Chardonnays and Sauvignon Blancs has increased dramatically in recent vintages. The 1994 and 1995 harvests have amply demonstrated that, between £3.99 and £4.99, Chile's whites offer more elegance and intensity of flavour than anyone's. Wineries such as Caliterra, Casablanca, San Pedro, Errázuriz, Santa Rita, Valdivieso, Carmen and Santa Carolina can be proud of what they've achieved.

Chile overshadows its neighbour Argentina on the UK market, but there's a lot more wine produced in the latter than the former. Most of it gets consumed on the domestic market (which is just as well), but we're starting to see a few Argentinian wines on retail shelves in the UK. The best to date have come from Catena and Bodegas Norton, but we expect to see more wineries attempt to overcome the dreaded Falklands Factor in the next year or so.

The United States was the first New World country to broach the UK market with those famous Californian carafes (the things we all keep our coppers in), but lost out to Australia in the late 1980s and early 1990s because of an inability to provide inexpensive 'entry point wines' to guide consumers towards the delights of the West Coast's best Chardonnays, Cabernets and Pinot Noirs.

This has changed in the last two years, thanks to the efforts of wineries like Fetzer, J. Lohr, Bonny Doon, Glen Ellen, Arciero, Firestone, Sebastiani and even our good friends Ernest and (the late) Julio Gallo. As a result, California wines are finally set to become a New World force in the UK.

The Nelson Mandela effect

California's progress notwithstanding, the New World country which really captured the public's collective palate in 1995 was South Africa. When President Nelson Mandela appeared at the Rugby World Cup dressed in captain François Pienaar's Number 6 shirt, it was hard to feel unmoved.

The Mandela effect has done great things for Cape wines too. When the South African leader turned up at a dinner in London two years ago with a bottle of Nederburg in hand, it effectively ended the lingering consumer boycott of South African produce. Sales of South African wine have gone into orbit since 1993. We purchased 1.9 million cases of it in 1994 and it looks as if that figure could double in 1995.

A time for celebration in the Cape? Yes and no. South Africa is not without its problems. Its vineyards are dominated by one rather boring grape (Chenin Blanc, or Steen as it's known locally), many of its vines are diseased and in need of replanting and several of its volume-producing co-operatives desperately need to invest in modern technology.

Another long-term trap is the so-called Bulgaria Syndrome – whereby South Africa will be perceived solely as a producer of cheap wines. The huge volume increases in the UK are largely thanks to sales of cheap Chenin Blanc and Colombard-based whites. As Kim Tidy of Thresher warns: 'South Africa doesn't have a strong image yet, so there's a risk that it will end up as a producer of commodity wines. If that happens, it will lose all the value that being part of the New World bestows.'

As things stand, South Africa is losing out to Chile, Australia, the United States and New Zealand in the middle market. We're starting to see some very good things from the likes of Fairview and Danie De Wet, but the Cape is still under-represented in the £4 to £6 range.

A day of rest?

Sunday, as has been apparent for some years now, is no longer a time of respite. Even the booze trade has to work weekends these days. Since 1 August 1995, off-licence and convenience stores in England and Wales have been allowed to open from 10.00am to 10.30pm on Sundays. It means more work for the poor underpaid souls who have to work in British off-licences, but on balance we approve of this move to bring the UK into line with more civilised continental practices.

Star turns of 1995

As we've already mentioned, Chilean white wines were the divas of 1995. We've also seen welcome improvements from Bulgaria (especially in the quality of its white wines), Hungary (which is beginning to make the most of its native grapes, such as Furmint and Kekfrankos, as well as producing some extremely good flying-winemaker Chardonnays), Bordeaux (for its whites) and California.

Areas that we mentioned last year have continued to please. Northern Spain, southern Italy and the Languedoc-Roussillon are all producing brilliant value wines with a genuine local accent. Not everything which emerges from these regions is worth buying. On the contrary, a lot of it is actively nasty. But if you're planning to spend under £5 on a bottle of wine, these are among the first places you should look.

Cold versus warm climate wines

In fact, we think we're witnessing a power shift in the world of wine, from cool to warm climates. Until the advent of temperature-controlled, stainless steel fermentation and New World techniques such as night harvesting and must-chilling, warm climates found it hard to make intensely flavoured, fresh wines.

Now all that is changing – the Australian Riverland, Puglia, La Mancha, California's Central Valley, South Africa's Olifantsriver and the Languedoc are replacing the cooler climates of Northern Europe as sources of quaffing wines. Liebfraumilch, Muscadet, red Bordeaux, Mâcon Blanc, Sancerre and Bourgogne Rouge are slowly being supplanted on dinner tables and restaurant lists by wines such as Vin de Pays d'Oc Merlot, Australian Semillon/Chardonnay, La Mancha Tempranillo and Puglian Negroamaro.

We may still look to the Mosel, Burgundy, Piedmont and Bordeaux for more expensive fine wines, which at their sublime best combine elegance with staying power, but just because something says Bordeaux or Burgundy on the label, it doesn't mean we have to like it. In poor vintages, and all too often in good ones too, we're better off turning elsewhere for our everyday drinking. One day, even the French might catch on to what's happening in the Languedoc-Roussillon.

Must improve

Is it a coincidence that red Bordeaux has yet again failed to stack up under £5? As already mentioned, we've had some wonderful white

Bordeaux this year, but we struggled to find more than a handful of drinkable reds. Too many cheap clarets taste thin, tart and green.

Who else are we going to dump on? Well, Beaujolais again seemed anxious to prove that it's yesterday's wine. We had two spectacularly good crus from Majestic and Lay & Wheeler, but the quality of basic Beaujolais is a disgrace.

So, increasingly, is that of inexpensive Australian reds and whites. The desire of supermarkets to offer something – anything – from Down Under for less than £3 is damaging the image of Australia. It's time the big companies in Australia put their size-11 boots down.

Other underwhelming wines this year came from Brazil, Canada and Romania. Despite what we said at the beginning of this Introduction, we're concerned that, in their search for something new, supermarkets are buying sub-standard wines.

Signage and shoppability
And finally, as they say on the *News at Ten*, we've been introduced to a new language in 1995 – marketingspeak. It's a sign of how seriously the major chains take the booze business when their staff start talking about 'premiumising', 'empowerment', 'brand propositions', 'signage' and (our favourite) 'shoppability'. Whatever happened to a person standing behind a counter selling wine?

See you next year.

ASDA ***

Head Office: Asda House, Southbank, Great Wilson Street, Leeds LS11 5AD

Telephone: 01132 435435

Number of branches: 203 including seven Dales

Credit cards accepted: Access, Visa

Hours of opening: Monday to Saturday 9.00am to 8.00pm; Sunday 11.00am to 5.00pm

By-the-case sales: Yes

Glass loan: Yes

Home delivery: From December 1995

Clubs: No

Discounts: On cases and mixed cases

In-store tastings: Yes, in selected stores

Top ten best-selling wines: Asda Liebfraumilch; Lambrusco la Vigna Bianco; Asda Hock; Bulgarian Cabernet Sauvignon; Asda Frascati; Asda Portuguese Rosé; Asda Chianti; Asda Claret; Asda Côtes du Rhône; Montepulciano Cantine Tollo

Range: GOOD: Southern France, Germany, Italy, Australia, Chile
AVERAGE: Spain, Portugal, Eastern Europe, Loire, New Zealand, Burgundy, Bordeaux, Champagne and sparkling wines, California
POOR: Alsace, Beaujolais

Well, we said last year that there were changes in the air at Asda. What we hadn't appreciated was that it was action man Philip Clive, not Nick

Dymoke-Marr, who would be pedalling his mountain bike out of the Asda wine department.

The irrepressible *Loaded* magazine reader Dymoke-Marr now heads the new team, which, with trainee buyer, Illy Jaffar, has been boosted by the arrival of Alistair Morrell from Booths of Preston.

In the 1995 edition of *Grapevine*, we mentioned the Sauna Project – not a Julie Burchill flesh and shopping novel, but the offspring of customer research, suggesting that customers wanted more information about the wines they were buying.

Dymoke-Marr explains: 'A year ago, we decided that we weren't doing things properly and that there must be another way of showing what we had to offer. We went back to the customers who said "Your wine department has no soul." It really hurt. So we asked them what they wanted and they said "We want an easier way to select wines, a department that's interesting and allows us to spend a bit more time, plus some information on how to enjoy the wines." '

After a brainstorming session, the formula was slimmed down to three main factors: taste, money and country of origin, in that order. The order of priority was chosen after Dymoke-Marr approached a confused-looking shopper one evening. When she complained of being unable to find anything medium dry, Dymoke-Marr helpfully suggested a Cape white or Hungarian Muscat. 'Why don't you normally do things by taste?' said the shopper, switching on the light bulb in Dymoke-Marr's head.

After convincing Allan Leighton, Asda's deputy chief executive, that people who buy wine spend more money on groceries, the team got the backing for putting its new scheme into place. Before the beginning of 1995, the new format was up and running. Wines are now organised by style, and the intimidating fine wine section (with fine wines slashed from 120 to 60) has been replaced by an unpretentious looking 'bookshelf', with information on how best to enjoy more expensive fare. With a copy of *Loaded* in one hand, perhaps?

Does this make Asda style victims or style leaders? A number of competitors have expressed reservations about this new approach – revolutionary for a supermarket – to selling wines. What if you're specifically looking for an Anjou Rouge or a claret and you don't know which style category it falls under? Despite the reservations, Dymoke-Marr says it has done wonders for sales, helping Asda, under the dynamic Archie Norman, to go from shipwreck to shipshape in the space of just three years.

With 320 wines, the range is relatively small, but Dymoke-Marr claims to prefer a small-but-perfectly-formed range to a vast Tesco-sized 775 range, which he thinks can be confusing. 'It's not a smaller range, but more condensed. There is no duplication.' He admits that it has given customers less opportunity to trade up, but he says the department will be adding new Chilean, Argentinian, South African and Italian wines to provide customers with a leg-up to higher-priced, better quality wines.

In an effort to get customers to try out new things, the Asda team are introducing what they call 'Wow!' wines – 'wines, that is, which are not cheap, but which people won't believe we can sell at such incredible prices,' says Dymoke-Marr. 'It's our equivalent of the Oddbins Fine Wine store.' The aim at this stage is to get 10 white and 10 red 'Wow!' wines into the top 35 stores.

At the cut-price, cut-throat end of the market, Dymoke-Marr makes no secret of the fact that he is in favour of the £1.99 wine as long as it's a 'good, wholesome, decent wine' and Asda don't lose money on it. In fact, the lad in him is rather proud of it.

'We started the £1.99 club. We don't make any money. That's not the object. We started it because it was obvious there are some people who never spend more than £2 on a bottle of wine. A lot of people who would not normally drink wine are buying as well as, not instead of, their normal purchase.'

Training staff in the stores is another extension of the Sauna Project, with 300 staff having passed the Wine and Spirit Education Trust's basic certificate and 50 who've achieved Higher Certificate status. 'It's a stake in the ground. And doing tastings with customers in-store means we're getting closer to our customers. People are saying we're beginning to realise how ripped off we were by wine merchants.'

As sources of decent wine under £2.99 dry up, sooner or later, Asda will be forced to abandon the £2.99 pricepoint which is so vital to its lucrative position as a cheaper alternative to Sainsbury's and Tesco. For the time being, there are enough good wines under £3 (the main sources, says Dymoke-Marr, are Italy, Argentina and Eastern Europe) for Asda to provide that alternative. 'It's a challenge to persuade people to go over £3,' he concedes.

One thing is for sure. Whichever way the customers go, we doubt that the Asda wine department will be borrowing the company's slogan for its successful Brolly Patrol promotion, featuring porters with umbrellas bearing the legend: 'Another drier Asda buyer'.

White

Under £3

FRANCE

Muscadet de Sèvre-et-Maine, Cellier du Bellay
0 / 3 / ⁑   10/20

Tart, tiring, unbalanced white from the Nantes region of France. Not one of Muscadet's better efforts.

1994 Le Pigoulet, Vin de Pays de Gers
£ / 3 / ⁑   12/20

Appley, sweetish white from Gascony's Plaimont co-operative in Armagnac country. Basic stuff.

Asda Vin de Pays des Côtes de Gascogne
£££ / 2 / ⁑   14/20

Made by the Plaimont co-operative's great rival, Yves Grassa, this is a much crisper, fruitier Gascon white for only 30 pence more. A fresh, grapefruity quaffer.

1994 Vin de Pays du Gard 'Les Garrigues'
££ / 2 / ⁑   13/20

Clean but rather heavy and alcoholic southern French white from an indecipherable mix of grapes.

1994 Bordeaux Sauvignon, Château le Désert
£££ / 2 / ⁑   14/20

One of a number of good value Bordeaux white wines to have emerged in the last year, showing the crunchy, citrus-peel fruit of the Sauvignon grape.

1994 Chardonnay Vin de Pays du Jardin de la France, Domaine Baud
£ / 1 / ⁑   13/20

Asda selected this cuvée with the specific aim of 'offering a good quality Chardonnay at an affordable price'. They achieved the latter half of the aim, but the Chardonnay tastes more like Loire Valley Chenin to us.

GERMANY

Liebfraumilch, St Ursula
£££ / 5 / ⚑   13/20

One of the best Liebfraumilchs on the market. Not hard, perhaps. But at least this is fresh, clean and grapefruity without the cloying sweetness or excessive chemical addition that so often mars cheap German whites.

1993 Asda Wiltinger Scharzberg Riesling Kabinett
£££ / 4 / ⚑   14/20

Asda's recent change of supplier to the Mosel's Rudolf Müller Estate has yielded promising results. Why buy Liebfraumilch when you can get hold of something as genuine as this grapey, tangy Riesling?

HUNGARY

1994 Asda Hungarian Pinot Blanc
0 / 3 / ⚑   12/20

Made by the St Ursula Winery in Bingen – and it shows. The is a vegetal, oversulphured effort, rather like a drier version of Liebfraumilch.

1994 Asda Hungarian Muscat
£££ / 3 / ⚑   14/20

Fresh and grapey with lots of orange peel and lychee-like spice. Great label and brilliant value.

ITALY

Lambrusco Bianco 8%
0 / 6 / ⚑   10/20

Our sample was five months old, so perhaps that's why it was showing signs of fatigue. Sour apples and candyfloss sweetness.

Moscato Frizzante
££ / 6 / ⚑   13/20

If you like Aqua Libra, you'll love the sweet melon, cucumber and ginseng notes of this frothy, mildly alcoholic lemonade.

1994 Frascati Superiore
££ / 2 / ♪   **13/20**

It's rare to find a drinkable Frascati these days at under £3, so we're not surprised that this typically baked, southern dry white is one of Asda's top ten best-sellers.

ROMANIA

1994 River Route Sauvignon/Muscat
£ / 3 / ♪   **13/20**

Sightings of Romanian whites in the UK are as rare as jokes in the *International Herald Tribune*. Produced by a German-Romanian partnership, this bizarre blend of grapes foxed us with its flavours of plum, raisin and tea-leaf. If that sounds a bit over the top, try the wine.

SOUTH AFRICA

Asda Cape White
£ / 4 / ♪   **13/20**

Off-dry peardrop and banana style white made from local grapes, amongst which Steen, known as Chenin Blanc outside South Africa, predominates. Also available in party-pack three-litre size for pouring over your feet.

£3–5

AUSTRALIA

1994 Penfolds Bin 202 Riesling
££ / 3 / ♪   **14/20**

Until recently Penfolds has been better known for its reds than its whites. This is a sweetish, soft pear and banana style white with citrusy acidity. A good introduction to the joys of Australian Riesling.

1994 Asda South Australia Chardonnay
££ / 2 / ♪   **14/20**

A classic Australian Chardonnay with lots of bold pineapple and melon fruitiness. It's less oily than some, but it still has plenty of oaky stuffing.

1994 Rawsons Retreat Penfolds Bin 21 Semillon/Chardonnay
£££ / 2 / ▮   15/20

A good example of the new-style Penfolds whites. With its spicy vanilla oak, herby Semillon and Chardonnay richness, these two grapes combine harmoniously to produce a sundae of vanilla ice cream and lemony fruit.

CHILE

1994 Asda Chilean Sauvignon
£££ / 2 / ▮   15/20

Made by up-and-coming Chilean winemaker Andres Ilabaca at Canepa, this fresh, grapefruity Sauvignon has been rounded out with a touch of the Semillon grape.

1994 Cono Sur Chardonnay
0 / 2 / ▮   12/20

In its first vintage, Cono Sur established itself as one of the most exciting new wineries in Chile for its Pinot Noir and Cabernet Sauvignon. This boring, fruitless Chardonnay is not yet up to scratch.

1993 Rowanbrook Chardonnay Reserve
£££ / 2 / ▮   16/20

This has to be one of Chile's best value Chardonnays. Andres Ilabaca has excelled himself, creating a complex, buttery Chardonnay with attractive oak character and crisp, refreshing acidity.

FRANCE

1994 Domaine St François, Sauvignon Blanc, Vin de Pays d'Oc
£££ / 2 / ▮   16/20

The Foncalieu co-operative has obviously picked up a trick or two from flying winemaker Hugh Ryman, who was instrumental in setting up the domaine. This is a modern, summery white with zesty varietal fruitiness. Great value.

1994 Chardonnay Vin de Pays d'Oc, Montagne Noire
££ / 2 / ▮   14/20

The result of a new joint venture between Foncalieu and Michael

Goundrey from Australia's Mount Barker Region. It's a bit isolated there, so perhaps he fancied some company. If so, it was the right move, because the result is an appealing melon and citrus fruit flavoured Chardonnay with a strong dose of smoky oak.

1993 Muscadet de Sèvre-et-Maine Sur Lie, Domaine Gautron
££ / 1 / ⚱   15/20
Miles better than Asda's basic Muscadet, proving that if you want to buy a bottle of the Nantais' best-known white, it's always worth looking for the magic words 'sur lie' on the label. It's fresh with good weight and tangy fruit and a hint of pepper to add complexity.

GERMANY

1993 Hochheimer Hölle Riesling Kabinett, Aschrott
££ / 4 / ⚱   15/20
From one of the Rheingau's leading estates, this is a floral, almost peachy Riesling with sweetness balanced by crisp acidity. A good buy.

ITALY

1994 Soave Classico Lenotti
£££ / 2 / ⚱   15/20
Good value Soave from Carlo Lenotti, with beery, green olive aromas. If that sounds unpleasant, it shouldn't.

1994 Ca' Pradai Pinot Grigio
£££ / 2 / ⚱   15/20
Made by a Chilean-based French winemaker in Italy – this internationalism is getting a bit confusing – this is a fresh, peachy, almondy Pinot Grigio with a dash of Pinot Bianco for added zest.

1994 Ca' Pradai Chardonnay
£££ / 2 / ⚱   15/20
From the same winery in the Friuli region of northeastern Italy, this is a crisp, modern style of Chardonnay with a touch of butteriness.

1994 Frascati 'Colli di Catone' Superiore
£££ / 2 / 🍷   16/20

This is the sort of wine that could give Frascati a good name. Produced by the quality-conscious Antonio Pulcini, it's a blend of Malvasia di Candia, Malvasia di Lazio and 10 per cent Chardonnay. We detected touches of ginger spice, lime and honey in this attractive dry white.

1994 Lugana Sanrosela Boscaini
£ / 2 / 🍷   14/20

A dry, almost Chablis-like Italian white from the Boscaini estate in Valpolicella. A little austere for some, perhaps.

1990 Recioto di Soave Castelcerino
0 / 7 / 🍷   13/20

We were underwhelmed by this rather stale, barley-sugar-like sticky, which needs more freshness and life.

UNITED STATES

1993 Arius Californian Chardonnay
0 / 3 / 🍷   10/20

A confected California white combining artificial flavours of desiccated coconut and pineapple juice. Yum . . .

£5–8

AUSTRALIA

1994 Goundrey Langton Chardonnay
££ / 3 / 🍷   15/20

Not quite up to the high standard of the previous two vintages, but this lightly oaked melon and citrus fruit cocktail is still one of Australia's most attractive Chardonnays. Shame they weren't able to keep the price under £5.

FRANCE

1994 Domaine des Deux Roches, St Véran
£££ / 2 / ♪   16/20
From one of the leading estates in the Mâconnais region, this spicy, modern Chardonnay has much in common with the best wines of neighbouring Pouilly Fuissé. Serious white Burgundy at a less than serious price.

1993 Asda Chablis, Guy Mothe
££ / 1 / ♪   15/20
Good quality grower's Chablis with some of the minerally character we look for in Chablis and the emphasis firmly on fruit rather than oak.

GERMANY

1994 Wiltinger Braunfels Riesling Kabinett, Jordan and Jordan
££ / 4 / ♪   15/20
From the Van Volxem Estate in the Saar Valley, this is a highly aromatic Riesling with lots of green apple tang and sharp acidity.

1994 Graacher Himmelreich Riesling Kabinett, Reichsgraf Von Kesselstatt
£££ / 3 / ➤   16/20
Made by Annegret Reh-Gartner, the wines from this Mosel estate are some of the finest in Germany, showing elegance and considerable poise. Like biting into a juicy Cox's apple.

1993 Kreuznacher Bruckes Riesling Spätlese, Von Plettenberg
£££ / 5 / ♪   16/20
A riper style of Riesling from the Nahe region's Von Plettenberg estate, combining modern, peachy sweetness with zest and elegance.

1993 Niersteiner Pettenthal Riesling Auslese, Graf Wolff Metternich
££ / 6 / ➤   15/20
From one of the Rheinhessen's best-known estates, a fragrant, honeyed Auslese with spicy fruit and enough acidity to prevent it from cloying.

HUNGARY

1988 Tokaji Five Putts Havas Hill
£ / 7 / ⌘   14/20

An old-fashioned, massively sweet, tea-leaf, toffee and raisin style Tokaji with biting acidity.

NEW ZEALAND

1994 Stoneleigh Sauvignon Blanc
££ / 2 / ⌘   15/20

Typical Marlborough Sauvignon Blanc, packed with enticing flavours of gooseberry and green bean and the ripe fruit of a good southern hemisphere vintage.

Red

Under £3

BULGARIA

Bulgarian Country Wine, Cabernet Sauvignon/Merlot, Burgas
£££ / MB / ⌘   14/20

A little bit on the rustic side, but this chunky, blackcurrant-pastille, Bordeaux-style blend is typical of the improving reds emerging from Eastern Europe.

1994 Bulgarian Liubimetz Merlot
£££ / MB / ⌘   14/20

A modern (allelujah!), lush, chocolatey Bulgarian Merlot with a chewy, dry aftertaste.

FRANCE

Asda St Chinian
££ / FB / ⌘   14/20

A robust, full-throated winter warmer from the Languedoc's biggest producer, showing high acidity and plenty of spice. Time to get out the sheepskin rug.

Asda Claret, Paul Barbe
££ / MB / 🌡   14/20
On the light side, but with enough fresh, grassy, aromatic character to make it an attractive thirst-quencher.

Asda Bordeaux Supérieur
0 / MB / 🌡   13/20
Basic, tannic, old-fashioned claret that makes you long for the smoother flavours of the New World – unless you were born before VE Day.

HUNGARY

1994 Asda Hungarian Kekfrankos
£££ / MB / 🌡   15/20
Made by Australian Adrian Wing, who liked Hungary so much that he married a native, this soft, peppery, juicy red is Hungary's answer to Côtes du Rhône.

ITALY

1994 Montepulciano d'Abruzzo Tollo
£££ / LB / 🌡   15/20
Winemaker Ricardo Tiberio is clearly doing great things at the Tollo winery. This juicy, savoury Montepulciano, with a pleasing rustic bite, is amazing value at well under £3.

1994 Coltiva Il Rosso
£££ / LB / 🌡   14/20
Made by Chilean flying winemaker Andres Ilabaca from the Sangiovese grape, this is a fresh, fragrant cherry-scented rosso with lots of colour and fruit.

Asda Valpolicella
£ / LB / 🌡   13/20
Pleasant, light Valpol with a nutty twist. It's not easy to spot the 10 per cent Cabernet Sauvignon allegedly added for backbone.

MOROCCO

Domaine Mellil Moroccan Red
£ / FB / 🍾   13/20
Porty, tannic, pruney North African plonk with that authentic whiff of camel dung. One to make the going easier.

PORTUGAL

1994 Bela Fonte Portuguese Red
£ / MB / 🍾   13/20
Full-bodied, rustic Portuguese Tinto with a little bit of sweetness.

ROMANIA

1994 River Route Romanian Pinot Noir
0 / MB / 🍾   11/20
Nik Schritz of Kendermans, who presumably had something to do with this wine, believes that Romania is an ace place for red wines. On the evidence of this sickly, fruitless example, we beg to differ.

SOUTH AFRICA

Asda Cape Red
0 / MB / 🍾   11/20
This is a confected, insipid concoction which may remind our cross-dressing male readers (both of them) of their nail varnish.

SPAIN

1994 Terra Alta Cabernet Garnacha
£££ / MB / 🍾   14/20
Made in tandem by Nick Butler of Australia and Spain's Jorge Vidal, this wine is profoundly influenced by New World winemaking methods, but retains some Spanish earthiness.

£3–5

AUSTRALIA

1992 Berri Estates Cabernet/Shiraz
£ / MB / ♪   14/20

With its cinnamon oak spice and warm, chocolatey fruit flavours, this is an accessible, typically Australian blend from one of the country's most reliable producers.

1993 Penfolds Rawsons Retreat Bin 35
££ / MB / ♪   15/20

In typical Penfolds mould, this Cabernet Sauvignon/Shiraz blend has masses of sweet plum and blackberry fruit overlaid by a forest of spicy American oak. But don't tell Greenpeace.

BULGARIA

1991 Bulgarian Suhindol Cabernet Merlot
0 / MB / ♪   12/20

Oak-chippy, charry red. Poor person's Rioja.

CHILE

1994 Asda Chilean Cabernet Merlot
£££ / MB / ♪   15/20

Adorned with one of Asda's smartest labels, this is a successful Bordeaux blend from Chile's Canepa winery, full of juicy blackcurrant and spearmint fruitiness and soft tannins.

1994 Terra Noble Chilean Merlot
£ / MB / ➡   14/20

Another Chilean red, this time with the input of Gamay specialist Henri Marionnet. Using the Beaujolais method of carbonic maceration for softness of texture, it's halfway there, but finishes up just a little too dry for its own good. It may tone down in the bottle.

1993 Rowanbrook Cabernet Reserve
0 / MB / ♪   12/20
Coarse green oak is the dominant flavour in this disappointingly dour
wine. Unfortunately.

1993 Cono Sur Cabernet Sauvignon
£ / MB / ♪   13/20
Chilean Cabernet Sauvignon is often lean and rather lacking in fruit. We
found this suffered from similar failings, but the follow-on vintage is a
big improvement. So look out for the '94.

FRANCE

Asda Fitou
0 / FB / ♪   12/20
Rustic, foursquare Fitou with a tarry aftertaste and hardish tannins.

1994 Mas Segala Côtes du Roussillon Villages
££ / FB / ♪   15/20
Owned by Charles Faisant, export director of the Foncalieu winery, Mas
Segala has established itself as one of the best-value reds from the
Roussillon region. Juicy, chunky, attractively oaked red with a good dose
of the Syrah grape.

1993 Domaine de Grangeneuve, Coteaux du Tricastin
££ / MB / ♪   15/20
A soft, spicy, southern French red dominated by the Grenache grape,
backed up by Cinsault, Syrah and Mourvèdre.

1994 Beaujolais Villages, Domaine des Ronzes
£ / LB / ♪   14/20
It's halfway to a rosé, but this is an easy-drinking, refreshing Beaujolais,
probably more suited to summer picnics than those après-ski moments.

ITALY

1994 Spanna del Piemonte, Cantina Gemma
£ / MB / ♪   13/20
From the Gemma estate, this is a northeastern Italian red with lots of

tannic, grip and bitter almond and damson fruitiness. Powerful stuff that needs food to mop up the chewy tannins.

1993 Chianti Salvanza, Colli Senesi, DOCG
££ / MB / 🍷   15/20
Made at the Piccini winery in the Colli Senesi sub-region of Chianti, this is one of the best-value Italian reds on the market, with plenty of wild, robust Sangiovese fruit and backbone.

1993 Barbera d'Asti, Cantina Gemma
££ / MB / 🍷   14/20
From an area better known for its sweet sparkling wines, this is a light, savoury, bitter almond scented red with a nip of biting acidity.

1992 Rozzano Villa Pigna
£££ / FB / 🍷   16/20
A serious red in an imposing Italian designer bottle. Appealingly priced at under £5, this wine from Montepulciano in Tuscany is packed with spicy plum, vanilla and coconut oak flavours. A substantial mouthful.

SOUTH AFRICA

1994 Fairview Estate Shiraz
£££ / MB / 🍷   16/20
As well as being a cheesemaker of considerable repute, Charles Back is one of South Africa's most inventive winemakers. This soft, modern, chocolatey, deeply coloured Shiraz shows him at his innovative best.

£5–8

AUSTRALIA

Penfolds Kalimna Shiraz, Bin 28
£££ / FB / 🍷   16/20
Made with grapes from vineyards situated to the north and west of the world-famous Barossa Valley in South Australia, this sweet, massively oaked, blackberryish Shiraz is typical of the winning Penfolds style.

FRANCE

1993 Château de Parenchère, Bordeaux Supérieur
££ / MB / 🌢   15/20

The follow-on vintage to last year's 1991 is similar in style, showing lots of polished coffee bean oak and green pepper and blackcurrant Cabernet Sauvignon based fruitiness.

SOUTH AFRICA

1994 Woodlands Pinot Noir Western Cape
0 / LB / 🌢   13/20

The Asda team think that this wine would normally sell for £11 to £12. The fact that it's only selling for half that suggests that it's worth nowhere near Asda's exalted estimate. Made at Meerlust in the Cape, it's light on fruit and heavy on alcohol. If it came from Romania, this wine would normally sell at £2–3.

UNITED STATES

1993 Arius Neuf California Red Wine
££ / MB / 🌢   15/20

An all-Grenache, Rhône-style red wine picked up on the California market by whizz-kid New York broker Jason Korman. Rich, sweet and alcoholic, with typical peppery fruitiness.

Rosé

£3–5

SOUTH AFRICA

1994 Fairview Dry Rosé
££ / 3 / 🌢   15/20

Another characterful wine from Charles Back's goat pen in Paarl, showing soft, attractive mint and strawberry fruitiness and just the right amount of residual sweetness.

UNITED STATES

1994 Sebastiani White Zinfandel
0 / 4 / ⅟   11/20

Sweet, cloying alcoholic fruit juice without the redeeming freshness you're entitled to expect from a rosé. This is what used to be called Blush. And so it should.

Sparkling

£3–5

AUSTRALIA

Chandlers Point Australian Brut NV
£ / 3 / ⅟   13/20

Made by the family firm of McWilliams, this is a frothy, basic tank-method sparkling wine.

£5–8

AUSTRALIA

Victoria Park Pinot Chardonnay NV
£££ / 2 / ⅟   16/20

Yalumba are responsible for some of the best value sparkling wines in Australia, notably Angas Brut. This blend of the Champagne grapes Pinot Noir and Chardonnay is pleasingly complex, with some Champagne yeastiness and tangy, elegant fruit.

Over £8

FRANCE

Nicolas Feuillatte, Blanc de Blancs Chardonnay NV

££ / 2 / 🍷   16/20

Asda wine buyer Nick Dymoke-Marr likes the style of wine made by Nicolas Feuillatte so much that he's also taken on the Champagne house for Asda's own-label Champagne. This well-priced 100 per cent Chardonnay shows a hint of toastiness and real finesse.

UNITED STATES

Scharffenberger Brut NV

£££ / 2 / 🍷   16/20

A consistent *Grapevine* favourite from the Veuve-Clicquot-owned Scharffenberger operation in California's cool Anderson Valley, this Pinot Noir-based fizz is savoury, malty and mouthfilling. It also remains excellent value at under £9.

Fortified

£5–8

PORTUGAL

1989 Asda Late Bottled Vintage Port

££ / FB / 🍷   15/20

This is one of the many good quality Smith Woodhouse Ports available in the high street. Rich, chocolatey, well-made Port that will be ideal for Christmas.

BUDGENS **

Head Office: Budgens Stores Limited, 9 Stonefield Way, Ruislip, Middlesex HA4 0JR

Telephone: 0181 422 9511

Number of branches: 102, of which 10 are Fresh Save stores

Credit cards accepted: Visa, Access, Switch

Hours of opening: Monday to Friday, 8.30am to 8.00pm; Saturday 8.00am to 8.00pm; Sunday 9.00am to 6.00pm

By-the-case sales: Yes

Glass loan: No

Home delivery: No

Clubs: No

Discounts: 5 per cent on case sales

In-store tastings: Yes

Top ten best-selling wines: Budgens Vin de Table Red; Bordeaux Blanc; Budgens Claret; Château Bassanel, Minervois; Blanc de Blancs Special Cuvée; Budgens Liebfraumilch; Budgens Lambrusco Bianco; Merlot del Veneto; Frascati Superiore; Budgens Hock

Range: GOOD: Italy, Champagne and sparkling wine, Eastern Europe
  AVERAGE: Regional France, Germany, South Africa, Bordeaux, Loire, Sherry, Alsace, Australia, New Zealand, Spain, California
  POOR: Burgundy, Chile

Budgens published a mission statement this year. Its philosophy, apparently, is to provide 'quality, value and friendly service on the high street and in the heart of the community'. This is no simple task – the high street has been through some torrid times in the last decade, what with the growth of the out-of-town superstore and the boom in what the marketing bods call 'one-stop shopping'. The days when John Budgen opened his first grocery stores in Maidenhead, East Anglia and the Thames Valley, 124 years ago, seem to belong to a different millennium, never mind another century.

How does a company of Budgens' size compete with the likes of Tesco, Sainsbury's and Safeway? Well, by keeping staffing levels low, for a start. Tony Finnerty, the man who single-handedly runs the booze department at Budgens, remains the wine trade's answer to the Lone Ranger. 'Tonto's not arrived yet,' he says. 'He's still chasing squaws.' Lesser men would whinge about their lot, but Finnerty accepts it all with a smile.

At least he's managed to get away from Ruislip this year, visiting France, Spain, Italy and Germany on buying trips. 'It's still very difficult for me to visit places that demand more than a five-day visit,' he says. So don't expect to come across any of the Finnerty blarney in Chile, South Africa, Australia or California.

Of course, Finnerty doesn't *have* to visit a region to find good wines. He picked a couple of really good California reds from Sebastiani's Pepperwood Grove range without straying from his desk. But we'd still like to see him given the chance to visit the New World and expand his range further.

As things stand, he's done a pretty good job over the last year. Wine sales are up 32 per cent by volume and 12 per cent by value, and Finnerty appears pleased with the progress of his crusade 'to get people away from Liebfraumilch and Lambrusco and buying something else at a comfortable price level'.

Finnerty has been forced to compete with the major supermarket groups. 'We've done lots of cut-price activity,' he says, 'but where possible I've tried to reduce a wine from £3.99 to £2.99 rather than from £2.99 to £1.99 or less.' Nevertheless, Finnerty concedes that deals are a big draw. The aim is to get customers into a store and 'increase their average spend'. Local shoppers are appraised of 'cut-price specials' via leaflet drops. These are offered every three weeks, with anything up to five wines in the frame.

As a 'convenience supermarket', Budgens relies on what are termed secondary rather than primary shoppers – in other words, on the person who wants to top up his or her weekly shop on the way home from work. The drinks department is a major beneficiary of Budgens' high street locations, which is why Finnerty sees his main competition as off-licences rather than the larger supermarkets.

There has been a certain amount of restructuring at Budgens over the last year. Penny Market has been scrapped and replaced with something called Fresh Save (who thinks up these names?). As its snappy moniker suggests, this is geared to selling fresh, as opposed to frozen or possibly stale, food. The new stores will stock a larger range of wines than the discount-style Penny Market did. More work for the beleaguered Mr Finnerty? 'No, they'll take things from the Budgens list,' he says. Out of a total Budgens range of 360 lines, Fresh Save will have 50 or so.

Back in the parent store, Finnerty has taken on another 20 wines this year, expanding his imports from South Africa, Australia, Chile and California. Some of these listings are fairly obvious choices, but Finnerty also makes an effort 'to pick up wines from smaller producers and get away from the norm. We can buy restricted volumes of certain wines and gear distribution to availability.'

Finnerty has been at Budgens for four years now, a period which has coincided with what he calls 'vast improvements' in the organisation of the stores. Under his guidance, the wine range has nearly doubled in size and now includes a decent selection of sub-£5 bottles, with good choices from Italy, Spain, France and Eastern Europe.

In the face of his customers' continuing preference for Lambrusco and Liebfraumilch, we applaud Finnerty's determination to list unusual things, such as a Trebbiano from Australia, a Cabernet Franc from California, a German Dornfelder and a South African Pinot Noir. These are the sort of wines that will entice more sophisticated wine drinkers through the doors of their local Budgens. Who knows, if they buy enough bottles, Tony Finnerty may have an assistant by next year. Step forward, prospective Tontos.

White

Under £3

BULGARIA

1994 Vinex Preslav Chardonnay/Sauvignon Blanc
££ / 3 / ♪   14/20
Lemony, boiled sweets style blend of Chardonnay and Sauvignon Blanc
in an encouragingly accessible, modern style. More please, Bulgaria.

FRANCE

Blanc de Blanc Cuvée Spéciale, Jean Bellay
0 / 3 / ♪   12/20
A Chenin Blanc based Loire quaffer with rather unappealing sweet and
sour characters.

GERMANY

1994 Bereich Bernkastel, Peter Mertes
0 / 5 / ♪   12/20
This tastes more like a Euroblend than a Mosel. At this price, perhaps
it is.

ITALY

Tocai del Veneto, Vino da Tavola, Gambellara
0 / 3 / ♭   10/20
Stale, confected and sadly limping beyond its sell-by date. Should be
poured into Lake Garda, but beware, the fish might bite back.

SPAIN

Espuma Prima, La Calda de Siete Aguas, 5%
£ / 6 / ♪   13/20
Frothy demerara sugar and ice cream soda scented white made from the
Muscat grape. Spain's answer to Lambrusco.

£3-5

AUSTRALIA

1995 Flinders Creek South East Australia Trebbiano
£££ / 2 / ♦   15/20

An unusual find by the elusive Tony Finnerty – a lemony, vibrantly fruity white with peardrop and cinnamon spiciness. It's rare to see the normally undistinguished Trebbiano mentioned on an Australian label, but the quality here justifies its use.

1993 Brown Brothers Dry Muscat
££ / 2 / ♦   15/20

Fresh, floral, lime-juicy Victorian white, which has just made the transition from a flute to a Burgundian bottle. The wine remains as good as ever.

FRANCE

1994 Domaine l'Argentier Terret, Vin de Pays des Côtes de Thau
£ / 3 / ♦   14/20

From the fusillage of flying winemaker Jacques Lurton, this is an unoaked, boiled sweets and banana style Languedoc white made from the local Terret grape, traditionally reserved for vermouth.

1994 Chardonnay, François Dulac, Vin de Pays de l'Ile de Beauté
£ / 2 / ♦   13/20

From Corsica's flat eastern seaboard, this is a basic, faintly buttery, unoaked Chardonnay made by the Languedoc's Skalli Fortant de France. The name is more attractive than the over-£4 price.

1993 Tuilerie du Bosc, Côtes de Saint Mont, Cave de Plaimont
0 / 2 / ♦   13/20

A bungled attempt at a Graves-syle Gascon white, in which the oak tastes bitter and sawdusty. Less oak and a lot more fruit would be preferable.

1994 Mâcon-Igé, Les Vignerons d'Igé
££ / 2 / ♦   15/20

Well done to the Igé co-operative for keeping this spicy, unoaked

Chardonnay under £5. The bottle looks good and the wine is fresh and comparatively complex for a Mâcon-Villages.

GERMANY

1993 Flonheimer Adelberg Auslese
££ / 6 / 1   14/20
Inexpensive for an Auslese at just over £3.50, this is a peachy, perfumed Müller-Thurgau-based white with a grapey hint of Scheurebe-like spiciness.

1993 Klüsserather St Michael Kabinett
£ / 5 / 1   13/20
Not an attempt, we are assured, to pass off a Budgens wine as a Marks & Spencer own-label. Instead, this is a clean, grapey German quaffer for which Budgens and presumably Saint Michael himself are happy to take full responsibility.

1991 Baden Gewürztraminer Reserve, Badischer Winzerkeller
0 / 3 / 1   10/20
Not badisch, just plain bad.

HUNGARY

1993 Tokaji Furmint Chateau Megyer
££ / 1 / 1   14/20
With its unusual tea-leaf and ginger-spice nose, this dry Hungarian white made in the Tokaji region, famous for its sweet dessert wines, is an off-the-wall style. It's well worth a punt, but be warned – it may be a bit austere for some palates.

ITALY

1994 Lugana Villa Flora, Zenato
££ / 2 / 1   15/20
Distinctively Italian in flavour, this is a nutty, peachy, weighty Lake Garda white with a knife blade of fresh acidity and a bitter twist.

1994 Frascati Superiore, Casale del Grillo
££ / 2 / ♩   14/20
Lemony, aromatic, aniseedy Frascati with good body and a nutty
Mediterranean tang.

UNITED STATES

1993 Glen Ellen Proprietor's Reserve Chardonnay
£ / 3 / ♩   13/20
Basic, sweetened up, oak-chippy Californian white, which needs more
concentration on the wine and a little less on the packaging – at least
for the discerning British market.

Red

Under £3

BULGARIA

1992 Stara Zagora, Merlot/Cabernet Sauvignon
£ / MB / ♩   13/20
From a winery that sounds like a cross between a Czech brewery and a
football team, this is an oaky, chunky, deeply coloured, modern red with
fresh acidity and green pepper notes.

FRANCE

Vin de Pays des Coteaux de l'Ardèche
£ / MB / ♩   13/20
Warm, soft, carbonic maceration style southern French red with hefty
alcohol.

ITALY

Merlot del Veneto, Vino da Tavola, Gambellara, Zonin
££ / MB / ♩   14/20
Grassy, unoaked northern Italian red with attractive ginger spice
and refreshing, thirst-quenching acidity.

£3–5

AUSTRALIA

1994 Brown Brothers Tarrango
££ / MB / 1   15/20
After a wobble last year, this unusual Beaujolais style Australian red, made from a rare crossing of Touriga Nacional and Sultana grapes, has returned to form. Juicy, fresh and packed with succulent fruit. Guaranteed not to swear at tennis umpires.

CHILE

1992 Undurraga Pinot Noir
0 / FB / 1   13/20
Chunky, plummy, bizarrely flavoured Pinot Noir from a traditional Chilean winery which is finally starting to move in the right direction. Judging from this wine, the promising new Pinot Noir plantings have not made it into the bottle yet.

FRANCE

1993 Château Bassanel Minervois, Jeanjean
£ / FB / 1   13/20
A Languedoc red whose robustly sweet Grenache-like flavours reminded us more of a Côtes du Rhône than a Minervois.

Budgens Claret, Dulong
££ / MB / 1   14/20
A smooth, pleasantly grassy, modern-style claret from the house of Dulong, which shows that paying a little extra for Bordeaux is often well worthwhile.

1993 Faugères, Jeanjean
0 / FB / 1   12/20
Stale, tannic, overextracted plum-skin red which bears as much resemblance to decent Faugères as we do to Tom Cruise and Matt Dillon.

1994 Le Haut Colombier, Vin de Pays de la Drôme
£ / MB / ♪   13/20
Soft, peppery, sweetish Granache-based red with a plonky aftertaste.

1993 Crozes Hermitage, Quinson
0 / LB / ♪   12/20
Made by a Fleurie-based *négociant*, this tastes more like an over-sugared Beaujolais than a Crozes Hermitage. Did someone muddle the vats up, or was it just an exceptionally light vintage in the northern Rhône?

1992 Domaine Bosquet-Canet, Listel, Vin de Pays des Sables du Golfe du Lion
££ / MB / ♪   14/20
Made by Listel, the company which produces large quantities of indifferent rosé, this is a surprisingly well-made, modern Cabernet Sauvignon with elegant fruit and polished new oak character.

1994 Château Rousseau, Côtes du Rhône-Villages
££ / FB / ▬   15/20
Heady, spicy, densely fruity Rhône with just the right amount of chewy rusticity and alcohol. A fireside or barbecue red.

1993 Costières de Nîmes
££ / FB / ♪   15/20
Chocolatey, rich, alcoholic Provence red with a hint of Mediterranean spice.

1993 Tuilerie du Bosc, Côtes de St-Mont, Cave de Plaimont
££ / MB / ♪   14/20
A claret-style blend of Cabernet Sauvignon and Gascony's homegrown Tannat grape, this is a well-made, oaky red with an astringent bite on the finish.

GERMANY

Rheinhessen Dornfelder

£ / LB / ♪   13/20

A highly aromatic, lightly fruity red, which smells and tastes more like
the white Müller-Thurgau than the red Dornfelder grape. Close your
eyes and dream of Liebfraumilch.

NEW ZEALAND

1993 Montana Marlborough Cabernet Sauvignon

£ / MB / ♪   13/20

A wine which has suffered from the cool growing conditions of the 1993
New Zealand vintage, this grassy, oaky red is showing too many weeds
and vegetables.

PORTUGAL

1990 Dão Dom Ferraz, Caves Primavera

£ / FB / ♪   13/20

Robust, rustic, old-fashioned Dão (pronounced 'dung'). On second
thoughts . . .

SOUTH AFRICA

1994 Table Mountain Pinot Noir, Stellenbosch

£ / MB / ♪   13/20

Jammy, morello cherry style red with a sweet touch of Pinot Noir
character.

SPAIN

1989 Viña Albali

£ / MB / ♪   13/20

A Garnacha-based Rioja-style Spanish red with charry, spearminty oak
and drying tannins. Badly needs food.

UNITED STATES

1993 Sutter Home Merlot
££ / MB / 🜚   14/20

From the people who invented California Blush, this is a real wine, showing the grassy, chocolatey sweetness of the Merlot grape to good effect. Well-priced at around £4, especially given the current fad for Merlot on the United States' mellow West Coast.

1993 Pepperwood Grove Cabernet Franc
££ / MB / 🜚   15/20

Made by the dynamic Sebastiani winery, this is a concentrated mouthful of grassy, blackcurranty California red wine in an attractive package based, unusually, on the lesser-known Cabernet Franc grape.

1993 Pepperwood Grove Zinfandel
£££ / MB / ➤   16/20

From the same winery, this is even more expressive, with plenty of colour, tobaccoey, ripe fruit and restrained, fine-grained tannins. The raspberry sweetness of California's native Zinfandel grape is nicely framed by American oak.

£5–8

SPAIN

1987 Gran Condal Rioja Gran Reserva
£££ / MB / 🜚   16/20

Made by the Rioja Santiago Bodega, this is a mature, old-fashioned, sweetly fruity Rioja with dry, leafy tannins and a sheen of vanilla. Exceptional value for a Gran Reserva at just over £5, but don't allow it to linger in your wine rack.

Sparkling

£3–5

AUSTRALIA

Flinders Creek Brut Rosé
££ / 3 / ♪   14/20
Pale, strawberry cup and rhubarb style rosé. Good value at under £5, but
don't expect too much complexity.

£5–8

GERMANY

1993 Schmitt Vom Schmitt Rheinhessen Sekt, Magnum
£ / 4 / ♪   13/20
Germany has to think of somewhere to put its unripe grapes, which
explains this light, magnum-sized, appley, off-dry fizz. At least the bottle
looks good.

NEW ZEALAND

Lindauer Brut
££ / 3 / ♪   14/20
The lesser of Montana's two New Zealand sparkling wines – Deutz
Marlborough Cuvée being the other – this is a well-made, large-bubbled
fizz with fresh, tangy, cool climate fruit. Still good value at under £7.

CO-OP **(*)

Head Office: CWS Retail, National Buying, Marketing & Distribution Group, PO Box 53, New Century House, Manchester M60 4ES

Telephone: 0161 834 1212

Number of branches: 2,500 licensed branches

Credit cards accepted: All major credit cards

Hours of opening: Varies from store to store

By-the-case sales: In selected superstores

Glass loan: In selected superstores

Home delivery: Arranged at local level

Clubs: Offers to Co-op members

Discounts: Occasionally on large orders

In-store tastings: Regularly in selected superstores

Other facilities: Regular monthly promotions across the range

Top ten best-selling wines: Co-op Lambrusco Bianco; Co-op Liebfraumilch; Co-op Chianti; Co-op Valencia Red; Co-op Laski Rizling; Co-op Claret; Co-op Portuguese Rosé; Co-op Vino de la Tierra, Valle de Monterrey; Co-op Vin de Pays Côtes Catalanes; Co-op Hock

Range: GOOD: Chile, Spain
　　　　AVERAGE: Australia, Portugal, regional France, Eastern Europe,
　　　　　　　　Bordeaux, Beaujolais, South Africa, Italy
　　　　POOR: Germany, United States

Two years ago we got rather excited about a new range of wines supposedly on its way to the Co-op's 2,500 licensed stores. Gosh, we thought to ourselves, this should bring a bit of excitement to the shelves of our local Co-op. We stood back and waited for the deluge of thrilling wines, but in most cases they didn't materialise.

The Co-op's two buyers, Master of Wine Arabella Woodrow and Paul Bastard, have been very busy over the last 12 months, increasing the list to a biggest-ever 482 wines and taking on all sorts of fancy things, from Supertuscan reds to £9 Spanish Chardonnays. If we were of a more cynical disposition, we might ask: Haven't we been here before? Not so, according to Bastard. 'This time the stuff will make the stores.'

To be fair to the Co-op team, it can't be easy buying for an organis-ation with more limbs than an octopus. Believe us, the structure of the Co-operative Retail Trading Group is complicated. We've had it ex-plained to us three times and we're only just beginning to understand it.

Briefly, this is how it works. The Co-op is an umbrella organisation for 51 different co-operative societies, the largest of which is the Co-operative Wholesale Society Retail. Woodrow and Bastard buy for CWS, but not necessarily for other parts of the co-operative movement. Groups such as the Co-operative Retail Society (which includes Co-op, Leo's, Lo-Cost and Pioneer) take some of the Co-op range but are also free to source their own wines.

Still with us? 'It is complicated,' admits Woodrow, and she's got a PhD in biochemistry, 'but by its very nature, co-operation isn't simple. The Co-op is not one but a number of different societies. So you won't find every one of our wines in every store.' You sure won't – at least 30 per cent of the Co-op doesn't have to buy any of the wines sourced by Woodrow and Bastard. The places you're least likely to find them (the wines, rather than the buyers, that is) are Wales, the Southwest and central Manchester. In other parts of the country, you're in with a shout.

The other problem is the size of the stores, which vary from 'com-munity stores to hypermarkets with every possible permutation in between', according to Woodrow. As such, the Co-op reminds us of the London street system – quaint, unwieldy and developed with little or no central planning.

Only two of the CWS's 1,288 licensed stores carry the whole wine range – Aberdeen and Benton near Newcastle. Elsewhere, you may or may not find some of the better wines bought by Woodrow and Bastard during the last year. Nevertheless, Bastard denies that the more interesting wines are a façade. 'We need those wines in our biggest stores.'

He also says that 'the Co-op's never been as organised and controlled as it is now. It's only in the last two years that there's been any form of co-ordinated central buying.' There is even the distinct possibility that the CWS and the CRS could merge in the medium term. Such a merger would certainly make the job of the Co-op's wine buyers, not to mention its customers, a lot easier.

These caveats apart, the Co-op wine range has been through wholesale, and much-needed, changes over the last two years. 'Our list was very traditional,' says Woodrow, 'with an awful lot of German QbAs that tasted the same.' The New World has been the main beneficiary of the revamp, with new wines from Chile, Australia and South Africa. 'We've also tried to expand traditional areas with more exciting wines.'

It's good to see the Co-op initiating projects of its own, rather than buying off the peg. Hungaroo Pinot Gris and the Chilean Long Slim White and Red are encouraging examples of this trend. To some extent, the Co-op has been forced to be more pro-active. Bastard and Woodrow found that, because they couldn't shift the volumes of a Tesco or a Sainsbury's, they were being fobbed off with older vintages of certain wines.

The new ideas have gone down well with Co-op customers, in so far as one can generalise about such a diverse group. CWS wine sales are up 20 per cent in volume and 'not far off in value' according to Bastard. 'We're selling more expensive wines than we've ever done before and people are buying across the range.'

This is just as well, as several of the Co-op's most basic wines are deeply uninspiring. The German selection in particular needs an urgent blood transfusion. Further up the range, as we have indicated, there are interesting wines from Italy, Spain, France, Portugal and Chile. There's also evidence that the Co-op is keen to avoid 'me-too' brands where possible.

Set against all this is the threat of what Bastard calls 'commercial pressures from above' to list cheap, large volume wines to compete with the £1.99 offerings from competitors. 'There's a lot of strong character in this department holding out against the cheap and nasty.'

We hope it stays that way. 'You have to remember,' adds Bastard, 'that we're coming from miles off the pace. We're five years behind some of the big players and we've got a lot of ground to make up.' Things are certainly moving in a positive direction at the Co-op. The organisation is still hamstrung by the structure and size of its retail operation, but provided some of the Co-op's new wines trickle down into the smaller stores, we should see further progress in 1996.

White

Under £3

BULGARIA

1994 Debut Sauvignon Blanc Fumé, Russe
£ / 3 / 1   13/20
A combination of fruit sweetness and oak chip make this modern Bulgarian white a pleasant, if slightly confected, drink.

1994 Bear Ridge Chardonnay, Lyaskovets, Kym Milne
£££ / 3 / 1   14/20
Fresh, grapefruity, zesty Chardonnay made by Kym Milne in Bulgaria. It's encouraging to see Bulgaria producing white wines like this at under £3.

CHILE

1995 Chilean White
££ / 3 / 1   14/20
Made at the excellent Canepa winery, this is a good example of the clean, pure fruit flavours emerging from Chile. Predominantly made from the Sauvignon Blanc grape by Andres Ilabaca, it's agreeably fresh and gooseberryish.

CROATIA

Co-op Laski Rizling, Kontinentalna Hrvalska
0 / 5 / 1   10/20
From the bad old days of Balkan winemaking, this is a baked, gluey, resinous white that's halfway to a retsina. We'll leave you on your own for the second half of the journey, if that's OK with you.

GERMANY

Co-op Hock
0 / 5 / ♪   10/20
Nasty, bitter, souped-up German sweetie from the Rheinhessen co-operative.

Co-op Liebfraumilch
0 / 5 / ♪   11/20
From the same operation, this is a marginally more interesting, slightly fresher, grapey white.

Co-op Morio Muscat
£ / 4 / ♪   12/20
Slightly drier than the previous two whites, this is the best of the Co-op's basic German offerings, although we wouldn't cross an autobahn to drink it.

ITALY

Co-op Lambrusco Bianco
0 / 5 / ♪   11/20
Produced by the large Fratelli Martini set-up, this is a bog-standard, sweet and fizzy Lambrusco with rather sharp acidity.

Co-op Sicilian White
£££ / 2 / ♪   14/20
Packed with local character, this fresh, nutty Mediterranean white has an attractive lime-like streak and plenty of flavour, especially for a wine at this undemanding price.

SPAIN

Co-op Valle de Monterrey, Vino de la Tierra
£ / 2 / ♪   13/20
From Galicia's Costa Verde, this is a light, apple-crisp white made mainly from the local Trincadeira grape. A decent tapas bar quaffer.

£3–5

AUSTRALIA

Murrumbidgee Estate Fruity Wine

£ / 4 / 1   13/20

To keep Aussie wine under £3.50, producers such as Cranswick-Smith are resorting to basic grapes such as Frontignac, Gordo and Colombard. The result in this fruit salad blend is a simple marmaladey white with sweetness to round it out.

1994 Co-op Australian Chardonnay, Angoves

£ / 3 / 1   14/20

For an extra £1, you can buy yourself something with Chardonnay on the label. This is a ripe, buttery, commercial style with oak character and a slice of lemony freshness.

CHILE

1994 Long Slim White Chardonnay/Semillon

£££ / 2 / 1   15/20

Blended specially for the Co-op at the Errázuriz winery by winemaker Kym Milne, the name of this exciting, superfresh white is a Chilean homage to Australia's Long Flat White. The flavours are altogether different though – zesty, grapefruity and unoaked.

1994 Carmen Chardonnay

£££ / 2 / 1   15/20

Another super Chilean white, this time from the hand of Alvaro Espinosa, one of Chile's most exciting young winemakers. It's a riper, smokier style with rich, buttery fruit and tangy acidity.

1994 Caliterra Casablanca Chardonnay

£££ / 2 / 1   17/20

Star winemaker Ignacio Recabarren has produced a brilliant value Chardonnay from Chile's most exciting white wine area, the Casablanca Valley, halfway between Santiago and the port of Valparaiso. Fresh, clean-cut, citrus-fruit flavours with a grapefruity tang and a touch of oak.

FRANCE

1994 Vignerons des Ramparts Sauvignon Blanc

££ / 2 / ⁀   14/20

Not quite as fresh and well-defined as other Foncalieu whites we've had
this year, but this soft, asparagusy Sauvignon Blanc is still a good drink
at under £4.

Co-op Vin de Pays d'Oc Chardonnay

0 / 2 / ⁀   11/20

Hello, anyone awake? This wine went into a coma some time ago and
hasn't come round yet.

GERMANY

Kirchheimer Schwarzerde Beerenauslese, half-bottle

£££ / 7 / ↩   16/20

Something of a bargain, this smoky, honeyed, buttered Brazil nut-like
dessert wine is unctuously rich in apricoty lusciousness and dried fruit
flavours, but still remarkably fresh.

HUNGARY

1994 Hungaroo Pinot Gris

££ / 3 / ⁀   14/20

Made by Australian Nick Butler at the Neszmely winery, this ripe, spicy,
peachy white is one-third of the way to Alsace in style, with attractive
softness and full-bodied weight.

ITALY

1994 Chardonnay del Piemonte Alasia

£ / 2 / ⁀   14/20

A new venture combining the talents of Martin Shaw, the original
Australian flying winemaker, and the excellent Araldica co-operative in
northwestern Italy's Piemonte region. This rich, full-fruited, unoaked
Chardonnay marries the best of the New and Old Worlds. Our only
worry is that it seems to be ageing quickly.

MOLDOVA

Kirkwood Moldovan Chardonnay

£ / 3 / ∄   13/20

An attempt to revamp the Hincesti Moldovan Chardonnay, this is Hugh Ryman's best effort yet, but still tastes rather confected, with a boudoir aroma of talcum powder and a curious touch of baked banana.

SOUTH AFRICA

1995 Kumala Chenin Chardonnay

£ / 3 / ∄   13/20

From the Sonop Co-op, this is a cool-fermented, peardrop and banana style white padded out with sweetness.

1994 Oak Village Chardonnay

££ / 2 / ∄   14/20

More of a wine than the Kumala, this is a crisper, zestier, better-defined white with attractive lemony freshness and some well-judged oak flavour.

SPAIN

1991 Berberana Carta de Oro Rioja, Crianza

£££ / 2 / ∄   15/20

A modern take on an old-fashioned Spanish style, this is a coconutty, lightly oaked Viura-based white with fresh, citrus-fruit character and some appealing, peachy depth.

£5–8

FRANCE

Le Pavois d'Or Sauternes, 50cl

££ / 5 / ∄   15/20

Made by the reliable Bordeaux *négociant* firm of Ginestet, this is a stylishly packaged, well-made blend of Sauternes vintages with unusual marzipan and liquorice flavours that reminded us of a cross between a Jurançon and a Monbazillac.

ITALY

1994 Boscaini Monteleone Soave
££ / 2 /   14/20
A nutty, soft, pleasantly rounded Soave made in a modern style by the
merchant firm of Boscaini with a touch of buttery character derived from
contact with its fermentation lees.

Over £8

SPAIN

1994 Augustus Chardonnay, Cellars Puig i Roca
££ / 2 /   16/20
One of a growing number of Chardonnays produced in the Penedés
region of Spain, this is an opulent fudge, toast and vanilla style white
with enough acidity to keep it fresh for another year or two. At nearly
£9.50 a bottle, it's not cheap, but José Puig's Chardonnay is one of
Spain's finest.

Red

Under £3

BULGARIA

Russe Country Red Cabernet/Cinsault
££ / MB /   14/20
When the Co-op offered this wine to its customers at the knockdown
price of £1.99, it sold 20,000 cases in a month. Even at around £2.70,
this juicy, unoaked, plummy red from the modern Russe winery is still a
bargain.

CHILE

1994 Chilean Red
££ / MB / ♪   14/20

Blended at the Concha y Toro winery by American Ed Flaherty, this is a deeply coloured blackcurrant pastille style Chilean red with a slightly old-fashioned edge. Good at the price, though.

ROMANIA

1993 Prahova Valley Pinot Noir
££ / MB / ♪   14/20

More modern in style than most Romanian reds, this is a fresh, vibrant, violet and damson-fruity Pinot Noir with a touch of jammy rusticity.

SPAIN

Co-op Valencia Red
£ / MB / ♪   13/20

An unoaked, no-frills, Levante red from the ubiquitous Vicente Gandia operation. Light and beetrooty.

Marqués de Parada, Garnacha, Calatayud, Bodegas Maluenda
££ / MB / ♪   14/20

An extra 20 pence will buy you this juicier, fruitier, more substantial Spanish red, albeit with a firm, dry tannic bite.

£3–5

AUSTRALIA

1993 Co-op Australian Cabernet
£ / MB / ♪   14/20

Fresh, minty, commercial red with pleasant liquorice and green pepper characters and marked, but well-judged, sweet American oak influence from Angoves in Australia's Riverland.

BRAZIL

Amazon Cabernet Sauvignon
£ / MB / ♪   13/20
A charry, minty, oak-chipped novelty from Brazil with a brilliant
Amazon-jungle parrot label. One for the Copacabana posing pouch.

CHILE

Long Slim Red Cabernet/Merlot
££ / MB / ♪   14/20
The partner to Kym Milne's enjoyable Long Slim White made at the
Errazuriz winery north of Santiago, this is fresh, juicy and unoaked with
a typically chewy Chilean aftertaste.

FRANCE

1994 Co-op Vin de Pays d'Oc, Merlot, Boutinot
££ / MB / ♪   14/20
Blended by Englishman Paul Boutinot, this is a sweet, grassy, chocolatey
style of Merlot, which, as David Coleman might have said, asks all sorts
of questions of inexpensive Bordeaux.

1994 Co-op Vin de Pays d'Oc, Syrah, Boutinot
£ / MB / ♪   13/20
From the same English merchant, this is a chunkier, fuller, southern red
with youthful flavours of black olive and unripe plums. A little too
chewy for our taste.

1994 Domaine de Conquet, Merlot, Vin de Pays d'Oc
£££ / MB / ♪   15/20
An attractively priced, soft, lusciously fruity Merlot from the south of
France made with his customary sureness of touch by flying winemaker
Jacques Lurton. Another good claret substitute.

Bad-Tempered Cyril, Vin de Pays d'Oc
£ / FB / ♪   13/20
Made by Australian Nick Butler at Domaine de Raissac in the Languedoc,
Bad-Tempered Cyril is a blend of Tempranillo and Syrah (the name is a

way round the ludicrous laws imposed by the French *appellation* authorities, which forbid the use of more than one grape variety on the label of a vin de pays wine). Sadly, the wine doesn't live up to its name, showing rather too much dry tannin and green fruit.

Co-op Claret, Dourthe
£ / MB / ⁑   13/20
Chewy, basic claret for people who haven't discovered the often better value Merlots and Cabernet Sauvignons emerging from the Languedoc-Roussillon.

1994 Domaine Serjac Grenache, Vin de Pays d'Oc
££ / FB / ⁑   14/20
One of the few decent red wines we've had this year from Domaines Virginie, this is a warmly fruity Grenache with a touch of oak and rich, faintly minty depth.

ITALY

1993 Co-op Chianti, Piccini
£ / MB / ⁑   13/20
Soupy, raisiny, dry Chianti which lacks a bit of concentration. The sort of thing they used to sell in wicker flasks – and probably still do.

1993 Le Trulle, Primitivo del Salento
£ / FB / ⁑   13/20
Despite the fact that this is made by Kym Milne from the local Primitivo grape, we found that the oak-chip sweetness rather got in the way of any indigenous character. Chewy stuff.

1991 Ceppi Storici, Oak-aged Barbera
££ / MB / ⁑   15/20
A meaty, gamey, well-oaked Barbera from the excellent Araldica co-operative. Chocolatey softness, spice and an appealingly funky character make this an interesting buy at under £5.

1993 Boscaini Le Canne, Bardolino
£ / LB / ⁑   14/20
Light, fresh, cherried quaffing red with an attractive purple label. A teeny bit overpriced for a basic Bardolino.

PORTUGAL

1991 Co-op Bairrada Tinto, Sogrape
££ / FB / ⚑   14/20

A peppery, Rhône-like northern Portuguese red in which the Baga grape's natural acidity has kept the wine fresh and fruity, despite what are comparatively rustic tannins.

1991 Quinta de Pancas Cabernet Sauvignon
££ / MB / ⚑   15/20

A fluent Portuguese attempt at a modern, international style of Cabernet Sauvignon. We enjoyed this soft, spicy, elegantly oaked red, and so, we trust, will you.

1991 Duas Quintas, Douro, Ramos Pinto
£££ / FB / ⤙   16/20

Made by the Louis Roederer-owned house of Ramos Pinto, this is a rich, structured, minty, concentrated red made from native Douro grape varieties, which are so good that normally they'd be reserved for fortified winemaking.

SOUTH AFRICA

Kumala Cinsault/Pinotage, Sonop
£££ / FB / ⚑   15/20

A juicy, modern, banana-scented blend made by the softening carbonic maceration process, and showing masses of sweet, gluggable, come-hither fruit. Warmer than the embrace of the Springbok back row.

SPAIN

1994 Santara Cabernet/Merlot, Conca de Barbera
££ / MB / ⚑   14/20

From the *appellation* which sounds like a medieval Hollywood epic, this is an Australian-influenced red made by flying winemaker Hugh Ryman and showing spicy, charry oak in abundance. The underlying fruit is a mite green and bitter.

UNITED STATES

1992 Glen Ellen Merlot, Proprietor's Reserve
£ / MB / 🍷   13/20

Sweetened-up, rather confected Merlot made by the price-fighting varietal specialists Glen Ellen, in California. This tastes like a blackberry and rhubarb juice cocktail.

£5–8

AUSTRALIA

1992 Leasingham Domaine Cabernet/Malbec
£ / MB / 🍷   15/20

They're no longer the bargain they once were, but the red wines from the Clare Valley's Leasingham Domaine are still supremely drinkable Aussie styles. This sweetly oaked blend is fresh, medium-bodied and softly succulent.

FRANCE

1993 Morgon Les Charmes, Domaine Brisson
££ / MB / 🍷   15/20

A regular listing at the Co-op, Gérard Brisson's well-made Morgons are serious, honest examples of what a Beaujolais *cru* should be: sweet, ripe and attractively cherried.

SPAIN

1992 Enate Tempranillo/Cabernet, Crianza, Somontano
£££ / MB / 🍷   16/20

A cool-climate, almost Rioja-like blend from one of Spain's most exciting up-and-coming regions, this is lightly oaked, refreshing and finely balanced. Great value at just over £5.

Rosé

Under £3

PORTUGAL

Co-op Portuguese Rosé
£ / 4 / ½   13/20
From the company which inflicted Mateus Rosé on the wine-drinking public, this medium sweet Mateus lookalike is bubblegummy, soft and suitably bland. Has anyone managed to get one of these lampshade bottles into a bottle bank yet?

Sparkling

£5–8

AUSTRALIA

Barramundi Sparkling
£ / 4 / ½   13/20
A sweet, hefty, unctuous fizz made from neutral grapes but showing a touch of Opal Fruits character. Made to make you pass water.

Fortified

£3–5

SPAIN

Co-op Moscatel de Valencia, Vinival
££ / 8 / ½   14/20
Almost the only Moscatel we've tasted in this country that doesn't come from Gandia, this old-fashioned, orange-coloured fortified dessert wine is a super-ripe, supersweet, marmalade and raisin like concoction, with a surprising amount of character.

DAVISONS ***

Head Office: Davisons Wine Merchants, 7 Aberdeen Road, Croydon, Surrey CR0 1EQ

Telephone: 0181 681 3222

Number of branches: 77

Credit cards accepted: Access, Visa

Hours of opening: Monday to Saturday 10.00am to 2.00pm and 5.00pm to 10.00pm; Sunday 12.00pm to 2.00pm and 7.00pm to 9.00pm

By-the-case sales: Yes

Glass loan: Free

Home delivery: Free in local area

Clubs: No

Discounts: Eight-and-a-half per cent on mixed or unmixed cases

In-store tastings: Yes, occasionally

Top ten best-selling wines: Jacob's Creek Semillon/Chardonnay; Pampette Blanc Dry; Hardy's Nottage Hill Chardonnay; Pampette Blanc Medium; Bulgarian Cabernet Sauvignon; Jacob's Creek Red; Liebfraumilch Huesgen; Hardy's Stamp Series Semillon/Chardonnay; Hardy's Stamp Series Cabernet-Shiraz; Nottage Hill Cabernet Sauvignon

Range: GOOD: Bordeaux, Burgundy, Australia, regional France, Port
AVERAGE: Loire, New Zealand, South Africa, Rhône, Italy, Eastern Europe, Germany, Chile, Champagne and sparkling wines, Spain
POOR: United States, Portugal

As he stood us a round of beers at the bar of JT's, Michael Davies seemed to have put the gloomy prognostications of the previous year behind him. The managing director of Davisons was his chirpy self again as he sensed the feel-good factor returning to Croydon and the leafy suburban parades in which Davisons plies its traditional trade. Davisons' swanky, expensive refit of the now-defunct Master Cellar was looking good. A second JT's would shortly be opening in Banbury. And a brand new shop had opened in a prime Croydon site.

These were just the icing on the wedding cake, however. The marzipan was Mayor Sworder. Having taken a fancy to the traditional city wholesaler, Michael Davies proposed on Beaujolais Nouveau Day 1994 and finally got hitched in July 1995. 'It's a perfect match,' said Davies, licking his lips at the thought of the post-nuptial arrangements. 'Their customers are basically city institutions. They're desperate to get their hands on our clarets. They need access to our bulk buying. We will go through both ranges and pick the best of the two.'

Despite the chirpiness, Davies confessed that things had not looked at all good for a long time, culminating in a dreadful 1994. So much so that he had entertained doubts whether he would be taking the independent chain, founded by his great-grandfather John Thomas Davies in 1875, into the next millennium. 'Last year it was very worrying. Supermarkets have knocked out the specialists. It was getting to the stage where had trade continued to decline the way it had been over the last three years, it simply wouldn't have been any fun any more.

'There have always been the two sides to the business. As a company, we've had pubs (40) and shops (77), and one has always performed better than the other. Since 1989, neither side was doing well. But things have changed for the better. It seems that we're getting it back. Not suddenly, but since February, we have started to gain ground consistently. It's still bloody difficult. Customers are very much attuned to bargains. Sales go down by two-thirds if you go over £2.99 to £3.25, and they'll transfer their allegiance for pence.'

Despite this promiscuous approach to the range, Davisons' customers are among the most loyal – and traditional – of any off-licence chain. 'We get hell for knocking stuff on the head that's been going for years, like Commanderie St John or Emva Cream.' Davisons may have an old-fashioned appearance about it, but the look is almost studied. 'We have a great relationship with our customers. Managers tend to be middle-aged couples who become friends. If you want slightly old-fashioned service, the better managers know your name, where you live and will deliver. A lot of people like the slightly old-fashioned country wine merchant image.'

For Davies, being user-friendly also means being able to respond to the supermarket competition. 'We have increased the range of Romanian and Spanish wines. We're not dropping prices, but bringing in more wines at £2.99. Our lowest price is £2.49 – on a Romanian country wine. They are adequate wines. The price per bottle had gone down in the last few years, but quality has gone up. Ten years ago, if you wanted a decent red, it had to be either claret or Burgundy.'

Almost all of Davisons' 77 shops are freehold sites, a fact which gives Davisons a cushion against escalating revenue costs. But a survey on where their profits were coming from showed that the shops were doing better than they thought. 'If the shops went, we would be crucified as a trading operation. Without the shops side, the city wholesale business couldn't cover the cost of distribution and warehousing.' So even if each shop does not necessarily make a profit, the whole would appear to be greater than the sum of the parts.

There are now 400 wines in the Davisons range. From the New World, Australia had remained static because of price increases, and New Zealand, limited. In common with much of the retail trade, South Africa and Chile have streaked ahead in 1995. Even so, claret, a Davisons stalwart, remains buoyant. 'You come to us for decent aged clarets. In the 1980s, we bought all but 1980, 1984 and 1987s. In the 1990s, we haven't bought 1991, 1992 or 1993, but we have bought some 1994s to appear as and when they're ready.' Davies has some 40,000 cases of fine wines stashed away for a wet day.

Davisons doesn't go out to woo the 18 to 35 Oddbins crowd, although Davies admits he's 'trying to make the London sites more fun as the age group comes down'. But with shops in places such as Ongar, Dagenham, Doddinghurst, Orpington, Penge and Paddock Wood, Davies is canny enough to know that even if money doesn't grow on trees, there's still a treasure trove in the tree-lined suburban towns which are Davisons' stronghold. When he says, 'I'm building towards being here in 100 years' time,' we'll drink to that.

White

Under £3

AUSTRIA

1994 Servus, Burgenland
££ / 3 / ♪   14/20
A successful attempt to prove that Austria can make fresh, drinkable
whites at under £3. This Grüner Veltliner-based blend is zesty,
grapefruity and flecked with white pepper.

£3–5

AUSTRALIA

1994 Peter Lehmann, Chenin Blanc, Barossa, South Australia
££ / 2 / ♪   14/20
Tea-leafy, lemon meringue scented Chenin from the Baron of the Barossa
Valley, Peter Lehmann, whose value-for-money wines are making a big
impact on the British market.

1994 Penfolds Koonunga Hill Chardonnay
££ / 2 / ♪   15/20
From the ever reliable Penfolds stable (or should that be ranch, given the
weight of American oak on this and most other Pennie's wines), this is a
rich, smoky Aussie white with tropical sweetness and balancing acidity.

CHILE

1994 Sauvignon Blanc, Caliterra
£££ / 2 / ♪   16/20
Crispy, zesty, engagingly aromatic Chilean Sauvignon made by the
passionate Ignacio Recabarren. This is midway between the elegance of
Sancerre and the pungency of a Marlborough Sauvignon Blanc, showing
flavours of grapefruit and melon, and tremendous concentration for a
wine at under £4.

FRANCE

1994 Château de la Jannière, Muscadet de Sèvre-et-Maine Sur Lie
££ / 1 / ♪   15/20
Attractively creamy aromas and rich, weighty fruit lifted by a *sur lie*
prickle and fresh acidity. Well-made domaine Muscadet, which shows
that it's worth paying the extra for a genuine *sur lie* wine.

1994 Domaine de Pierre Jacques, Chardonnay, Vin de Pays d'Oc
£ / 2 / ♪   14/20
Soft, modern, peardroppy white from the Languedoc-Roussillon, which
finishes up on the green, austere side. Has anyone seen Pierre's brother?

1994 Chardonnay, James Herrick, Vin de Pays d'Oc
££ / 2 / ♪   15/20
Probably the best release yet from Englishman James Herrick's extensive
Chardonnay plantings near Narbonne, this is a peachy, lightly oaked
white with hints of butter and greengage, and an RSJ of supporting
acidity.

ITALY

1994 Nuragus di Cagliari DOC, Dolianova, Vino di Sardinia
££ / 2 / ♪   14/20
Full, weighty, Sardinian white from the go-ahead, giant Dolianova co-
operative. Baked apple Mediterranean character balanced by fresh,
lemony acidity.

SOUTH AFRICA

1994 Cape Cellars Colombar
£ / 3 / ♪   13/20
Fresh, basic boiled sweets style white from South Africa's sprawling
KWV operation.

1993 Cape Cellars Sauvignon Blanc
£ / 3 / ♪   13/20
Faintly nettley, technically sound white from the same source. Yer pays
yer money . . .

SPAIN

Oak-aged Viura, Valencia, Gandia
£ / 2 / ▮   13/20

Not unlike an old-fashioned white Rioja in style, this is a strongly oaky, Levante white with neutral fruit and lime-juicy acidity. Fans of Don Darias should enjoy this one.

El Coto Bianco. Rioja, Bodegas El Coto
£££ / 2 / ▮   15/20

This is the real thing – a modern apple and pear like white Rioja with nicely integrated oak and appealing freshness and complexity.

£5–8

AUSTRALIA

1994 Ironstone Semillon/Chardonnay Margaret River
££ / 2 / ▮   15/20

Blended by David Hohnen, the man behind Western Australia's Cape Mentelle winery and New Zealand's Cloudy Bay, this is an exuberant, refreshingly grapefruity, lightly oaked blend, which could almost be made from Sauvignon Blanc.

1992 Craigmoor Chardonnay, Mudgee, New South Wales
0 / 2 / ▮   14/20

Deeply coloured, rather leaden-footed Aussie white made from super-ripe fruit and showing flavours of oak, honey and toffee-fudge – attractive enough in themselves, but lacking a little freshness.

CHILE

1993 Chardonnay Reserva, Caliterra
£££ / 2 / ▮   16/20

One of a number of outstanding Chilean whites we tasted in 1995, this is the oakier of Ignacio Recabarren's two Chardonnays from Caliterra. Made in the warm Maipo Valley, it's a richly buttery, medium-bodied style, showing well-judged oak and fresh grapefruity acidity.

FRANCE

1994 Bourgogne Aligoté Bouzeron, Domaine Carnot, Bouchard Père et Fils
££ / 1 / ♪   15/20
Bouzeron makes the best Aligoté in Burgundy. In fact, it's the only village entitled to its own *appellation* for this often austere grape. This one, from merchants Bouchard Père et Fils, is more rounded than most, showing ripe, almost exotic aromas and a streak of Chablis-like acidity.

1993 Château Boyrein, Graves, Jean Medeville
££ / 1 / ♪   15/20
A fresh, nettley, modern white Bordeaux which owes more to the Loire Valley than the Graves in flavour and texture.

1994 Château de Sours, Bordeaux Blanc
££ / 2 / ♪   15/20
Intensely flavoured, barrel-fermented, Entre-Deux-Mers white from ex-Majestic Wine director Esme Johnstone, made under the guidance of Hugh Ryman. Creamy and spicy when we tasted this from the barrel; we hope it maintains this level of quality in bottle.

1993 Pouilly Blanc-Fumé, Domaine Jean-Claude Chatelain, St Andelain
££ / 2 / ♪   16/20
On the ripe side for a Pouilly Fumé, this is a complex, concentrated Sauvignon Blanc with a faint prickle of carbon dioxide adding zip and life to its gooseberry and honey flavours.

ITALY

1993 Chardonnay del Friuli, Villa del Borgo
££ / 2 / ♪   15/20
Floral, unoaked, pear-scented northeastern Italian white with an admirable, piercingly clean Chardonnay character. Stylish stuff.

NEW ZEALAND

1994 Nobilo Sauvignon Blanc, Marlborough
££ / 2 /]   15/20

With its asparagus and tinned pea nose, this soft, juicy, ripe Sauvignon could only come from the South Island's Marlborough region. And it does.

1994 Oyster Bay Sauvignon Blanc
££ / 2 /]   16/20

From the dynamic brother-and-sister duo of Rose and Jim Delegat, this is a crisper, more elegant, but still intensely gooseberry fruity Marlborough Sauvignon Blanc edged with a grapefruity tang.

1994 Nautilus Sauvignon Blanc, Marlborough
££ / 2 /]   17/20

Made by Australia's Yalumba winery, this is even more concentrated, essence-of-assertive Marlborough Sauvignon. A stylish, beautifully crafted white made by Simon Adams under the supervision of Yalumba's chief winemaker, Brian Walsh.

SOUTH AFRICA

1994 Sauvignon Blanc, Saxenburg Estate
£ / 2 /]   14/20

Saxenburg is one of the KWV co-operative's best labels, producing wines of attractive varietal character, such as this grassy, crisp Sauvignon Blanc. We just found it a little expensive.

Over £8

FRANCE

1993 St-Romain Clos sous Roche, Domaine Coste Caumartin
0 / 1 /]   14/20

High in the hills behind Burgundy's Côte de Beaune, the village of St-Romain makes fresh, if occasionally austere, Chardonnays. This rather expensive white has an attractive vanilla fudge nose and an overlay of well-judged oak, but is marred by the harsh acidity typical of the vintage.

1993 Sancerre, Domaine Jean-Max Roger
£££ / 1 / ⌐   17/20
Made in the village of Bué by one of the best producers of
Sancerre, this is a complex, concentrated, minerally Sauvignon
Blanc with smoky, aniseedy flavours. If Sancerre was always as
good as this, it wouldn't be losing out to the New World quite so
dramatically.

GERMANY

1992 Oppenheimer Sackträger Kabinett, Halbtrocken, Guntrum
0 / 5 / ⌐   11/20
A lot of words for your money, but not enough fruit or flavour. Tart,
sugary and overpriced.

Red

£3–5

AUSTRALIA

1994 Grenache, Peter Lehmann
££ / FB / ⌐   15/20
Rich, alcoholic, vibrantly fruity Aussie red made by Barossa Valley
specialist Peter Lehmann. It's an unashamedly gluggable, strawberryish
red which shoves most Beaujolais into the nearest corked hat.

1993 Penfolds Bin 2 Shiraz/Mourvèdre
£ / FB / ▬   14/20
Sawdusty, minty, robustly flavoured Rhône style Australian blend in the
classically oaky Penfolds style.

CHILE

1993 Cabernet Sauvignon, Caliterra
££ / MB / ⌐   14/20
Fruit-dominated, blackberry-fresh style of Cabernet Sauvignon with

lashings of sweet, chunky flavour. A good New World alternative to claret from Chilean wizard winemaker Ignacio Recabarren.

FRANCE

1993 Domaine de Limbardie, Vin de Pays des Coteaux de Murviel
££ / MB / **1**   14/20

From Henri Boukandoura's estate in the Languedoc, this is another well-made Bordeaux-style red with fleshy, softly grassy fruit flavours, using the carbonic maceration technique for maximum suppleness.

1993 Domaine de Montpezat, Cabernet/Syrah, Vin de Pays d'Oc
££ / MB / **1**   14/20

Light, easy-drinking, tobaccoey red with hints of green pepper Cabernet and black pepper Syrah. A successful duo of grapes.

1993 Domaine St-Martin, Cabernet/Merlot, Vin de Pays des Côtes de Thongues
£ / MB / **1**   14/20

A chewier, more rustic southern French red with evident oak input. Concentrated, if a little short on subtlety.

ITALY

1993 Merlot del Veneto, Via Nova
£ / LB / **1**   13/20

Simple, cherryish, refreshing Merlot from northeastern Italy. Decent trattoria rosso.

SPAIN

Gandia Tempranillo
0 / MB / **1**   11/20

Basic browning, raisiny, oak chipped plonk from Spain's Utiel-Requena region. Not a great advertisement for the Tempranillo grape, supposedly Spain's best red variety.

£5–8

AUSTRALIA

1992 Church Block, Wirra Wirra Vineyards, McLaren Vale
£££ / FB / ↙   16/20

A blend of Cabernet Sauvignon, Shiraz and Merlot from Greg Trott's first-rate McLaren Vale winery, showing the ripe, full-bodied elegance and judicious oak handling for which Wirra Wirra is justly celebrated.

1992 Ryecroft Peppertree Shiraz/Cabernet
£ / FB / ↙   15/20

A more obvious McLaren Vale red with hefty flavours of mint, caramel and ground pepper which don't quite knit together.

1992 Ironstone Cabernet/Shiraz
0 / FB / ↕   13/20

Blended by David Hohnen of Cape Mentelle and Cloudy Bay fame, this is a hard, slightly overoaked Western Australian red. Go for the Ironstone white instead.

1990 Craigmoor Cabernet Sauvignon, Mudgee
0 / FB / ↕   12/20

Mature, raisiny, drying Cabernet which combines overripe fruit and confected, bitter oak. Smudgy Mudgee.

FRANCE

1993 Moulin à Vent, Domaine de la Tour du Bief, Georges Duboeuf
£ / MB / ↕   15/20

One of the few Duboeuf Beaujolais to be aged in new oak, this serious, well-made Gamay is halfway to red Burgundy in style. As such, it's overpriced at nearly £8.

1990 Château Mendoce, Côtes de Bourg
££ / MB / ↕   14/20

Attractively aromatic, mature Merlot from the Right Bank *appellation* of Côtes de Bourg opposite the Médoc, showing a touch of toasted oak, smooth, supple fruitiness and a rustic edge.

1988 Château de Cardaillan, Graves
££££ / MB / 🍷   16/20

This is the sort of wine that Davisons does best – mature, well-made claret with a few years' bottle age under its neck label. Supple, farmyardy and full of character.

SOUTH AFRICA

1993 Cabernet Sauvignon, Saxenburg Estate
££ / MB / 🍷   15/20

An inky, densely coloured Cape Cabernet from one of the KWV's many tentacles, this is a minty, perfumed red with good concentration and plenty of sweet French and American oak character. Comparatively elegant for a South African red.

Over £8

AUSTRALIA

1992 E & E Black Pepper Shiraz, Barossa Valley
£ / FB / ⌐   14/20

The best thing about this strappingly oaked, hugely alcoholic Hardy's red is its evocative name. A free copy of *Grapevine* to the first reader who can tell us what E & E stands for.

FRANCE

1989 Bourgogne Pinot Noir, Domaine J M Morey
££ / MB / 🍷   15/20

Not cheap for a basic red Burgundy, but this declassified Chassagne-Montrachet is supple, aromatic, savoury Pinot Noir, which has benefited from six years in bottle. No ordinary Bourgogne Rouge.

1989 Savigny-lès-Beaune, Domaine Pavelot
££ / MB / 🍷   16/20

From the same well-considered Burgundy vintage, this is a finer, more concentrated style with lots of new oak and flavours of plum and dark chocolate, reflecting the ripeness and easy drinkability of the vintage.

1987 Santenay, Le Chainey, Domaine J M Morey
££ / MB / 🍷   15/20
Mature, gamey red Burgundy from an unspectacular vintage, which
shows you what a good grower (and Davisons) can come up with in
lesser years. Spicy, complex, mature Pinot Noir, perfect for drinking
now.

1988 Château Beaumont, Médoc, Cru Bourgeois
££ / MB / ⌐   16/20
Since insurance company GMF took over this gigantic Médoc estate,
investment has brought about significant improvements. This is a
modern, coffee-bean oaky, well-balanced claret in the classic 1988
vintage mould. It should age with distinction.

1986 Château Villars, Fronsac
££ / FB / ⌐   15/20
Showing the weight and tannic concentration of the 1986 vintage, this
is a claret with appealing cigar-box spiciness, rich fruit and plenty of
oak. Another one for the wine rack.

1990 Château Coudert, St-Emilion Grand Cru
£££ / MB / ⌐   16/20
A good advertisement for the sprawling St-Emilion *appellation*, this is a
classic, concentrated, minty Merlot from a great vintage with succulent,
chocolatey fruit flavours and real finesse.

1993 Châteauneuf-du-Pape, Domaine Font de Michelle
££ / FB / ⌐   15/20
Made by the broad-shouldered Gonnet brothers, this is well-made,
aromatic, Grenache-based Châteauneuf-du-Pape, with plenty of
underlying spice and zip, especially for such a light vintage in the region.

UNITED STATES

1989 Cabernet Sauvignon, Everest Estate
0 / FB / 🍷   10/20
Leathery, dry, charry, overserious California Cabernet. Should have been
double-glazed and deep-sixed at birth.

Rosé

£3–5

FRANCE

1994 Château de Sours, Bordeaux Rosé
££ / 3 / ♪   15/20
A soft, juicy, just off-dry rosé with plenty of colour and green pepper and
strawberry fruitiness from the former Majestic director, Esme Johnstone,
and Bordeaux star winemaker Michel Rolland.

Sparkling

£5–8

AUSTRALIA

Killawarra Brut, South Australia, Bottle Fermented
££ / 3 / ♪   14/20
Hugely popular peardrop and lemon sherbet style fizz from Penfolds.
Still good value at just over £5.

Killawarra Rosé, South Australia, Bottle Fermented
££ / 3 / ♪   14/20
Similar, but pink – a frothy, strawberry ripple sparkler.

FULLER'S ***(*)

Head Office: Fuller, Smith & Turner PLC, Griffin Brewery, Chiswick Lane South, London W4 2QB

Telephone: 0181 996 2000

Number of branches: 65

Credit cards accepted: Visa, Access, Switch

Hours of opening: Monday to Saturday 9.30am to 10.00pm; Sunday 11.00am to 10.00pm

By-the-case sales: Yes

Glass loan: With deposit of 50 pence per glass

Home delivery: Free locally

Clubs: No

Discounts: One free bottle with every unmixed case

In-store tastings: Every Saturday in all stores

Top ten best-selling wines: Le Gascony Blanc, Vin de Pays des Côtes de Gascogne; Chardonnay, Vin de Pays du Jardin de la France; Le Gascony Rouge, Vin de Pays des Côtes de Gascogne; Casa del Marqués Rioja; Liebfraumilch Egbert; Lambrusco Bianco Zonin; Berticot Sauvignon Blanc, Côtes de Duras; Penfolds Bin 21 Semillon/Chardonnay; Nottage Hill Chardonnay; Nottage Hill Cabernet

Range: GOOD: Red Bordeaux, New Zealand, Australia, Rhône, Burgundy, Spain, Chile

AVERAGE: Champagne and sparkling wines, regional France, Germany, United States, South Africa, Loire, Italy

POOR: Eastern Europe, Portugal

Fuller's can't stop winning awards for its wonderful, flavoursome ales.

There we were preparing to taste our way through the London off-licence chain's wine range, when news of yet another triumph arrived from the brewery. London Pride had been named 'Champion Best Bitter' by the beardies at the Campaign for Real Ale's Great British Beer Festival at Olympia.

All in all, 1995 was a memorable year for Fuller's. As well as a visit from old big ears himself, Prince Charles, in February and the CAMRA award, the brewery celebrated its 150th anniversary in business. It also witnessed the first full year in action for roller-blading wine buying controller, Roger Higgs, the former Oddbins employee who has brought much-needed zip and character to the Fuller's range.

When we assessed the Fuller's list a year ago, Higgs had just swept into the forecourt of the Griffin Brewery. With characteristic energy, he set about the wine range with a sharpened meat cleaver. In the space of a few weeks, he'd hacked away the silly range of Greek wines and introduced a host of goodies from Bordeaux, the Rhône, regional France, New Zealand and Australia. Some of these were finds from his Oddbins' days, but others were new to the UK market, or at least the high street.

So how did things progress in 1995? Rather well, as it happens. The frenetic activity of the first few months – Higgs' equivalent of The Terror – has been replaced by a more leisurely period of consolidation, but it's still been an exciting year. 'I reckon you need two years to put a wine range together,' Higgs told us after 15 months in the job. 'And we're two-thirds of the way there. It was a question of priorities at the start – I looked at Chile, Australia and South Africa first, then regional France, then Spain. Italy is my next big project.'

Changing the range has been hampered by external factors – wine shortages in Spain and Australia and the performance of the pound against the mark and French franc. 'In places like Spain, the prices went ape this year,' says Higgs. 'But with the lira at 2,600 to the pound, Italy is looking more and more interesting. I'm taking on lots of new things in the £3–6 range.'

Fuller's wine list has grown to 590 wines in the last year, with 150 new additions. The top 36 stores (known as Gold stores at Fuller's) get the whole lot, whereas the Silver and Bronze shops tend to be smaller and stock a selected range.

Nothing on the list is priced below £2.85. 'I don't see the point of selling wine at £1.99,' says Higgs. 'All it does is convince people who thought they didn't like wine that they were right. The guys in our stores don't want to do cheap wines, and neither do I. Everyone wants good prices, but I don't see the point if it means sacrificing quality.'

The 'guys in the stores' have also done a lot to promote the New World – *the* growth area at Fuller's. 'Chile, South Africa and Australia are producing a lot of exciting wines at the moment,' says Higgs, 'and I'm impressed by the stuff we're starting to see from Argentina.' To his evident delight, New World sales are growing at the expense of Liebfraumilch and Lambrusco.

The enthusiasm of Fuller's managers is vital to the future of Fuller's, one of the few independent chains left in Britain. 'I've spent a lot of the last year motivating the people who run the shops. You have to make them feel part of the business, which is why we give them tastings, product information and plenty of incentives.' Without good managers, Higgs says he might as well be out on his roller blades. 'There are lots of people who can put together a decent wine range. It's selling it that matters.'

Fuller's off-licences also shift large volumes of company beer, 'but the brewery regards us as quality wine merchants in our own right'. The advantage of having a comparatively small number of stores is that Higgs can indulge his enthusiasms to a certain extent. 'I can buy small parcels of 50 cases and get the wine into all the stores.' Naturally, they're more likely to sell in flagship sites, such as Richmond and Maidenhead, than in some of Fuller's less up-beat locations.

Responding to the criticism that Fuller's is turning into an Oddbins lookalike, Higgs says that 'there's as little cross-over as is humanly possible. If I put together an Oddbins range, there's no point in people coming to Fuller's.' This is true enough. There *are* a few Oddbins' refugees on the Fuller's list, but Higgs has imposed his own forceful personality on it, too. The Burgundy, Spanish, southern French, Australian and South African ranges are all proof of that.

So, thumbs up overall. If Roger Higgs is only two-thirds of the way towards completing the revamped Fuller's range, we're looking forward to tasting the remaining third. Once that's in place, Fuller's brewery may not be the only part of the business which wins the odd award.

White

Under £3

FRANCE

1994 Winter Hill, Vin de Pays de l'Aude
£ / 3 / ⅟   13/20
Fuller's price-fighting French white is made by Australians, as the label
helpfully informs you. It's better than the companion red, but we still
can't understand why they'd come all that way to produce an appley,
off-dry white of little distinction.

ITALY

1994 Chardonnay del Triveneto
££ / 2 / ⅟   14/20
A crisp, peachy, aromatic, unoaked Italian Chardonnay which smells and
tastes like a Pinot Grigio. A good basic quaffer.

SPAIN

1994 Castillo de Montblanc, Conca de Barbera
££ / 2 / ⅟   14/20
Made in Catalonia by itinerant winemaker Hugh Ryman, this blend of
Macabeo and the local Parellada grapes in an expensive-looking bottle
is a crisply refreshing, lemony party white.

£3–5

ARGENTINA

1993 Alamos Ridge Chardonnay, Mendoza
££ / 2 / ⅟   15/20
Smoky oak, lemon and lime-juicy Chardonnay with some buttery lees
character and plenty of alcohol. Surprisingly fresh and well made, given
the body and weight of the wine. Good value.

AUSTRALIA

1994 Chenin Blanc, Peter Lehmann
££ / 3 / ⚊   14/20

Gluggable, sweetish Barossa Valley white with attractive guava and boiled sweets fruitiness. The sort of ripe, easy-drinking white for which the Barossa is renowned.

1994 Lindemans Cawarra Semillon/Chardonnay
££ / 3 / ⚊   14/20

A commercial, winningly made, warm climate blend with flavours of marmalade and fresh peach and a herby note. It's refreshing to come across an inexpensive Australian white in which oak is not the dominant flavour.

1994 Rawsons Retreat Penfolds Bin 21 Semillon/Chardonnay
£££ / 2 / ⚊   15/20

A good example of the new-style Penfolds whites. With its spicy vanilla oak, herby Semillon and Chardonnay richness, these two grapes combine harmoniously to produce a sundae of vanilla ice cream and lemony fruit.

1993 Rothbury South East Australia Chardonnay
£ / 3 / ⚊   14/20

A ripe, pineappley, oaky Australian Chardonnay with barley sugar fruitiness from the Hunter Valley based Rothbury winery.

1994 Moondah Brook Verdelho
££ / 3 / ⚊   15/20

A grassy, elderflower-like Western Australian Verdelho from the BRL-Hardy group, which reminded us of a full-bodied Sauvignon Blanc with its ripe cassis and melon fruitiness. A nice change from Chardonnay – even if it does taste like a Sauvignon.

CHILE

1994 Cono Sur Chardonnay
0 / 2 / ⚊   12/20

In its first vintage, Cono Sur established itself as one of the most exciting new wineries in Chile for its Pinot Noir and Cabernet Sauvignon. This boring, fruitless Chardonnay is not yet up to scratch.

1994 Caliterra Casablanca Chardonnay
£££ / 2 / ❦   17/20
Star winemaker Ignacio Recabarren has produced a brilliant value Chardonnay from Chile's most exciting white wine area, the Casablanca Valley, halfway between Santiago and the port of Valparaiso. Fresh, clean-cut, citrus-fruit flavours with a grapefruity tang and a touch of oak.

1994 Valdivieso Barrel Fermented Chardonnay
£££ / 2 / ❦   16/20
Veteran winemaker Luis Simian's attempt to out-Burgundy the Côte d'Or, using the traditional techniques of barrel fermentation and lees-stirring. This is a super-rich, butterscotch and toffee style Chardonnay in a slightly more fruity style than the equally enjoyable 1993.

FRANCE

1994 La Serre Chardonnay, Vin de Pays d'Oc
££ / 2 / ❦   14/20
A reliable, highly drinkable New World-influenced Languedoc Chardonnay with a tropical fruit salad of flavours blended by Simon Farr, of independent merchants Bibendum.

1994 James Herrick Chardonnay, Vin de Pays d'Oc
££ / 2 / ❦   15/20
Probably the best release yet from Englishman James Herrick's extensive Chardonnay plantings near Narbonne, this is a peachy, lightly oaked white with hints of butter and greengage, and an RSJ of supporting acidity.

1994 Domaine de Raissac Viognier, Vin de Pays de l'Aude
££ / 2 / ❦   14/20
Plump, ripe, peachy Viognier which lacks the acidity and definition of the best southern French examples of the northern Rhône's star white grape, but is still well-priced at under £5.

1994 Mâcon-Igé, Les Vignerons d'Igé
££ / 2 / ♪   15/20

Well done to the Igé co-operative for keeping this spicy, unoaked Chardonnay under £5. The bottle looks good and the wine is fresh and comparatively complex for a Mâcon-Villages.

1994 Bourgogne Chardonnay, Joseph Bertrand
££ / 2 / ♪   15/20

Fresh, crisp, lemony white Burgundy with an Aligoté-like zestiness and buttery flavours. Clean, well-made and highly drinkable.

1994 Domaine Vieux Manoir de Maransan, Côtes du Rhône Blanc
£££ / 2 / ♪   15/20

A highly successful, well-priced southern Rhône white with flavours of toast and ginger spice and far more fresh fruitiness than you usually find in a white Côtes du Rhône. Perhaps Australian Nick Butler's influence had something to do with it.

ITALY

1994 Pinot Grigio del Friuli, Pecile, Bidoli
£££ / 2 / ♪   15/20

A smartly packaged, stylish Italian white with crisp lemon and apricot flavours and a tang of fresh acidity. A good apéritif white.

NEW ZEALAND

1993 Highfield Estate Sauvignon, Marlborough
£ / 2 / ♪   14/20

A crisp, almost tart Marlborough Sauvignon with characteristic elderflower notes. The coolness of the vintage is evident in the wine's faintly vegetal character.

1992 Highfield Estate Chardonnay, Marlborough
££ / 2 / ♪   15/20

Also from a cool New Zealand vintage, this is a lemony, lightly oaked Chardonnay with a hint of butterscotch and plenty of bracing acidity.

SOUTH AFRICA

1994 Fairview Crouchen Chardonnay
££ / 2 / ‡   14/20

Characteristically adventurous blend of Cape grape varieties from the innovative Charles Back, in which the foxiness of Crouchen is balanced by the softness of the Chardonnay. It also helps to keep the price under £4.

SPAIN

1994 Castillo de Montblanc Chardonnay, Conca de Barbera
££ / 2 / ‡   14/20

From a recently elevated Spanish *denominación*, this ripe, rounded, melony Chardonnay made by Hugh Ryman at the Concavin winery is decently priced at under £4, but slightly affected by oak bitterness.

1994 Can Feixes, Penedés
££ / 1 / ‡   15/20

An encouraging blend of the native Parellada and Macabeo with the more international Chardonnay, which proves that the Penedés can make more interesting things than Cava. Crisp, aromatic, citrus-flavoured white with elegant dryness.

1994 Barrel-fermented Rioja, Muga
££ / 1 / ‡   15/20

An old-fashioned, smoky, Sherry-like white Rioja, which reminded us of the idiosyncratic Marqués de Murrieta. It's a dry and fairly demanding style, which needs food to show at its best. We hope Spain continues to maintain the tradition of wines like this.

£5–8

ARGENTINA

1993 Catena Agrelo Vineyard Chardonnay
££ / 2 / ‡   16/20

A savoury, buttery, barrel-fermented Argentinian Chardonnay with a rich array of fruit flavours and attractive toasty oak characters. The most complex Argentinian white we've tasted. One for the polo club bar.

AUSTRALIA

1992 Wynns Coonawarra Estate Chardonnay
0 / 2 / 🖁   13/20
Made in a love-it-or-leave-it, heftily oaked, weighty style, this is a one-glass wonder. Great if you've got five other people round for dinner and just the one bottle.

CHILE

1994 Caliterra Reserve Chardonnay
£££ / 2 / 🖁   16/20
Another first-rate South American white, this time from Chile's excellent 1994 vintage. It's an oaky, grapefruity, richly complex Maipo Valley white made by *Grapevine* winemaker of the year, Ignacio Recabarren. Wonderful value at under £6.

FRANCE

1993 Mâcon Davayé, Domaine des Deux Roches
£££ / 2 / 🖁   16/20
From a forward-thinking Mâconnais estate, which makes the most of low yields and modern winemaking to produce extremely fresh, concentrated Chardonnays, this is a minerally, unoaked white in which the spicy clarity of the village *appellation* shines through.

1993 Saint Véran, Domaine des Deux Roches
£££ / 2 / 🖁   16/20
From the same estate, this spicy, modern Chardonnay has much in common with the best wines of neighbouring Pouilly Fuissé. Serious white Burgundy at a less than serious price.

Over £8

AUSTRALIA

1994 Ninth Island Chardonnay, Tasmania Wine Company
£ / 2 / ⅃ 15/20

Made by Dr Andrew Pirie, the thinking woman's winemaker, this is a crisp, grapefruit and melon style Chardonnay from Tasmania's picturesque, cool climate vineyards.

1994 Devil's Lair Chardonnay, Margaret River
£££ / 2 / ⅃ 16/20

A brilliant label advertising a brilliant wine. John Wade's rich, lime and vanilla flavoured Chardonnay with its coating of toasty oak and powerful alcohol is one of the best Western Australian whites we've come across this year. Well worth its £10 price tag.

FRANCE

1993 Puligny-Montrachet, Henri Clerc
££ / 2 / ⤙ 16/20

A spicy, almost Muscat-tinged Côte de Beaune Chardonnay from the bracing 1993 vintage, with considerable complexity and backbone. It's traditional in style, but characterful with it, and should age well.

NEW ZEALAND

1994 Dashwood Sauvignon, Marlborough
££ / 2 / ⅃ 15/20

Dashwood is the second label of Marlborough-based winery Vavasour in the Awatere Valley, but it's still among the better South Island Sauvignons. This is a green pepper and asparagus-laden white with a tartish finish.

1994 Hunters Sauvignon, Marlborough
££ / 2 / ⅃ 16/20

An intense, tropical fruit Sauvignon Blanc from Jane Hunter, OBE. As ever, it's fresh, grapefruity, concentrated and highly aromatic with flavours of passion fruit and melon. We slightly preferred the previous vintage, but this is still a super wine.

SOUTH AFRICA

1994 Bouchard Finlayson Chardonnay Kaaimansgart Vineyard
££ / 2 / ¶   15/20
Situated in Hermanus, one of the coolest growing regions in the Cape, Bouchard Finlayson is a collaboration between Paul Bouchard and South African Peter Finlayson, dedicated to producing Burgundian-style Chardonnay and Pinot Noir. The estate is promising, as this elegant, attractively oaked Chardonnay demonstrates, but its vines are not yet sufficiently old to give the concentration the owners aspire to in their wines, especially at nearly £9 a bottle.

SPAIN

1994 Augustus Chardonnay, Puig i Roca
££ / 2 / ¶   16/20
One of a growing number of Chardonnays produced in the Penedés region of Spain, this is an opulent, fudge, toast and vanilla style white with enough acidity to keep it fresh for another year or two. At nearly £9.50 a bottle, it's not cheap, but José Puig's Chardonnay is one of Spain's finest.

Red

Under £3

FRANCE

1994 Winter Hill, Vin de Pays de l'Aude
0 / MB / ¶   11/20
'French wine made by Australians', reads the label. Why anybody would bother travelling thousands of miles to make this rustic Carignan/Merlot plonk is a mystery to the lads at *Grapevine* HQ.

ITALY

Gabbia d'Oro Rosso
0 / LB / ♪   **11/20**

A light, sweetish red that could come from virtually anywhere. Italy's lame response to Piat d'Or. We can't see the Italians adoring this plonk.

SPAIN

Don Gulias Tinto, Vino de Mesa, Bodegas Vitorianas
0 / LB / ♪   **10/20**

Tart, raisiny, sub-Don Darias Spanish plonk. If wine has to be this bad to creep under the £3 price point, we suggest you dig a little deeper into your pocket.

£3–5

ARGENTINA

1993 Alamos Ridge, Cabernet Sauvignon
££ / MB / ♪   **15/20**

Lots of juicy, oaked Cabernet Sauvignon aromas. Coffee bean and spicy, drying oak with well made, youthful blackcurrant fruit and none of the bitterness Chile often seems to produce in its Cabernets.

AUSTRALIA

1994 Grenache, Peter Lehmann
£££ / MB / ♪   **15/20**

Rich, alcoholic, vibrantly fruity Aussie red made by Barossa Valley specialist Peter Lehmann. It's an unashamedly gluggable, strawberryish red which shoves most Beaujolais into the nearest corked hat.

1992 Rouge Homme Coonawarra Cabernet/Shiraz
££ / MB / ♪   **15/20**

An animaly, smoky, blackcurrant-like blend from the cuddly Greg Clayfield, one of the Coonawarra region's best winemakers. There's a lot of wine and complexity here for under £5.

CHILE

1993 Caliterra Cabernet
££ / MB / ▮   14/20

Light, elegant blackcurrant pastille-like Chilean Cabernet from the Maipo Valley, which could do with a little more richness to balance the slightly tart acidity. Well-priced, though, at under £4.

1993 Caliterra Estate Maipo Cabernet
£££ / MB / ▬▬   16/20

It's worth paying the extra £1 for this intensely spearminty, vibrant, cassis-scented Cabernet Sauvignon, with its ripe but substantial tannins, spicy oak and youthful, succulent fruitiness all in perfect balance.

FRANCE

1994 Cabernet/Syrah Les Limouxins, Vin de Pays d'Oc
££ / MB / ▮   14/20

Light, fresh, easy-drinking southern French blend from the excellent Limoux co-operative, with the emphasis on gluggability at an inexpensive sub-£3.50 price.

1994 Domaine de Raissac Tempranillo/Syrah, Vin de Pays d'Oc
£ / FB / ▮   13/20

Made by Australian Nick Butler at Domaine de Raissac in the Languedoc, this is an unusual blend of Spain's Tempranillo and France's Syrah. Sadly, the wine shows rather too much dry tannin and green fruit.

1993 Mas de Montel Syrah, Vin de Pays d'Oc
££ / MB / ▮   15/20

Juicy, aromatic, medium-weight Syrah with fresh, unoaked black olive and blackberry fruit flavours. A mini-Crozes-Hermitage from the Languedoc at an un-Crozes-like price.

1993 Château de Coupe-Roses, Minervois
££ / FB / ▮   15/20

Peppery, spicy, old-fashioned Minervois in which the rustic tannins are more than compensated for by the chocolatey, full-bodied weight of fruit.

1994 Mâcon Igé Les Roches Rouge
££ / MB / 🍷   14/20

A Beaujolais-style thirst-quencher from the Mâconnais region of southern Burgundy, showing bright, raspberry fruitiness, a touch of mint and refreshing acidity. A decent bistrot Burgundy.

1993 Côtes du Roussillon, Jean-Luc Colombo
££ / FB / 🍷   15/20

Michel Rolland disciple Jean-Luc Colombo is one of the most dynamic and controversial oenologists in southern France, travelling huge distances from his base in Cornas to advise winemakers from Perpignan to the suburbs of Lyon. New oak is the Colombo hallmark. It doesn't always work to the advantage of the wine, but this chunky, alcoholic, Syrah-based red has sufficient fruit to cope with the splinters.

ITALY

1993 Montepulciano d'Abruzzo, Citra
££ / MB / 🍷   14/20

A light, modern-style Italian red from the Adriatic coast with fresh, cherried fruit, a nip of acidity and robust, savoury tannins.

1993 Teroldego Rotaliano, CA Donini
££ / MB / 🍷   15/20

Soft, smooth, plummy northern Italian red made from the local Teroldego Rotaliano grape, and showing effusive alcohol sweetness and liquorice spice.

SOUTH AFRICA

1993 Dieu Donné Cabernet Sauvignon, Franschoek
££ / MB / 🍷   15/20

Not quite God-given, but this minty, refreshing Cabernet Sauvignon from one of the Cape's comparatively cool pockets, with its attractive oak character and elegant fruitiness, should appeal to Catholic tastes.

1993 Fairview Shiraz/Merlot
££ / MB / 🍷   15/20

Yet another intriguing blend from master wine and cheese maker

Charles Back, this is a smoky, eucalyptus-like red with masses of vibrant fruit and fresh acidity. Just the job for wine and cheese parties.

SPAIN

1994 Rioja Baja Garnacha Artadi
££ / FB / ▰▬   15/20
Usually dismissed as an area which produces bread-and-butter Rioja, this rich concentrated, peppery Grenache is so beefy and extracted that you could almost mistake it for a Zinfandel, or even a Douro red. Traditional Rioja drinkers may do a double-take, but we were impressed by the wine's flavours and stylish packaging.

£5–8

ARGENTINA

1993 Catena Agrelo Vineyard Cabernet Sauvignon
££ / MB / ▰   15/20
A wine which combines claret-like aromas with a whack of charry, toasty oak, from American winemaker Paul Hobbs. Now into its stride, this is a farmyardy Argentinian red from one of South America's most promising wineries.

AUSTRALIA

1993 Château Reynella Basket Pressed Shiraz
££ / FB / ▰▬   16/20
There's no shortage of mint and spicy coffee bean American oak on show here. If that sounds unappealing, it shouldn't do, because there's plenty of lush, chocolatey McLaren Vale Shiraz in the bottle too. We're not sure what the bearded Rocky O'Callaghan, the inventor of the original Basket Press Shiraz, thinks of the name, but we reckon he'd happily put a few bottles of this away – probably at one sitting.

1993 Rockford Dry Country Grenache
£££ / FB / ▰▬   16/20
From the cult figure himself, this is a soft, super-rich, heart-warming

Grenache made from old Barossa Valley bush vines. The Barossa's characterful answer to Gigondas.

CHILE

1993 Cono Sur Pinot Noir Reserve
££ / MB / ♪   15/20
Made by American winemaker Ed Flaherty at the Concha y Toro owned Cono Sur Chimbarongo Estate Winery in the Rapel region, this second release was the best Pinot Noir we came across from South America last year. Rich and chocolatey, but the voluptuous loganberry and raspberry fruit flavours have faded a bit. Drink up.

FRANCE

1990 Château Caroline, Cru Bourgeois, Listrac
£££ / MB / ⌐   16/20
A wine which is just beginning to develop into something really interesting, this is a concentrated, chocolatey claret with a hint of the farmyard and the backbone normally associated with the Listrac appellation.

1993 Hautes Côtes de Nuits Denis, Denis Philibert
££ / MB / ♪   15/20
An aromatic, if rustic, Pinot Noir, showing the firm tannins of the 1993 vintage, but enough blackberry fruitiness to make it worth its £7 price tag.

1994 Côtes du Rhône-Villages, Cairanne, Max Aubert, Domaine de la Présidente
£££ / FB / ⌐   16/20
Made by elderly autodidact Max Aubert, this is an attractively fruity, Grenache-based southern Rhône red with chocolatey spice and layer upon layer of flavour. Aubert's hours of study have clearly been fruitful.

ITALY

1990 Chianti Riserva, Villa Antinori
££ / MB / ﹜   15/20

Mature, typically Tuscan red from a large volume producer which can still turn out good Chiantis as well as its higher profile vini da tavola, Sassicaia and Tignanello.

SPAIN

1990 Señorio de Nava Crianza Ribera del Duero
£ / FB / ﹜   14/20

The follow-on vintage to the apparently voluminous 1987 – we always wondered who stole the wines in between – this solid, chunky, oaky Tempranillo with its rather raw, green edge is nothing like as appealing as its predecessor. Bring back the 1987.

Over £8

AUSTRALIA

1993 Wirra Wirra Original Blend, McLaren Vale
£££ / MB / ﹈   17/20

An exceptional blend of Grenache and Shiraz from McLaren Vale winemaker Ben Riggs. Like nearly all Wirra Wirra's red wines, this is rich, supple, concentrated and beautifully judged, with Ovaltine and savoury fruitiness balanced by the judicious use of oak.

1992 Leasingham Classic Clare Shiraz
£ / FB / ﹈   15/20

This is Leasingham Domaine's attempt at a premium Clare Valley red. It's impressive, concentrated stuff with masses of minty fruit flavours, but we found the American oak a little too charry and obtrusive for our taste. Maybe it needs more time for the elements to fuse.

FRANCE

1990 Château Teyssier, St-Emilion Grand Cru
££ / MB / ▬   16/20

From a British-owned property in St-Emilion, which has recently benefited from investment in new technology, this is a mature, medium-bodied St-Emilion with plenty of colour and ripe, silky tannins.

1992 Nuits St-Georges, Caves des Hautes Côtes
££ / MB / ♪   15/20

Beguiling, aromatic Pinot Noir with fresh raspberry and chocolate fruit flavours and a leafy touch of rusticity for added complexity.

1992 Fixin Philippe Naddef
£££ / MB / ♪   16/20

A more modern style of Pinot Noir with plenty of spicy oak, good weight and mulberry fruitiness from one of the Côte de Nuits' less well-known appellations.

UNITED STATES

1993 Saintsbury Pinot Noir Garnet
££ / LB / ♪   16/20

The lightest of the three styles of Pinot Noir made at David Graves' and Dick Ward's celebrated Carneros winery, this is a charming, lightly oaked Pinot Noir with soft strawberry fruitiness and fresh acidity. It's also a rival to red Burgundy at under £10.

Rosé

£3–5

FRANCE

1994 Domaine de Raissac Cabernet Rosé, Vin de Pays d'Oc
££ / 2 / ♪   14/20

An interesting southern French rosé made by Australian Nick Butler at the Domaine de Raissac. The grassiness and structure of the Cabernet Sauvignon grape give the wine added body and piquancy.

Sparkling

Over £8

FRANCE

Champagne Brossault Brut
£ / 3 / 1   14/20

Fuller's house Champagne is a frothy, sweetish blend with the accent on youthful strawberry fruitiness.

Château de Boursault Brut Champagne
£££ / 2 / 1   16/20

An extra £4 will buy you a classier Pinot-dominated fizz with less sugar, more elegance and appealing length of flavour.

Joseph Perrier Brut Champagne, Cuvée Royale
£££ / 2 / 1   17/20

A malty, traditional Champagne from the underrated Châlons-sur-Marne house of Joseph Perrier. It's a weighty, characterful, chocolatey style that's excellent value for a Grande Marque Champagne at around £16.

GREENALLS CELLARS
(INCLUDING WINE CELLAR ***,
BERKELEY WINES **(*) AND CELLAR 5 **)

Head Office: Greenalls Cellars Ltd, PO Box 476, Loushers Lane, Warrington, Cheshire WA4 6RR

Telephone: 01925 444555

Number of branches: 467 (incorporating 24 Wine Cellar stores, 99 Berkeley Wines, 310 Cellar 5 and 34 Greenalls Food Stores and Night Vision)

Credit cards accepted: Access, Visa, Delta, Switch, Amex

Hours of opening: Monday to Saturday 10.00am to 10.00pm; Sunday 12.00pm to 2.00pm and 7.00pm to 10.00pm

By-the-case sales: Yes

Glass loan: Yes

Home delivery: Yes for Wine Cellar. By arrangement with Berkeley Wines

Clubs: Under discussion for Berkeley Wines and Wine Cellar

Discounts: Party planning, sale or return offers and quantity discounts up to 15 per cent on wine

In-store tastings: Yes, every Saturday in Wine Cellar stores

Top ten best-selling wines:

Wine Cellar: Lindemans Cawarra Semillon/Chardonnay; Bulgarian Cabernet Sauvignon, Sliven; Lindemans Cawarra Shiraz/Cabernet; House Claret, Calvet; Campo Viejo Rioja Crianza; Côtes du Ventoux, Les Lys; James Herrick Chardonnay; Hardy's Stamp Series Shiraz/Cabernet; Peter Lehmann Grenache; Peter Lehmann Chenin Blanc

Berkeley Wines: Liebfraumilch; Lambrusco Bianco; Lindemans Cawarra

Semillon/Chardonnay; Bulgarian Cabernet Sauvignon, Sliven; Lindemans Cawarra Shiraz/Cabernet; Peter Lehmann Grenache; Frascati San Caio; Piesporter Michelsberg; Campo Viejo Rioja Crianza; Hungarian Chardonnay, Nagyrede

Cellar 5: Liebfraumilch; Lambrusco Bianco; Hock Deutscher Tafelwein; Piesporter Michelsberg; Bulgarian Cabernet Sauvignon, Sliven; Hungarian Country White; Leziria Red; Soave Illasi; Hungarian Chardonnay, Nagyrede; Niersteiner Gutes Domtal

Range: GOOD: Champagne and sparkling wines; Australia; red Burgundy; South Africa; Chile; North America; Portugal; Ports and Sherries
AVERAGE: New Zealand; regional France; Bordeaux; white Burgundy; Rhône; Loire; Spain; Italy
POOR: Eastern Europe; Germany

A new verb entered the English language this year – to Naderise. Taken from the first name of Greenalls Cellars' dynamic managing director, Nader Haghighi, the word's definition is simple: to bring zip and a *frisson* of excitement to the British high street.

The latest town to experience naderisation is Epsom. From his swanky new Wine Cellar off-licence in the London hydrangea belt, Haghighi has plans to conquer the high streets of the south of England. A year after the trade paper *Off-Licence News* predicted that Cellar 5 was about to 'look south', Haghighi has delivered the cases of wine. And there is more, much more, to come. The Epsom store, he says, will be 'the launch pad for a new generation of wine shops'. It could become the Cape Canaveral of Surrey.

As we pointed out in last year's edition of *Grapevine*, Haghighi has never lacked self-belief. He reminds us of Salvador Dali's celebrated confession that 'at the age of seven I wanted to be Napoleon. And my ambition has been growing steadily ever since.' From his lowly beginnings as a child street trader in an Iranian street market to his present, chauffeur-driven position, Haghighi brings chutzpah to everything he does.

The formula certainly seems to be working in Warrington. Since he took over Greenalls Cellars 18 months ago, he's transformed Britain's third largest off-licence chain (behind the Thresher/Wine Rack/Bottoms

Up trio and Victoria Wine) from a sleepy regional chain into a dynamic, newsworthy operation – opening new shops, listing hundreds of new wines and generally scaring the hell out of his competitors.

With 467 stores in the North and Midlands, Cellar 5 (as it used to be known in pre-segmentation days) always had potential, but it needed investment and a sense of leadership. Parent company The Greenalls Group has provided the former; Haghighi the latter. Within weeks of his arrival in April 1994, the rumours were whirling. Was Haghighi about to buy Unwins? Or would it be Davisons, Fuller's or even Oddbins?

Instead, he concentrated on his own shops – introducing a Thresher-style retail pyramid, with Wine Cellar at the apex, Berkeley Wines in the middle and Cellar 5 at the (broad) base. Since then, he's added Greenalls Food Stores and a handful of video/drink stores called Night Vision, all under the Greenalls Cellars banner.

The resemblance is not that surprising, given that Haghighi used to be operations director at Thresher. If the retail structure owes much to Thresher, the Wine Cellar list looks rather like that of Oddbins. A case of joining, rather than beating the competition, perhaps?

From the start, Haghighi has made no secret of his ambition to make Greenalls Cellars a national force, rather than just a regional chain. Hence the Epsom store – a cross between an Oddbins, a Victoria Wine and a Wine Rack with a few extra innovations thrown in. The Wine Cellar stores are certainly attractive – bright, roomy and well-designed, with everything from cheese to hyper-expensive Cognac on offer. And the wine range isn't bad either.

This is where Wine Cellar, and Greenalls Cellars as a whole, will succeed or fail. To compete with the likes of Oddbins, Thresher and Victoria Wine, the chain has to offer customer service and plenty of good wines at enticing prices.

Can it be done? Enter Kevin Wilson, the former buyer for William Low supermarkets in Scotland. Wilson and fellow buyer David Vaughan, who used to work for Augustus Barnett, have had the difficult task of making Greenalls Cellars live up to Haghighi's expectations. In 12 months, they've dumped much of the old range and introduced more than 600 new lines.

Wilson's approach is simple: 'I always have a bowl of fruit on my desk to remind suppliers what sort of wines I like.' And his skill as a buyer is already apparent in the revamped range, with lots of interesting stuff on the shelves.

Our main criticism is that some of the prices are distinctly uncompetitive. Out of an impressive 151 Australian, Chilean and New Zealand wines, only 21 cost less than £4. Window dressing is a necessary part of the exercise, but the key to success will be performance. The tough part is to come: delivering quality in the £2.99 to £3.99 range, and the right mix of £4 to £8 wines.

The other problem is that, while Wine Cellar looks smart and ABC1-customer-friendly, the Cellar 5 estate (the core of Greenalls Cellars' business) still contains some pretty dowdy-looking stores. We're also concerned that the best wines won't trickle down into the more basic off-licences.

Will Greenalls Cellars succeed where other regional chains have failed? Haghighi believes that, in the medium term, there will be room for only two specialist off-licence chains. The supermarkets are squeezing them at one end, cross-Channel shopping at the other. Faster than we imagine, it could come down to a three-way scrap between Victoria Wine, Thresher and Greenalls Cellars.

If so, Haghighi won't back down. 'To me, determination is everything, it's the key to success,' he says. 'To do what I've done, you have to be determined and clear about what you want. When I have a vision of something, I make it happen.'

Haghighi may be bullish, but large question marks remain. The 1994 Greenalls Group annual report promised a £7 million investment in 'further brand development' in 1995. A more telling phrase is 'full year profit down by 4.7 per cent to £4.3 million but improved second half performance'.

As only one part of a successful hotel and pub group, Greenalls Cellars has got to deliver better figures fast. Nader Haghighi and his two wine buyers have done an impressive job over the last 18 months, but if they're going to keep shareholders happy they'll have to continue the push towards quality and greater profitability.

For Haghighi to turn Greenalls Cellars into a major retail presence, he has to persuade his masters to sink more beer money into one of the smaller independent high street chains, such as Davisons or Unwins. For the moment, neither appears willing to sell. The more expensive alternative is to buy non-off-licence sites and convert them. Whatever happens, it's going to be another lively year at Greenalls Cellars.

White

£3-5

AUSTRALIA

1994 Chenin Blanc, Peter Lehmann
££ / 3 / ▮   14/20
Gluggable, sweetish Barossa Valley white with an attractive guava and boiled sweets fruitiness. The sort of ripe, easy-drinking white for which the Barossa is renowned.

1994 Bucklow Hill White
££ / 3 / ▮   15/20
Aromatic, grapey Aussie white made predominantly from the Riesling grape by Penfolds' value-conscious Tollana operation. Lots of flavour and zest for your money. With wines like this, perhaps Aussie Riesling could catch on.

1994 Rawsons Retreat Penfolds Bin 21 Semillon/Chardonnay
£££ / 2 / ▮   15/20
A good example of the new-style Penfolds whites. With its spicy vanilla oak, herby Semillon and Chardonnay richness, these two grapes combine harmoniously to produce a sundae of vanilla ice cream and lemony fruit.

CHILE

1994 Sauvignon Blanc, Villard
£££ / 2 / ▮   16/20
One of Chile's best Sauvignon Blancs, which producer Thierry Villard proudly boasts is made from the lesser Sauvignonasse clone. It just shows that if the winemaker knows what he is up to, even Sauvignonasse can produce complex, grapefruity whites with some tropical passion fruit notes.

FRANCE

1994 Bergerac Blanc Sec, Domaine du Pigeonnier
££ / 2 / ▮   15/20
Made by Scottish winemaker Jon Alexander in southwestern France, this

blend of Sauvignon Blanc and Semillon is a highly aromatic dry white with pear-drop fruitiness and crisp grapefruity acidity. One for Auld Lang Syne.

1994 Sauvignon Blanc, Vin de Pays d'Oc Les Fumées Blanches, Lurton

£ / 2 / ♪   14/20

Flying winemaker Jacques Lurton has taken grapes from the Mediterranean plain near Béziers, added a few oak chips and come up with a smoky, honeyed Sauvignon that ought to be under £4.

1994 Marsanne sur lie, Les Terres Noires, Vin de Pays de l'Hérault

££ / 2 / ♪   15/20

Made in the Languedoc from the northern Rhône's Marsanne grape, this is an aromatic, honeysuckle and lime scented white with attractively rounded fruit and a bite of acidity.

1994 Chardonnay, Vin de Pays d'Oc, Lurton

£ / 2 / ♪   13/20

A slightly disjointed southern French Chardonnay in which the constituent elements, of oak chip, fruit richness and acidity aren't quite speaking the same lingo.

1993 Chardonnay, Vin de Pays d'Oc, Baudin

££ / 2 / ♪   15/20

A similar idea better executed in this ripe, pineappley Chardonnay. Good balance is a feature of the wines made at Hardy's Domaine de la Baume near Béziers.

1994 Sauvignon du Haut Poitou, Domaine Tour Signy

££ / 1 / ♪   15/20

Fresh, grassy, easy-drinking Loire Sauvignon Blanc in a modern, mini-Sancerre mould.

1994 Château Mylord Entre-Deux-Mers, Large

0 / 2 / ♪   13/20

Nothing to do with Shakespeare's *Measure for Measure*, as far as we know, this Bordeaux château has produced a decent, if unexciting, white with an overdose of tart acidity.

GERMANY

1993 Riesling Qualitätswein Moselland, Mosel-Saar-Ruwer
0 / 4 / 1   12/20

From the co-operative that sounds like an extension of the Walt Disney empire, this is an acid-drop and sugar confection that leaves your gums contemplating a visit to the dentist.

1991 Hochheimer Königin Victoriaberg Riesling Kabinett
£££ / 4 / 1   16/20

This famous Rheingau vineyard is named after Britain's Queen Victoria and produces rich, honeyed, full-flavoured Riesling with lots of petrolly intensity. Ignore the kitsch label and enjoy this terrific bargain at under £5.

HUNGARY

1994 Sauvignon Blanc, Gyöngyös Estate
0 / 3 / 1   9/20

Like sweetened-up mushy peas, this Hungarian Sauvignon Blanc appears to be going downhill with each passing vintage. Now that the estate has been bought by Germany's St Ursula, we hope investment will reverse the unaccountable slide.

1993 Tokaji Furmint Château Megyer
££ / 1 / 1   14/20

With its unusual tea-leaf and ginger-spice nose, this dry Hungarian white made in the Tokaji region, famous for its sweet dessert wines, is an off-the-wall style. It's well worth a punt, but be warned – it may be a bit austere for some palates.

ITALY

1994 Chardonnay del Piemonte Alasia
£ / 2 / 1   14/20

A new venture combining the talents of Martin Shaw, the original Australian flying winemaker, and the excellent Araldica co-operative in northwestern Italy's Piemonte region. This rich, full-fruited, unoaked Chardonnay marries the best of the New and Old Worlds. Our only worry is that it seems to be ageing quickly.

1994 Soave Classico Vigneto Monte Tenda Tedeschi
£££ / 2 / 🍾   15/20
Tedeschi is one of the top estates in the Veneto region, and this fresh, modern, green-olive-scented Soave, with its commendable richness of fruit and flavour, shows why.

1994 Pinot Grigio Friuli Pradio
£££ / 2 / 🍾   16/20
Well-priced for a Friuli white at just under £5, this is a fragrant, juicy, pear-flavoured unoaked white with excellent balance and intensity.

SOUTH AFRICA

1994 Chenin Blanc, Paarl Ridge
0 / 3 / 🍾   11/20
Simple, sweetened-up Chenin Blanc from the Cape. More of a hollow than a ridge.

SPAIN

1993 Rueda Hermanos Lurton
£ / 2 / 🍾   14/20
An equal blend of the local Viura and Verdejo grapes made in northwestern Spain's Rueda region (arguably the country's best white wine region), this is a well-made, appley, cool-fermented, dry quaffer for the tapas bar.

UNITED STATES

1993 Late Harvest Riesling, Madrona 37.5cl
££ / 7 / 🍾   15/20
Madrona is a label developed by British wine merchant Simon Loftus in concert with wacky American barrel-broker Mel Knox. This sweet, concentrated, softly peachy, barley sugared dessert wine is excellent value at under £5.

£5–8

AUSTRALIA

1993 Chardonnay Goundrey, Mount Barker
£ / 2 / ⌇   14/20

A *Grapevine* favourite last year, the 1993 Chardonnay from Michael Goundrey's Western Australian base is starting to show more than a few wrinkles with its dry, over-insistent oak character starting to drown out the fruit. It's also more pricey at Greenalls than elsewhere.

FRANCE

1993 Bourgogne Aligoté, Domaine Pillot
£ / 1 / ⌇   14/20

From Chassagne-Montrachet's Domaine Pillot, this is a lemony and somewhat austere Aligoté that needs food to soften its hard edges.

1994 Laforêt Bourgogne Chardonnay, Drouhin
0 / 2 / ⌇   12/20

A depressingly dull and very basic white Burgundy from one of the Côte d'Or's most respected *négociants*. Underfruited and old-fashioned.

GERMANY

1989 Graacher Himmelreich Riesling Kabinett, Dr Loosen
££ / 4 / ⌐   16/20

Ernie Loosen is one of the most dynamic and outspoken winemakers in the Mosel Valley, producing elegant, pure-flavoured whites of integrity and intensity. At around £8, this might seem a little expensive for a Kabinett, but we loved its steely, lime juice and petrol-like Mosel crispness.

UNITED STATES

1993 Fumé Blanc, Murphy Goode
££ / 2 / ⌇   15/20

Based in Sonoma's Alexander Valley, Murphy Goode specialise in complex Bordeaux-style whites. This is a toasty Sauvignon-based fumé

(American for oaked), closer to the Graves than New Zealand in style.

1992 Riesling Reserve, Argyle Oregon
£££ / 4 / ⌐   17/20
From Petaluma's Oregon venture, this is a very unusual botrytis-affected white that, by an accident of nature, failed to complete its fermentation in tank, leaving a little bit of residual fruit sweetness behind. The result is a one-off white with luscious lime juice aromas and fresh citrusy acidity.

Over £8

AUSTRALIA

1993 Semillon, Amberley Estate
£££ / 2 / ⌐   17/20
Isolated from the main body of Australia's winemaking regions, the vineyards of Western Australia are sometimes overlooked by white wine lovers. Wrongly in our view. As this sumptuous, toasty, barrel-fermented Semillon demonstrates, Margaret River is capable of producing stunning, ageworthy whites.

FRANCE

1992 Mâcon Viré Domaine Emilian Gillet, Thévenet
£££ / 3 / ⌐   17/20
A very unusual Chardonnay from the Mâcon region of southern Burgundy, made by the wiry Jean Thévenet in a deliberately off-dry style. Thévenet believes that, in the past, many Mâconnais whites contained a degree of residual sugar, and claims that his wines reflect this tradition. Whatever the historical truth, the resulting wines can be spectacular. This super-ripe, honeyed cuvée makes the point fluently.

1990 Meursault, Domaine Matrot
£££ / 2 / ⌐   17/20
From earring-wearing Thierry Matrot, this is a contrast in style, but no less traditional or well-made. It's a rich, leesy, minerally

Meursault white of great complexity and class, reflecting the excellence of the 1990 vintage.

1993 Château Thieuley Cuvée Francis Courselle
££ / 2 / ▌   16/20
Owned by Francis Courselle, a winemaking academic at the University of Bordeaux, Château Thieuley is a pioneering estate producing extremely modern styles of dry white Bordeaux often totally or partially fermented in new oak. This smoky, Graves-style white is loaded with intense grapefruit and buttered toast flavours.

ITALY

1992 Recioto di Soave, I Capitelli, Anselmi 37.5cl
££ / 8 / ▌   16/20
Made from dried grapes in the time-sanctioned Veneto manner by leading producer Anselmi, this is nevertheless a modern style of Recioto, with fermentation in new oak barrels adding a sheen of cream and vanilla to the wine's richly concentrated natural sweetness. Drink on its own or with a ripe peach or pear.

NEW ZEALAND

1993 Brancott Estate Sauvignon Blanc, Montana
£££ / 2 / ▌   17/20
Identified on the label by the enigmatic letter 'B', Brancott Estate is one of three designated vineyard sites owned by leading New Zealand producer Montana. This is the only Sauvignon among the trio, and represents a marked contrast in style to the value-for-money, unoaked style for which the winery is best known. At close to £12, it's not cheap, but we think it stands comparison with a fine white Graves.

UNITED STATES

1993 Chardonnay Carneros Benziger
££ / 2 / ▌   16/20
Located at the cool southern end of California's Napa Valley, the Carneros district is now established as one of the West Coast's foremost

vineyard areas for premium Chardonnay and Pinot Noir. This well-made, barrel-fermented white, made by varietal specialists Glen Ellen in Sonoma, is a successful Californian attempt at a neo-Burgundian style.

Red

£3–5

AUSTRALIA

1994 Grenache, Peter Lehmann
£££ / MB / ⚑   15/20
Rich, alcoholic, vibrantly fruity Aussie red made by Barossa Valley specialist Peter Lehmann. It's an unashamedly gluggable, strawberryish red which shoves most Beaujolais into the nearest corked hat.

CHILE

1993 Cabernet/Merlot, Andes Peaks
££ / MB / ⚑   14/20
With its chunky, unyielding tannins and robust blackcurrant fruitiness, this is a wine which gives you plenty of flavour for your money.

FRANCE

1993 Chinon, Domaine Giraudier
££ / MB / ⚑   15/20
Soft, rounded, classic cool climate Cabernet Franc which needs to be lightly chilled to be at its best. It's surprising to find a wine with this level of concentration from the rainy 1993 vintage.

1994 Merlot/Cabernet Sauvignon, Les Terres Noires, Vin de Pays de l'Hérault
££ / MB / ⚑   14/20
Made by Delta Domaines near Béziers in the Languedoc, this is a modern, spicy, pistachio-tinged Mediterranean blend, with plenty of chunky depth.

1991 Corbières Château des Mattes
££ / FB / ☝   15/20

A traditional, robust Languedoc red, matured in spicy French oak for extra oomph and flavour. Big, smoky and powerful.

ITALY

1993 Montepulciano d'Abruzzo, Umani Ronchi
££ / MB / ☝   14/20

A good value Italian quaffer showing plenty of coffee bean and almond aromas backed up by soft fruit sweetness and a twist of Italianate acidity.

1994 Refosco Tuaro Friuli, Pradio
£ / MB / ☝   14/20

Made from the snappily named Refosco del Peduncolo Rosso, this northeastern Italian red is a vibrantly fruity, densely coloured, raspberry and cherryish pasta enhancer.

1994 Dolcetto d'Asti, Alasia
££ / MB / ☝   15/20

Another wine made by the successful partnership of Martin Shaw (nothing to do with the actor of the same name) and northwestern Italy's Araldica co-operative. Once again, Shaw has avoided oak and plumped for the fresh, fruity succulence of the Dolcetto grape. We hope his contract is renewed annually.

PORTUGAL

1994 Terras do Sado Pedras do Monte
££ / MB / ☝   15/20

We found this smoky, damson-skin red among the most enjoyable of Greenalls' extensive Portuguese range. Perhaps it had something to do with the name of the winemaker, Antonio Rosa.

1993 Alentejo Tinto da Talha
£ / MB / ☝   14/20

Soft, spicy southern Portuguese quaffer made in an approachable, easy-drinking style.

SOUTH AFRICA

1993 Welmoed Pinotage
££ / FB / ⌘   15/20
From an estate in the Stellenbosch region of the Western Cape, this ripe,
raspberry-fruity Pinotage belongs firmly in the modern winemaking
camp. Good value at under £5 and no mistaking the distinctive grape
behind the label.

SPAIN

1993 Priorato Tinto Scala Dei
££ / FB / ⌘   15/20
Priorato on Spain's Mediterranean coast is not the most commercial of
denominations. It's normally big, tarry and tannic with levels of alcohol
than can approach those of a fortified wine. This one is more modern
than most, but still shows plenty of baked, rustic fruitiness. Best drunk
with robust food.

1994 Tempranillo Hermanos Lurton
£ / MB / ⌘   14/20
Chunky, inky, modern Tempranillo from winemaking consultant
Jacques Lurton. It's still a bit closed at the moment, but should open out
in time.

URUGUAY

1991 Tannat Castel Pujol, Las Violetes
££ / FB / ⌘   15/20
Still the only drinkable wine we've come across from Uruguay, this
savoury, beefstockish interpretation of Madiran's Tannat grape is an
unusual buy at under £5.

£5–8

AUSTRALIA

1992 Shiraz, Peter Lehmann
££ / FB / 🌶   15/20

Shiraz is arguably what Peter Lehmann, one of the Barossa Valley's great characters, does best. This oaky, pepperminty red is certainly not short of abundance of flavour and sweet, juicy fruitiness.

CHILE

1992 Merlot Villard, Cachapoal
£ / MB / 🌶   15/20

Light, elegant, spearminty Chilean Merlot from Frenchman Thierry Villard. We liked the wine, but felt that it should have come in at under £5.

FRANCE

1994 Brouilly Domaine des Nazins, Duboeuf
££ / MB / 🌶   15/20

From the largest of Beaujolais' 10 *crus*, superblender Georges Duboeuf has come up with a fruity, strawberry-fruity Gamay, showing the sort of drinkability that once made Beaujolais famous.

1993 Gigondas, Cave de Vacquéyras
££ / MB / 🌶   16/20

A heady, perfumed, southern Rhône red from an appellation which often outperforms neighbouring Châteauneuf-du-Pape in the value-for-money department. This is less alcoholic than some and shows a delightful spicebox of aromas and flavours.

1990 Saint Joseph les Larmes Alain Paret
££ / MB / 🌶   16/20

Saint Joseph is such a sprawling northern Rhône appellation that the quality of its wines can vary wildly. This typically aromatic, elegant Syrah has developed extra complexity with a bit of age.

ITALY

1993 Campo ai Sassi Rosso di Montalcino
£ / MB / ♪   15/20

Dense, chewy, oaky, tannic Italian made, believe it or not, for earlier drinking than its more classic stablemate, Brunello di Montalcino.

PORTUGAL

1991 Cabernet Sauvignon, Quinta de Pancas
££ / MB / ♪   15/20

A fluent Portuguese attempt at a modern, international style of Cabernet Sauvignon. We enjoyed this soft, spicy, elegantly oaked, red, and so, we trust, will you.

SPAIN

1991 Navarra Crianza Guelbenzu
£££ / MB / ♪   16/20

A smooth, modern blend of Spain's Tempranillo grape with Bordeaux's Cabernet Sauvignon and Merlot, this shows that Navarra has the ability to produce wines every bit as complex as its more illustrious neighbour, Rioja.

1990 Ribera del Duero, Reserva Vega Cubillas
£££ / FB / ☞   16/20

Aficionados may remember the excellent 1987 Señorio de Nava, a vintage which seemed to go on for ever. Nothing to do, of course, with the fact that it won a Gold Medal in international competition. Well, this is the follow-up vintage you've been waiting for – a super-oaky, powerfully concentrated, Tempranillo-based red, which is still in short trousers.

UNITED STATES

1993 Cabernet/Merlot Hedges Cellars, Washington State
£££ / MB / ♪   16/20

Washington State has emerged as a serious value-for-money alternative to California, as evidenced by this silky, beautifully proportioned

Bordeaux blend with its attractive cool climate elegance and length of flavour.

1993 Madrona Cabernet Sauvignon, North Yuba
££ / MB / ➠   16/20
Another wine sourced under the Madrona label, this time North Yuba's religious community at the Renaissance winery. We can all thank the Lord for this finely crafted, minty Cabernet Sauvignon with its sweet fruit middle and robust tannins (and when we say Lord, we're not referring to Simon Loftus).

Over £8

FRANCE

1992 Savigny lès Beaune Fourneaux, Domaine Chandon de Briailles
££ / MB / ⌘   16/20
Lightly oaked, cherryish Pinot Noir with a core of delicious sweet fruit from an often undervalued Côte de Beaune appellation.

1992 Volnay, Domaine Marquis d'Angerville
££ / MB / ➠   16/20
As you'd expect from a Volnay, this is a denser, more powerful red Burgundy with rich, smoky, concentrated fruit and oaky backbone. Not cheap at nearly £15, but then Volnay, in the first rank of Côte d'Or appellations, rarely is.

1992 Clos du Marquis Saint Julien
££ / MB / ⌘   17/20
Clos du Marquis is the second label of the Saint Julien star second growth Léoville Lascases owned by Bordeaux *éminence grise*, Michel Delon. It's consistently one of the best second labels, and considering that it's from the light 1992 vintage, this elegant, chocolatey claret is a terrific effort.

ITALY

1988 Chianti Rufina Riserva, Marchese Gondi, Villa di Bossi
£ / FB / 🍴   15/20

Leafy, leathery, raisiny Chianti in the old-fashioned style. It's nicely aromatic but the hefty tannins cry out for a plate of wild boar – or something similar, anyway.

SOUTH AFRICA

1993 Pinotage Kanonkop
££ / FB / ➤   16/20

Made by Beyers Truter, the Pinotage king of South Africa, this is a textbook example of South Africa's indigenous crossing of Pinot Noir and Cinsault. It still has the rich aromas and big flavours associated with Kanonkop reds, but we've noticed a perceptible lightening of style in recent vintages.

UNITED STATES

1993 Saintsbury Pinot Noir Garnet
££ / LB / 🍴   16/20

The lightest of the three styles of Pinot Noir made at David Graves' and Dick Ward's celebrated Carneros winery, this is a charming, lightly oaked Pinot Noir with soft strawberry fruitiness and fresh acidity. It's also a rival to red Burgundy at under £10.

Rosé

£5–8

FRANCE

1994 Château de Sours Bordeaux Rosé
££ / 3 / 🍴   15/20

With its day-glo hue and bubblegum and redcurrant fruitiness, Esme Johnstone's Bordeaux Rosé is consistently one of the best on the market.

It would be even better if it were cheaper – perhaps that's the exchange rate for you.

Sparkling

Over £8

FRANCE

Ariston Brut, NV
££ / 2 / 〗   15/20
Made at a small six-hectare family estate, this Champagne with its garish yellow label is made in equal parts from the Pinot Noir, Pinot Meunier and Chardonnay grapes. It's a fruity, full-bodied style with lots of zip and zest, and is exclusive to Greenalls.

Dom Ruinart 'R' Brut, NV
£ / 2 / 〗   16/20
With its rich, creamy, bottle-aged character and broad, mouthfilling mousse, this is a hedonist's Champagne at a masochist's price of nearly £25.

1988 Henriot Brut
££ / 2 / 〗   16/20
For £4 less, you can line yourself up with a bottle of this excellent vintage Champagne, made in a mature, toasty style which the French call *le goût* (as opposed to *le vice*) *anglais*.

UNITED STATES

Quartet Roederer Estate NV
£££ / 2 / 〗   17/20
Made by Frenchman Michel Salgues in northern California's ultra-cool Anderson Valley, this is a brilliant New World sparkling wine in which the company's French parentage shines through. A blend of 70 per cent Chardonnay and 30 per cent Pinot Noir, it's a vividly complex fizz with yeasty-toasty complexity, the faintest hint of oak, and a dry, lingering aftertaste.

Gloria Ferrer Brut

££ / 2 / ♪   15/20

Another European-backed Californian venture, in this case by the giant
Spanish Cava producer, Freixenet. For those who find Cordon Negro
disappointing, this frothy, full-flavoured fizz will come as an agreeable
surprise.

Fortified

£3–5

ITALY

1994 Moscato di Pantelleria Pellegrino 37.5cl

£ / 7 / ♪   14/20

From the Mediterranean island of Pantelleria off the southern coast of
Sicily, this is a rich date and raisin dessert wine with unctuous grapey
sweetness. We found it a bit cloying, but the sweet of tooth should
happily slurp it up.

KWIK SAVE **(*)

Head Office: Warren Drive, Prestatyn, Clwyd LL19 7HU

Telephone: 01745 887111

Number of branches: approximately 950

Credit cards accepted: No, but Switch and Delta in some stores

Hours of opening: Monday to Wednesday and Saturday 9.00am to 5.00pm; Thursday and Friday 9.00am to 8.00pm; Sunday 12.00pm to 3.00pm

By-the-case sales: No

Glass loan: No

Home delivery: No

Clubs: No

Discounts: No, whole range 'competitively priced'. Sometimes one-off special offers and there is usually a monthly promotion

Top ten best-selling wines: Liebfraumilch; Hock; Lambrusco Bianco 5%; Rouge de France; Lambrusco Rosé 5%; Lovico Suhindol Cabernet Sauvignon/Merlot; Cadenza Italian Red Vino da Tavola; Flamenco Red; Flamenco Medium White; Lambrusco Bianco Light 3%

Range: GOOD: Regional France, Eastern Europe, Bordeaux, Australia
AVERAGE: Spain, Portugal, South Africa, Chile, United States, Italy
POOR: Germany

For wine, as much as sliced white bread and frozen burgers, Kwik Save has always concerned itself with what an Istanbul bazaar hawker once called 'big cheapness'. It's a basic, but extremely effective approach to retailing aimed at a very specific type of customer – essentially the meaner rich and the genuinely poor. As ace wine buyer Angela Muir asked us with a cheeky smile: 'We only operate in one of your price brackets, don't we?'

In fact, this is more or less accurate. Wines retailing over the talismanic £2.99 mark *chez* Kwik Save are as rare as scorching spring mornings in Lapland. Leave out the three-litre wine boxes, Le Piat d'Or, Champagne, a couple of Australians and a pair of sparkling wines and we're talking the nether reaches of the market here.

Cheap doesn't have to mean undrinkable, though. For over the last three years, Muir and assistant Deborah Williams have assembled one of the best inexpensive ranges in the high street – demonstrating an admirable obsession with value for money matched only by the wine buying teams at Asda, Somerfield and Morrison's.

Not that Muir finds the job easy. 'The public insists on wine at £2.99,' she says, 'and the more duty goes up and the currency markets work against you, the harder it gets.' Still, 90 per cent of the Kwik Save offering has to satisfy the chain's thriftiest drinkers, with Liebfraumilch and Lambrusco seemingly unshakeable at the top of the pile.

What encourages Muir is that customers are increasingly willing to venture off-piste in their purchases. At Kwik Save, this means the New World or, to be more precise, anything that isn't sweet and sticky. 'Our sales of South African and Chilean wines are up hugely, as are those of red wines,' she points out. 'So while I find the popularity of Lieb and Lambrusco depressing, the overall market is moving upwards.'

Kwik Save's margins are some of the lowest around – discounting the chains who seem to regard wine as a loss leader or a substitute for television advertising. Customers clearly appreciate what they find on the shelves. Volumes have doubled in three years and the average price of a bottle of wine has increased by 27 pence. Small mercies perhaps, but it's still part of a pleasing trend.

'What I'm trying to do,' adds Muir, 'is make sure that someone who buys a bottle of wine at Kwik Save enjoys it.' It is to her credit that she has, in the main, succeeded. There are duff bottles at Kwik Save – we weren't terribly impressed by the German whites or basic Spanish reds – but the overall standard is remarkably high given the price constraints.

The main reason for this is that Muir is a very astute buyer. She tastes samples of the whole range on a weekly basis. 'And if there are any signs of deterioration,' she warns, 'I scream and shout at the supplier.' Don't know about you, but it's not a position we'd like to find ourselves in.

The South of France is the area Muir rates the highest on value for money at the moment, closely pursued by Spain, Portugal, South Africa and Chile. For the time being, Australia's wine shortage and correspondingly high prices have halted Kwik Save's planned assault on the wine market Down Under. So the wine producers of the Hunter and Barossa Valleys have been spared a confrontation with Angela Muir. When it does happen, we'll be first in the queue for tickets.

White

Under £3

AUSTRALIA

Pelican Bay Dry White
££ / 2 / 1   15/20
Fresh from the 1995 vintage Down Under, this is a grapey Riesling-based dry white showing commendable citrus-fruit zing. OK, it's in a dwindling category, but this is the best sub-£3 Aussie white around.

Pelican Bay Medium Dry White
££ / 4 / 1   14/20
Sharing the same smart olive-green livery as its drier cousin, this has a touch of Muscat-like fragrance and well-balanced sweetness. Try it with spicy food.

BULGARIA

1994 Bear Ridge White, Lyaskovets
£££ / 2 / 1   14/20
Flying winemaker Kym Milne has achieved the near-impossible in producing a drinkable white wine from Bulgaria. It's fresh and lightly spiced with a good dose of the panache Mr Milne brings to even the lowliest blend. Could this be the start of a revolution?

1994 Chardonnay Sauvignon, Preslav, Domaine Boyar
£££ / 2 / 1   14/20
Another surprisingly well-made Bulgarian white, showing flavours of

green bean and white pepper. Domaine Boyar supplies the descendants of the Bulgarian monarchy – but that needn't put you off.

CHILE

White Pacific Sauvignon Blanc
££ / 2 / 🖤   13/20
From Curicó in southern Chile, this is a good, if slightly neutral, example of the Sauvignon Blanc grape, made by Australian Kym Milne. If you concentrate hard enough, you can just about spot the grapefruit character.

FRANCE

Blanc de France, Selection Cuvée VE
£ / 2 / 🖤   12/20
VE, just in case you're wondering, is a French pun on the name Kwik Save (Vite Epargne). Geddit? Perhaps Kwik Save could have spared us this plonk de plonk from the Loire Valley, but at the price, it's decent, clean and reasonably fruity.

1994 Vin de Pays des Côtes de Gascogne
££ / 2 / 🖤   13/20
Produced at the usually impressive Plaimont co-operative, this is a crisp, summery white from Three Musketeers country. One for all . . .

1994 Bordeaux Sauvignon, Cuvée VE
£££ / 2 / 🖤   15/20
Well done Kwik Save, for unearthing a fresh Bordeaux Blanc with lots of aroma and typically grassy fruit. If only a few more wine merchants could produce inexpensive Sauvignon Blanc of this quality on a regular basis.

1994 Domaine la Gravenne Vin de Pays d'Oc Sur Lie
£ / 2 / 🖤   13/20
From the Domaines Virginie operation in Béziers, this is a cool-fermented, New World influenced white with a faintly bitter twist.

1994 Steep Ridge Chardonnay/Sauvignon Vin de Pays d'Oc
££ / 2 / ▮   14/20
Another modern dry white from the Languedoc, with a little more
character and depth of flavour. An easy-drinking, unoaked quaffer.

GERMANY

1994 Hock, K. Linden
0 / 3 / ▮   12/20
Recognisably German (unfortunately), this proves that even Angela Muir
is fallible. Hock it certainly isn't.

1994 Liebfraumilch, K. Linden
0 / 3 / ▮   11/20
Sales of Liebfraumilch are still increasing at Kwik Save. The depressing
thing is that quality seemingly has little to do with it. Could it have more
to do with the price? Answers on a postcard to Angela Muir at Kwik
Save.

HUNGARY

1994 Hungarian Country Wine, Kiskoros Region
££ / 3 / ▮   13/20
A Rizling-based off-dry, spicy white in a full-bodied Alsace mould. The
main difference is that it's half the price.

1994 Hungarian Chardonnay
£££ / 2 / ▮   14/20
Made by Akos Kamocsay under the supervision of Australian Nick Butler,
this is a lightly oaked, citrus-scented Chardonnay with a sharp edge.

1994 Hungarian Pinot Gris, Aszar-Neszmely
£££ / 2 / ▮   14/20
From the same winemaking duo, this is a rich, weighty, Alsace-like white
with an attractive texture.

ITALY

Lambrusco Bianco Light, 3%
£ / 7 / ▮   12/20
Sweet, massively grapey fizz. Pleasant, but closer to fruit juice than wine.

Lambrusco Bianco '5'
££ / 6 / ▮   13/20
The extra 2 per cent alcohol shows, adding body and weight to this
more grown-up Lambrusco. Banana split and lemonade in a glass.
Mmm . . .

Cavalino Moscato Piemonte 5%
££ / 4 / ▮   14/20
Ditto, but a little bit drier.

1994 Soave, Cantina Sociale di Soave
£ / 2 / ▮   13/20
The all-singing, all-dancing Soave co-operative has come up with a
typically clean, respectable Veneto white with a faint whiff of almond.

Cadenza White, Vino da Tavola
££ / 3 / ▮   13/20
A perfumed, off-dry Italian white with a Muscat-like perfume and a
background of baked Mediterranean fruit.

1994 Frascati Superiore, Villa Pani
£££ / 2 / ▮   14/20
One of the more interesting of Kwik Save's Italian whites, thanks to
plenty of weight, and a characterful combination of resin, nuttiness and
fresh acidity.

Puglian White, Country Collection, Vino da Tavola
£££ / 2 / ▮   14/20
An extremely well-made white from the heel of southern Italy, showing
spice, zip and rich fruit in abundance. At last Italy seems to be making
the most of its storehouse of white grape varieties.

Atesino Chardonnay, Concilio

£££ / 2 / 🌓   14/20

Textbook flying-winemaker Chardonnay from Kym Milne with typical
buttery flavours and a smidgeon of oak character. It's hard to find
Chardonnay this good under £3.

SOUTH AFRICA

Clearsprings Cape Medium White

£££ / 4 / 🌓   14/20

From the go-ahead Simonsvlei co-operative, this is a cool-fermented,
talcum-powder-scented, off-dry white, with attractive fruit salad
flavours. Great value, but make sure you chill it down.

Landema Falls Colombard Chardonnay

£££ / 2 / 🌓   14/20

Another super value Springbok white, noticeably drier than the
Clearsprings, and with a distinctly peachy Chardonnay character.

£3–5

AUSTRALIA

1994 Angoves Chardonnay, Classic Reserve

££ / 3 / 🌓   15/20

An all-day breakfast of toast, melon, peach and butter. The sort of wine
that gave Australia a good name in the UK. Short on subtlety perhaps,
but long on flavour and enjoyment. Get the bacon on the griddle.

FRANCE

1994 Marsanne, Domaine Fontenille, Vin de Pays d'Oc

£££ / 2 / 🌓   15/20

It's unusual to find Marsanne, the great white grape of the northern
Rhône, down in the wilds of the Midi, but this oatmealy, full-bodied dry
white might set a trend.

HUNGARY

1994 Furmint, Château Megyer
£££ / 2 / ♦   16/20

It's a brave move by a cut-price operation like Kwik Save to list a wine at over £4, never mind one as unusual as this dry, spicy, complex Hungarian white made by French château owner Jean-Michel Arcaute. Thanks to foreign investment, the Tokaj region is fast reclaiming its historic position as Eastern Europe's finest wine region.

UNITED STATES

1994 Barefoot Cellars Chardonnay
0 / 2 / ♦   12/20

Nice footprint label, but leaves no impression on the palate.

Red

Under £3

BULGARIA

Lovico Suhindol, Cabernet Sauvignon/Merlot, Bulgarian Country Wine
££ / MB / ♦   13/20

Well-executed, oaky red, closer to an affordable Rioja than a Bordeaux in style.

1992 Iambol Merlot/Pamid, Domaine Boyar
££ / MB / ♦   13/20

In contrast, this more mature red is more like a Bordeaux, showing soft, green pepper fruitiness and a touch of spicy oak.

FRANCE

Rouge de France, Sélection Cuvée VE
0 / LB / 🍷   11/20
This coarse southern blend would have been enough to dampen even the most enthusiastic VE day celebrations. One for collaborators rather than war heroes.

Vin de Pays de l'Hérault
£ / MB / 🍷   13/20
From pasta magnate Robert Skalli, this bubblegummy southern French plonk is wonderful with cous-cous. *N'est-ce pas*, Robert?

Minervois, Val d'Orbieu
££ / MB / 🍷   14/20
From France's largest wine company, this is a chunky Mediterranean red exuding the herbal aromas of the *garrigue*.

1994 Steep Ridge, Grenache/Shiraz, Vin de Pays d'Oc
£ / MB / 🍷   13/20
As the name suggests, this is a modern, New World-influenced southern French blend with plenty of softly quaffable fruit.

Claret, AC Bordeaux, Cuvée VE
££ / MB / 🍷   14/20
It's almost impossible to find drinkable claret under £3 any more, so well done, Kwik Save, for finding this fresh, agreeably grassy example.

1993 De Belfont Cuvée Spéciale, Vin de Pays de l'Aude
£ / MB / 🍷   13/20
A blend of the unusual Portan grape with more familiar Merlot, this is a muscular, broad-shouldered red with a lot of dry tannins.

1994 Skylark Hill Merlot, Vin de Pays d'Oc
££ / MB / 🍷   14/20
A youthful, vibrant red made by flying Australian winemaker Nick Butler, who has moved his landing strip from Hungary to the South of France.

1994 Château de Pouzols, Cuvée Prestige, Minervois
0 / MB / 〗   11/20

If this is the cuvée prestige, we shudder to think what the vin ordinaire tastes like. Undistinguished farmyard fare.

ITALY

Cadenza Red, Sangiovese del Rubicone, Vino da Tavola
£ / LB / 〗   12/20

A grand name for such a basic, light, cherried Italian red. We wouldn't cross the Rubicon, or even a puddle, for this one.

1994 Valpolicella, Cantina Sociale di Soave
£ / LB / 〗   14/20

From the reliable Soave co-operative, this is a juicy, gluggable rosso with plenty of colour and oomph.

Puglian Red, Country Collection, Vino da Tavola
0 / FB / 〗   12/20

Unusually for flying winemaker Kym Milne, this is a poorly judged, old-fashioned southern red with leathery tannins. Not one for our country collection.

MACEDONIA

1993 Macedonian Country Red, Povardarie
£££ / MB / 〗   14/20

A meaty, densely coloured Balkan red with plenty of rich, ripe, spicy fruit. Continuity of supply might be a problem.

1993 Macedonian Merlot, Steve Clarke's Blend
0 / FB / 〗   10/20

We've no idea who Steve Clarke is, and after tasting this rubbery, overoaked effort, we don't really care.

PORTUGAL

Villa Moresco Tinto, Benfica Co-operative
£££ / MB / ⚱   15/20
From Eusebio country (anyone remember him from 1966?), this is an
attractively spicy, peppery red made from native Portuguese grape
varieties.

1994 Alta Mesa Estremadura
££ / MB / ⚱   13/20
You might be surprised to find this juicy, peppery, modern red at high
table, but it's the sort of thing cheapskate Oxbridge dons serve up in
decanters to deserving students.

SOUTH AFRICA

Landema Falls Cinsault/Cabernet Sauvignon
££ / MB / ⚱   14/20
Livingstone's dog was named after these falls discovered in the Orange
Free State in 1868. Or was it? Good, well-made, easy drinking red with a
claret-like touch and a little bit of fruit sweetness.

SPAIN

1994 Don Fadrique Cencibel
0 / FB / ⚱   11/20
Angela Muir describes this eggy vino tinto as a wine Kwik Save 'did not
have to buy'. Why did it?

Flamenco Red, Cariñena
0 / MB / ⚱   10/20
Long on tannin and matchstick oak, but short on fruit. Not one to stamp
your feet to.

Promesa Tinto Joven, Cosecheros y Criadores
££ / MB / ⚱   14/20
Another wine with a name that sounds like an out-take from a Spanish
language school. But no complaints about the wine, which is gluggably
juicy in a Beaujolais style. Worth learning by rote.

UNITED STATES

California Cellars Red, Mission Bell Winery
0 / LB / ♪   12/20
Sweetened up, boring California red. Strictly for use in the missionary position.

£3–5

AUSTRALIA

1993 Angoves Butterfly Ridge, Cabernet Sauvignon/Shiraz
£ / MB / ♪   13/20
This one emerged from its chrysalis rather too long ago. Drinkable but tiring.

CHILE

1994 Cono Sur Cabernet Sauvignon
£££ / MB / ♪   15/20
Cono Sur made a name for itself in the UK with its excellent 1993 Pinot Noir, and this one builds on the promising start. Made by curly-haired Californian beanpole, Ed Flaherty, it's a plummy, tobaccoey Cabernet with lots of succulent fruit. One of the best-value Chilean reds on the market.

FRANCE

1994 Grenache Noir, Vin de Pays d'Oc, Fortant de France
£ / MB / ♪   14/20
Soft, alcoholic southern French red from the Skalli stable. Marginally overpriced given the ready availability of the Grenache grape in the Languedoc.

1994 Pinot Noir, Vin de Pays d'Oc, Domaine St Martin
0 / FB / ♪   12/20
Headbanger's Pinot Noir with masses of bitter tannin, colour and chewiness. Could be made from anything – except Pinot Noir (*is this libellous*, Ed?)

UNITED STATES

Barefoot Cellars Cabernet Sauvignon
££ / MB / ♪   14/20
This blackcurranty, coffee bean scented California red makes more of an impression than the white. Not indelible, unless you pour it on your shirt.

Rosé

Under £3

FRANCE

1994 Rosé de Syrah, Vin de Pays d'Oc, Domaines Virginie
£££ / 3 / ♪   14/20
Orange-tinged, bubblegummy, off-dry rosé from an Australian-influenced operation in the Languedoc. Fresh, crisp and well-made.

ITALY

Lambrusco Rosato '5'
££ / 5 / ♪   13/20
One of a bewildering line-up of Lambruschi at Kwik Save. Fizzy, alcoholic strawberry juice by another name.

PORTUGAL

1994 Promesa Rosado
0 / 4 / ♪   12/20
Mateus Rosé lookalike with a sweet, confected fruitiness and a slight spritz. Strictly for those sepia-tinted, chockie box moments.

Sparkling

Over £8

FRANCE

Champagne Brut, Louis Raymond
££ / 2 / ⅟   14/20
Paul Raymond's brother Louis has come up with another racy fizz – a
favourite with Soho residents. Fresh, frothy and well-priced. More than
you can say for Raymond's Revue Bar. Allegedly.

Fortified

Under £3

SPAIN

Castillo de Liria, Moscatel, Valencia
£ / 9 / ⅟   13/20
A considerable improvement on last year's effort, this fortified Spanish
white is almost gaggingly sweet, with honey and raisin sweetness and
an element of citrus peel acidity. Try it with trifle.

MAJESTIC WINE WAREHOUSES ****

Head Office: Odhams Trading Estate, St Albans Road, Watford WD2 5RE

Telephone: 01923 816999

Number of branches: 50

Credit cards accepted: Visa, Access, American Express, Diners, Switch

Hours of opening: Generally Monday to Saturday 10.00am to 8.00pm; Sunday 10.00am to 6.00pm. A few stores have slightly different hours.

By-the-case sales: Exclusively, but cases can be mixed and ordered in any quantity after that. They do not have to be in multiples of 12.

Glass loan: Yes

Home delivery: Free within a 15-mile radius of the store

Clubs: No

Discounts: 'Substantial' discounts on Champagne and sparkling wines over £5.99; 10 per cent off six unmixed bottles; 15 per cent off an unmixed case; and 20 per cent off five cases. Discounts on multi-buys. A large number of special offers and deals always available.

In-store tastings: Ten theme tasting weekends per year. Special feature wines every weekend, plus well-stocked tasting counter in stores at all times. Tastings for private groups welcome.

Top ten best-selling wines: Pinot Grigio, Pasqua; Chardonnay, Vin de Pays d'Oc, Bessière; Blanc de Blancs, Henri Lambert; Le St Cricq, Blanc de Blancs; Lindemans Cawarra Semillon/Chardonnay; Il Paesano, Merlot del Veneto; Côtes du Rhône, Chevalier aux Lys d'Or; Mâcon Blanc, Les Chazelles; Angas Brut; GF Cavalier Sparkling

Range: GOOD: Bordeaux, Champagne and sparkling wines, Loire, Germany, regional France, Rhône, Port, Australia, Spain, Beaujolais

AVERAGE: Burgundy, South Africa, California, Italy, New Zealand, Alsace, Portugal

POOR: Eastern Europe, Chile

When Majestic trading director Tony Mason appeared in a black and white photograph in *Wine* magazine recently, the image captured him in characteristic pose – negotiating a 'deal' with one of the best-known winemakers in Savigny over the bonnet of a car. Mason likes nothing better than the haggle and barter of the market. Send him on a buying trip and the man grows in stature.

Mason's streetwise approach to wine has finally started to pay dividends – four years after Wizard Wines bought an ailing Majestic for a bargain-basement £2.5 million in September 1991. As a former Majestic director and one of the best wheeler-dealers in the business, Mason was the ideal man to rescue the wine warehouse chain. But even he couldn't conquer the recession singlehandedly. For two years, Majestic just hung in there, backed by the money of frozen food king John Apthorp and the loyalty of its customers.

As we reported last year, things started to improve in 1994. And the trend continued on an upward curve in 1995. So much so, that Majestic celebrated the opening of its fiftieth store in Southampton and announced impressive financial results showing a 91 per cent increase in pre-tax profits over the previous year. 'The results,' according to managing director Tim How, 'just prove what we are capable of achieving, and adding another store to our portfolio puts us one step nearer to our goal of 100 stores in the year 2000.'

Bullish words. How and Mason are now in charge of a wine warehouse empire which extends from Southampton to Stockport, with a move into northern Europe a future possibility. The biggest problem facing Majestic, says Mason, is finding appropriate new sites at the right price. 'We need somewhere with at least 2,500 square feet and parking for 15 cars in an upmarket area. Most of those kinds of sites are taken by exhaust businesses.' Still, Majestic has managed to add three new stores, including Southampton, in the last 12 months, so Kwik-Fit doesn't always get to the estate agents first.

Mason is happy with the way things are progressing. 'It took us two years just to get the business sorted out and improve the staffing,' he says. 'The recession has demolished a lot of small regional businesses.

And the supermarkets are clearly pulling out of the £2.99 to £4.99 range. So there's a fantastic opportunity for us in the middle market.'

Not that Mason has avoided the £1.99 end of the business. His attitude, as ever, is that if it's good for business, it's worth doing. 'The £1.99 wines are essentially a marketing tool,' he says, 'to show people that we're serious about being in business and not an expensive place to buy wine. It reassures customers that we're offering wines at all levels.' Mason admits that he doesn't make much money on £1.99 wines. But they account for 40,000 cases of Majestic's one million case throughput, so they're obviously popular with customers.

All the same, Majestic is hardly a cut-throat discount operation. It's one of the few national retailers that can shift significant volumes of what Mason calls 'blue chip wines'. And its 700-strong range is one of the best in Britain, full of good regular lines as well as unusual parcels picked up by Mason at auction, from the receiver or, allegedly, off the back of the nearest *camion*.

Majestic has a number of things in its favour – good staff, substantial stocks of individual wines, car parking and a rapid turnover of new products. Its image was burnished further this year by Tim How's suave appearance in an American Express TV ad. 'The ad cost more to make than we paid for Majestic,' smiles Mason.

The range is still strongest in France, especially Bordeaux, Champagne, the Loire and the Languedoc. France accounts for 50 per cent of sales, followed, in order of importance, by Australia, Italy and Spain. But French sales have been uneven – Bordeaux and the Midi have done well, while the Loire and Burgundy have slipped in the last 12 months.

The real casualty of 1995, however, was Eastern Europe. 'We lost 50 per cent of sales,' says Mason. 'It just seems to be in terminal decline.' Our feeling is that Majestic hasn't yet taken advantage of the new-style reds and whites emerging from Hungary and Bulgaria. The same is true of Chile, a country which is dramatically under-represented down on the warehouse floor. We were also a little disappointed by the results of Tony Mason's visit to California, which seemed to result in a lot of listings for Beringer and Mondavi – hardly the super-sharp cutting edge of West Coast winemaking.

Nevertheless, we're impressed overall by what Majestic has achieved in the last two years. Crucially, it's encouraged people to spend more money on wine at a time when supermarkets are pushing average prices through the tiled floor. Majestic's average transaction is over £90 and, at £4.04 (excluding sparkling wines, Champagne and spirits), its average bottle price is one of the highest in the high street. You can see why Majestic's not keen to open a branch in Peckham or Moss Side.

The encouraging thing is that Mason believes Majestic can sell more fine wine. Indeed, he's taken on a buyer, Chris Hardy, whose job is to source blue chip bottles alongside the less fancy stuff bought by Tony Mason and Jeremy Palmer. 'We want to be able to sell to the public at auction prices,' says Mason. 'We see this as an area where we can grow our business, particularly as fine wine prices have hardened dramatically in the last year.'

American Express ads apart, Majestic relies on word of mouth and regular mailings to bring in the punters. 'We've got an active list of 150,000 people who are very loyal to Majestic,' says marketing director Debbie Worton. The profile of the typical Majestic customer remains pretty much what it always has been – fortysomething professional males with enough spare cash to spend £25 or more in one go on booze and mineral water – but it's getting a little younger.

Eighty per cent of Majestic's customers are graduates, according to Worton – a figure which would surely plummet overnight if Majestic were to open a warehouse in the maelstrom of Calais. 'We don't want to set up in Calais,' confirms Mason, 'but maybe we should be looking at Paris or Germany.' Knowing Mason, he probably is already. After all, the closer he is to the vineyards of Europe, the closer he is to the deals. 'Cutting out the middle man,' he adds, 'is what Majestic is all about.'

White

Under £3

FRANCE

1994 Chardonnay-Pierre Bonnet, Vin de Pays du Jardin de la France
£ / 2 / 1   13/20
Clean, buttery, unoaked Loire Chardonnay. Pleasant, crisp quaffing at the price.

ITALY

Trebbiano Gaviola
0 / 3 / 🌢   11/20
Majestic's response to the rash of supermarkets cheapies, this is a very
basic quinine and almond scented white with a rough, nail polish-like
rasp.

£3–5

AUSTRALIA

1993 Wynns Coonawarra Riesling
£££ / 4 / 🌢   15/20
Recently transferred from the old Germanic flute to a more commercial
Burgundy-shaped bottle, this fresh, zesty, lemon and lime style Riesling
from South Australia's Coonawarra region is a really attractive example
of what Australia can do to bring the Riesling grape alive.

CHILE

1995 Undurraga Chardonnay, Santa Ana Valle, Maipo
£ / 2 / 🌢   13/20
A peardroppy attempt at a modern-style Chardonnay by one of Chile's
more old-fashioned wineries. Simple, rather dilute stuff, which relies too
much on new technology and yeast strains for flavour.

FRANCE

1993 Sur Lie, Vin de Pays d'Oc
0 / 2 / 🌢   12/20
Made by the giant Listel operation which specialises in dull southern
French rosés, this is a baked, basic Languedoc white allegedly made from
the Sauvignon Blanc grape. We weren't detained long enough to find
out.

1994 Cheverny Blanc, Oisly et Thésée
££ / 1 / 🌢   14/20
A blend of Sauvignon Blanc with 10 per cent Chardonnay, unusual for a

French *appellation* white, this is a crisp, nettley, modern white from the go-ahead Oisly (pronounced 'Wally') ét Thésée co-operative.

1993 Muscadet de Sèvre et Maine Sur Lie, Château de Rochefort
£ / 2 / ⚫︎   14/20

Getting on a bit at two years old, but this is a rich, full-bodied, appley Muscadet with enough *sur lie* zip to keep both hands on the zimmer frame.

1994 Sauvignon Blanc Fortant de France, Vin de Pays d'Oc
£ / 2 / ⚫︎   14/20

Grapefruity, soft Sauvignon Blanc from the style-conscious Skalli Fortant de France operation in the port of Sète. As is often the case with Fortant, the handsome package promises a little bit more than the wine delivers.

1992 Château Haut Mazières, Bordeaux
££ / 2 / ⚫︎   15/20

Deeply coloured, rich, grassy, oaky Graves-style white Bordeaux showing attractive bottle-aged maturity. Well-priced at under a fiver.

GERMANY

1993 Jacob Zimmermann Kabinett, Herxheimer Herrlich, Pfalz
£ / 5 / ⚫︎   13/20

Soft, grapey, honeyed, superliebfraumilch in a Bordeaux bottle.

1993 Jacob Zimmermann Spätlese, Bockenheimer Gräfenstöck, Pfalz
££ / 6 / ⚫︎   15/20

From the same producer, this is a sweeter, more complex style with exotic mango and peach fruit flavours balanced by fresh acidity.

ITALY

1994 Chardonnay Atesino, Kym Milne
££ / 2 / ⚫︎   14/20

Made by Kiwi winemaker Rebecca Salmond under the fuselage of flying winemaker Kym Milne in Trentino, this is a fresh, crisp, peachy northern Italian Chardonnay with good concentration for a wine under £4.

SOUTH AFRICA

1995 Two Oceans Sauvignon Blanc
£ / 3 / 1   13/20

The two oceans here are the Atlantic and the Indian, in case you were reaching for the nearest atlas. This faintly grassy, sweetish white is an improvement on last year, but it's still two decks short of a liner.

SPAIN

1994 Marqués de Riscal Rueda Blanco
£ / 2 / 1   14/20

Produced in what is arguably Spain's best white wine region by the traditional Rioja winery, Marqués de Riscal, this is an attractively modern, fresh tapas bar white made from the local Verdejo and Viura grape varieties.

UNITED STATES

1993 Apple Hill Semillon/Chardonnay
0 / 3 / 1   12/20

One of a bewildering array of California wines blended for the UK market by superbroker Jason Korman, formerly of the La Crema Winery. This soft, confected, flat white is not one of his greatest finds.

£5–8

AUSTRALIA

1992 Chateau Tahbilk Marsanne
££ / 2 / 1   15/20

A highly unusual Australian white made from the rare Marsanne grape in Victoria's Goulburn Valley by the ultra-traditionalist Chateau Tahbilk. It's an ageworthy white showing complex, peaty aromas of green malt, eucalyptus and even tea-leaf. Give it a try, especially if you like malt whisky.

1987 Lindemans Botrytis Semillon
£ / 7 / 🍾   14/20

This deep, golden, mature Semillon wine is rich in honey and barley sugar sweetness, but has lost the refreshing acidity it once had. Now that the European Union and Australia's winemakers have settled their differences over sweet wines, we are seeing better value stickies than this from Down Under.

1994 Ironstone Semillon/Chardonnay, Margaret River
££ / 2 / 🍾   15/20

Blended by David Hohnen, the man behind Western Australia's Cape Mentelle winery and New Zealand's Cloudy Bay, this is an exuberant, refreshingly grapefruity, lightly oaked blend, which could almost be made from Sauvignon Blanc.

1992 Wynns Coonawarra Estate Chardonnay
0 / 2 / 🍾   13/20

Made in a love-it-or-leave-it, heftily oaked, weighty style, this is a one-glass wonder. Great if you've got five other people round for dinner and just the one bottle.

1994 Cape Mentelle Semillon/Sauvignon
£££ / 2 / 🍾   17/20

David Hohnen's Western Australian base is less famous than Cloudy Bay, his New Zealand offspring. But the wines can be just as good. This fresh, zippy, Bordeaux-style blend with its subtle oak and tropical melon and grapefruit flavours is one of Australia's most exciting and underrated white wines.

FRANCE

1994 Pouilly Fumé Les Logères, Guy Saget
£ / 1 / 🍾   14/20

Crisp, lightly fruity Sauvignon Blanc, which could do with a bit more concentration of fruit, even at the comparatively cheap – for Pouilly Fumé – price of £7.

1993 Blanche de Bosredon, Bergerac

£££ / 2 / ⚑
16/20

A classy, barrel-fermented Bordeaux-style blend of Semillon and Sauvignon Blanc, showing stylish, smoky oak aromas and ripe, delicately toasty fruitiness.

1993 Limoux, Toques et Clochers

£££ / 2 / ⚑
16/20

From the excellent Limoux co-operative in the cool hills of the Aude department, this is one of a number of Burgundian-style Chardonnays produced specially for an annual auction, complete with French celebrities and media razzmatazz. Citrus fruit intensity and well-judged, new vanilla oak make this a brilliant alternative to Côtes de Beaune whites.

1992 Grand Ardèche Chardonnay, Louis Latour

£ / 2 / ⚑
15/20

Also from the South of France, this is Burgundian *négociant* Louis Latour's attempt at a value-for-money, premium Chardonnay. With its charry, toasty oak and toffee-fudge like flavours, this crafted Chardonnay could easily come from the New World.

1993 Chardonnay de Bourgogne, Cuvée des Ducs, Dufouleur

££ / 2 / ⚑
15/20

Another *négociant* Chardonnay, this time from the Nuits St-Georges based house of Dufouleur, but the style is entirely different, with the emphasis on fresh, citrus-fruit, almost Chablis-like character and little or no oak.

1993 Hautes Côtes de Nuits Blanc, Vaucher

£ / 2 / ⚑
15/20

Another *négociant*, another Chardonnay. Crisp, lemony and elegant in a classic Hautes Côtes style.

1992 Mercurey, Château de Chamirey

£££ / 2 / ⚑
16/20

The best of *négociant* Antonin Rodet's Côte Chalonnaise whites, this shows why the 1992 white Burgundies have such a high reputation. It's fresh, well-oaked and beautifully balanced with a length of flavour typical of the vintage.

1990 Château Doisy Dubroca, Barsac

££ / 7 / 🖢   15/20

An exotic, waxy, honeycomb and barley sugar sticky, showing richness, toasted oak and a degree of botrytis character from a good vintage for sweet Bordeaux whites.

GERMANY

1993 Rüdesheimer Drachenstein, Georg Breuer

££ / 4 / 🖢   15/20

From one of the best producers in the Rheingau, this is a modern, medium-bodied Riesling with talcum powder and white pepper aromas and an elegant, grapefruity tang of acidity.

1994 Schlossböckelheimer Kupfergrube Riesling Kabinett, Staatliche Weinbaudomäne Niederhausen Schlossböckelheim, Nahe

££ / 4 / 🖢   15/20

A smoky, earthy Riesling from the Nahe region with vibrant fruit ripeness and balancing sweet and sour acidity. Try saying the name backwards while gargling.

1990 Piesporter Goldtröpfchen Riesling Auslese, Reichsgraf von Kesselstatt

£££ / 6 / 🖢   16/20

Typically flavoursome Riesling from Annegret Reh-Gartner, one of the few Mosel producers to have made a dent in the UK market. It's packed with elegant, complex flavours of apple and honey with a smidgeon of coconut and refreshing acidity.

1994 Wiltinger Braune Kupp Riesling Kabinett, Egon Müller-Scharzhof

£££ / 4 / 🖢   17/20

About as good as a Riesling Kabinett gets, this is a super-fragrant, delicate Mosel white with flavours of lime and fresh pears balanced by a blade of crisp acidity. Can be drunk now, but will develop extra complexity in the bottle.

ITALY

1994 Chardonnay del Salento Barrique, Vigneto di Caramia, Kym Milne

££ / 2 / 🍾   15/20

A single-vineyard Chardonnay produced by Australian Kym Milne in conjunction with producer Augusto Càntele near Brindisi in southern Italy. This spicy, modern, richly fruity, oaked Chardonnay shows that Kym Milne is capable of making fine whites as well as chippy cheapies.

NEW ZEALAND

1994 Oyster Bay Sauvignon Blanc

££ / 2 / 🍾   16/20

From the dynamic brother-and-sister duo of Rose and Jim Delegat, this is a crisp, elegant, but still intensely gooseberry fruity Marlborough Sauvignon Blanc edged with a grapefruity tang.

1993 Oyster Bay Chardonnay, Marlborough

£££ / 2 / 🍾   16/20

A zesty, stylish, lightly oaked Marlborough Chardonnay with sweet butterscotchy fruit. You can see why Chardonnay has taken over from Müller-Thurgau as the most planted grape variety in New Zealand.

SPAIN

1993 Viñas del Vero Barrel Fermented Chardonnay, Somontano

££ / 2 / 🍾   15/20

From Somontano, a northern Spanish region, which is emerging as a promising source of Burgundy-style wines, this is a rich, smoky, barrel-fermented Chardonnay with a buttery texture and lots of flavour.

Over £8

FRANCE

1994 Sancerre Les Roches, Vacheron

££ / 1 / 🍾   16/20

Consistently one of the most enjoyable whites produced in the eastern

Loire's best-known *appellation*, Vacheron's Sancerre is lively and zesty with bracing gooseberry and citrus fruit flavours.

UNITED STATES

1992 Jekel Gravelstone Chardonnay
£ / 2 / ♪   15/20

Oaky, well-made southern California Chardonnay with some elegant, cool climate intensity and a refreshing aftertaste. This winery has been through some choppy waters over the last decade, but its most recent owners seem to have steadied the rudder.

1991 Cuvaison Chardonnay
££ / 2 / ♪   16/20

Made by John Thacher, one of the best makers of white wines in California's Napa Valley, this aged Carneros Chardonnay has developed an attractive nuttiness to complement the crisp, cool climate elegance of the underlying fruit.

Red

Under £3

ITALY

Sangiovese Gaviola, Basilicata & Puglia
£ / MB / ♪   12/20

This is Majestic's price-fighting red made in a perfumed, jammy, but recognisably southern Italian style. It's drinkable – which is more than you can say for most £1.99 bottles.

PORTUGAL

1994 Pedras Do Monte
0 / FB / ♪   12/20

Rustic, foxy, slightly jammy Portuguese plonk made from the widely planted Periquita grape. The sort of thing you could only drink happily in an Algarve restaurant.

£3-5

AUSTRALIA

1993 Rawsons Retreat Bin 35, Cabernet/Shiraz, Penfolds

££ / FB / ⅃　　　　　　　　　　　　　　　　　　　15/20

Mint, sage and rosemary scented Aussie red, made in a typically unstuffy style by the giant Penfolds operation. Less oaky than some Penfolds reds, it shows attractive blackberry fruitiness and rounded tannins.

1993 Bin 45 Cabernet Sauvignon, Lindemans

£ / MB / ⅃　　　　　　　　　　　　　　　　　　　14/20

True to the Lindemans formula, this is softer, more velvety and blackcurranty than stablemate Penfolds' reds. We could drink more of the cheaper Rawsons Retreat.

CHILE

1993 Undurraga Cabernet Sauvignon, Santa Ana Valle, Maipo

££ / MB / ⅃　　　　　　　　　　　　　　　　　　　14/20

One of many Undurraga wines available at Majestic, this light, grassy, quaffable Cabernet Sauvignon with its soft blackberry fruitiness is the one to go for.

1993 Montenuevo Oak-aged Cabernet Sauvignon, Vinicola Mondragon

£ / MB / ⅃　　　　　　　　　　　　　　　　　　　13/20

From the normally reliable Canepa winery, this is a deeply coloured but rather over-oaked Chilean red with a chewy, charry finish.

FRANCE

1992 Monastère de Trignan, Coteaux du Languedoc

£££ / FB / ⅃　　　　　　　　　　　　　　　　　　　16/20

A great follow-up to the superb 1991, even though it's now crept over £4. Super-aromatic Languedoc, old vine Syrah, using the carbonic maceration technique to maximise fruit flavours and smooth textures. A massively spicy, rosemary and thyme infused red. All that's missing is the basil.

1990 Côtes du Ventoux, Vidal Fleury
£ / FB / ♪   14/20

Ageing, soft, alcoholic southern Rhône red from Guigal-owned
négociant, Vidal Fleury. There's a core of raspberry fruitiness, but we
found the tannins on the robustly dry side.

1993 Château Camplong, Corbières
£££ / MB / ⬆   15/20

Juicy, smooth, concentrated Corbières, with angostura spiciness and
well-handled tannins, at an exceptional price.

1990 Le Page de Vignelaure, Coteaux d'Aix-en-Provence
£ / MB / ⬆   14/20

Recently acquired by former Majestic director Esme Johnstone's Rystone
group, this picturesque Provençal château in Cézanne country came
with huge stocks of old vintages in the cellar. This light Cabernet-based
red, with its Italianate, bitter-cherry fruit, is one of a number of selected
vintages at Majestic.

1993 Rully Rouge, Louis Page
£ / MB / ♪   13/20

A rather coarse, oaky Côte Chalonnaise red with little if any Pinot Noir
character from Nuits St-Georges *négociant* Labouré-Roi.

1994 Claret, Yves Barry
££ / MB / ♪   14/20

Fresh, grassy, well-made Bordeaux rouge with a hint of oak character
and lively acidity. Exactly the sort of wine the Gironde should be
producing to compete with the lure of the New World.

Oaky Claret, Raoul Johnston
£ / MB / ♪   14/20

Youthful, solidly oaked claret from the Médoc *négociant* firm of Raoul
Johnston. A good example of what used to be called luncheon claret.

ITALY

1993 Montepulciano d'Abruzzo, Barone Cornacchia
£££ / MB / ♪   15/20
Robust, raisiny, traditional Italian red brimming with black cherry and damson fruitiness and chunky, dry tannins. Needs equally robust food.

1994 Negroamaro del Salento, Kym Milne
£££ / MB / ♪   15/20
An interesting contrast in style, showing the aromatic spice and juicy Mediterranean fruit of Puglia's Negroamaro grape. It's nice to see flying winemaker Kym Milne making the most of a local, albeit under-appreciated, variety.

1994 Bardolino, Cavalchina
££ / MB / ♪   14/20
Fresh, cherried Beaujolais-style Italian red. Perfect for sipping on the shores of Lake Garda. It almost tasted as good in Balham.

PORTUGAL

1991 José de Sousa, J M da Fonseca
£££ / FB / ♪   15/20
From the plains of southern Portugal's baking Alentejo region, this is a modern take on what used to be known as Tinto Velho, one of the few red wines to be traditionally fermented in Ali Baba style earthenware jugs. Made by California-trained winemaker Domingos Suarez Franco, it's a leafy, chocolatey red with raisiny fruit and a bite of tangy acidity.

1994 Bright Brothers Estremadura
££ / MB / ♪   14/20
Soft, juicy, modern Portuguese tinto with peppery fruitiness and smooth, supple tannins from Peter Bright, an old hand – and a sure one – with Portuguese grape varieties.

SPAIN

1992 Marqués de Griñon, Rioja
£ / MB / ♪   14/20

Bodegas Berberana has apparently bought the Toledo-based Marqués de Griñon winery, and is now using the brand name on some of its Riojas too. All of which explains the Berberana style on offer in this modern, judiciously oaked, vanilla-scented red.

£5–8

AUSTRALIA

1993 Yalumba Bush Vine Grenache
£££ / MB / ♪   17/20

A smoky, opulent Grenache from old Barossa Valley vines, matured in French oak for extra flavour. This peppery spicy, full-bodied red from the Yalumba winery is everything you expect from a good southern Rhône red, but seldom receive.

1992 Ironstone Cabernet/Shiraz
0 / FB / ♪   13/20

Blended by David Hohnen of Cape Mentelle and Cloudy Bay fame, this is a hard, slightly overoaked Western Australian red. Go for the Ironstone white instead.

1993 Wynns Coonawarra Shiraz
£ / FB / ⌐   14/20

A powerful, peppery, cinnamon-flavoured Coonawarra Shiraz in which the oak is just a little too forceful.

1991 Wynns Coonawarra Cabernet Sauvignon
£££ / FB / ⌐   16/20

Another red from the hand of Wynns' Peter Douglas, this is a more elegant, better balanced Cabernet with supple tannins, coffee-bean oak and cool climate grassy fruitiness.

FRANCE

1994 Chénas Domaine des Pierres, Trichard
£££ / MB / 🍷   17/20
One of the best Beaujolais we tasted in 1995, this is a lively, well-structured, immensely drinkable Beaujolais *cru*, showing the concentration which Gamay can attain in an *appellation* like Chénas.

1992 Fixin, Labouré-Roi
££ / MB / 🍷   15/20
Light, aromatic, raspberry fruity Pinot Noir from one of the Côte de Nuits' most northerly *appellation*s. It would make a decent house red Burgundy.

1990 Chinon Les Garous, Couly-Dutheil
££ / MB / 🍷   16/20
Made by the *négociant* house of Couly-Dutheil, this is a leafy, complex, sweetly fruity Cabernet Franc from one of the best recent vintages in the Loire.

1994 Château Flaugergues Sommelière, Coteaux du Languedoc
£££ / FB / 🍷   16/20
From vineyards situated within the city limits of Montpellier, this is one of the best Languedoc reds on the market. With rich, concentrated, bush-vine derived colour and flavour, the emphasis in this Grenache-based red is on gutsy, spicy fruit rather than oak.

1993 Château Beauséjour, Fronsac
££ / MB / 🍷   15/20
Supple, easy-drinking claret showing stylish Right Bank Merlot character and good succulent fruit for the vintage.

1992 Château Haut Mazières, Bordeaux
££ / MB / 🍷   15/20
An oakier, equally modern style of affordable claret with good length of flavour and elegance.

ITALY

1990 Capitel San Rocco Ripasso, Tedeschi
££ / MB / 🍷   15/20

Made from a blend of Valpolicella grapes fermented on the lees of an
amarone wine, this is a pungent, damson-like Veneto red with the fresh,
cherry-skin bite typical of the ripasso technique.

SOUTH AFRICA

1991 Backsberg Shiraz
£££ / FB / ↤   16/20

Fresh, minty, beautifully made, mature Cape Shiraz from the Old-
Testament-bearded Michael Back. Backsberg is one of the most
consistent producers in the Cape.

1992 Backsberg Klein Babylonstoren
£££ / FB / ↤   16/20

From the same winery, this is a blend of the Bordeaux grapes Cabernet
Sauvignon and Merlot, and represents a less rustic, more modern step
up in quality from previous vintages. Named after the local Tower of
Babel rock, it's a grassy, chocolatey, full-flavoured red with a lot of
character.

SPAIN

1994 Balbas Tradición, Ribera del Duero
£ / FB / ↤   14/20

Touted as Spain's most exciting red wine region, Ribera del Duero
frequently fails to live up to its name. This chunky, robust, orange peel
scented Tinto Fino red may improve with age, but is on the pricey side
at £7.

1991 Viñas del Vero Pinot Noir, Somontano
£££ / MB / 🍷   16/20

We're far more excited by what's going on in Somontano than Ribera del
Duero, where this complex, spicily oaked, wild strawberry perfumed
Pinot Noir is typical of the elegant Burgundy styles on offer.

1989 Marqués de Riscal Rioja Reserva, Rioja Alavesa
£££ / MB / ⌐ 16/20
After a decade when cellar problems damaged the quality and reputation
of its red wines, Riscal is once again producing concentrated, aromatic,
savoury, old-fashioned red Riojas such as this.

UNITED STATES

1992 Eagle Peak Merlot, Fetzer
£ / FB / ⌐ 14/20
Solid, four-square Merlot with youth and tannin on its side from lifestyle
specialists Fetzer of Mendocino County. It's a shade extracted and hard
on the aftertaste, but may soften over the next two years.

Napa North Mourvèdre (Bin 703)
£ / FB / ⌐ 14/20
Tarry, jammy, richly alcoholic California Mourvèdre from ubiquitous
blender Jason Korman.

Over £8

AUSTRALIA

1990 Coonawarra Cabernet, Penfolds
££ / FB / ⌐ 15/20
Massively oaked Coonawarra Cabernet with macaroon-like coconut
oakiness framing densely packed, blackcurranty flavours. Fine if you like
a splintery style of red.

FRANCE

1989 Beaune Clos de la Féguine, Domaine Jacques Prieur
£££ / MB / ⌐ 17/20
**The best of the Antonin Rodet-owned Jacques Prieur wines,
showing classic Pinot Noir characters of game and succulent,
voluptuous ripe fruit concentration. What top-class red Burgundy
should taste like all the time.**

1990 St-Julien, Tipsy Club
££££ / MB / 👆   17/20
A classic Tony Mason deal, this declassified Ducru-Beaucaillou
was picked up from a defunct Paris dining club. Showing the
power and concentration of the vintage, it's a rich, coffee-bean,
oaky style with typical St-Julien elegance.

1992 Château Haut Bages Averons, Pauillac
£££ / MB / 👆   16/20
With its come-hither vanilla oak and supple, green pepper fruitiness, this
claret, the second wine of Château Lynch Bages, shows all of the easy-
drinking advantages and little of the leanness of the 1992 vintage. Well-
priced at under £10.

1990 Château Cantemerle, Médoc
£££ / MB / 👆   17/20
A rich, well-upholstered claret which is still in its youth, but has
the sweet middle and savoury concentration to drink relatively
young. Château Cantemerle is a Fifth Growth claret, which in
good vintages often outperforms its classification.

1993 Le Second du Mouton-Rothschild, Pauillac
0 / MB / 👆   16/20
You'd never guess it from the rather tacky label, but this is the second
wine of First Growth, Château Mouton-Rothschild. It's fine and elegantly
poised with plenty of vanilla oakiness, but, as you'd expect from a 1993,
lacks a bit of stuffing. Cheap at half the price.

SPAIN

1987 Castillo Ygay Tinto, Rioja Alta
££ / MB / 👆   16/20
Produced in what owner Marqués de Murrieta considers to be the best
vintages, Castillo Ygay is a Gran Reserva Rioja which normally takes
years of bottle age to reach its peak. This old-fashioned, concentrated
tinto has the acidity, tannin and depth of fruit for a long life. Rioja
neophytes may find the style a little austere.

UNITED STATES

1992 Ridge Santa Cruz Cabernet Sauvignon
££ / MB / ➼   17/20

Made by goatee-bearded Paul Draper, one of the West Coast's leading wine producers, this is an aromatic, concentrated, briary red with masses of fruit and structure and soft, beguiling tannins. It's almost as good as the Ridge Montebello, one of California's most outstanding Cabernets.

1991 Beringer Cabernet Sauvignon, Napa Valley
£££ / MB / ⏏   16/20

Unusually for a Napa Valley Cabernet Sauvignon, this juicy, deeply coloured style is not overstuffed with tannin and extracted macho bitterness. An elegant, mint and cigar-box style with supple, fine-grained tannins, which is also sensibly priced at around £9.

1992 Mondavi Napa Pinot Noir, Napa Valley
£ / MB / ⏏   15/20

Not quite up to the standard of the more expensive Reserve Pinot Noir (also listed by Majestic), Tim Mondavi's basic release is succulently strawberryish, fresh and juicy with a smattering of oak.

1992 Ridge Lytton Springs Zinfandel, Sonoma County
£££ / FB / ➼   16/20

Believe it or not, this is the most forward of Paul Draper's Ridge Zinfandels. Not that it's a wine for quiche eaters – showing masses of colour, sweetly spicy, almost porty flavours and toasty American oak. Serious Zin.

1991 Beringer Howell Mountain Merlot, Bancroft Ranch
££ / MB / ⏏   16/20

From the slopes of the Napa Valley's Howell Mountain, this is Beringer's answer to top St-Emilion, with lush, ripe, chocolate and tobacco flavours and a £20 price tag to match.

Rosé

£3–5

ITALY

1994 Bardolino Chiaretto, Cavalchina
£££ / 2 / ∤   16/20
Fresh, dry, elegant, redcurrant and rose-hip syrup style rosé with lively
acidity and a nip of tannin. Rosé for grown-ups.

£5–8

FRANCE

1994 Château de Sours, Bordeaux Rosé
££ / 3 / ∤   15/20
A soft, juicy, just off-dry rosé with plenty of colour and green pepper and
strawberry fruitiness from the former Majestic director, Esme Johnstone,
and Bordeaux star winemaker Michel Rolland.

1994 Côtes du Rhône Rosé, Jamet
£££ / 2 / ∤   16/20
Picked up by buyer Tony Mason during a typical deal-hunting foray into
the Rhône Valley, this spicy, full-flavoured rosé is a 100 per cent Syrah
made from declassified Côte Rôtie grapes using the *saignée* method of
fermentation. Jamet is one of the stars of Côte Rôtie.

Sparkling

Under £3

ITALY

Torrerossa Moscato del Piemonte, Abbazia
££ / 5 / ⅃   14/20
Sweet, fresh, grapey, lemonade-like Muscat fizz. A featherweight
charmer.

Over £8

FRANCE

De Telmont Grande Réserve
££ / 2 / ⅃   15/20
A regular listing at Majestic, this creamy, youthful, good value
Champagne is consistently enjoyable at around £13.50.

Oeil de Perdrix, Leonce d'Albe
£££ / 2 / ⅃   16/20
French for 'partridge eye', Oeil de Perdrix is a reference to this attractive
Champagne's delicate onion-skin colour rather than a weird food and
wine pairing. It's a complex, fruity, Pinot-based fizz with a hint of
biscuity richness and good depth of flavour.

Louis Roederer Rich Sec
££ / 4 / ⅃   16/20
An off-the-chalk-cellar-wall Champagne from the Reims-based house of
Louis Roederer with rich, chocolatey Pinot Noir fruit, crisp acidity, and,
as the name suggests, a subtle coating of sweetness.

NEW ZEALAND

Nautilus, Cuvée Marlborough
££ / 2 / ⅃   16/20
Pungent, aromatic, golden-coloured fizz from Australia's Yalumba

winery, which is unmistakably New World in character, showing malty flavours and exotic richness.

SPAIN

1990 Freixenet Vintage Brut
0 / 2 / 1   11/20

Basic, earthy, stale, apple-like Cava. Does anyone really want to drink vintage Cava? A case to Michael Portillo.

UNITED STATES

Quartet Roederer Estate NV
£££ / 2 / 1   17/20

Made by Frenchman Michel Salgues in northern California's ultra-cool Anderson Valley, this is a brilliant New World sparkling wine in which the company's French parentage shines through. A blend of 70 per cent Chardonnay and 30 per cent Pinot Noir, it's a vivid fizz with yeasty-toasty complexity, the faintest hint of oak, and a dry, lingering aftertaste.

Gloria Ferrer Brut
££ / 2 / 1   15/20

Another European-backed Californian venture, in this case by the giant Spanish Cava producer, Freixenet. For those who find Cordon Negro disappointing, this frothy, full-flavoured fizz will come as an agreeable surprise.

Fortified

£5–8

SPAIN

Hidalgo Manzanilla La Gitana
£££ / 1 / ♪   16/20
Fresh, savoury, Marmite-yeasty Manzanilla from one of the best fortified
wine producers in Spain. It's salted almonds time.

Over £8

PORTUGAL

1978 Feuerheerd Vintage Port
£ / MB / ♪   14/20
A little light for a vintage Port – we thought it was a mislabelled tawny.
But then you don't often see 1978 vintage Port at under £9.

1980 Quarles Harris
£££ / FB / ♪   16/20
This is a bit more like it – a fiery, peppery, powerfully juicy and aromatic
Port from the underrated 1980 vintage. It would make the perfect
Christmas Day tipple.

SPAIN

Lustau Old East India Sherry
££ / 9 / ♪   15/20
So sweet that it almost resembles a superconcentrated Pedro Ximenez
Sherry in style, this is a liquid raisin and toffee-like fortified wine of
considerable character and depth.

MARKS & SPENCER ***

Head Office: 57 Baker Street, London W1A 1DN

Telephone: 0171 935 4422

Number of branches: 283

Credit cards accepted: From autumn 1995, Switch and Delta as well as Marks & Spencer's own card

Hours of opening: Variable

By-the-case sales: Yes

Glass loan: No

Home delivery: Marks & Spencer Wine Cellar is a home delivery service for a minimum of one case within most of the UK. This service is guaranteed within 48 hours. The fee per delivery, whatever the size of the order, is £3.99

Clubs: No

Discounts: Twelve bottles for the price of 11, whether the case is mixed or unmixed

In-store tastings: Yes

Top ten best-selling wines: White Lambrusco; Oudinot Champagne; Chablis; Vin de Pays du Gers; Prosecco; Classic Claret; Italian Chardonnay; Bucks Fizz; Italian Table Red; Valencia Red

Range: GOOD: Champagne and sparkling wines, Bordeaux, Burgundy, Australia, Sherry
AVERAGE: Italy, Loire, Rhône, South of France, New Zealand, South Africa, Chile, Spain, Portugal, Germany
POOR: Eastern Europe, Argentina

If all publicity is good publicity, as Hugh Grant might say, 1995 has been a corker for M&S. First there was the tabloid splash about John Major Jr having a fling with a married store manager. Then M&S shareholders wanted to know why M&S was buying fish from the whale-slaughtering Faroe Islanders, and Lisa Bruce complained that M&S £20 swimsuits bore a striking resemblance to her rather more exclusive designs.

To cap it all, the company's £809,000-a-year chairman, Sir Richard Greenbury, got his St Michael boxer shorts in a twist when he disowned his own 'fat cat' committee's plan to tax executive share options. 'If I had been able to read the future, I would never have taken this job on,' said Greenbury, referring, presumably, to the committee, rather than his chairmanship of M&S.

Against such an action-packed background, the wine department's steady performance this year has been a little more low-key. Head buyer Chris Murphy summed it up matter-of-factly: 'We have focused more and more on getting involved in how the wines are made and blended and when they change from one vintage to the next.' Fewer headline-grabbing forays into *terra incognita*, and more concentration on long-term relationships with suppliers.

Given the M&S wine department's Great Leap Forward last year, the 'partnership' strategy is paying off. 'Our philosophy is to work in partnership with our suppliers,' says Murphy. 'When we went to Australia, we explained we thought that there had been a drift in quality. On our second trip, we got first choice. We think we've put together the best blend. A lot of what we do is about communication and getting what we think our customers want. You have to build up the contacts.'

Chris Murphy's other half, as it were, Jane Kay, one of the few high street buyers with a degree in oenology, has travelled to Australia twice to buy wines. The Australian range is still well-chosen and extensive, but because supplies from Australia have been drying up faster than a Brisbane cricket pitch, Murphy & Co. have sensibly turned more of their attention to South America.

'Chile is fantastic,' says Murphy. 'Their investment strategy is paying off, particularly on reds. We've seen a quantum leap in quality.' The Chilean range is based on value-for-money varietals from Alvaro Espinoza's Carmen and San Pedro, the latter much improved since Frenchman Jacques Lurton's arrival. 'South Africa is motoring,' says Murphy, presumably referring to his latest safari since the two wines from the producer KWV could hardly be described as fast-lane material. Argentina, a hard nut to crack, is resisting the nutcracker, while

California, too, remains a token presence.

Last year M&S won our award for most improved wine retailer. Despite the improvements, we criticised the range for including too many wines from boring suppliers. 'We've made no conscious decision to increase or restrict the number of suppliers,' says Murphy. 'It's the wine or the quality of the wine. Carmen is right for us. Alvaro Espinoza is an exciting winemaker. We have broadened, as it happens, as we've expanded into South America and South Africa a bit. If we get a brilliant deal, does it matter that it comes from the same winery?'

No, not if it comes from Carmen in Chile, Giordano in Italy, Mandeville in the South of France, La Chablisienne in Chablis or Australia's Rosemount. But Girelli (14 wines) and St Ursula still, frankly, represent the ultra-safe choice for Marks & Spencer's admittedly conservative customers. The golden touch even seems to have deserted Domaines Virginie, a New-World-influenced M&S find in the South of France.

The high street battle for the hearts and pockets of the wine-consuming public has not escaped M&S. But it has, as least, resisted any temptation to go the downmarket route of the £1.99 bottle. 'The only £1.99 bottle we sell is water,' says Murphy wryly. 'Sales are for vanity and profit is for sanity. This company is about giving value for money, year in, year out. Anyone can giver £1 notes away for 50 pence. It destabilises the whole market. We've been told there are people who buy over the telephone and don't even bother to taste a sample first.'

Which isn't to say that M&S have been idle in the promotions department. There's 50 pence or £1 off the wine of the month, featured in store. There are promotions linking wine with food. More of the variety offering £1 off all Champagnes, linking strawberries and bubbly, mind, than the 20 pence off a pack of frozen peas with every bottle of Liebfraumilch.

The wine department has also increased its core range at the £2.99 price level, suggesting willingness to take a more flexible approach to profit margins. Despite the bottles at £2.99, M&S has, says Murphy, 'concentrated in the £3–5 area, which is our strength.' He refutes the idea that a large range is a good thing *per se*. 'How do you find your way around a range of 700-plus wines? We're trying to do the selection for customers.'

France remains the M&S stronghold, with some 40 to 50 per cent of sales. Yet traditional as M&S customers remain, they still like a deal, even though they don't want what Murphy calls 'the £1.99 crap end'. The standing offer of 12 for the price of 11 is 'huge and growing', according to Murphy. M&S manage to sell a fair number of 'dinner party wines' off their 30-strong list, which in most other stores would be little more than window-dressing.

M&S finds it hard to compete with the supermarkets on car parking, but all stores do have a 'collect by car' point, and branching out into more exclusive wines in home delivery enables M&S to list parcels of fine wines, which would otherwise be too small for the main list. 'We can buy in small quantities, and customers like to dabble in and out of exciting little numbers,' says Murphy. A leaflet goes out every month to a nucleus of customers who use the M&S charge card regularly.

Despite the 'safe' tag, M&S has continued to respond to the growing demand for good value wines, and to fine-tune existing quality. The pioneering introduction of plastic corks, for instance, has gone a long way towards eradicating the cork taint which afflicts so many everyday wines. 'The challenge over the next 12 months is going to be to keep value for money going,' says Chris Murphy. 'The customer is no longer king, he's a dictator.' A thought which should keep the dynamic duo on the balls of their feet over the coming year.

White

Under £3

FRANCE

1994 Côtes de Gascogne, Vin de Pays, Plaimont
£ / 3 / 1   13/20
A basic, grapefruity Gascon blend of mainly Ugni Blanc and Colombard from the giant Plaimont co-operative. An off-dry quaffer.

SPAIN

1994 Conca de Barbera, Concavin, Hugh Ryman
££ / 2 / 1   14/20
Made in Catalonia by itinerant winemaker Hugh Ryman, this blend of

Macabeo and the local Parellada grapes is a crisply refreshing, lemony party white.

£3–5

AUSTRALIA

Australian Medium Dry, South Eastern Australia, Lindemans
££ / 4 / ♪   14/20
Lemon and lime
Aussie Rhine.
Does this qualify us for a stab at the Poet Laureateship?

1994 Barossa Valley Semillon, Peter Lehmann
£ / 2 / ♪   14/20
From the Baron of the Barossa, this is a basic, herby Semillon with a touch of lemon curd and Bakewell tart sweetness.

CHILE

1994 Lontue Sauvignon Blanc, Viña San Pedro
££ / 2 / ♪   14/20
Made by Frenchman Jacques Lurton, who has revitalised Chile's giant San Pedro in the space of a couple of vintages, this is a deliciously fresh, melon and grapefruit flavoured Sauvignon Blanc.

1994 Lontue Chardonnay, Viña San Pedro
££ / 2 / ♪   15/20
Same Frenchman, same winery, and another great value white, this stainless-steel-fermented Chardonnay shows plenty of buttery richness enlivened by zesty acidity.

FRANCE

1994 Bordeaux Sauvignon, Yves Pagès
££ / 2 / ♪   15/20
The result of a joint venture between Lancastrian wine broker Paul Boutinot and Yves Pagès, this is a New World influenced Sauvignon

Blanc from the Entre-Deux-Mers region. Summery, fresh, stylish and crunchy white Bordeaux.

1994 Chardonnay Viognier, Vin de Pays des Coteaux de l'Ardèche

££ / 2 / ♣   14/20

A Chardonnay-dominated blend from the southern French Ardèche region, in which the Viognier character is rather muted. All the same, it's an attractive, unoaked white with some lees-derived richness.

1994 Gold Label Chardonnay, Vin de Pays d'Oc, Domaines Virginie

£ / 2 / ♣   14/20

A little overpriced for a basic southern French Chardonnay, this is a fresh, cool-fermented white with some smoky oak and peardrop character.

1994 Sauvignon, Domaine de l'Etang, Vin de Pays d'Oc, Domaines Virginie

£ / 2 / ♣   13/20

Also made by Domaines Virginie in Béziers, this is a clean, if rather dilute, Sauvignon Blanc with a hint of varietal character.

1994 Chardonnay Domaine de Mandeville, Vin de Pays d'Oc, Olivier de Mandeville

£££ / 2 / ♣   15/20

One of two outstanding white wines from Olivier de Mandeville's model vineyards in the Aude department of southern France, this is a bright, lemony, richly fruity, New World-influenced Chardonnay.

1994 White Bordeaux Matured in Oak, Joanne

£££ / 2 / ♣   16/20

A rich, spicy, smoky Graves-style white made by the Casteja family of Château Doisy-Védrines, using new oak fermentation techniques pioneered by Bordeaux University professor and vineyard owner Denis Dubourdieu.

1994 Viognier Domaine de Mandeville, Vin de Pays d'Oc, Olivier de Mandeville

£££ / 2 / 🌡   16/20

One of the best value Viogniers we've come across, this is a pungently aromatic, ripe, apricoty, unoaked dry white with masses of flavour, freshness and balance. Producers of Condrieu, look to your laurels.

1994 Sauvignon de Touraine, Jacky Marteau

££ / 2 / 🌡   15/20

From the village of Pouillé in the heart of the Touraine region, this is a fresh, extremely well made, nettle and cassis scented Sauvignon Blanc, which could almost be a Sancerre – if it weren't for its relatively modest price.

1994 White Burgundy, Cave de Lugny

££ / 2 / 🌡   15/20

Spicy, pure, unoaked white Burgundy from the Mâconnais region's Lugny co-operative, for readers who prefer fruit to splinters.

GERMANY

1992 Deidesheimer Hofstuck Riesling Kabinett, St Ursula

£ / 3 / 🌡   13/20

Faintly petrolly superlieb to go with your Chicken Kiev.

ITALY

Italian Table Wine, Girelli, 1 Litre

0 / 3 / 🌡   12/20

From the Trento-based winery which still supplies rather too many of Marks & Spencer's basic Italian requirements, this blend of Trebbiano and Garganega is neutral and on the sweet side.

Pinot Grigio delle Tre Venezie, Vino da Tavola, Girelli

0 / 2 / 🌡   13/20

Faintly peachy, boring Veneto white, at least £1 overpriced.

1994 Giordano Chardonnay, Chardonnay del Piemonte
££ / 2 / 🍾   15/20

Perhaps someone should hand a bottle of this cool climate, melon and angelica spice Chardonnay to the owners of Girelli. For 20 pence more than the Pinot Grigio, it's a vastly superior proposition.

1994 Frascati Superiore DOC (Estate Bottled), Pallavicini
££ / 2 / 🍾   15/20

A blend of three grapes (Malvasia del Lazio, Malvasia di Candia and Trebbiano Toscano), this is Frascati with character, weight, and aromatic, peachy fruit.

1994 Pinot Grigio della Toscana, Le Rime, Villa Banfi
££ / 2 / 🍾   15/20

With its stylish gold and black designer label, this blend of Pinot Grigio with a touch of Sylvaner, made by Ezio Rivella in Montalcino, is spicy, perfumed and crisp on the tongue.

NEW ZEALAND

1994 New Zealand Medium Dry, Averill Estate
££ / 3 / 🍾   14/20

An off-dry, green bean style blend of Semillon and Müller-Thurgau made under an alternative Montana label. Close your eyes and you could almost be drinking Marlborough Sauvignon.

1994 Kaituna Hills Marlborough Sauvignon Blanc, Averill Estate
£££ / 2 / 🍾   16/20

You can keep your eyes open here – you are drinking Marlborough Sauvignon. It's a crisp, essence-of-New-Zealand style with masses of elderflower, gooseberry fruitiness and ultra-fresh acidity.

1994 Kaituna Hills Gisborne Chardonnay, Averill Estate
£££ / 2 / 🍾   16/20

Another Montana corker with melony, stone-fruit flavours, a hint of oak and a buttery richness derived from malolactic fermentation.

£5–8

AUSTRALIA

1994 Rosemount Estate Fumé Blanc
££ / 2 / ▸   15/20

Hunter Valley-based Rosemount have sourced this delicately smoky, full-bodied Sauvignon Blanc from South Australia's McLaren Vale. Fumé Blanc normally implies ageing or fermentation in barrel, but we're assured that this one didn't come within spitting distance of an oak stave.

1994 Barrel Fermented Chardonnay, Rothbury Estate
££ / 2 / ▸   15/20

From the reliable Rothbury Estate, this is a ripe, richly textured, spicy Hunter Valley Chardonnay with refreshing citrus-like acidity.

1994 McLaren Vale Chardonnay, Rosemount Estate
££ / 2 / ▸   16/20

The best of M&S's Australian Chardonnay range, made in a lightly oaked style by the laconic Philip Shaw at Rosemount's vineyard in the McLaren Vale. Peach and guava fruit underpinned by crisp lemony zest make for a perfectly balanced white.

CALIFORNIA

1994 Canyon Road Sauvignon Blanc, Geyser Peak
£ / 2 / ▸   14/20

A clean, grapefruity Sauvignon made in Geyserville, California, by Australian winemaker Daryl Groom; Penfolds half-owns the winery. It's pleasant enough, but lacks the grassy tang we expect from the Sauvignon Blanc grape. But then again, such a character is considered anathema in California.

FRANCE

1993 Vouvray, Château Gaudrelle
££ / 3 / ▸   16/20

The more expensive of M&S's two Vouvrays, but in our view the better by some distance. With its baked apple fruitiness, fresh acidity and honeyed texture, it's a classic style with restrained, rounded fruit sweetness. The estate owner, Alexandre Monmousseau, is clearly a producer to watch.

1994 Mâcon Villages, Rodet
£ / 2 / ▮   13/20
Less exciting than the cheaper Cave de Lugny white Burgundy, this is a pleasant, if rather fat and one-dimensional, unoaked southern Burgundian Chardonnay.

1992 Montagny Premier Cru, Cave de Buxy
£ / 2 / ▮   14/20
From the Côte Chalonnaise's Buxy co-operative, this is a laudable attempt at a complex white Burgundy. We felt that there was rather too much oak for the weight of fruit.

1993 Chablis AC, La Chablisienne
££ / 2 / ▮   16/20
The Chablisienne is one of those rare co-operatives that seems to find it difficult to make poor wine, producing a string of highly enjoyable Yonne whites from *jeunes vignes* to *grand cru*. This is a fresh, minerally, unoaked Chardonnay with a buttery texture and excellent length of flavour.

SOUTH AFRICA

1994 Madeba Reserve Chardonnay
0 / 2 / ▮   13/20
Made by Pieter Ferreira at Graham Beck's state-of-the-art Robertson winery, this is a tart, coarsely oaked Cape Chardonnay with insufficient fruit. You'd be better off buying your whites up the road from Danie de Wet's cellar door.

Over £8

AUSTRALIA

Orange Vineyard Chardonnay, Rosemount Estate
0 / 2 / ▸   14/20

With its New Labour Party style rose label and Bordeaux bottle, this Chassagne Montrachet wannabe is a triumph of style over content. Maybe Tony Blair's spin doctors have been called in.

FRANCE

1993 Domaine Laporte Sancerre, La Terre des Anges
£ / 2 / ▸   15/20

Made in the Sancerre commune of Bannay, this is a crisply grassy, if rather overpriced, Sauvignon Blanc. We'd rather drink something from Chile or New Zealand.

1990 Chablis Premier Cru, Grande Cuvée, La Chablisienne
££ / 2 / ▸   16/20

Closer to the Côte d'Or than Chablis in style, this is a rich, toasty, butterscotchy Chardonnay with plenty of spicy and almost savoury depth of fruit. Some may find the new oak a little too powerful, but we thought it was well-judged in the context of the richness of fruit.

1992 Meursault, Domaine Louis Jadot
£££ / 2 / ▸   17/20

Made by the obsessive Jacques Lardière at *négociant* Louis Jadot's cellars in Beaune, this is a highly complex, Côtes de Beaune Chardonnay showing nutty richness and the creamy ripeness of the vintage. Worth spending £17 on if you've got it.

1990 Chablis Bougros, Grand Cru, La Chablisienne
£££ / 2 / ▸   17/20

From the top-notch 1990 vintage, this beautifully balanced Chablis is still extremely fresh for its age, showing intensely minerally flavours, firm backbone, concentration and delicately integrated oak.

Red

Under £3

FRANCE

French Country Red, Vin de Pays des Pyrénées Orientales, Vignerons Catalans
£ / MB / 🍷   13/20
Decent, carbonic maceration red from the Roussillon region of southern France made from a blend of traditional varieties – Carignan, Grenache and Cinsault.

£3–5

AUSTRALIA

1993 Australian Shiraz, Bin 50, Lindemans
£ / MB / 🍷   14/20
Produced from a pot-pourri of vineyards in Padthaway, McLaren Vale, Barossa Valley, Coonawarra, Riverland and the Adelaide Hills, this is a smooth, toffee-oaky Shiraz which lacks a little bit of concentration. Perhaps it lost something on its travels.

CHILE

1993 Maipo Cabernet Sauvignon Reserve, Carmen Vineyards
££ / MB / 🍷   15/20
Alvaro Espinoza, one of Chile's home-produced crop of talented winemakers, has come up with an exuberantly fruity, modern style of Cabernet Sauvignon and aged it in French oak barrels. Our feeling is that it was left in oak a little too long.

FRANCE

French Full Red, Côtes du Roussillon Villages, Vignerons Catalans, 1 Litre

£ / FB / ♪   14/20

Spicy, peppery, robust Roussillon red made from old-vine Carignan, Syrah and Grenache. A bit pricey for a basic rouge.

1994 Cabernet Sauvignon Domaine de Mandeville, Olivier de Mandeville

££ / MB / ♪   15/20

Aromatic, modern style, unoaked Cabernet Sauvignon with juicy, cassis-flavoured fruit from the promising Olivier de Mandeville.

1993 Gold Medal Cabernet Sauvignon, Vin de Pays d'Oc, Domaines Virginie

£ / FB / ♪   13/20

Chewy, tannic, extracted Cabernet Sauvignon from Domaines Virginie in the Languedoc. It may have something to do with the quality of recent vintages, but we've had a number of disappointing wines from the Virginie stable this year. Has the cutting edge been blunted?

1992 Fitou, AC, Les Producteurs du Mont Tauch

££ / FB / ♪   14/20

A traditional blend of Carignan and Grenache in equal proportions, made by the dynamic Mont Tauch co-operative in an angostura spicy, robustly Mediterranean style.

1993 Domaine St Germain Minervois, Cave Co-opérative du Haut Minervois La Livinière

£££ / MB / ♪   15/20

A wine which shows you what the addition of Syrah to Grenache and Carignan can accomplish. The rosemary and thyme-like perfume, soft, raspberry fruitiness and fresh acidity are enhanced by the carbonic-maceration vinification technique.

1994 Château Cazeau, Classic Claret, AC Bordeaux, La Guyennoise

££ / MB / ♪   15/20

From the comparatively unfashionable Entre-Deux-Mers region, this is a soft, juicy claret with attractive green pepper notes. It just shows why it's sometimes worth paying a little bit extra for Bordeaux Rouge.

1991 Bordeaux Matured in Oak, AC Bordeaux, Dourthe Frères
£ / MB / 🥄   14/20

A Cabernet Sauvignon dominated blend from various growers in the Médoc, showing coffee-bean oak, green pepper fruitiness and dryish tannins. One to drink up rather than squirrel away.

ITALY

Italian Table Red, Girelli, 1 Litre
0 / MB / 🥄   12/20

Sweetened-up Italian plonk made from Merlot and Schiava – Italy's response to Piat d'Or.

1994 Montepulciano d'Abruzzo, DOC, Girelli
££ / MB / 🥄   14/20

A blend of 90 per cent Montepulciano and 10 per cent Sangiovese grapes from two co-operatives in Abruzzo's L'Aquila province. Of the cheaper Girelli wines stocked by M&S, this savoury, plummy, softly fruity red is the one to go for.

Bradesco, Giordano
£££ / MB / 🥄   16/20

Giordano winemaker Enzo Barbero has blended Barbera, Dolcetto, Merlot and Montepulciano grapes in an engagingly succulent and red-blooded style, with spicy notes and savoury, fresh acidity. As mishmashes go, this one's an unexpected triumph.

1992 Il Caberno, Giordano
£££ / MB / 🥄   16/20

Another Barbero special, building on the success of last year's brilliant début. With a handsome package that belies its price tag, this minty, chocolatey blend of Nebbiolo with 15 per cent Cabernet Sauvignon adds polish to the Piemontese repertoire.

1993 Rubilio, Casa Vinicola Calatrasi
££ / MB / 🍷   15/20

Made in a modern, family-owned winery near Palermo, this Sicilian blend of Nero d'Avola, Cabernet Sauvignon and Sangiovese is a robust but concentrated rosso with plenty of savoury fruit sweetness and bite.

SOUTH AFRICA

1993 South African Cabernet Sauvignon Reserve, Simonsvlei
££ / MB / 🍷   14/20

The Simonsvlei co-operative has adapted faster than many Cape producers to the demands of the British palate. This aromatic Cabernet Sauvignon is a fruit-dominated style with accessible ripeness and some vanillin oak character.

SPAIN

1991 Carretala, Raimat
££ / MB / 🍷   15/20

A curious combination of no fewer than six grape varieties (presumably the kitchen sink wouldn't fit into the bottle), from Catalonia's innovative Raimat winery. With its spicy American oak character, and fresh cherryish fruit, this is a red of considerable character.

1991 Roseral Rioja, Crianza, Bodegas AGE
££ / MB / 🍷   15/20

Unusual for Rioja in that it contains no Garnacha grapes, this blend of Tempranillo with 30 per cent Mazuelo is a fragrant, attractively mature Iberian red with restrained oak and sweet ginger spice.

£5–8

AUSTRALIA

1993 Langhorne Creek Cabernet Sauvignon
££ / MB / 🍷   15/20

Made by Michael Potts in a traditional style using open fermentation tanks, this is a smoky, minty, subtly crafted South Australian Cabernet Sauvignon with supple blackcurrant fruit.

1993 Rosemount Estate Shiraz
£££ / FB / 👒   16/20
An attractive package and an equally attractive wine. This is a rich, smoky, mouthfilling Shiraz with notes of pepper, plum and strawberry. Good value at under £6.

FRANCE

1994 Côtes du Rhône Villages, Visan, Domaine du Rastelet
£ / FB / 💧   14/20
A single estate Côtes du Rhône Villages produced under the auspices of the Visan co-operative, this is a soft, full-bodied, Grenache-based red that could do with another dimension or two.

1994 Vacquéyras, Domaine de la Curnière
£££ / FB / 👒   16/20
From the Vacquéyras co-operative, this is also a Grenache-based southern Rhône red. But this time, the warm, chocolatey richness of the grape backed up by the spice and pepper of Syrah has produced a vastly superior wine for no extra cost.

1990 St-Emilion, JP Moueix
££ / MB / 💧   15/20
From the generally excellent 1990 vintage, this Merlot-dominated claret from the Moueix stable is rich and weighty with a judicious dose of subtle oak.

ITALY

1993 Basilica Cafaggio, Chianti Classico
££ / MB / 💧   15/20
Sourced by Girelli from Stefano Farkas's Cafaggio estate in Chianti Classico's Greve commune, this modern, attractively balanced Tuscan rosso is an improvement on the heftier 1992 vintage. A handsomely packaged buy at just over £5.

SPAIN

1986 Marqués del Romeral Gran Reserva
££ / MB / 🍷   15/20
An inexpensive Gran Reserva from the giant AGE operation made in a
delicate, sweetly oaked, traditional style. At nearly 10 years old, it's
rapidly approaching its sell-by date.

Over £8

AUSTRALIA

1992 Rose Label Coonawarra Cabernet Sauvignon, Rosemount Estate
£££ / MB / ➻   16/20
Another wine which appears to reflect M&S's changing Party allegiance,
this red rose Coonawarra Cabernet is a complex, deeply coloured,
tobacco-pouch style, showing the region's characteristic elegance. New
rather than hard Labour.

FRANCE

1992 Châteauneuf-du-Pape, Les Couversets, Quiot
£ / MB / 🍷   14/20
Considering that half the southern Rhône vineyards were washed away
in 1992, this is a commendable effort from a property owned by the
President of the Institut National de Appellations d'Origine (INAO to you
and us), but an element of greenness still seeps through.

1989 Volnay, Louis Jadot
£ / MB / 🍷   15/20
The *négociant* house of Louis Jadot is better known for its whites than
its reds, but this village Pinot Noir is fragrant, spicy and commendably
lively for the vintage. It would make a good red Burgundy for Christmas.

1988 Château L'Hospitalet, JP Moueix
££ / MB / 🍷   16/20
The second label of Château Gazin, a Pomerol estate which has seen
dramatic improvements in the last eight years, Château L'Hospitalet is

normally a good buy. This fleshy, plump, oak-aged, Merlot-dominated red is drinking beautifully at the moment.

ITALY

1989 Brunello di Montalcino, I Due Cipressi, Val di Suga
£££ / FB / ➡ 17/20
Names after two cypress trees on the Val di Suga estate, I Due Cipressi is classic Brunello di Montalcino – smoky, succulent, seriously structured Sangiovese (we're in an alliterative mood today). Drink now or before the millennium is out.

Rosé

£3–5

FRANCE

1994 Gold Medal Rosé de Syrah, Domaines Virginie
££ / 2 / ▌ 14/20
Fresh, bubblegummy, day-glo rosé with lots of soft, gluggable fruitiness and an attractively dry finish.

SPAIN

Rosé de Valencia
£ / 2 / ▌ 13/20
Made from the local Bobal grape, this is a light, clean, raspberry fruity rosado from Valencia's Gandia operation.

Sparkling

£3–5

ITALY

NV Prosecco, Zonin
££ / 3 / ⌐   15/20
Made from the local Prosecco grape, this aromatic, perky Veneto fizz
with its hint of sweetness is one of the best cheap sparkling wines on
the market.

£5–8

AUSTRALIA

**1991 Australian Chardonnay, Blanc de Blancs, Bottle Fermented
Brut**
£ / 3 / ⌐   15/20
Frothy, rich, tropical fruity sparkling Chardonnay with perceptible
sweetness. Overpriced at nearly £8.

Over £8

FRANCE

Oudinot Brut NV Champagne
££ / 2 / ⌐   15/20
An M&S stalwart, Oudinot Brut is a crisp, fruity, Pinot-dominated blend
from an independent company. Good value at just over a tenner.

Veuve de Medts, Premier Cru Brut, NV Champagne
£££ / 2 / ⌐   16/20
From a co-operative situated in the heart of the Côte des Blancs, this is a
Chardonnay-based blend largely from the excellent 1990 vintage. It's
toasty, buttery and rich with commendable depth of flavour. Excellent
value at around £13.

NV, Champagne, Chevalier de Melline, Premier Cru, Blanc de Blancs, Brut, Union Champagne
£ / 2 / ½   15/20
An all-Chardonnay fizz also produced at the Union Champagne co-operative, this is an aromatic, if slightly austere, style.

1988 Vintage Champagne, St Gall, Premier Cru, Brut, Union Champagne.
£££ / 2 / ½   17/20
A *Grapevine* favourite two years on the trot, this toasty, Pinot Noir dominated Champagne is a rich, well-structured fizz reminiscent of Bollinger in body and complexity. Well-priced at around £18 for a vintage Champagne.

Fortified

£3–5

SPAIN

Marks & Spencer Pale Dry Sherry
£ / 3 / ½   14/20
A good, fresh, salty Fino with a touch of sweetness, although we're still not convinced by the chocolate-box label.

Marks & Spencer Medium Rich Cream Sherry
££ / 7 / ½   15/20
With its Newcastle Brown-hue, this is a liquorice, treacle and date-style for those who enjoy a lot of sweetness with their Sherry.

MORRISON'S **(*)

Head Office: William Morrison Supermarkets PLC, Junction 41 Industrial Estate, Carr Gate, Wakefield, West Yorkshire WF2 0XF

Telephone: 01924 870000

Number of branches: 81

Credit cards accepted: Access, Visa, Switch, Delta

Hours of opening: Majority 8.30am to 8.00pm weekdays; 8.00am to 6.00pm Saturday; Sunday 10.00am to 4.00pm

By-the-case sales: No reductions

Glass loan: Free in all stores

Home delivery: No

Clubs: No

Discounts: No

In-store tastings: Occasional tastings in selected stores

Top ten best-selling wines: Hock Deutscher Tafelwein; Soveral, Vinho de Mesa; Carreras Dry Red; Gabbia d'Oro Rosso; Morrison's red Rioja; Morrison's Liebfraumilch; 1985 Romanian Cabernet Sauvignon; Morrison's Lambrusco; Morrison's Portuguese Rosé; Vin de Pays de l'Aude Red

Range: GOOD: Regional France, white Bordeaux, Australia, Germany
AVERAGE: Champagne and sparkling wines, Spain, Italy, Chile, Loire, Bulgaria, New Zealand, South Africa
POOR: Beaujolais, Romania, Hungary

'People in the south don't know about Morrison's,' says Stuart Purdie, the store's wine buyer. 'Even the weather forecast is biased towards

London.' If you're from London or the Southeast, the closest you've probably come to Morrison's is via Morrison's Carpets or Morrison's Mortgage Brokers. If you live in Blackpool, Burton or Bradford, then you would no doubt far rather be wheeling your supermarket trolley in and out of your nearest Morrison's than listening to the weather forecast anyway.

Morrison's would be a sort of Waitrose of the North and Midlands if it weren't for its ultra-competitive prices. After last year's tour of the giant Morrison's in-store off-licence in Bradford we took ourselves to Sheffield this year (at this rate, we should be done in the year 2085), where the drinks department is almost as large. As in Bradford, it's a store within a store, with aisles which turn corners to mitigate the forbidding austerity of long, straight rows of bottles.

Not convinced by arch-rival Asda's initiative of displaying wines by style, rows of white wines by country are mirrored in the row opposite by reds set out in similar fashion. The middle of each row proudly displays a fine-wine rack of wines mostly over £5, including Mouton Cadet. Morrison's wine buyer is not keen on the term 'fine wine' – he thinks it's too fancy – so a free bottle of Mouton Cadet to any reader who can come up with a solution. In fact, only 5 per cent of sales are over a fiver, but just having the rack, according to Purdie, adds a bit of Cadet – sorry, cachet – to the range.

Morrison's also stock a huge number of interesting beers with promotions to lure customers away from boring lagers to some of their more interesting offerings. During the Rugby World Cup, if you bought two bottles of Carling Black Label you could get one Merrimans Old Fart free.

Purdie is proud of the fact that wine sales at Morrison's have doubled in three years, even if they are still small beer by the standards of the Big Four supermarkets. There are just under 400 individual wines in the range, which has the added advantage – unlike many a supermarket range – of being available in all Morrison's stores.

The New World continues to grow dramatically, particularly Australia and South Africa. But Purdie feels that now that Australia has more or less given up at the £2.99 price level, Chile's time has come.

His whistle-stop tour of the South of France's Vinisud exhibition paid dividends with some attractive offerings from France's most competitive region, in particular the modern styles of Penfolds' Laperouse, Delta Domaines' Grenache/Merlot and Big Frank's Red Minervois, even if the latter's garish packaging is a little too bold for some of Morrison's more traditionally minded customers.

For the Liebfraumilch drinker who wants something better, Morrison's German range has been overhauled and now includes a number of superior quality wines from Franz Reh in the £2.99 to £3.99 price range. Purdie would like to devote more time to Spain, even if prices are edging up there. Italy, with the exchange rate so strongly in Britain's favour, is also an area ripe for exploration.

Logically, Hungary and Bulgaria, where flying winemakers have transformed much of the basic, raw material into good value wines in the £2.79 to £3.99 price range, are Morrison's country. The problem is that because Morrison's is not big enough to employ flying winemakers direct, it has to pick up the crumbs from Lazarus' – make that Kym, Warren, Wayne and Bruce's – table.

A bigger problem still is the downward pressure on price caused by the battle of the £1.99 bottle. 'We have two £1.99 wines on a regular basis,' says Purdie. 'The effect is to treble sales. Anything will sell at £1.99. A lot of people are simply £1.99 buyers, not new people coming into wine. We're building a more loyal customer base at the £2.99 price level.'

So, if £2.99 is the critical threshold price for most Morrison's customers, how does Purdie go about luring customers over £2.99 into the more exciting pastures of the £3.99 wine? Or even the likes of Australia's delicious 1994 Penfolds Rawsons Retreat Semillon/ Chardonnay, at £4.49? 'I think we've got to break that £2.99 barrier, which we're doing by putting quality there. But we have to ensure we are building confidence by selling value for money.'

Like all new Morrison's stores opened since 1986, the Sheffield store that opened in April 1991 – a converted barracks – returns to Morrison's roots as a late Victorian grocer. The store design is based on a street market, complete with Chef's Larder, master baker, pie shop, fishmonger and butcher on the outside – and even a Granny's Attic, selling second-hand knick-knacks – and wide aisles.

Ken Morrison, the family company's active chairman and managing director, plans to have 82 stores up and running by the end of 1995, with new outlets opening in Burton, Cleethorpes, Darlington, Doncaster, Huddersfield, Nottingham, Tamworth and Widnes, reaching 90 by the end of 1996.

Although the drink department's buying team consists of three buyers (and one of them, Grant Eastwood, buys the fortified wines), Stuart Purdie effectively, *is* the Morrison's wine department. Asda, by contrast, with a similarly sized range, now has three buyers in its wine department.

Stuart Purdie would like to bolster the range by concentrating on more individual wines, but, on his own, he stands about as much chance as a trussed and headless chicken does of laying a golden egg. He could go further towards weaning loyal Morrison's customers off their precious £2.99 bottle if he had a bit more help. So, come on Ken. With after-tax profits up 15.7 per cent to £73.1 million, how about that helping hand?

White

Under £3

FRANCE

1994 Bordeaux Sauvignon, Yves Pagès
£££ / 2 / 1   15/20
The result of a joint venture between Lancastrian wine broker Paul Boutinot and Yves Pagès, this is a New World influenced Sauvignon Blanc from the Entre-Deux-Mers region of Bordeaux. Summery, fresh, stylish and crunchy white Bordeaux.

1994 Muscadet de Sèvre et Maine, Vincent de Valloire
0 / 2 / 1   12/20
Appley, basic white with a faintly earthy flavour. Muscadet as we used to know – and dislike – it.

GERMANY

Morrison's Hock Deutscher Tafelwein, Zimmermann-Graeff
£££ / 5 / 1   14/20
Fresh, appealingly floral and grapey, this Müller-Thurgau-based white is one of the best inexpensive German whites on the market, and a top ten seller at Morrison's. Better and cheaper than the Lieb.

1993 Franz Reh Kabinett, QmP

£££ / 5 / ⚑   14/20

With its honey and ginger spice aromas and soft, grapey sweetness, this is another fresh and well-balanced German quaffer.

ITALY

1994 Orvieto Classico Uggiano

££ / 2 / ⚑   14/20

Cheap, fresh, fruity Umbrian dry white with some attractively honeyed fruitiness.

Eclisse White, Vino da Tavola di Puglia

££ / 2 / ⚑   14/20

Blended specially for Morrison's by flying winemaker Kym Milne from local Puglian grapes, this is a well-made, modern white with some peardrop fruitiness and backbone. We haven't yet worked out what a French name is doing on the label of an Italian white. Any suggestions?

Morrison's Lambrusco, Bianco dell'Emilia

£ / 5 / ⚑   13/20

A classical sherbety confection with freshness to grope its way through the sweetness.

SOUTH AFRICA

1994 Fair Cape Chenin Blanc

££ / 3 / ⚑   14/20

A well-priced, cleverly made cheap white, showing flavours of butter and boiled sweets. Clean, fresh and rounded out with a dollop of sweetness.

£3–5

AUSTRALIA

1994 Coldridge Estates Chenin Blanc/Chardonnay

0 / 3 / ⚑   12/20

A Stuart Purdie favourite from his days at the late Peter Dominic (RIP). This neutral, dilute Aussie white is not as good as it has been in previous vintages. But then Australia generally is struggling at the £2.99 to £3.49 level.

1994 Rawsons Retreat Penfolds Bin 21 Semillon/Chardonnay
£££ / 2 / ♪   15/20

A good example of the new-style Penfolds whites. With its spicy vanilla oak, herby Semillon and Chardonnay richness, these two grapes combine harmoniously to produce a sundae of vanilla ice cream and lemony fruit.

1994 Lindemans Bin 65 Chardonnay
£ / 3 / ♪   14/20

By comparison, this sweeter, oakier Aussie white tastes a little clumsy and old-fashioned. It's still a respectable benchmark for the under-£5 Chardonnay from Down Under, however.

CHILE

1994 San Pedro Sauvignon Blanc
£££ / 2 / ♪   15/20

Zesty, grapefruity Chilean Sauvignon Blanc with fresh melon characters. One of winemaking consultant Jacques Lurton's best whites.

FRANCE

1994 Touraine Sauvignon Plouzeau
£ / 1 / ♪   13/20

Austere, tart, vaguely nettley Sauvignon Blanc from the Loire Valley, this is 50 pence more expensive than the San Pedro, and nothing like as good.

Vin de Pays Chardonnay, 'La Source'
0 / 2 / ♪   12/20

Made at Domaines Virginie near Béziers, this is a fat, oak-chippy white which has suffered from heavyhandedness in the winery.

1994 Vin de Pays des Côtes de Gascogne, Domaine du Rey
££ / 2 / ♪   14/20

It may have something to do with the fact that it was produced from organically grown grapes, but this grassy, zesty blend of Colombard and Ugni Blanc is one of the best cheap Gascon whites on the market.

1994 Laperouse, Vin de Pays d'Oc

££ / 2 / ‌   15/20

The offspring of a joint venture between Penfolds of Australia and France's largest wine company, Val d'Orbieu, this unoaked blend of Chardonnay, Marsanne, Grenache and Colombard is like fresh pears spiced with aniseed. A very promising start.

1993 Gewürztraminer, Preiss-Zimmer, Turckheim

££ / 2 / ‌   14/20

Appealingly light for a Gewürztraminer – a grape which can taste rather gooey at times – this is a fresh, well-priced, spicy white with some fragrant, rose petal fruitiness.

GERMANY

1993 Franz Reh Spätlese, QmP

££ / 5 / ‌   14/20

Sold in an attractive blue flute bottle, presumably to appeal to bubble bath consumers, this is a fragrant, Müller-Thurgau-based white with appley acidity for balance.

HUNGARY

1994 Chapel Hill Chardonnay

££ / 2 / ‌   14/20

Very well priced at just over £3, Kym Milne's oaked Hungarian Chardonnay from the Balatonboglar co-operative has good, buttery concentration and fresh, peachy fruit.

NEW ZEALAND

1994 Timara Dry

££ / 2 / ‌   14/20

Though apparently made from Müller-Thurgau and Semillon grapes, this crisp, tinned pea-like Kiwi white tastes like a Sauvignon Blanc. Which makes this Montana blend pretty good value at under £4.

ROMANIA

1985 Late Harvest Chardonnay, Murfatlar
£ / 6 / ⅛   13/20

It's rare to find late-harvest Chardonnays on the market – never mind one that comes from pre-Berlin Wall Romania. This is an oddity which tastes like a cross between a fortified Muscat and a bottle of Robinson's Lemon Barley Water. Just about worth a punt at £3.30 a bottle if you don't object to politically incorrect dessert wines.

Over £8

FRANCE

1988 Chablis Grand Cru, Valmur
££ / 2 / ⅛   15/20

Morrison's fine wine selection begins and ends here. Under £9 is a very good price for a mature Grand Cru Chablis, and this old-fashioned, minerally white has sufficient character to demonstrate that Stuart Purdie's nostrils can appreciate a bargain.

Red

Under £3

CHILE

Entre Rios Red
££ / MB / ⅛   14/20

Blended by Frenchman Jacques Lurton, this blend of Cabernet Sauvignon and Merlot is soft and juicy with some peppery sweetness and a hint of toffeeish oak character.

FRANCE

Coteaux du Languedoc, Tradition
£ / FB / ♟   13/20
Dry, traditional, rustic southern French red with some rosemary and
angostura bitters aromas and warm climate, robust tannins. Carolyn
Purdie is still partial to a drop of this one.

1994 Winter Hill, Vin de Pays de l'Aude
0 / MB / ♟   11/20
'French wine made by Australians', reads the label. Why anybody would
bother travelling thousands of miles to make this rustic Carignan/Merlot
plonk is a mystery to the lads at *Grapevine* HQ.

1994 Côtes du Ventoux, Jean-Paul Léon
£ / MB / ♟   13/20
Basic Provençal plonk with plenty of alcohol and rough-edged fruitiness.

ITALY

Gabbia d'Oro Rosso
0 / LB / ♟   11/20
A light, sweetish red that could come from virtually anywhere. Italy's
lame response to Piat d'Or. We can't see the Italians adoring this plonk.

Eclisse Red, Vino da Tavola di Puglia
££ / MB / ♟   14/20
With its baked southern fruitiness and flavours of plain chocolate and
liquorice, this robust, well-made red is yet another winner from the fleet-
footed Australian winemaker, Kym Milne.

MOROCCO

Moroccan Red
£ / FB / ♟   13/20
Raisiny, chunky north African red which has had the winemaking fatwa
removed from it by the input of flying oenologist Nick Butler.

PORTUGAL

Soveral, Vinho de Mesa
££ / FB / ♪   13/20
Tannic, chewy, Douro-style Portuguese red with robust, hot climate fruitiness.

SPAIN

1987 Carreras Dry Red, Valencia, Egli
0 / MB / ♪   10/20
A wine which still seems to be suffering from a headcold. Tart plonkissimo red. We'd rather drink Pavarotti's perfume.

£3–5

AUSTRALIA

1994 Coldridge Estates Shiraz/Cabernet
£ / MB / ♪   13/20
More enjoyable than its white counterpart, but this sweetish, raspberry-fruity Aussie blend still tastes confected and slightly medicinal.

BRAZIL

Amazon Cabernet Sauvignon
£ / MB / ♪   13/20
A charry, minty, oak-chipped novelty from Brazil with a brilliant Amazon-jungle parrot label. One for the Copacabana posing pouch.

CHILE

1993 Gato Negro Cabernet Sauvignon
£ / MB / ♪   13/20
A light, easy drinking, grassy claret substitute made by Bordeaux's Jacques Lurton at the San Pedro winery in Chile.

FRANCE

1990 Côtes du Rhône-Villages, Vinaton
£ / MB / 🍷   13/20
From a well-known Beaujolais *négociant* (we were given the info off the record, and we're still respecting our sources), this Grenache-based quaffer has lost some of its vibrancy over the last 12 months.

1994 Big Frank's Red Minervois
££ / MB / 🍷   14/20
Produced by eccentric Polish-American painter Frank Chludinski, this counterpart to Big Frank's White is a ripe, juicy, undemanding introduction to the Languedoc.

1991 Château Tour Camillac
££ / MB / 🍷   15/20
Mature, attractively grassy claret with structured tannins, a hint of oak and good honest fruitiness. Good value at under a fiver.

1991 Château de Lastours, Arnaud de Berre
£ / FB / 🍷   14/20
From a picturesque estate which also houses a community of disabled people, this is an old-fashioned, leathery blend of Carignan and Grenache made in a ripe, warm-hearted style. If you're in the Languedoc, the winery restaurant is worth a visit (but ring first).

1994 Château Jougrand, St-Chinian
££ / FB / 🍷   14/20
Deeply coloured, tarry, southern French red with some attractive underlying raspberry fruitiness and dry, warm climate tannins.

1993 Domaine Terres Noires Grenache/Merlot, Vin de Pays de l'Hérault
££ / MB / 🍷   14/20
From Delta Domaines near Béziers, this is a soft, approachable, unoaked, modern red with attractive cherry-spice and thirst-quenching acidity.

1993 Côtes de Buzet, Renaissance
£ / MB / **ʝ**   14/20

From the Buzet co-operative in France's southwestern corner, this is a grassy, almost claret-like red with a shaving or two of oak and a pleasantly rustic bite.

ITALY

1992 Chianti Classico Uggiano
£ / MB / **ʝ**   13/20

Heftily oaked for a basic Chianti, this is a spicy if rather confected Tuscan red.

1992 Barbera d'Alba Feyles
££ / MB / **ʝ**   15/20

An old-fashioned Piedmontese Barbera with tarry, chocolatey tannins, juicy fruit and fresh acidity. Among our favourite reds at Morrison's, but newcomers to Italy may find this grower's wine a little unusual.

ROMANIA

1986 Romanian Cabernet Sauvignon, Dealul Mare
££ / MB / **ʝ**   14/20

An enormously popular style with Morrison's customers, this is a mint and tomato-skin flavoured red with a core of soft fruit. Well-priced at just over £3, but still old-fashioned.

SOUTH AFRICA

1991 KWV Shiraz
0 / FB / **ʝ**   12/20

Chewy, earthy, old-fashioned Cape red which is just about hanging on in there. The question is where?

SPAIN

1994 Morrison's Rioja Tinto, Bodegas Navajas
£ / MB / **ʝ**   13/20

Oak-chippy, basic Rioja. If you like the Don Darias style of tinto, you should love this coconutty, dry red.

1989 Mosen Cleto Crianza, Campo de Borja
0 / MB / 🌡   7/20

This sawdust-speckled bottle wins the *Grapevine* award for the worst bit of packaging in 1995. It takes some doing to come up with a bottle that doubles as a loofah substitute. The wine inside is worthy of the packaging – cooked, volatile and seriously unpleasant.

1992 Torres Sangredetoro
£ / MB / 🌡   14/20

A Mediterranean blend of Garnacha and Cariñena from Spain's highest profile winery, this is a robust quaffer which would be 50 pence cheaper if it didn't have the illustrious Torres brand name to support.

£5–8

AUSTRALIA

1992 Jamiesons Run Red
££ / MB / 🍷   16/20

A deeply coloured blend of Cabernet Sauvignon, Shiraz, Malbec and Petit Verdot with sweet American oak flavours of vanilla and spice. The wine's juicy blackcurrant fruit still shows the elegance of fine Coonawarra reds.

FRANCE

1990 Michel Lynch Rouge
£ / MB / 🌡   15/20

Blended by Jean-Michel Cazes of Château Lynch Bages wearing his *négociant* hat, this is a full, ripe Bordeaux Rouge with firm tannins and some well-judged oak influence.

ITALY

1990 Chianti Riserva, Uggiano
£ / MB / ♪   14/20
Like its *normale* stablemate, this rather confected Chianti Riserva suffers
from too much oak interference. Fine if you like bog-standard,
commercial Chianti with no Tuscan character.

Rosé

Under £3

PORTUGAL

Morrison's Portuguese Rosé
0 / 3 / ♪   12/20
With sweetness to soften its raw acidity, this is a tannic, old-fashioned
Mateus Rosé imitation, which doesn't even live up to the low standards
of its rôle model.

£3–5

FRANCE

1994 Vin de Pays d'Oc, Syrah Rosé, La Source
£ / 2 / ♪   13/20
From Domaines Virginie, this is a rather clumsy, bubblegummy rosé
with insufficient fruit flavour.

Sparkling

£3–5

FRANCE

Reminger Brut, Blanc de Blancs, Ackermann Laurance
££ / 3 / ▮   14/20
Appley, sweetish, Chenin Blanc-based fizz from the Loire Valley made
by the cuve close method. At under £4 a bottle, it's a good party fizz,
especially if concentrated with fresh orange juice.

ITALY

Asti Gianni
£ / 5 / ▮   13/20
Grapey, soft, sweet fizz with orange peel zest and refreshing bite.
Inoffensive stuff for quaffing with your Madeira cake.

£5–8

FRANCE

Saumur Brut, Gratien et Meyer
££ / 2 / ▮   15/20
Complex, mouthfilling fizz from one of the best sparkling wine
producers in the Loire Valley, showing flavours of aniseed and baked
apple. Good value at under £6.

GERMANY

Deinhard Yello
£ / 3 / ▮   13/20
No, not a spelling mistake, it really is called Yello. But quite why, we
can't tell you. A sweetish blend of German Riesling and northern Italian
Chardonnay. What will Deinhard think of next? How about Brazilian
Doradillo or Chinese Petit Manseng?

INDIA

1988 Omar Khayyam
£ / 2 / ▮   14/20

A sparkling wine which has established a small but loyal following in the UK, largely among Indian-restaurant-goers. This mature, nutty, toasty fizz is far better than Carling Black Label.

Over £8

FRANCE

Nicole D'Aurigny Champagne, Réserve Brut
££ / 3 / ▮   15/20

Among the best cheap Champagnes on the market, this £9 Pinot Noir based fizz from the Union Auboise co-operative is malty, soft and on the sweet side.

Paul Hérard Champagne, Demi-Sec
££ / 4 / ▮   15/20

Selected with Morrison's sweet-toothed customers in mind, this is a comparatively unusual, off-dry Champagne with creamy richness and a chocolatey tang.

NICOLAS ***(*)

Head Office: 157 Great Portland Street, London W1N 5FB

Telephone: 0171 436 9338

Number of branches: eight, all in the London area

Credit cards accepted: Visa, Access, Switch, Amex

Hours of opening: Varies from store to store

By-the-case sales: Yes

Glass loan: Free (deposit required)

Home delivery: Yes, free within central London

Clubs: No

Discounts: Ten to 20 per cent off selected wines and Champagnes (no minimum purchase). Twice a year, 'three for the price of two' offer on some Bordeaux and 15 per cent discount on 40-odd makes of Champagne (no minimum purchase)

In-store tastings: Yes. Full details from individual shops

Top ten best-selling wines: Petites Récoltes Vin de Pays des Côtes de Thau; Prieuré d'Amilhac Chardonnay, Vin de Pays des Côtes de Thongue; Jurançon Grain Sauvage; Montagny Premier Cru Cuvée Spéciale; Petites Récoltes Vin de Pays de la Cité de Carcassonne; Domaine du Bois du Garn, Côtes du Vivarais; Réserve Nicolas Bordeaux; Clos de la Coutale, Cahors; Château de Sabazan, Côtes de Saint-Mont; Gris de Cabernet, Coteaux de l'Ardèche

Range: GOOD: Bordeaux, southwestern France, Loire, Champagne and sparkling wines, Beaujolais, Savoie, Jura, white Burgundy
AVERAGE: Alsace, Provence, red Burgundy, Rhône
POOR: Languedoc-Roussillon

Alain Favereau, Nicolas' Paris-based head honcho, was interviewed in a French magazine a few months ago after being voted best wine buyer in the country by *La Revue Vinicole*. In response to a question about his taste in wine, he was adamant that: 'I don't buy liquids. I buy wines which are true to their *terroir*.'

Ho hum, we thought, we've heard that one before – yet another Frenchman who believes that God makes wine without much in the way of human intervention. The news that Monsieur Favereau has been doing the slurping and spitting at Nicolas for over 30 years was even more worrying.

From his public pronouncements, Favereau sounded as if he'd be suspicious of modern French winemaking – what the French dismiss as *vins de cépage* – and any form of New World influence. The impression we had before we arrived at Nicolas' shop in the Fulham Road was one of staid traditionalism.

On our previous, brief visits as window shoppers to some of Nicolas' London shops, all of them in areas which estate agents describe as 'desirable', we'd also been put off by some uncompetitive prices and the sense that France's self-styled 'leading fine wine merchant' was struggling to understand the tastes of the British public.

In fact, the quality of what we tasted at Nicolas was a revelation. From his most basic lines – a series of smart vins de pays called *les petites récoltes* – to his selection of clarets and Champagnes, our friend Monsieur Favereau clearly knows his *oignons*.

He's also adept at selecting unusual, characterful wines from more obscure *appellations*, such as Savoie, Jurançon, Cheverny, Madiran, Palette and Savennières. In short, Nicolas confounded our expectations.

The French chain has taken a softly-softly approach to the British market since it arrived here eight years ago. It's got 280 shops in France (200 of which are in and around Paris), but only eight in the UK. Nicolas set up here in 1988, when it took over five premises from the defunct Buckingham's chain. It closed one of them and opened another four, in Kew, Richmond, St John's Wood and Kensington Church Street, in 1993.

It doesn't sound like a rapid expansion programme. 'We don't intend to compete with Thresher or Victoria Wine,' explains operations director Eric Gandon. 'We are aiming at a maximum of 20 shops in London at the top end of the market in order to sell good quality wines. Our approach is that of artisans, not industrialists. We're not interested in competing by offering discounts on what we sell.' This isn't altogether true. Nicolas does offer occasional discounts on things like Champagne and Bordeaux second wines, but this is hardly competition for the £1.99 brigade.

Nicolas specialises in French wines, lots and lots and lots of them. Indeed, we reckon it has one of the widest selection of Gallic bottles in this country, matched only by a quirky specialist such as La Vigneronne. The total range runs to 1,500 wines – 1,000 of which make it to the UK. There is a minor concession to prevailing British tastes (10 per cent of the stuff on the shelves is non-French) in the London shops, but Gandon is adamant: 'We're good at buying and selling French wines and that's why we're in business in the UK.'

The shops have a Gallic feel to them, too. Most of the staff are French and each branch has a slightly different range, as managers are allowed to select their own wines from the 1,000-strong list. 'The image we're after is very French,' adds Gandon. 'Good quality, service and breadth of selection.' There are also, if you wander into the Fulham Road shop on the right day, freshly baked and extremely moreish *gougères*.

Some might argue that Nicolas' approach to retail margins is rather French too. On many wines – from Fitou's Château de Ségure to Bordeaux's Château Margaux – Nicolas' prices are £1 to £10 more expensive than its high street competitors. You could argue that, for people who live in Holland Park or Kensington, such matters are irrelevant, but we wouldn't agree. Gandon says that rents and rates are higher in England than in France and that 'to make an impact here was easy; to make it work financially was much harder.'

Nicolas' high prices cost it half a star in our rating system. If it could be a little more competitive across the board, the chain would be a real force. As it is, there's no better place to find unusual French wines, such as Vin Jaune, Corsica's Comte de Peraldi and Jurançon Sec. There's also in-depth coverage of the class areas. The only weak corner of the list is the Languedoc-Roussillon, where the thrilling developments of the last five years appear to have escaped the scrutiny of the master wine buyer Alain Favereau. It's reassuring to know the man is fallible after all.

Most of these wines are also available at Nicolas' Caen and Le Havre outlets, as well as in London.

White

£3–5

FRANCE

1994 Petites Récoltes Vin de Pays des Côtes de Thau, Cave Les Gruchottes
££ / 2 / ❶   14/20
A fresh pear and aniseed scented white from the shores of the Mediterranean, made from an unusual four-way blend of Terret, Ugni Blanc, Chardonnay and Sauvignon.

1994 Réserve Nicolas, Bordeaux, Léon d'Aubert
££ / 2 / ❶   14/20
Crisp, grapefruity, lemon curd-like blend of Sauvignon Blanc and Sémillon. Aromatic, well-balanced stuff.

£5–8

FRANCE

1993 Cépage Chardonnay, Coteaux de l'Ardèche, Vignerons des Coteaux de l'Ardèche
£ / 2 / ❶   14/20
A modern, buttery, New World-influenced Chardonnay from the southern Rhône with flavours of stone fruits and honey and an undertow of crisp lemony acidity.

1993 Chasselas 'Vieilles Vignes', Pierre Sparr
££ / 2 / ❶   15/20
A honeyed, peachy, almost Pinot Gris-like Alsace white with soft aromatics and rich, concentrated fruit. The lively acidity of the Chasselas grape keeps the wine attractively fresh.

1993 Domaine de la Désoucherie, Cheverny, Christian Tessier
££ / 1 / ❶   15/20
A blend of mainly Sauvignon with 20 per cent Chardonnay from the

Loire Valley's Cheverny *appellation*, this is a nettley, bracingly tart seafood white.

1994 Jurançon Grain Sauvage, Cave des Producteurs de Jurançon
£££ / 2 / ⚱   16/20

From the co-operative which dominates the *appellation* of Jurançon in the Pyrenean corner of southwestern France, this is a dry, grapefruity white with unusual, exotic flavours of cinnamon, nutmeg and tropical fruits. Just the sort of curiosity that Nicolas does best.

1993 Alsace Muscat, André Senner
££ / 2 / ⚱   15/20

A blend of two-thirds Muscat d'Alsace and one-third Muscat Ottonel, this is dry and comparatively restrained by the boudoir standards of aromatic Alsace varieties. It's smoky and fresh with a touch of rose petal perfume.

1993 Pacherenc du Vic Bilh, Cave de Plaimont, 50cl
££ / 4 / ⚱   15/20

Another find from the old curiosity shop, this is a blend of the local southwestern French Arrufiac, Petit Courbu, Gros Manseng and Petit Manseng grapes. It's a medium dry, honeyed style with attractive lemon peel freshness.

1993 Prieuré d'Amilhac Chardonnay, Vin de Pays des Côtes de Thongue, Cazottes
£ / 2 / ⚱   14/20

An oaky, grilled almond white with lots of alcohol and fat buttery fruit. Specially selected for the UK market, apparently. If so, the wine should have been £1 cheaper.

1992 Saumur, Cave de Saumur
£ / 1 / ⚱   14/20

An appley, minerally blend of Chenin Blanc, Chardonnay and Sauvignon from the extensive, subterranean St Cyr co-operative, with some bottle-aged maturity.

Over £8

FRANCE

1994 Château La Gentilhommière, Roussette de Savoie, Dominique Allion
£££ / 1 / ⌡   16/20
A yeasty, tobaccoey Soave-style white with good weight and fresh Alpine acidity. Another characterful wine from a relatively obscure region.

1992 Château d'Epiré, Bizard-Pitzou, Savennières
££ / 1 / ⌡   16/20
A rich, honeyed bottle-aged Chenin Blanc from a Loire *appellation* famous for the longevity of its dry white wines. Drink with *sandre au beurre blanc* by the banks of the Loire. Failing that, sardines at Little Venice will do.

1988 Montagny Premier Cru Cuvée Spéciale, Cave de Buxy
0 / 1 / ⌡   12/20
A bitter, old-fashioned, rancid white Burgundy. Thank you and *bonne nuit*.

1990 Château de l'Etoile, Vandelle
£££ / 1 / ⌀   16/20
A curio made from a combination of Chardonnay with the rustic local Poulsard and Savagnin grapes in eastern France's remote Jura region. It's an austere, tangy, Sherry-like white with highly unusual salty and smoky flavours. Not one for Liebfraumilch drinkers.

1993 Kaefferkopf, Vin d'Alsace, Kuehn
££ / 3 / ⌡   16/20
A powerfully spicy, lychee-like blend of aromatic Gewürztraminer and Tokay Pinot Gris, with soft peach and ginger fruit and refreshing acidity.

Red

£3–5

FRANCE

1994 Chaintreuil, Corbières, Cave des Gruchottes
££ / FB / ♪   14/20
A spicy, robust, full-throated blend of Carignan and Grenache with firm tannins and a whiff of the Mediterranean *garrigue*.

1994 Domaine du Bois du Garn, Côtes du Vivarais
0 / MB / ♪   13/20
A carbonic maceration style southern French blend of Grenache, Cinsault and Syrah with pleasant cherryish fruit. Pricey at around £5.

1992 Latour de France, Côtes du Roussillon-Villages, Cave des Gruchottes
££ / FB / ♪   15/20
Nothing to do with bicycle races, although one glass of this would be enough to knock you out of the saddle. It's a chewy, smoky, richly upholstered Roussillon red made from a Mediterranean pot-pourri of Carignan, Grenache, Syrah, Cinsault and Mourvèdre.

1994 Petites Récoltes Vin de Pays de la Cité de Carcassonne, Cave des Gruchottes
£ / MB / ♪   13/20
A youthful, bubblegummy, foursquare red from the Nicolas house selection. OK, in a plonky sort of way.

1991 Réserve Nicolas, Côtes de Castillon, Léon d'Aubert
£ / MB / ♪   13/20
A soft, mature Merlot-dominated claret with a rustic bite of tannin. A decent sub-£5 claret from the Right Bank hills of Castillon.

£5-8

FRANCE

1988 Baron d'Ardeuil, Les Vignerons de Buzet
0 / MB / 🍷   14/20

A composty, laughably priced southwestern French red made in a claret style. The mature characters of wet leaves and well-hung game are starting to dominate. Drink up before the maggots arrive.

1991 Chevaliers des Arènes, Costières de Nîmes
££ / FB / 🍷   15/20

At under £6, this is a considerably better priced and more attractive red from the Languedoc/Provence borders, blending Syrah, Grenache, Mourvèdre and Carignan in a traditional, sweetly ripe, bottle-matured style.

1992 Clos de la Coutale, Cahors, Bernède et Fils
££ / MB / 👄   15/20

With its tea-leaf and tar aromas, this is typical Malbec, or Cot, as it's known in Cahors, leavened with a proportion of Tannat and Merlot. Showing oodles of plum and cherry fruitiness, this is comparatively accessible for a Cahors.

1992 Domaine de la Désoucherie, Cheverny, Tessier
£ / LB / 🍷   14/20

A light, fruity red made from Gamay and Pinot Noir and showing delicate, pure fruit flavours and a rasp of acidity. The Loire's answer to Bourgogne Passetoutgrains.

1994 Le Masoulier, Vin de Pays de l'Hérault, Cave des Vignerons de Villeveyrac
0 / FB / 🍷   12/20

A solid, if slightly fecal, southern French co-op plonk which ought to be at least £2 cheaper.

1990 Madiran Collection, Cave de Plaimont
££ / FB / 👄   15/20

A claret-style Gascon red made from Tannat, Cabernet Sauvignon and the local Fer Servadou grape, this is a well-made, oaky blend with soft, chocolatey fruit sweetness and some coffee bean and oak character.

1994 Réserve Nicolas, Côtes du Rhône, Jean de Rochebrune
£ / MB / ➖   14/20
Spicy, deeply coloured blend of Grenache, Cinsault, Mourvèdre and Syrah, showing youthfully robust tannins and full, liquorice-like fruitiness.

Over £8

FRANCE

1989 Beaune Premier Cru Clos de la Mousse, Bouchard Père et Fils
0 / MB / ♪   13/20
From one of Burgundy's least impressive *négociants*, this is a soupy, over-alcoholic Pinot Noir which lacks definition and the supposedly superior character of a Premier Cru. We can think of better ways to spend £21.50. About a thousand of them.

1992 Château Bel Air, Lussac-St-Emilion
££ / MB / ♪   16/20
An attractive, modern, Merlot-based Right Bank claret showing sweet oak and the supple fruitiness of the best 1992 Bordeaux reds. Good value at under £10.

1985 Château Côte l'Eglise, Pomerol
0 / MB / ⸮   11/20
Shagged-out, tomato-skin-style plonk masquerading as Pomerol. There ought to be a law against wines like this.

1988 Château Villars, Fronsac
££ / MB / ♪   16/20
Fresh, elegant, attractive Right Bank claret from a recent vintage overshadowed by its two more seductive successors. Polished vanilla oak and minty fruit make this an appealing buy at around £12.50.

1990 Château de Sabazan, Côtes de St-Mont, Cave de Plaimont
££ / FB / ➤ 16/20
The flagship red wine from the reliable Plaimont co-operative, marrying Tannat, Pimenc, Cabernet Sauvignon and Cabernet Franc grapes with a heavy dose of new oak to produce a youthful, almost Pauillac-like red with plenty of dark chocolate and blackcurrant fruitiness.

1993 Château Raspail, Gigondas, Christian Meffre
££ / FB / ⌇ 16/20
A heady, aromatic, orange peel scented southern Rhône red with lashings of the *appellation*'s characteristic alcohol and peppery spiciness. Plenty of character for a rather average vintage.

1990 Clos du Marquis, St-Julien
££ / MB / ➤ 17/20
It's an old wine trade adage that the best time to buy second labels is in brilliant vintages. This silky, moreish, beautifully proportioned claret, the second wine of Château Léoville Lascases in St-Julien, is rich in cinnamon and vanilla spiciness and will reward a five-year spell in your cellar or under the bed.

1985 Cru du Paradis, Madiran
££ / FB / ⌇ 15/20
It's unusual to find a Madiran of this age on a British retail shelf, but we rather enjoyed this mature, sweetly fruity, tea-leafy red, which retains its robust, bitter chocolate tannins, even at 10 years of age.

1990 La Baronnie Madeleine, Chinon, Couly-Dutheil
£ / MB / ⌇ 15/20
Structured, grassy, oaky Chinon from one of the Loire Valley's better *négociants*, with attractive green pepper perfume and firm tannins.

Rosé

£3-5

FRANCE

1994 Petites Récoltes, Vin de Pays des Maures, Cave des Gruchottes
££ / 2 / ╏ 14/20
Fresh, dry, strawberryish rosé made from a blend of Grenache and Cinsault grapes. Needs food to show at its best.

Gris de Grenache, Vin de Pays des Coteaux de l'Ardèche, Vignerons Ardèchois
££ / 2 / ╏ 15/20
A delicately pale, all-Grenache rosé from the southern Rhône with smoky aromas and good mid-palate weight and richness.

£5-8

FRANCE

1994 Réserve Nicolas, Côtes de Provence, de Rochebrune
£ / 2 / ╏ 14/20
A teeny bit expensive at nearly £6, but this well-coloured, commercial blend of Grenache and Carignan, with its sweet herb and berry fruitiness, is fine for those overwintering on the Côte d'Azur.

Sparkling

£5-8

FRANCE

François de Sécade, Blanquette de Limoux
££ / 2 / ╏ 15/20
Ignore the cheap and tacky label if you can, and proceed to the superior

stuff in the bottle. Toasty, fresh and crisp with attractive apple and pear fruitiness.

Over £8

FRANCE

Champagne Bruno Paillard Première Cuvée
££ / 2 / ♪   16/20
A Pinot Noir dominated fizz from one of the few Champagne houses to have sprung up in the last decade. It's a malty, mouthfilling blend with lots of reserve wine weight and concentration.

1991 Crémant de Loire Brut Rosé Millésimé
££ / 2 / ♪   15/20
An unusual pink sparkling wine made entirely from the Loire's Cabernet Franc grape at the St Cyr co-operative, and showing fresh summer pudding and green pepper fruitiness with plenty of zippy acidity.

Fortified

Over £8

PORTUGAL

Grand Madeira Sercial, La Vieille Réserve
£££ / 5 / ➥   17/20
At £27 a bottle, this needs to be good to justify its price tag. And good it is, with masses of raisin, nut and crème brûlée characters, smoky concentration and tangy, zesty acidity. Like all the best fortified wines, this mature Madeira conceals its alcoholic punch with skill.

ODDBINS **** (*)
ODDBINS FINE WINE STORES *****

Head Office: 31–33 Weir Road, London SW19 8UG

Telephone: 0181 944 4400

Number of branches: 206 plus 6 Fine Wine stores

Credit cards accepted: Visa, Access, American Express, Switch

Hours of opening: Generally Monday to Saturday 10.00am to 9.00pm; Sunday opening times vary. Please ask your local branch for details.

By-the-case sales: Yes

Glass loan: Yes (with deposit)

Home delivery: Free within locality of shop (minimum one case)

Clubs: Oddbins wine club members receive *The Catalyst* magazine

Discounts: Ten per cent on mixed cases during Saturday tastings; 5 per cent on mixed cases at any time; seven bottles for the price of six on Champagne and sparkling wine at £5.99 and above

In-store tastings: Every Saturday, from 2.00pm to 5.00pm

Top ten best-selling wines: Mumm Cuvée Napa Brut; Lindemans 1994 Cawarra Colombard/Chardonnay; 1993 Glenloth Shiraz/Cabernet; 1994 Oddbins White, Domaine de Jöy, Vin de Pays des Côtes de Gascogne; 1994 Glenloth White; Perrier Jouët Champagne; Mumm Cuvée Napa Rosé; 1994 James Herrick Chardonnay; Oddbins Red, Vin de Pays Catalan; Heidsieck Dry Monopole Champagne

Range: GOOD: Australia, Burgundy, Bordeaux, Rhône, Alsace, South of France, Chile, California, Italy, Spain, New Zealand, Germany, Champagne and sparkling wines

AVERAGE: Loire, South Africa
POOR: Eastern Europe, England

'It's been a tough year,' said Oddbins' buyer Steve 'Richard Gere' Daniel, and he wasn't referring to the departure of deputy managing director John Ratcliffe, hitherto his inseparable partner. Ratcliffe has been beamed up to Oddbins' parent, Seagram, apparently for a spot of corporate grooming as Oddbins' new managing director.

Steve Daniel was more preoccupied with life in the high street, where Bottoms Up, Victoria Wine Cellars and the new toddler on the block, Greenalls' Wine Cellar, had all been helping themselves to the honeypot marked 'Oddbins – Keep Out'. But Daniel was in no mood to admit that the competition was hurting too badly. 'We're doing very well in the £3–£5 price category and we don't think our competitors are. The specialists are having a shit of a time. They're getting crucified.'

To cope with the tougher conditions, Oddbins has been asking more of its store managers. 'They've got to generate customers, be more active and aggressive, offer tastings and do more of a specialised wine merchant's job,' says Daniel, who's well aware that the range is only as good as the calibre of the people selling it.

'We've got good guys in the shops, which is possibly the difference between us and the rest of the competition.' It's true that Oddbins' customers don't want to be nannied or patronised. They want shop staff who are on the same wavelength and know what they're talking about. Enthusiasm, knowledge and an ability to communicate are Oddbins CV essentials.

At the bottom end of the market, for what Daniel calls 'the wavering voter', Oddbins stocks some pretty good £2.99 products like the 1995 Santa Carolina white and the southern French Cuvée de Grignon. It hasn't abandoned the sub-£3 market entirely, but Oddbins has lost ground in the area thanks to supermarket price-cutting, which Daniel sees as creating a 'something for nothing' culture.

'When you take a £2.99 or £3.49 product and sell it at £1.99, the consumer takes advantage and starts to think "why pay the full price for anything?" The supermarkets' aggressive pricing activity in offering a £3 bottle at £2 is making the consumer more deal orientated. But they are finding that only the special offers are selling and as a result their ranges are shrinking and the more esoteric wines are not selling.'

Oddbins instead offers case discounts and promotions such as the regular seven for six offer on Champagnes and sparkling wines over £5.99, and in-store tastings. The annual Oddbins Wine Fair goes from strength to strength and a newsletter, *The Catalyst*, keeps members informed. And this autumn, the wacky Steadman list features Samuel Morewood, an obscure Victorian Collector of Excise, plus snippets from those well-known alcohol connoisseurs, Hunter S. Thompson and William Burroughs.

In 1994, Oddbins fired a broadside at the independent wine merchants by selling large quantities of top-class 1992 white Burgundy. Encouraged by this success, it shifted another 1,500-odd cases of the 1993 whites in 1995, with a selective offer of some of the excellent 1993 reds (including wines from Jayer-Gilles, Mongeard-Mugneret, Domaine de l'Arlot and Carillon) coming up at Christmas.

Does this all mean that Oddbins has shed T-shirts, jeans and nose rings for monocles and pin-stripes? Hardly, but the Burgundies have brought in the sort of well-heeled customer who used to think of Oddbins as a source of the cheap, the cheerful and the Australian, and had the classics delivered to the tradesman's entrance by the Wine Society or Berry Bros & Rudd of St James's.

With the shops carrying more fine wines than before, especially from Burgundy and California, the new Oddbins Fine Wine stores are a convenient extension of this side of the business. The Oxford store opened in 1995, bringing the total to six stores capable of stocking unusual wines available in quantities too limited to appear in the main shops.

The Fine Wine stores, with a range of some 500 to 550 wines and an average spend of £15, have done well, but the market for the likes of Sulbric, a Piedmontese Barbera/Nebbiolo blend at £22.99, or Sean Thackrey's Orion, a £23.99 Californian old vine Syrah, is not bottomless. To the relief, presumably, of the beleaguered independent wine merchant, ten Fine Wine stores is the maximum Oddbins foresees.

Australia, assiduously built up by John 'the Rat' Ratcliffe and top seller at Oddbins last year, is still big bucks. In fact it's big bucks that are the problem. Prices have caused Oddbins to think twice about carrying quite so many Aussie eggs in the picnic basket, as the summer list lamented: 'Unfortunately, with demand outstripping supply, particularly at the everyday end of the range, you may see some of your favourite wines inching up in price, or even disappearing altogether over the coming months.'

From 40 per cent of sales, Australia is shifting back down a gear to an estimated 30 per cent of sales this year. 'Australia is a case of natural wastage,' reassures Daniel. 'There hasn't been that much of a cutback. We expect to lose around 5 to 6 per cent of the range this year, but we'll still have around 300 wines.' Not bad for a diminishing New World country.

Some of the slack has been taken up by developments elsewhere in the New World, notably Chile, South Africa and California. There is obviously plenty of life left in Chile, which has shot up to nearly 10 per cent of sales, and is well-represented at Oddbins by some of the country's top names, among them Santa Carolina, Errázuriz, Carmen, Caliterra and Cono Sur.

An uncharacteristically world-weary Daniel told us that 'there are not that many places left to develop'. But there are only two Argentinian wines on the list, and with production of the equivalent of two billion bottles, a 100 per cent increase should be a doddle. At the top end, South Africa has been developed to good effect with the likes of Kanonkop, Glen Carlou and Danie de Wet, but the £3.49 to £4.49 range needs attention.

Steve Daniel's claim to be 'ahead of the game' in California is justified. 'We're the only people who take California seriously. The competition finds it difficult because of price.' Good value varietals and blends from Franciscan, Sterling, Fetzer, Randall Grahm and broker Jason Korman's Havenscourt range have done well, although there are problems in sight as the current glut dries up and bulk prices rise.

At the top end, Ridge, Calera, Matanzas Creek and Newton are among California's best estates. Here, the Oddbins' list reflects the fact that in Bordeaux and Burgundy styles, and increasingly in Rhône and Italian, the quality and range of California's wines often outstrips the rest of the New World. Future prospects, however, will depend heavily on the stability of the dollar.

In Europe, Italy was Oddbins' biggest seller after France, but it slipped into fourth place behind Spain. 'Italy was offering bad value. We were disgusted with the general level of quality. Bad vintages in Piemonte created problems with overpriced Barolo. We've pruned back at the top end.' With more modern, reasonably priced styles of wine, however, from less established areas such as Sardinia, Puglia, and the Mediterranean south, Italy is back in business.

Spain, too, has become a fixture, not so much in Rioja, which has suffered price and quality problems, but in the less traditional, up-and-coming areas such as Navarra and La Mancha. And with estates such as Toni Jost, Kurt Darting, Franz Künstler, Müller-Catoir and von Kesselstatt, Oddbins is still the best high street venue for fine German wines.

In France, lost ground in the classic regions has been compensated for as deficiencies in the South of France have been rectified. 'Long term, the South can produce wines whose intrinsic quality is as good as anywhere in France. Things would be even better if the exchange rate were better.' New to the list, Domaine Lascaux and Mas Cal Demoura, Olivier Jullien's father's property at Pic Saint Loup, join forces with a couple of superb Costières de Nîmes, from Paul Blanc and Mas Carlot.

It was brave, given the exchange rate and the notorious difficulty in selling the region's wines, to feature Alsace during the year, but top properties Schoffitt, Domaine Weinbach, Schaetzel and Hugel have apparently sold well. 'You have to cater for the cutting-edge consumer who wants something other than Chardonnay. The core Oddbins consumer is very well educated about wines, not that far behind buyers and journalists.' (Yes, he did say journalists, and we're holding him to it.)

If they're looking for interest beyond Chardonnay in their white wines, Oddbins' inquisitive customers are equally excited about New World Syrah and Pinot Noir, which have become increasingly popular styles at the expense of Cabernet Sauvignon. 'Consumers are increasingly making up their own minds,' says Daniel.

So, as the supermarkets head downmarket, all credit to Oddbins for continuing to paddle against the flow and to champion quality and innovation. Oddbins may not have the high street to itself any longer, and no doubt its rivals are still practising acupuncture on little Oddbins dolls, but the high street without Oddbins would be like Las Vegas in a power cut. Perish the thought.

White

Under £3

CHILE

1995 Santa Carolina Dry White
£££ / 3 / ♪   14/20

Made by Chilean Pilar González, this is a soft, melony, flavoursome white produced entirely from the Sauvignon Blanc grape. At this sort of price, the Loire and New Zealand simply can't compete.

£3–5

AUSTRALIA

Glenloth South Eastern Australia Private Bin No 106
££ / 3 / ♪   14/20

Fresh lime-citrus Riesling aromas and flavours made under another label by the Penfolds winery. One of the best cheap Australian wines on the market, proving that you have to go to £3.50 to find something attractively drinkable.

1994 Lindemans Cawarra Colombard/Chardonnay
££ / 3 / ♪   14/20

A slightly fuller, lemon curd and smoky oak chip Aussie white, also from the voluminous vats of the Penfolds group. Almost impossible to dislike – unless you're French.

1994 Lindemans Cawarra Semillon/Chardonnay
££ / 3 / ♪   14/20

A commercial, winningly made, warm climate blend with flavours of marmalade and fresh peach and a herby note. It's refreshing to come across an inexpensive Australian white in which oak is not the dominant flavour.

1989 McWilliams Eden Valley Riesling

£££ / 3 / 🌡   16/20

Aged Riesling is one of Australia's trump cards, and this mature, nutty, unoaked white, with its rich Mosel-kerosene and coconut-like flavours, is a classic. Great value at under £4.

1993 Saltram Chardonnay, South East Australia

££ / 2 / 🌡   15/20

A golden oldie (in colour) from Australia, with ripe pineappley fruit, rich alcohol and charry oak balanced by well-judged acidity.

1994 WW Chardonnay, McLaren Vale

££ / 2 / 🌡   15/20

Close your eyes and the green bean aromas of this McLaren Vale could put you in mind of a Sauvignon Blanc. On the palate, the wine shows the peachy fruitiness of the Chardonnay grape topped off with a delicate coating of smoky oak.

1994 Rawsons Retreat Penfolds Bin 21 Semillon/Chardonnay

£££ / 2 / 🌡   15/20

A good example of the new-style Penfolds whites. With its spicy vanilla oak, herby Semillon and Chardonnay richness, these two grapes combine harmoniously to produce a sundae of vanilla ice cream and lemony fruit.

CHILE

1995 Santa Carolina Sauvignon Blanc

£££ / 2 / 🌡   16/20

From the Lontue region, this is an extremely full-flavoured, beautifully made, melon, peach and grapefruit zest style Sauvignon Blanc from Chile's excellent 1995 vintage.

1994 Caliterra Casablanca Chardonnay

£££ / 2 / 🌡   17/20

Star winemaker Ignacio Recabarren has produced a brilliant value Chardonnay from Chile's most exciting white wine area, the Casablanca Valley, halfway between Santiago and the port of Valparaiso. Fresh, clean-cut, citrus-fruit flavours with a grapefruity tang and a touch of oak.

1994 Caliterra Sauvignon Blanc
£££ / 2 / 🍷 16/20

Crisp, zesty, engagingly aromatic Chilean Sauvignon made by the passionate Ignacio Recabarren. This is midway between the elegance of Sancerre and the pungency of a Marlborough Sauvignon Blanc, showing flavours of grapefruit and melon and tremendous concentration for a wine at under £4.

FRANCE

1994 Oddbins White, Domaine de Jöy, Vin de Pays des Côtes de Gascogne
££ / 2 / 🍷 14/20

A refreshing, grapefruity Gascon blend of Colombard and Ugni Blanc from Domaine de Jöy. Zesty, enjoyable stuff.

1994 Grenache Blanc, Vin de Pays d'Oc Fortant
£££ / 2 / 🍷 14/20

Arguably the most Mediterranean of the wines made at Robert Skalli's futuristic showcase winery in Sète, this is a modern interpretation of one of the Languedoc region's workhorse grape varieties. It's fresh and full-bodied, with a tea-leaf and pear-like quality.

1994 Chardonnay, Vin de Pays d'Oc André Hardy
££ / 2 / 🍷 15/20

Another wine with a Skalli connection, as producer André Hardy was once one of Fortant de France's star Chardonnay growers. He's still a star, but now he's ploughing his own galactic furrow near Montpellier. This is a buttery, fat, unoaked style with considerable richness of flavour.

1994 Domaine St Hilaire, Vin de Pays d'Oc Chardonnay
££ / 2 / 🍷 15/20

Also made by André Hardy, this is another unoaked Chardonnay, in this case made from his own vineyard. It's concentrated, soft and buttery with some ripe peach and banana fruitiness and a minerally note.

1994 Touraine Sauvignon, Domaine de la Rénaudie
££ / 2 / 🍷 16/20

A crisp, nettley, well-made Touraine Sauvignon Blanc from an 18-hectare property in Saint Aignan-sur-Cher. It's as good as many a Sancerre, and even though it is 50 pence more than the previous vintage, the Rénaudie Sauvignon still offers brilliant value for money.

1994 Chardonnay, James Herrick, Vin de Pays d'Oc
££ / 2 / ⅃   15/20
Probably the best release yet from Englishman James Herrick's extensive Chardonnay plantings near Narbonne, this is a peachy, lightly oaked white with hints of butter and greengage, and an RSJ of supporting acidity.

ITALY

1994 Albana di Romagna 'Campo del Sole' Riva, Gaetane Carron
££ / 2 / ⅃   14/20
It's always been a matter of controversy in Italy that comparatively lowly Albana di Romagna was the first white wine to achieve DOCG (Denominazione di Origine Controllata e Garantita) status. The wines can be disappointing, but this appley, nutty example from Gaetane Carron is a pleasant surprise.

1994 Pinot Grigio del Friuli, Pecile, Bidoli
£££ / 2 / ⅃   15/20
A smartly packaged, stylish Italian white, overseen by consultant French winemaker Gaetane Carron, with crisp lemon and apricot flavours and a tang of fresh acidity. A good apéritif white.

1994 Vermentino di Sardegna, Sella & Mosca
£££ / 2 / ⅃   16/20
Made by Italian Mario Consorte, this is a fresh, appealingly aromatic, delicately pine-scented Sardinian white, showing the benefits of new technology and stainless steel fermentation. With its crisp acidity and lemony tang, this is an outstanding example of Sardinia's near-native white Vermentino grape.

1994 Terre Arnolfe, Colli Amerini Bianco, Umbria
£££ / 2 / ⅃   15/20
A spicy Umbrian blend of Trebbiano, Malvasia, Grechetto, Verdello and Garganega, with a refreshing bitter twist and a light spritz. Excellent value.

SOUTH AFRICA

1995 Namaqua Colombard
£ / 3 / ♪   13/20
Made at the Olifantsriver region's Vredendal co-operative, this is a simple, boiled sweets style white with peardroppy, technologically assisted flavours.

1995 Van Loveren Blanc de Blancs
£ / 3 / ♪   13/20
A dilute ginger and peardrop style blend of Sauvignon Blanc, Muscat and Colombard, with a prickle of carbon dioxide gas to prevent it from falling off the Table Mountain.

1995 Van Loveren Colombard/Chardonnay
££ / 2 / ♪   14/20
Another rather neutral Cape white from the Retief Brothers' Robertson winery. But with its hint of barrel-fermented oak and melon and grapefruit flavours, it's preferable to the Blanc de Blancs and Pinot Gris also stocked by Oddbins. A bit more flavour and the wine would be considerably more interesting.

1995 Danie de Wet Chardonnay Sur Lie
£££ / 2 / ♪   16/20
From 1995 *Grapevine* winemaker of the year Danie de Wet, this is a crisp, creamy, beautifully proportioned, unoaked Chardonnay with freshness, length of flavour and a prickle of gas. We'd like to present a bottle of this to almost every winemaker in the Mâcon region, but they'll just have to make do with the note instead.

SPAIN

1994 Santara Barrel-Fermented Chardonnay
£££ / 2 / ♪   15/20
A lightly oaked, northern Spanish Chardonnay from the Conca de Barbera region made by Hugh 'Grant' Ryman. Crisp, zesty and more complex than the unoaked version widely available on British shelves.

£5–8

AUSTRALIA

1994 Wirra Wirra Semillon/Sauvignon, McLaren Vale
£££ / 2 / ▶   16/20

The product of a cool vintage in McLaren Vale, this is a delightfully complex blend of Semillon and Sauvignon in which one-third barrel fermentation has brought extra depth and a toasty, Graves-like note to the wine. Flavours of gooseberry and melon are enhanced by grapefruity acidity.

1994 Wirra Wirra Chardonnay, McLaren Vale
££ / 2 / ▶   16/20

Also made by Ben Riggs, this is an oakier style with two-thirds barrel fermented and the rest made in tank to add zippy freshness. It's a full, fresh Chardonnay with seductively pure fruit flavours and stylishly judged oak treatment.

FRANCE

1994 Mâcon Davayé, Domaine des Deux Roches
£££ / 2 / ▶   16/20

From a forward-thinking Mâconnais estate, which makes the most of low yields and modern winemaking to produce extremely fresh, concentrated Chardonnays. As with the 1993, the spicy clarity of the village *appellation* shines through on this unoaked white, although the wine is slightly fuller in body and texture.

1994 St-Véran Les Chailloux, Domaine des Deux Roches
£££ / 2 / ▶   16/20

From the same estate, this spicy, lightly oaked Chardonnay has a lot in common with the best wines of neighbouring Pouilly Fuissé. Spice and grapefruit zest make this a serious Mâconnais white.

1994 Menetou-Salon, Cuvée Evelyn, Pellé
££ / 2 / ▶   16/20

A good alternative to Sancerre, this wine from a lesser-known *appellation* is a modern, zingy, elderfloral Loire white with soft Sauvignon Blanc characters.

1993 Montagny Premier Cru, Les Coères, Bertrand & Juillot
££ / 2 / ➳   15/20
Like many a 1993 white Burgundy, this is a fresh, almost austere style
whose minerally, lemony fruitiness needs a little more time to soften in
bottle. It's a well-made Côte Chalonnaise white with nicely balanced
oak.

GERMANY

**1993 Bacharacher Schloss Stahleck Riesling Kabinett, Mittelrhein,
Toni Jost**
£££ / 3 / ➳   16/20
From one of Germany's brightest talents, this is a superfresh, appley
Riesling with plenty of cassis-leaf concentration and a characteristic
lightness of touch.

1993 Josephshöfer Riesling Kabinett, Von Kesselstatt
£££ / 3 / ➳   16/20
From Annegret Reh-Gartner's best vineyard in the Mosel Valley, this is a
beautifully perfumed, violet-scented Riesling with typical Mosel green
apple bite and spicy depth of fruit flavour. Von Kesselstatt is building a
deservedly high reputation in this country for its outstanding Rieslings.

1993 Ungsteiner Honigsachel Riesling Auslese, Fuhrmann Eymael
£££ / 6 / ➳   16/20
An appropriately named honeyed white, with underlying flavours of
peaches and grapefruit segments and crunchy refreshing acidity to slice
through the wine's natural sweetness.

SOUTH AFRICA

1994 Rhebokskloof Chardonnay Sur Lie, Reserve
££ / 2 / ➳   15/20
A big, buttered brazil nut and toffee style South African Chardonnay
which almost goes over the top in its search for every ounce of flavour,
but just pulls back from the edge in time.

UNITED STATES

1993 Sterling Chardonnay, Napa Valley
££ / 2 / ∤   15/20

A good value Chardonnay from the Seagram-owned Napa Valley winery that looks like a Greek monastery. It's a soft, ripe, richly alcoholic style with plenty of flavour and well-handled oak for a wine at around £6.

Over £8

AUSTRALIA

1994 Wolf Blass President's Selection Chardonnay
££ / 2 / ∤   16/20

From the man with an unparalleled collection of bow ties, only some of which have been seen to revolve, this is a surprisingly elegant Chardonnay. Ronnie Corbett lookalike 'Wolfie' has blended a rich, alcoholic, smoky bacon style Chardonnay, using grapes from McLaren Vale and the Barossa and Eden Valleys.

1992 Heggies Vineyard Chardonnay, Eden Valley, South Australia
£££ / 2 / ∤   17/20

Made by Yalumba's Simon Adams from the company's best vineyards in the coolish Eden Valley, this is a freshly balanced, elegantly proportioned Chardonnay with well-integrated vanilla spice and a texture which reminded us of a New Zealand white.

1993 Cullen Chardonnay, Western Australia
££ / 2 / ∤   16/20

Unusually for an Australian Chardonnay, the surf-loving Vanya Cullen's distinctive Western Australian white undergoes full Burgundy-style malolactic fermentation, spending 12 months on its fermentation lees in barrel. The result is a complex, oatmealy Chardonnay with uncompromising flavours of butterscotch and fudge and refreshing acidity for balance.

FRANCE

1993 St-Aubin Premier Cru, Les Charmois, Bernard Morey
££ / 2 / ⇢   16/20

Made by one of the numerous Moreys in the Côte de Beaune, this is a slightly softer style with leesy richness, power and plenty of new oak. One of the best St-Aubins around.

1993 Puligny-Montrachet, Carillon
£££ / 2 / ⇢   17/20

Now acknowledged as one of the best white wine domaines in Burgundy, Carillon has produced a 1993 village white which is just as good as the excellent 1992s we're still working our way through. It's a nutty, complex Chardonnay with intense aromas and lots of seductive flavour. It may age even better than the 1992.

1992 Meursault Limozin, Mestre-Michelot
££ / 2 / ❭   16/20

A buttery, fat, old-fashioned Meursault from the cheeky, diminutive Bernard Michelot. It's a ripe, honeyed style from one of Burgundy's best recent white wine vintages, with lush fudge and butterscotch flavours and powerful supporting alcohol.

1994 Condrieu Vieilles Vignes Caillerets, Cuilleron
££ / 2 / ⇢   17/20

A follower of wine consultant Jean-Luc Colombo, the Cuilleron domaine produces concentrated, softly aniseedy Viognier with flavours of apricot jam and toast enlivened by fresh acidity.

1993 Chassagne-Montrachet, Maltroie, Fontaine-Gagnard
££ / 2 / ❭   17/20

Made by the tall former airline technician, Richard Fontaine-Gagnard, this is a pure, crisp, minerally Chassagne-Montrachet with plenty of new oak and an elegant citrus fruit streak.

1990 Château La Rame, Sainte-Croix-du-Mont
££ / 8 / ❭   16/20

Marmaladey, peachy, richly textured, nougat and almond like sweet white from a small and often underrated Bordeaux *appellation*. This botrytis-affected sticky is good enough to be mistaken for a Sauternes. Fine Wine shops only.

GERMANY

1993 Hochheimer Reichestal Stahleck Riesling Spätlese, Franz Künstler

££ / 5 / ➤   16/20

An exotic, grapefruity Rheingau white with refreshing, full-textured Riesling fruitiness and elegant balance. Künstler is another name to watch.

UNITED STATES

1993 Flora Springs Carneros Chardonnay

£££ / 2 / ➤   17/20

An unfiltered, unfined Chardonnay made with wild yeasts, as fashion now demands, from vineyards in the cool Carneros district at the southern end of the Napa Valley. Chardonnay specialists Flora Springs have made a wine with masses of complexity, plenty of oak, and honey and toffee flavours. What prevents the wine from tasting like a Ben & Jerry's ice cream is its saving freshness and crisp acidity.

1993 Beringer Vineyards Private Reserve Chardonnay

££ / 2 / ➤   16/20

A more old-fashioned Napa Valley Chardonnay in which rich, buttery, full-bodied flavours are enhanced by contact in barrel with the wine's fermentation lees. You almost need a knife and fork to eat, whoops, drink this.

1993 Woodward Canyon Reserve Chardonnay, Columbia Valley, Washington

££ / 2 / ➤   16/20

From Rick Small, one of the best winemakers in Washington State, this is a Burgundian-style barrel-fermented Chardonnay from his vineyards to the east of the scenic Cascade mountain range. It's a cool, fresh, toast and milk chocolate-like Chardonnay with spicy vanilla oak and lively, balancing acidity. Sold at Oddbins Fine Wine Shops only, at around £16.50.

Red

Under £3

FRANCE

1994 Cuvée de Grignon, Vin de Pays de l'Aude
£££ / MB / ♪   14/20
Disappointed by the quality, if that's the right word, of Winter Hill's rustic red wine, Oddbins' wine buyer Steve 'Armani' Daniel asked Michael Goundrey to beef it up with a bit of barrel-aged Cabernet Sauvignon. The result is a raspberryish red with attractive cinnamon spice. We wonder why Michael Goundrey didn't think of it himself.

CHILE

1995 Santa Carolina Dry Red
£££ / MB / ♪   14/20
Pilar González's blend of Cabernet Sauvignon, Merlot and the native País grape is a fresh, juicy, softly cherried, herby red at a more than attractive price.

SPAIN

1994 Andelos Red, Navarra
£ / FB / ♪   13/20
A light, rhubarby Spanish red made from the Garnacha grape, which is prematurely browning at the edges. Tinto plonko.

£3–5

AUSTRALIA

Glenloth South Eastern Australia Private Bin No 108
£ / MB / ♪   13/20
A sweet, minty, confected blend of Shiraz and Cabernet Sauvignon made by Australia's largest winery, Penfolds. Decently priced for a basic Australian red at around £3.50.

1993 Saltram Shiraz, South East Australia
0 / FB / **13/20**
An excessively extracted, eucalyptus-scented Shiraz with hefty, drying tannins and spicy oak.

BULGARIA

1991 Gamza Reserve, Suhindol
£ / MB / **13/20**
Made by winemaker Antim Dragiev from Bulgaria's native Gamza grape, this is a sweetish, fresh, peppery red with slightly confected blackcurrant pastille fruit flavours.

1990 Cabernet Sauvignon Special Reserve, Suhindol
£ / MB / **13/20**
By appointment to King Simeon II of Bulgaria no less, this is a dry, old-fashioned, oaky red. If we were royalty, we'd be drinking something a little more exciting.

CHILE

1995 Viña Concha y Toro Syrah
££ / MB / **15/20**
Soft, deeply coloured, youthful Chilean red which smells like a cross between a minty Cabernet Sauvignon and a tarry, blackberryish Syrah. It's lush and succulent with fruit and oak sweetness in attractive harmony.

FRANCE

1994 Oddbins Red, Vin de Pays Catalan
££ / MB / **15/20**
Softly robust, juicy southern French quaffer from the art-loving Roussillon property of Château de Jau. A suitable counterpart to the Oddbins white and another excellent party wine.

1994 Merlot, Vin de Pays d'Oc, Barton & Guestier
££ / MB / **14/20**
Deliberately made in a claret-like style by Bordeaux *négociant* Barton &

Guestier, using Merlot grapes from the Languedoc region to produce a grassy, robust country red at a sub-Bordeaux price. We preferred it to the same merchant's Vin de Pays d'Oc Syrah, also stocked by Oddbins.

1993 Costières de Nîmes, Mas Carlot
£££ / MB / ➥   16/20
A smoky, characterful, spicy blend of Syrah, Grenache and Cabernet Sauvignon with plenty of chocolatey, mid-palate lusciousness and a hint of claret-like grassiness.

1993 Costières de Nîmes, Paul Blanc
£££ / FB / ⌇   17/20
Softly concentrated Provençal red made entirely from the Syrah grape. If it weren't for a touch of Mediterranean spiciness, this concentrated, deeply coloured wine could almost be mistaken for a top-flight Crozes-Hermitage, or better.

ITALY

1993 Riva Sangiovese di Romagna Superiore, Podere San Crispino
££ / MB / ⌇   14/20
Made from 25-year-old Sangiovese vines by itinerant French winemaker Gaetane Carron, this new oak-aged red is fresh, dry and cherried with the sort of refreshing acidity that makes Italian red wines such a pleasure with food.

1992 Centare Rosso, Duca di Castelmonte
££ / MB / ➥   15/20
A modern, charry-oaky Sicilian blend of the indigenous Nero d'Avola and Nerello Mascalese grapes. Leathery, coconutty flavours and high acidity reminded us of a new-style Rioja crianza.

1993 Torrevento, Castel del Monte
£££ / MB / ⌇   15/20
A deliberately soft style made in Puglia from the local Uva di Troia and Aglianico grapes with juicy raspberry and damson-skin fruitiness and fleshy, supple tannins.

1994 Torre del Falco, Rosso della Murgia, Vino da Tavola
£££ / MB / ▮   16/20
A blend of Cabernet Sauvignon and the local Puglian Uva di Troia, which
further demonstrates that the heel of Italy can produce outstanding red
wines at under £5. It's minty, dry and lightly oaked with the green
pepper elegance of the Cabernet Sauvignon adding class to the Uva di
Troia. It's handsomely packaged too.

SOUTH AFRICA

1993 Stellenzicht Block Series Shiraz
£ / FB / ▮   14/20
A chunky, smoky, leafy Cape Red with sweet American oak but
insufficient fruit for balance.

SPAIN

1994 Tierra Seca, La Mancha
££ / MB / ▮   14/20
Made by American Ed Flaherty from Chile's Cono Sur winery, this is a
robust, oak-chipped, modern blend of Tempranillo and Cabernet
Sauvignon from the plains of La Mancha.

1991 Agramont Cabernet/Tempranillo Crianza, Navarra
£££ / MB / ▮   15/20
A minty, fresh, well-balanced Navarra version of the same two grapes,
this time with the benefit of whole oak barrels as opposed to what
Australians refer to as microcasks. This is still youthful and full of
promise, especially at only £4 a bottle.

1993 Palacio de la Vega Cabernet/Tempranillo, Navarra
££ / MB / ▮   15/20
This Cabernet/Tempranillo business is obviously habit-forming. Another
modern Navarra blend with the emphasis on juicy, vibrantly fruity,
cassis and blackberry flavours.

1992 Palacio de la Vega Crianza, Navarra
£££ / MB / ▮   16/20
A similar wine to the above but with the benefit of a year's oak ageing.

It's a sweetly succulent version in which the Cabernet Sauvignon character is nicely accentuated on the palate, and the fruit enhanced by spicy vanilla oakiness.

UNITED STATES

1993 The Monterey Vineyard Pinot Noir
££ / MB / ♪   14/20
From another of Oddbins' owner Seagram's California wineries, this is a jammy but honest Pinot Noir rounded out with a touch of oak and offering a good value alternative to red Burgundy at under £5.

£5-8

AUSTRALIA

1992 Leasingham Shiraz, Clare Valley, South Australia
££ / MB / ♪   15/20
A fleshy, blackberry and eucalyptus-like, spicy Shiraz with medium-weight tannins, plenty of supple fruit and well-judged oak influence.

1993 Saltram Mamre Brook Cabernet Sauvignon, South East Australia
££ / MB / ⊷   15/20
A blend of mainly Cabernet Sauvignon with 10 per cent Shiraz sourced from vineyards in the Barossa Valley and Langhorne Creek. Winemaker Nigel Dolan has produced an elegant, deeply coloured, cassis, mint and sweet oak flavoured red, which should continue to develop over the next couple of years.

1992 Peter Lehmann, Clancy's, Barossa Valley
£££ / FB / ⊷   16/20
From the Baron of the Barossa, Peter Lehmann, this is a typically heart-warming, minty blend of Cabernet Sauvignon, Cabernet Franc, Shiraz and Merlot. Lehmann pooh-poohs elegance in favour of wines with richness and density of flavour and texture.

1993 Château Reynella Basket Pressed Shiraz
££ / FB / ⌐   16/20

There's no shortage of mint and spicy coffee bean American oak on
show here. If that sounds unappealing, it shouldn't do, because there's
plenty of lush, chocolatey McLaren Vale Shiraz in the bottle too. We're
not sure what the bearded Rocky O'Callaghan, the inventor of the
original Basket Press Shiraz, thinks of the name, but we reckon he'd
happily put a few bottles of this away – probably at one sitting.

1994 Wirra Wirra Grenache/Shiraz, McLaren Vale
£££ / MB / ⌐   17/20

**An exceptional blend of Grenache and Shiraz from McLaren Vale
winemaker Ben Riggs. Like nearly all Wirra Wirra's red wines,
this is rich, supple, concentrated and beautifully judged, with
Ovaltine and savoury fruitiness balanced by the judicious use of
oak.**

FRANCE

1993 Côtes du Rhône, Arbousières, Domaine Réméjeanne
££ / FB / ⌐   15/20

A headily spicy, modern red made from old bush vine Grenache in a
ripe, alcoholic, almost Australian style.

1993 Cairanne Côtes du Rhône Villages, Richaud
££ / FB / ⌐   16/20

A wilder, more unruly wine with funky, richly textured flavours of
pepper, spice and strawberry fruit. When a Côtes du Rhône Villages is
this good, it's worth shelling out £6.50 on a bottle.

1993 Mas Cal Demoura, Coteaux du Languedoc
££ / FB / ⌐   16/20

Made by the talented Olivier Jullien, this is a super-ripe, superconcentrated, typical Mediterranean blend with aromas of demerara
sugar and *garrigue* spice and a sweetly fruity mid-palate richness.

1993 Château de Lascaux, Les Nobles Pierres, Pic St-Loup
££ / FB / ⌐   16/20

Spicy, oaky, gingery red from one of the Languedoc's finest and smallest wine areas. It's a concentrated, but extremely fresh red with plenty of character, colour and flavour.

1993 Côtes du Rhône Les Genevrières, Domaine Réméjeanne
££ / FB / ➴   16/20

A richly coloured, densely packed Grenache-led red with pepper, spice and robust tannins. It has the hallmarks of a good Châteauneuf-du-Pape – without the price tag.

1993 Château La Cardonne, Cru Bourgeois
££ / MB / ♪   16/20

From a large property in Bordeaux's Haut-Médoc, this is a well-made, softly fruity, green pepper influenced claret with remarkable concentration of fruit, given the somewhat watery harvest conditions. Perhaps Kevin Costner was involved in the production. On second thoughts, if he had been, the wine would have gone vastly over budget.

ITALY

1993 Uva di Troia, Cantele
£££ / FB / ➴   16/20

Made by Kym Milne at Augusto Càntele's Puglian winery, this is an oak-aged, sweetly pruney dry red produced from the local Uva di Troia variety. It's a tarry, tannic, but attractively fruity style which gets the best out of one of Italy's array of indigenous grapes.

SPAIN

1992 Palacio de la Vega Merlot, Navarra
£££ / MB / ♪   16/20

Aged in French oak, this is a modern, well-balanced Navarra red from one of the best producers in the region. It's got plenty of fresh acidity and green pepper fruitiness to balance the vanilla spiciness.

UNITED STATES

1993 Franciscan Pinnacles Pinot Noir, Monterey
££ / MB / ♪   16/20

A smokily aromatic, well-priced, raspberryish Pinot Noir from a cool area of California's central coast which is gaining a deserved reputation for elegant Pinot Noir and Chardonnay.

1993 Ravenswood Zinfandel, Sonoma
£££ / FB / ⊷   16/20

A big, plummy, tobaccoey, concentrated Zinfandel, sporting 14.5 per cent alcohol and lashings of full-flavoured American oak. When Zinfandel is as good as this, it's one of the world's most individual and attractive styles.

1991 Sterling DMR Cabernet, Napa Valley
££ / MB / ⊷   16/20

DMR stands for Diamond Mountain Ranch, in case you're an acronym freak. This Seagram-owned property has produced a pungently perfumed, typical Napa Valley mountain Bordeaux-style red with concentration and elegance in equal proportions.

Over £8

AUSTRALIA

1993 Rothbury Estate Reserve Shiraz, South East Australia
0 / FB / ⊷   14/20

Made by Keith Tulloch at one of the best-known wineries in the Hunter Valley, this is an unsubtle, massively oaky Shiraz with dry, extracted tannins, and an over-inflated price tag. It may improve with age but we wouldn't want to bet on it.

1993 Baileys 1920 Block Series Shiraz, Victoria
££ / FB / ⊷   16/20

A massively flavoured, ripely textured, peppery northeastern Victorian Shiraz from Glenrowan with a little (but not a huge amount) more subtlety than the styles produced in the Barossa Valley. So strapping it could almost be a Port.

1992 Ebenezer Malbec/Merlot/Cabernet, Barossa Valley
££ / FB / ⊷   16/20

There's nothing mean-spirited about this minty, youthful Bordeaux-style blend, which bears about as much resemblance to a claret as Jackie Collins does to Charles Dickens. Sweetly oaked and liquoricey with plenty of fine-grained tannins.

1993 Wirra Wirra The Angelus Cabernet Sauvignon, McLaren Vale
£££ / MB / ╰─   17/20

We haven't had a single disappointing wine yet from Wirra Wirra, McLaren Vale's outstanding winery. This supple, beautifully balanced Cabernet Sauvignon, which is named after the Wirra Wirra alarm system, is well up to standard. Where many Australian reds hit you over the head, this one takes you by the hand and leads you seductively to the dinner table.

1991 Lindemans Limestone Ridge Shiraz/Cabernet, Coonawarra
££ / MB / ╰─   16/20

Made by the cuddly Greg Clayfield, who assures us that there aren't many roots to be found in Coonawarra, this is one of a well-established trio of premium Lindemans reds. With pronounced American oak and blackberry fruit sweetness, it's a softly tannic, youthful blend which will ease comfortably into the next century.

1993 Stoniers Reserve Pinot Noir, Mornington Peninsula, Victoria
££ / MB / ▮   16/20

The cool, windswept Mornington Peninsula can produce some of the most elegant, Burgundian-style wines in Australia. This complex, aromatic, oak-matured Pinot Noir, made by Todd Dexter, is a good illustration. Available in Oddbins Fine Wine stores only.

FRANCE

1992 Cairanne, Côtes du Rhône Villages, L'Ebrescade, Richaud
£ / FB / ▮   16/20

This is aromatic and heftily extracted, but £8.50's pushing it a bit. That's enough Côtes du Rhône.

1993 Marsannay, Louis Trapet
£ / MB / ▮   15/20

Farmyardy, foursquare Pinot Noir without much in the way of style or supple fruit. Less tannic than some 1993s, but still on the dour side.

1993 Gevrey-Chambertin, Louis Trapet
£ / MB / ♪   15/20

From the same producer, this is a charry, extracted, rather oaky Côte de
Nuits village Pinot, which lacks the charm and subtlety we expect from
red Burgundy with the supposed class of Gevrey.

ITALY

1992 Lamaione Merlot, Frescobaldi, Vino da Tavola dei Colli della Toscana
£ / FB / ➤   15/20

A deeply coloured, bitter chocolate and tobacco style Merlot from
aristocratic producer Frescobaldi. With its chunky tannins, this is a
distinctively Italian style. Come back in five years' time.

1990 Sulbric, Azienda San Martino, Piemonte
££ / FB / ➤   16/20

A new-fangled Piedmontese blend of Nebbiolo and Barbera aged in new
oak barriques to push the price skywards. Shame about the £23 price
tag, because this is a soft, leathery, complex red with an attractively
untamed dimension. In Oddbins Fine Wine stores only.

UNITED STATES

1992 Ridge Santa Cruz Cabernet
£££ / FB / ➤   17/20

Made by goatee-bearded Paul Draper from declassified
Montebello Cabernet Sauvignon and 12 per cent Merlot, this is a
dense but supple Santa Cruz mountain red, with the mellow
elegance and fine-grained tannins which are the hallmark of
Ridge wines.

1992 Flora Springs Trilogy
£££ / MB / ➤   17/20

Trilogy is a Bordeaux blend of Cabernet Sauvignon, Merlot and
Cabernet Franc, and an example of what are known as Meritage
wines in California. This awkward term was coined because
producers of Bordeaux-style blends were legally prevented from
using the names of more than two grape varieties on the label. We

think this is the best Meritage red we've had yet – rich and claret-like with plenty of new oak and tobaccoey fruitiness backed up by substantial tannins.

1993 Edmunds St John Mourvèdre
££ / MB / 🍷   **16/20**
Made by Steve Edmunds, the original California Rhône Ranger, this is a fresh, peppery, Zinfandel-like red, produced from old Mourvèdre plantings. Available in Oddbins Fine Wine stores only.

Sparkling

Over £8

AUSTRALIA

1992 Croser Brut
£££ / 2 / 🍷   **16/20**
Modestly named after the man who made it, Brian Croser's Adelaide Hills fizz is an intensely lemony, weighty blend of Pinot Noir and 30 per cent Chardonnay with an idiosyncratic, almost savoury, smoky bacon note. It's one of Australia's classiest sparkling wines – just as well Mr Croser didn't call it Brian.

FRANCE

Champagne H Blin
££ / 2 / 🍷   **15/20**
A regular listing at Oddbins, this co-operative Champagne is a pleasantly biscuity, youthful fizz with good Pinot Noir fruitiness at an attractive price.

Heidsieck Dry Monopole Brut
£££ / 2 / 🍷   **16/20**
A considerable improvement on recent Monopole releases, this nicely balanced, broadly flavoured fizz tastes as if it has had a proportion of reserve wine added for a bit of toasty complexity. Little wonder that this

makes it into Oddbins' top ten best-selling wines. We hope that this new standard is maintained.

Perrier Jouët Grand Brut
£ / 2 / ♪   14/20
A more youthful Chardonnay-dominated style lacking the reserve wine richness of the Monopole and with little in the way of the expected yeast development either on nose or palate.

NEW ZEALAND

Deutz Marlborough Cuvée
£££ / 2 / ♪   16/20
A fine, elegantly crafted blend of Pinot Noir and Chardonnay made in New Zealand using the southern hemisphere's only Coquard Champagne press. The result of a fruitful partnership between Champagne house Deutz and New Zealand's Montana, Marlborough Cuvée has established itself as a complex, dry fizz of considerable tangy complexity.

UNITED STATES

Mumm Cuvée Napa
£ / 3 / ♪   14/20
Creamy, toasty and rather coarse California fizz from under-achieving Champagne house Mumm's Napa Valley outpost, with added sherbety sweetness to mask the wine's tangy acidity. We preferred last year's cuvée.

Mumm Cuvée Napa Rosé
££ / 3 / ♪   15/20
An improvement on the straight Cuvée Napa, this bronze-pink Napa Valley fizz is crisper and better-proportioned with its zesty strawberry flavour and aniseedy note.

SAFEWAY ***

Head Office: Safeway Stores plc, Safeway House, 6 Millington Road, Hayes, Middlesex UB3 4AY

Telephone: 0181 848 8744

Number of branches: 360

Credit cards accepted: Visa, Access, Delta, Switch

Hours of opening: Monday to Saturday 8.00am to 8.00pm; Sunday 10.00am to 4.00pm

By-the-case sales: A 5 per cent discount is given on any purchase of 12 bottles or more of wines costing at least £2.99 a bottle. This discount applies even when a wine is on promotion

Glass loan: Free in selected stores

Home delivery: No

Clubs: No

Discounts: May Wine Fair, selection of price promotions every week including Multisaves and Linksaves

In-store tastings: Occasionally

Top ten best-selling wines: Safeway Romanian Pinot Noir; Safeway Soave White; Safeway Hock; Safeway Bereich Nierstein; Safeway Liebfraumilch; Valhondo Country White; Quagga White; Safeway Lambrusco Bianco; Safeway Corbières Red; Safeway Claret

Range: GOOD: Eastern Europe, regional France, Italy, Spain, Australia, England, organic wines
AVERAGE: New Zealand, Chile, South Africa, Portugal, California, Burgundy, Bordeaux
POOR: Germany

Were we being a little uncharitable to the Green and English lobbies when we suggested last year that Safeway might spend a little less time on curiosities and a little more on up-and-coming regions? If so, Safeway itself seems to have heeded our advice.

While it still sponsors the annual Organic Fair, Safeway has scaled down its organic wine contingent from 17 to a dozen. The brave attempt to sell regional English wines from local stores has also collided with economic reality, as a result of which they too have been pruned back to fewer than a dozen.

By contrast, the up-and-coming regions are doing well. 'Sales of New World wines have galloped so fast that, if you take out our £1.99 promotions, they are not that far from an even split with the Old World,' says Lancastrian Master of Wine Liz Robertson. Given that Sainsbury's is nudging the 10 per cent mark and Tesco 20 per cent in the New World, the achievement is all the more impressive.

Safeway's New World launchpad was originally underpinned by Australia and New Zealand. But with prices in the South Pacific rising, the rest of the southern hemisphere could be set to take over. Brandishing value-for-money whites and the Springbok-inspiring, Mandela seal of approval, South Africa has forced its way rapidly into shopping trolleys as the best-selling New World wine country at Safeway.

After a trip to South America, Robertson is confident that this huge continent is a massive source of 'excitement and interest'. With prices to back it up, we would add. Chile has already established itself, and she believes that Argentina, very much the stubbly gaucho of the New World, is poised to ride to the front of the posse.

'The Old World is going to have to wake up extra fast,' says Robertson, who singles out Bordeaux as a region Safeway has sacrificed at the expense of Burgundy and the South of France. Even in the *terra cognita* of the Old World, the Safeway team are on the lookout for more modern, fruitier New World-influenced styles, especially from promising areas such as the South of France and southern Italy.

We thought Burgundy last year was a bit of a yawn. But Safeway has planted a smacker on Sleeping Beauty's lips, taking advantage of the fact that in almost every vintage since 1990, nature has been kinder to Burgundy than Bordeaux. The new list skirts the temptation to stock the cheapest *négociant* wines and contains a healthy mix of whites and reds from the likes of the Buxy co-operative, and the merchant Faiveley, as well as a handful of exciting domaines.

The pioneering work in Eastern Europe continues, with a little help from those airmiles specialists, Australia's Kym Milne and Nick Butler. Robertson does not subscribe to the school of thought which derides flying winemakers for reducing wines to the lowest common denominator. 'As long as they are doctoring and tending to awfulness, long may they reign.'

If there has been a switch of emphasis at Safeway over the past year or so, it has been away from the fun of buying wines towards the grubbier business of selling them. In response to market research, which indicated that Safeway was popular with the under-thirties and over-fifties, TV ads hit the screens, designed to lure the baby boomers and to show that Safeway was as competitive on price as its high street rivals.

Building on the success of its Spring Wine Fair, Safeway now holds a second Wine Fair in the autumn, with the emphasis on the New World. All well and good if the Wine Fair offers variety, novelty and value, but with only 11 out of 31 wines over £3, we felt there was a bit too much concentration on price, especially for a wine department with a reputation for innovation.

Likewise, the £1.99 promotions may help tackle public perceptions of Safeway as expensive, but Robertson does not disguise her dislike of the £1.99 wine. 'It clogs up the system. Stores are put through it just to service big lumps of stock for no money.' Multisaves seem to be a more effective form of promotion in that they actually encourage customers to drink better quality wines.

At the opposite end of the range, the fine wine racks have gone, although Robertson likes to see some expensive wines on the shelves, even if customers don't buy them. 'It gives customers confidence, even if it is beyond their price range. Wine sales are central to how people feel about us. There's a feeling of quality about Safeway.'

New this year is the Safeway vintage statement – the label bearing the vintage date. The fact that not all wines bear a vintage date allows less than scrupulous producers the opportunity to blend in surplus stocks from older vintages. 'There are inevitably differences in wines and it can be convenient for suppliers to put in bigger amounts of older vintages than they should.' Policing the supplier in this way gives customers more information and a guarantee (of sorts) that the wine is as fresh as possible.

Has Safeway become a little more cautious over the past year? We certainly feel so. The overall standard of the basic range is good, but some of the wilder, more interesting fringes have been trimmed. And with Australia producing relatively expensive wines, the focus on less expensive southern hemisphere wines suggests a knowing move downmarket. Innovation in a cut-throat high street isn't getting any easier.

White

Under £3

BULGARIA

1994 Chardonnay/Sauvignon, Preslav, Bulgaria
££ / 3 / ∤   14/20
An unusual combination of grape varieties allied to a touch of oak character has made this New World-influenced wine one of the more acceptable Bulgarian whites on the market.

FRANCE

1994 Safeway Vin de Pays de Vaucluse
£ / 2 / ∤   13/20
A rich pear, clove and ginger-flavoured dry white from the South of France. Soft and low in acidity.

1994 Blaye Blanc
0 / 2 / ∤   9/20
The kind of wine Bordeaux used to make. Fortunately, most people have moved on to more modern things than this woolly, oversulphured blend.

GERMANY

1994 Safeway Hock
0 / 5 / ∤   10/20
Oversulphured, stale sugar water. A wine that can only sell on price alone.

1994 Safeway Liebfraumilch
0 / 6 / ½   11/20

Just as much sulphur, but a bit more fruit. Or was it sugar?

ITALY

Safeway Lambrusco Bianco
0 / 6 / ½   11/20

Frothy, alcoholic lemonade substitute. Viva Italia.

SOUTH AFRICA

Quagga Colombard/Chardonnay, Western Cape
£ / 3 / ½   13/20

The most interesting thing about this neutral blend of South African
Colombard and Chardonnay is its Australian-sounding name. A quagga,
in case you didn't know, is an extinct half-zebra with a stripey bum,
according to those who've seen the pictures.

£3–5

AUSTRALIA

1994 Safeway Semillon/Chardonnay, South East Australia
£££ / 3 / ½   15/20

Made by Australia's largest wine company, Penfolds, this fresh, ripe,
exotically flavoured white is quite restrained by Australian standards.
Pleasant and easy-drinking.

1993 Hardy's RR Medium Dry White
£ / 5 / ½   13/20

RR stands for Rhine Riesling, the grape variety that prefers to whisper
rather than speak its name. Sweet, oily but full of lemon and marmalade
flavour.

BULGARIA

1994 Rikat, Rousse, Bulgaria
£ / 3 / ▮   13/20

Rikat is a clever abbreviation of the almost unpronounceable Rkatsiteli, one of Eastern Europe's native white grape varieties. This is a fragrant Muscat-style white with a touch of sweetness.

FRANCE

1994 La Coume de Peyre, Vin de Pays des Côtes de Gascogne
0 / 2 / ▮   12/20

Dilute, faintly musty Gascon white from the Plaimont co-operative, with some baked apple fruitiness.

1994 Safeway Bergerac Sauvignon
££ / 1 / ▮   14/20

Clean, crisp, bone-dry nettley Sauvignon Blanc from the Sigoules co-operative in southwestern France.

1994 Sauvignon Blanc, Vin de Pays d'Oc
0 / 2 / ▮   12/20

Made in the Roussillon region of southern France by the large Vignerons Catalans group, this is a fattish, basic white with barely detectable Sauvignon Blanc character.

1994 Safeway Côtes du Lubéron
0 / 2 / ▮   12/20

A bizarre set of aromas on show here, which reminded us of celery and cooking apples. Heavy, fruitless and old-fashioned stuff.

1994 Chardonnay, Vin de Pays du Jardin de la France
£ / 3 / ▮   13/20

Made by the Loire's Donatien Bahuaud winery, this crisp, commercial Chardonnay is a sweetish attempt at a Chablis style. Decent value at just over £3.

1994 Safeway Blanc de Bordeaux, Oak-aged
£££ / 2 / 🍷   16/20

Bordeaux merchants Prodiffu have come up with a real star here. Despite its humble *appellation*, this basic oak-aged Bordeaux with its zesty Sauvignon Blanc fruit reminded us of a fresh, toasty white Graves.

1994 Laperouse, Vin de Pays d'Oc
££ / 2 / 🍷   15/20

The offspring of a joint venture between Penfolds of Australia and France's largest wine company, Val d'Orbieu, this unoaked blend of Chardonnay, Marsanne, Grenache and Colombard is like fresh pears spiced with aniseed. A very promising start.

1994 Domaine Vieux Manoir de Maransan, Côtes du Rhône Blanc
£££ / 2 / 🍷   15/20

A highly successful, well-priced southern Rhône white with flavours of toast and ginger spice and far more fresh fruitiness than you usually find in a white Côtes du Rhône. Perhaps Australian Nick Butler's influence had something to do with it.

GERMANY

1992 Ruppertsberger Nussbein Riesling Kabinett, Pfalz
£££ / 4 / 🍷   16/20

There are so many words on this label that most consumers wouldn't know where to start. Our advice is to ignore the verbiage and acquaint yourself with the contents of the bottle – complex, minerally, lime-like Pfalz Riesling at a bargain price.

HUNGARY

1994 Matra Mountains Oaked Chardonnay, Nagyrede
£ / 3 / 🍷   13/20

From the normally reliable Australian flying winemaker Kym Milne, this greenish, oaky Chardonnay is probably more a reflection of a wet vintage than its producer.

1994 Chapel Hill Barrique-fermented Chardonnay, Balatonboglar
££ / 2 / ▮   15/20
Same winemaker, same vintage, but a more satisfactory result, partly, we suspect, because of the difference in location, and partly because of fermentation in oak barrels, giving this citrus-like Chardonnay better integrated oak flavours.

ITALY

1994 Safeway Pinot Grigio del Triveneto
££ / 2 / ▮   14/20
Not untypically neutral on the nose (the Italians are a bit suspicious of too much character in their white wines), this is an attractively put together greengage and ginger-flavoured dry Pinot Grigio from Italy's northeast.

1994 Safeway Chardonnay del Triveneto
££ / 2 / ▮   14/20
It's good to see well-made, unoaked Chardonnay in the high street. This is buttery and savoury with an almost yeasty character and a penetrating, crisp finish.

1994 Safeway Frascati Superiore Secco
£ / 2 / ▮   13/20
Soft, innocuous, baked Roman white with a bit of spritz. We felt the wine could have done with a bit more oomph.

1994 Grave del Friuli Pinot Grigio
££ / 2 / ▮   15/20
Made by Chilean-based French winemaker Gaetane Carron, this is a highly modern, cinnamon and banana-like, refreshing dry white from Italy's northeastern corner.

1994 'I Frari', Bianco di Custoza
£££ / 2 / ▮   15/20
In its imposing, heavyweight bottle, this green olive and angelica spicy Lake Garda white outperforms its modest price tag with style.

PORTUGAL

1994 Bright Brothers Fernão Pires/Chardonnay, Ribatejo
£££ / 2 / ¼   15/20

The Fernão Pires grape variety is one of the most interesting of an impressive array of indigenous grapes. Australia's Peter Bright has done a great deal to popularise this undervalued variety. Here he combines it nicely with the internationally acclaimed Chardonnay grape, adding a touch of oak to create an intensely flavoured dry white with a note of orange peel zest.

UNITED STATES

1993 Stoney Brook Chardonnay, California
££ / 3 / ¼   15/20

Lifestyle specialists Fetzer have done a lot to make California wine affordable in the UK. This modern, coconut-sweet white is a dangerously drinkable drop at under £5. Perhaps it should come with a warning label. It certainly does in the US.

£5–8

AUSTRALIA

1994 Hunter Valley Chardonnay, Rosemount Estates
£££ / 2 / ¼   16/20

The big exotic style of Hunter Valley Chardonnay is what converted a new generation of drinkers to Australian wine. This typically brash example from the pioneering Rosemount operation is chock full of honeydew melon and pineapple flavours topped with a serving of vanilla fudge. Ben and Jerry's couldn't do better.

1993 Hardy's Barossa Valley Chardonnay
£ / 2 / ¼   14/20

Like the Hunter Valley Chardonnay, but with knobs on. We found this a little too much of a good thing for our sensitive, retiring palates.

FRANCE

1993 Domaine de Rivoyre Chardonnay, Vin de Pays d'Oc
££ / 2 / ▮   15/20

We found this a little fuller than the excellent 1992, but Hugh 'Guru' Ryman has once again produced one of the best value Chardonnays in the South of France. The wine combines the ripe, tropical fruit of the New World with some well-judged French elegance.

1994 Gewürztraminer d'Alsace, Turckheim
££ / 2 / ▮   16/20

If you've ever wanted to know why Alsace tastes of lychees and rose petals, stick this floral bouquet under your nose and arrange accordingly. Rich, floral and spicy with good balancing acidity.

1994 Montagny Premier Cru, Cave de Buxy
££ / 2 / ▮   15/20

The 1994 vintage in Burgundy produced more voluptuous wines than the rather austere 1993 crop. This Côte Chalonnaise from the well-respected Buxy co-operative is full and attractive with plenty of characteristic spiciness.

NEW ZEALAND

1994 Private Bin, Villa Maria Sauvignon Blanc, Marlborough
££ / 2 / ▮   15/20

In price and style, this is halfway between Montana Sauvignon Blanc and the more exalted wines of Cloudy Bay and Jackson Estate. Refreshing, dry, zesty Sauvignon Blanc with plenty of elderflower cattiness.

1994 The Millton Vineyard Barrel-Fermented Chardonnay
££ / 2 / ▮   16/20

Organic farmer James Millton has declined to claim organic status for this barrel-fermented Gisborne white – presumably the elements defeated him in 1994. But otherwise it's well up to Millton's usual high standards, with elements of honeyed botrytis balanced by a Chablis-like acidity.

Over £8

FRANCE

1993 Mercurey, Les Mauvarennes
££ / 2 / ▮   16/20
Domaine Faiveley is one of the largest and most influential vineyard
owners in Burgundy. This beautifully balanced, spicy and citrusy Côte
Chalonnaise Chardonnay, one of the finest we've tasted from the 1993
vintage, comes from one of François Faiveley's best vineyards.

Red

Under £3

BULGARIA

1994 Safeway Young Vatted Merlot, Rousse
££ / MB / ▮   14/20
Originally conceived as what Australians call fruit-driven wine, the latest
vintage of Safeway's Bulgarian red has mysteriously picked up some oak
character along the way. Not that it detracts from the quality of the wine.
It's just that readers who've gone for the up-front fruity style may find
this oaky, almost claret-like red rather different

Safeway Bulgarian Country Wine, Pinot/Merlot, Sliven
££ / MB / ▮   13/20
A chunky, rustic, raisiny blend of Pinot Noir and Merlot, showing little
of either grape's soft fruitiness but plenty of dry tannins.

1991 Vinenka Merlot/Gamza Reserve, Suhindol
££ / MB / ▮   13/20
Sweet, sawdusty, blackcurrant pastille style fruit with plenty of colour
and fresh acidity make this a good value Bulgarian red.

1990 Cabernet Sauvignon Reserve, Sliven
0 / MB / 🌓   12/20

Dry, rooty, sawdusty red with insufficient charm to woo these two British palates.

1990 Cabernet Sauvignon Special Reserve, Suhindol
£ / MB / 🌓   13/20

By appointment to King Simeon II of Bulgaria no less, this is dry, old-fashioned, oaky red. If we were royalty, we'd be drinking something a little more exciting than this.

FRANCE

1994 Safeway Vin de Pays de l'Ardèche
£ / MB / 🌓   13/20

Light, modern, carbonic maceration-style red from the South of France. Preferable to a lot of cheap Beaujolais.

Safeway Corbières
£ / FB / 🌓   13/20

A faint whiff of the Mediterranean *garrigue* here, but we found the wine rather too dry and tannic for our liking.

Safeway Minervois
££ / FB / 🌓   14/20

Our sample of this wine was slightly marred by a touch of eggy hydrogen sulphide, but we felt the underlying wine, with its angostura bitters character, was fundamentally sound. If yours suffers a bit on the nose, drop a clean copper penny in the glass, swirl, and remember to remove before drinking.

Safeway Côtes du Roussillon Villages
0 / FB / 🌓   12/20

Dry and rather chunky southern French plonk with more tannin than fruit.

ITALY

Safeway Lambrusco Rosso
£ / MB / ∤   12/20

If you insist on drinking a sweet Lambrusco, this frothy, plumskin-scented fizz is marginally the best of the three on offer at Safeway.

1994 Tenuta Generale Cialdini Lambrusco Secco
££ / MB / ∤   15/20

Far better in our opinion to invest an extra 30 pence in this more grown-up, peppery, drier style, which, unlike the sweet versions, you can drink with food.

Safeway Sicilian Red
££ / FB / ∤   14/20

Fresh, aromatic, savoury, chocolatey red with plenty of Mediterranean spiciness and lively bite.

MOROCCO

Domaine Sapt Innour NV, Morocco
0 / FB / ∤   10/20

Old-fashioned, cooked North African red drunk on Foreign Legion picnics. No wonder the French left them to it.

£3–5

AUSTRALIA

1994 De Bortoli Shiraz/ Cabernet
££ / MB / ∤   14/20

Pleasantly elegant, minty Australian blend from New South Wales for people who find Australian reds rather too exuberant.

1994 Hardy's Stamp Shiraz/Cabernet
£ / MB / ∤   13/20

Sweet caramel oak and one-dimensional fruit. Fine if you like this sort of thing, but a bit on the obvious side.

1993 Penfolds Rawsons Retreat Bin 35
££ / MB / 🍷   15/20
In typical Penfolds mould, this Cabernet Sauvignon/Shiraz blend has
masses of sweet plum and blackberry fruit overlaid by a forest of spicy
American oak. But don't tell Greenpeace.

FRANCE

1994 Safeway Côtes du Rhône
£ / LB / 🍷   13/20
Light, juicy Côtes du Rhône with a hint of pepper.

1994 Safeway Côtes du Ventoux
££ / MB / 🍷   14/20
Made by Kiwi Mark Robertson, a pleasantly floral red with some
raspberryish fruit and good robust grip.

1994 Safeway Bergerac
££ / MB / 🍷   14/20
Attractive, easy-drinking claret-style red with fresh, grassy fruit that
reminded me of a Loire Cabernet Franc.

Safeway Claret, Bordeaux
£ / MB / 🍷   13/20
Meaty, concentrated red Bordeaux with green-edged acidity. Badly
needs food, but then don't we all.

1993 'Gabriel Corcol' St-Emilion
££ / MB / 🍷   14/20
It's rare to find St-Emilion under £5 these days, so this soft, oaky,
chocolatey, Merlot-based red is a good buy.

1993 Médoc, Oak-aged
££ / MB / 🍷   15/20
Lively, modern, well-made claret with attractively integrated oakiness
and a hint of green pepper, presumably from the Cabernet Sauvignon.

1993 Fortant de France Cabernet Sauvignon, Vin de Pays d'Oc
£ / MB / 🍾   13/20

For a wine from the warm South of France, this dry, if well-made, Cabernet Sauvignon could do with a tad more sweetness and concentration of fruit.

1993 Château La Tour de Beraud, Costières de Nîmes
£££ / MB / 🍾   15/20

A thrilling Syrah-based red from bull-fighting country in the South of France. Supple, aromatic and deliciously succulent, this wine reminded us of a good northern Rhône red.

1993 Domaine Rochevue, Minervois
£££ / FB / 🍾   16/20

Warm, spicy, chunky Languedoc red with oodles of the black olive and angostura spice of the *garrigue* poking through. A good substitute for central heating. Thanks to Cedric Brown, it's certainly cheaper.

ITALY

1993 Montepulciano d'Abruzzo, Cantina Miglianico
£££ / FB / 🍾   15/20

Vibrantly coloured ruby-purple rosso in the modern style, with lots of fresh acidity, medium-weight tannins and plummy fruit.

1993 Safeway Chianti Classico, Rocca delle Macie
££ / FB / 🍾   14/20

One of the most reliable names in Chianti, Rocca delle Macie makes wines that are difficult to get worked up about, one way or the other. Pleasantly savoury Sangiovese with a welcome touch of astringency.

1992 Safeway Casa di Giovanni, Vino da Tavola di Sicilia
£ / FB / 🍾   13/20

We're still trying to find out who Giovanni is. Mind you, after tasting this leathery, pruney, old-fashioned southern Italian red, we're beginning to have second thoughts.

PORTUGAL

1992 Vinho do Monte, Alentejo
££ / FB / 🏃   15/20

Made by Sogrape, the company which brought you Mateús Rosé, this is an excellent, plummy southern Portuguese red made from a trio of obscure indigenous grape varieties, namely João Santarem, Moreto and Alfrocheiro.

ROMANIA

1987 Safeway Romanian Cabernet Sauvignon Special Reserve
££ / MB / 🏃   14/20

Soft, minty, old-fashioned Cabernet Sauvignon from one of the few decent wineries we've come across in Romania.

1990 Safeway Romanian Pinot Noir Special Reserve, Dealul Mare
£ / LB / 🏃   13/20

Nicolae Dumitru, who's been beavering away at the Dealul Mare installation for the last 40-odd years, would like it known that he doesn't make most of the wine we see from Romania in this country. This old-fashioned, tomatoey Pinot Noir, which buyer Liz Robertson describes as a 'big furry animal', sells like videos of Ceaucescu's last moments.

SPAIN

1992 Safeway Castilla de Sierra, Rioja Crianza
££ / MB / 🏃   14/20

The garish yellow label failed to put us off this supple, mature, vanilla-scented Rioja. Old-fashioned Rioja with a degree of charm.

1990 Agramont Tempranillo/Cabernet, Navarra
££ / FB / ☛   15/20

The wines from Agramont in Navarra are getting better and better, and this chunky, modern blend of native Tempranillo and Cabernet Sauvignon from Bordeaux, topped off with lashings of spicy American oak, is one of the best Navarra reds at under £5.

1993 Berberana Tempranillo, Rioja
££ / MB / 🍾   15/20

Like the 1992, this 100 per cent Tempranillo combines the best of modern and traditional Rioja with well-judged oak and strawberry fruit, and the emphasis is on time in bottle, rather than years in old oak barrels.

1991 Cosme Palacio y Hermanos, Rioja
£££ / MB / 🍾   16/20

Similar to the Berberana Tempranillo, but showing an extra dimension of concentration of succulent fruit. Intensely flavoured, sweet chocolate and vanilla Rioja at its modern best.

UNITED STATES

1992 Stoney Brook Cabernet Sauvignon, California
££ / MB / 🍾   15/20

Californian winery Fetzer is determined to prove that the West Coast can produce drinkable wine at under £5. This minty, modern, sweetly oaked Cabernet does the job.

£5–8

AUSTRALIA

1993 Hardy's Barossa Valley Shiraz
£££ / FB / 🍾   16/20

A savoury, spicy, lavishly oaked Shiraz from South Australia's Barossa Valley. Like the 1992 vintage, it's a wine whose thick, robust flavours should grab you by the short and curlies.

1993 Wolf Blass Yellow Label Cabernet Sauvignon
££ / FB / 🍾   15/20

Wolf Blass is one of Australia's great showmen, producing wines which are impossible to dislike. They may be soft and commercial, but covering every square inch of the palate is what's made Australian reds so popular in this country. This oaky, eucalyptus and chocolate flavoured Cabernet is essence of Blass – give or take the bow tie.

1993 Penfolds Organic Cabernet/Merlot, Clare Valley
£££ / MB / ⌡   16/20
The follow-up release to Penfolds' successful, elegantly flavoured
organic white wine, this is a similarly subtle, attractive and
encouragingly restrained blend of Cabernet Sauvignon, Merlot, Petit
Verdot and Shiraz.

FRANCE

1993 Domaine La Tuque Bel-Air, Côtes de Castillon
££ / MB / ⌡   15/20
Succulent, aromatic Merlot-based claret from the eastern hills of
Bordeaux, close to its border with Bergerac.

1992s Safeway Château Canteloup, Cru Bourgeois, Médoc
£ / MB / ⌡   14/20
Not, as the name might suggest, a melon, but a modern, oaky medium-
weight claret from the Médoc. Like many 1992s, it's one to drink sooner
rather than later.

1993 La Cuvée Mythique, Vin de Pays d'Oc
££ / FB / ⌡   16/20
A southern French blend of Syrah, Mourvèdre, Carignan, Grenache and
Cabernet Sauvignon made from old vines by the go-ahead Val d'Orbieu
co-operative. This dense, oaky, complex red wine is oenologist Marc
Dubernet's homage to the Mediterranean's viticultural traditions.

1994 Regnié, Duboeuf
££ / MB / ⌡   16/20
At last! A Beaujolais that actually tastes of the Gamay grape. From King
of the Beaujolais Georges Duboeuf, this juicy raspberry-fruit red from the
Beaujolais cru of Regnié is a crowning achievement.

ITALY

1990 Barolo, Terre del Barolo
££ / FB / ►   15/20
It's quite something to unearth a Barolo under £7, never mind one from
the excellent 1990 vintage. The Terre del Barolo co-operative has

produced a leathery, truffley, mature Barolo with plenty of characteristically dry tannins to sink your teeth into.

PORTUGAL

1991 Duque de Viseu, Dão

££ / FB / **15/20**

From leading Portuguese producer Sogrape, this is a spicy, tobaccoey, encouragingly modern Dão region red with just enough chunkily Portuguese tannins to preserve its local character.

SOUTH AFRICA

1993 Kanonkop Kadette, Stellenbosch

££ / FB / **15/20**

A blend of South Africa's indigenous Pinotage and international superstar Cabernet Sauvignon, made by red wine specialist Beyers Truter, this is a deeply coloured, modern, oaky Cape number with the capacity to age.

SPAIN

1991 Viña Albali Cabernet Sauvignon, Valdepeñas

££ / FB / **15/20**

As far as we're aware, this is the first sighting of a Cabernet Sauvignon in eastern Spain's Valdepeñas region. It certainly represents an attempt by Viña Albali to produce a more international style of red. The wine's succulent, chocolatey, oaky ripeness suggests promise for the future.

Over £8

FRANCE

1992 Margaux, Barton & Guestier

£ / MB / **15/20**

A French wine which seems to have taken Australia's red wine styles to heart with a modern whack of coffee bean oak and ripe, supple fruit. This is quite an achievement in a wet vintage like 1992.

1990 St-Julien, Barton & Guestier
££ / MB / 🍷   16/20
For the same price as the 1992 Margaux, you can buy this fuller-flavoured, more concentrated 1990 St-Julien (a far better vintage), also from négociant Barton & Guestier. We found the oak better integrated on this one.

1992 Château de Chorey, Chorey-lès-Beaune
£££ / MB / 🍷   16/20
One of a number of pricey red Burgundies taken on by Safeway this year – and in our view the pick of the bunch. From Domaine Jacques Germain, it's a highly aromatic, pure Pinot Noir with some new oak influence and plenty of chocolatey, red fruit flavours.

Rosé

Under £3

FRANCE

1994 Domaine Bergerie Rosé, Vin de Pays d'Oc
£ / 2 / 🍷   13/20
A good value, fresh strawberry-like southern French rosé from wine merchant JeanJean.

ITALY

Safeway Lambrusco Rosé
0 / 6 / 🍷   11/20
Like the Lambrusco Bianco, but pink.

£3–5

FRANCE

1994 Côtes du Lubéron Rosé
£££ / 3 / ⌁   15/20
Another boiled sweets style rosé from the southern Rhône. Flying winemaker Hugh Ryman has produced an intensely fruity, zingy, exuberant rosé with a hint of sweetness.

1994 Fortant de France, Syrah Rosé, Vin de Pays d'Oc
£ / 2 / ⌁   13/20
There's a touch of peppery Syrah character in this well-packaged rosé from pasta merchant Robert Skalli, but not enough to make the wine really exciting.

HUNGARY

1994 Safeway Cabernet Sauvignon Rosé, Nagyrede
££ / 2 / ⌁   14/20
A coolish, green pepper style rosé made at Hungary's Nagyrede co-operative by Kym Milne's protégé, pony-tailed Mike Gadd. Like a drier version of good Cabernet d'Anjou – if that's not an oxymoron.

Sparkling

Under £3

ITALY

1994 Le Monferrine, Moscato d'Asti
£££ / 5 / ⌁   15/20
Highly scented, grapey Muscat with oodles of sweet but not cloying lemon sherbet fruit.

£3–5

ITALY

Safeway Moscato Spumante
0 / 5 / 👤   13/20
Dull, anodyne fizzy Muscat with 6.5 per cent alcohol. We'd much rather drink the Monferrine, especially at the price.

Safeway Asti Spumante
0 / 6 / 👤   14/20
A sound spumante from northwestern Italy with typically grapey and honeyed sweetness and zippy, fresh acidity.

Over £8

FRANCE

Safeway Albert Etienne Brut NV
££ / 2 / 👤   15/20
Consistently one of the best own-label Champagnes on the market, the Albert Etienne accent is on youthful, soft, but refreshing flavours at a sensible price. One for the feast of Stephen.

Fortified

£3–5

FRANCE

1994 Dom Brial Muscat de Rivesaltes
0 / 7 / 👤   12/20
Rivesaltes makes some of the most aromatic and characterful fortified Muscats in France. This spirity and heavy-handed example isn't one of them.

SPAIN

Lustau Manzanilla Sherry, 37.5cl
££ / 2 / ∤   14/20
Good straight-up Manzanilla with some salty, flor-yeast derived
character. The sample we saw could have been a little fresher.

Lustau Old Amontillado Sherry, 37.5cl
££ / 1 / ∤   15/20
Also from super-blender Emilio Lustau, known in Spain as an
almacenista, this amber-coloured, toffeed, nutty dry sherry is a
reasonably priced introduction to the style.

Lustau Old Dry Oloroso Sherry, 37.5cl
££ / 3 / ∤   16/20
The best of Safeway's Lustau Sherries, showing more richness, weight
and oomph than its colleagues. A mature, golden brown fortified with
lots of burnt almond fruit and fire.

Lustau Mature Cream Sherry, 37.5cl
£ / 6 / ∤   13/20
The nose on this sweeter style of Sherry showed a worrying touch of
mushroomy mustiness, but we preferred the coffeebean and prune-like
sweetness on the palate. Just as well, really.

1994 Safeway Moscatel de Valencia
0 / 8 / ∤   11/20
A sickly cocktail of honeydew melon, orange peel and dried fruits.
Massively sweet and extremely spirity, this is more of a trifle base than a
wine.

£5–8

PORTUGAL

Safeway Ruby Port
£££ / FB / ►   16/20
From the Portuguese-owned house of Calem, this is a soft, spicy,
liquoricey fortified wine with masses of fruit and velvety richness.

Safeway Vintage Character Port
££ / FB / ⌐   15/20
Also from Calem, this is more mature and better-structured than the
Ruby, with wild, peppery flavours and plenty of bite. Would benefit
from a couple of years under the stairs.

1988 Safeway LBV
££ / FB / ⌐   15/20
From the Symington family-owned firm of Smith Woodhouse, this Late
Bottled Vintage Port is powerfully blackcurrant and liquorice flavoured,
with lots of youthful, mouth-filling succulence.

Over £8

PORTUGAL

Safeway 10 Year Old Tawny Port
£ / FB / ▮   13/20
Closer to a Ruby than a more mature Tawny in appearance, this is an
easy-drinking, raspberryish style of Port from Smith Woodhouse.

1988 Taylors LBV
££ / FB / ⌐   16/20
Taylors is one of the most revered names in the Douro Valley, and this
strappingly rich, sweet, tannic Late Bottled Vintage is well up to the
house's high standards. A bold, but almost elegant wine.

SAINSBURY'S ****

Head Office: Stamford House, Stamford Street, London SE1 9LL

Telephone: 0171 921 6000

Number of branches: 355

Credit cards accepted: Visa, Access, Switch, American Express

Hours of opening: Branch specific. Regular late night opening

By-the-case sales: Not in stores, but case offers made through *Sainsbury's The Magazine*, Sainsbury's Wine Direct and on the Internet via Sainsbury's home page

Glass loan: No

Home delivery: Through *Sainsbury's The Magazine* and Wine Direct

Clubs: Wine Direct

Discounts: Multibuy offers, special offers and special purchases

In-store tastings: Yes, on an ad hoc basis

Top ten best-selling wines: Sainsbury's Liebfraumilch; Sainsbury's Hock; Sainsbury's Niersteiner Gutes Domtal; Sainsbury's Lambrusco Bianco; Sainsbury's Muscadet de Sèvre-et-Maine; Sainsbury's Vin Rouge de France 1.5l; Sainsbury's Navarra; Sainsbury's Bianco di Verona; Sainsbury's Rosso di Verona; 1989 Bulgarian Cabernet Sauvignon Reserve

Range: GOOD: Bordeaux, Loire, Languedoc-Roussillon, Australia, New Zealand, Chile, Italy, Bulgaria
AVERAGE: Beaujolais, Burgundy, Rhône, Alsace, Germany, Portugal, Champagne and sparkling wine, Spain, South Africa, Argentina, Hungary, England
POOR: California

We rather missed the chatty monthly update from Allan Cheesman's word processor when he left the Sainsbury's wine department for fresh produce, flowers and the deli five years ago. Over the course of 18 vintages, Cheesman had done much to put supermarket wines in general, and Sainsbury's in particular, in the retail limelight.

But the disco dancing by supermarket rivals on Cheesman's grave proved premature. By mid-1995, Allan Cheesman was back in charge. Was it Tesco's cheek in edging ahead of Sainsbury's that prompted his return? Whatever the truth of the matter, competition in the mid-1990s is much tougher than it was in the heady 1980s. Having proved himself in battle before, the not-so-veteran 45-year-old was the self-evident choice to steer the wine department towards the millennium.

Since Cheesman joined the business as a ruddy-faced trainee in 1972, the wine trade has seen dramatic changes. So much so that his early years at Sainsbury's are a throwback to a past era of dismal brands and stuffy, traditional wine merchants. Before the UK joined the Common Market in 1973, 'when Beaune,' as Cheesman says, 'came from Tunisia', Sainsbury's sold fortified Australian wine, old-style Spanish wines, Yugoslav wine, Vin du Midi, and Moroccan red bottled from 535-gallon safraps. And that was the extent of its wine list.

Unimpressed by the old farts of the wine trade, Cheesman was determined not to let the upper-middle classes keep the best things in life for themselves. He was instrumental (with Andrew Nunn) in pioneering Sainsbury's thrust into own-label wines. It was a move which gave customers the confidence to invite the boss for dinner and serve a Sainsbury's own-label without embarrassment. In the boom period of the 1980s, Cheesman estimates that consumption grew by a million new drinkers a year.

Thanks in large measure to the recession, things have changed dramatically in the five years Cheesman has spent grazing in flowers, fruit and veg. The boom came to a rapid halt, and, in the early 1990s, a rudderless Sainsbury's lost sight of the all-important three Vs espoused by Cheesman – value, variety and versatility. It nose-dived downmarket in a desperate attempt to compete with cross-Channel shopping and counter the cut-price challenge of the likes of Aldi, Netto and Kwik Save.

One of the legacies of this high street battle is the £1.99 bottle. Cheesman recognises it as a necessary evil, but says that he would love to see it disappear. 'Value, I believe, does not necessarily mean low prices . . . I am reminded how often in the past the extra centime, peseta or cent translated directly into the quality of the raw material in the bottle,' wrote Cheesman in the first of his new monthly salvoes.

'Buying to a price is the biggest mistake you can make. It can't do the industry any good. There's no reinvestment or desire to bring products into this market. It dawned on me in the 1970s that it was best to go for quality.' He concedes that the recession has moved price up the customer's shopping list, but if anyone can rid the high street of the pesky £1.99 bottle, Cheesman can. He still believes that 'the most important things are convenience, range, quality and increasingly; we're coming round to service.'

The biggest change in Cheesman's absence has been the growth of the New World: from close to nothing, to over 10 per cent. 'When I left, we were buying wine from 14 countries. Now it's 27. I didn't even realise Uruguay made wine,' he says. Sainsbury's belated discovery of Australia and New Zealand has left it top-heavy in this field. The range is good, but only 10 of the 58 Aussie and Kiwi wines listed are now under £4. As evidence of the value for money competition from the rest of the southern hemisphere, only 10 of the 33 South American and South African wines are over £4.

In 1990, Bulgaria was synonymous with Eastern Europe. Today, Eastern Europe accounts for up to 10 per cent of sales. For a period, when Bulgaria lost the plot, it looked as though the floodgates from Hungary, Romania and Moldova might open. Hungary's whites, thanks to flying winemaker input, have made the breakthrough. But Moldova and Romania are not there yet. And what do you know – Bulgaria itself is making a comeback with promising whites and more modern reds.

The influence of the elite, largely Australian, corps of flying winemakers has grown immensely in Cheesman's absence. Geoff Merrill has galvanised Sainsbury's new Italian range of white and red wines, while Peter Bright has strapped himself into flights to and from Portugal, Argentina and Italy on Sainsbury's behalf.

'When I left, flying winemakers had introduced technology, but all the wines were tasting the same,' says Cheesman. 'Geoff has brought the varietal character through. Peter works often with lesser known varieties. It's not just safety first. They bring something to the party.' Quite some party. Between them, Geoff Merrill and Peter Bright freight forward an estimated three-quarters of a million cases of wine to the celebrations. Ten per cent of the entire range is a lot of bottles in only two wine racks. Sainsbury's will need to keep a commercial eye on the cheeky duo to ensure their wines retain distinctive varietal character and regional identity – something which is not always apparent in some of their cheaper efforts.

With the range now approaching 500 wines, compared with 380 when he left, Cheesman has returned to a larger wine department. The bigger range and increase in staff are designed to make Sainsbury's more flexible in developing new products. Big volumes and direct relationships with suppliers also allow Sainsbury's to dictate price points in the high street.

Is there anything left for Cheesman to do? One area ripe for a major shake-up is France. 'As a classic bloke, I'm disappointed with Bordeaux and Burgundy,' he admits. 'I'm a francophile, and I'm not satisfied that they compete in value for money terms against their New World counterparts. We need to look at it.' He also acknowledges the superior service and range many independent wine merchants have to offer, and, while he cannot compete on range, he wants to put more into service and training.

The challenge facing Cheesman in a near-static market is a tough one, but he appears to have lost none of his appetite for a scrap. 'Sainsbury's must be a destination shop for wine. We should be the benchmark for quality. We are the biggest [Tesco may have different views on this], but we also want to be the best.' Having done so much to bring wine to the people in the first place, his new aim is to introduce better wines to a wider audience. Could this be a watershed year for Sainsbury's and Allan Cheesman?

NB Wines marked with an asterisk (*) are also available at J. Sainsbury Bières, Vins et Spiritueux in Calais (see page 573).

White

Under £3

AUSTRALIA

*Sainsbury's Australian White Wine

£££ / 2 / 1   14/20

Zippy, modern banana-fruity white from the de Bortoli winery in the snappily named Murrumbidgee Irrigation Area. One of the few good Aussie whites still available at under £3.

BULGARIA

1994 Rousse Rikat, Special Reserve

££ / 2 / ⅟   14/20

Well-made, lemon-fresh Bulgarian white with refreshing marmalade spice. Rikat, in case you're wondering, is supermarketese for the local white Rkatsiteli grape.

FRANCE

1994 Sainsbury's Blanc de Mer, Loire

0 / 2 / ⅟   12/20

Crisp, clean, basic Chenin Blanc-style white Loire.

Sainsbury's Muscadet de Sèvre-et-Maine

£ / 2 / ⅟   13/20

Decent, basic Muscadet with fresh apple fruitiness and a tart finish. It's worth paying the extra pound or so to buy Sainsbury's *sur lie* version.

GERMANY

*Sainsbury's Liebfraumilch

££ / 5 / ⅟   13/20

The best of Sainsbury's cheap, sweet German whites, this is grapey, soft and full of fragrant Müller-Thurgau character.

*Sainsbury's Hock

£ / 5 / ⅟   12/20

A faintly smelly aroma put us off recommending this basic German as highly as the Liebfraumilch.

*Sainsbury's Niersteiner Gutes Domtal

£ / 5 / ⅟   12/20

More of the same.

GREECE

Kourtaki Vin de Pays de Crète White

0 / 2 / ⅟   11/20

Labelled as a vin de pays – bewilderingly, given its Greek origins – this is the sort of baked, modernish Greek white that tastes fine after a day on a Mediterranean beach, but fails to reach Olympian heights once you're back in Britain.

ITALY

*Sainsbury's Bianco di Verona
££ / 3 / 1   13/20
From Fratelli Fabiano, a cool-fermented, soft, appley Italian quaffer with an added dose of sweetness to help the medicine go down.

*Sainsbury's Sicilian White
0 / 2 / 1   12/20
A heavy, baked, undistinguished island white. Not one for the violin case.

Sainsbury's Trebbiano Garganega, Vino da Tavola del Veneto
££ / 2 / 1   14/20
Spicy, fresh, gingery aromas and refreshing fruitiness make this Venetian dry white a perfect wine bar glugger.

Sainsbury's Lambrusco dell'Emilia Bianco
£ / 5 / 1   12/20
Low in sparkle, high in sugar.

MOROCCO

Sainsbury's Moroccan White
£ / 2 / 1   13/20
This clean, cool-fermented white could come from almost anywhere. In Morocco's case, that's a positive recommendation. Here's looking at you, folks!

PORTUGAL

Sainsbury's Do Campo Branco
££ / 2 / 1   14/20
This ripe, buttery Portuguese white made by Australian Peter Bright has been a justifiable success at Sainsbury's for combining local spice with

international taste. It would be nice to see more wines made from grapes like Fernão Pires.

ROMANIA

Sainsbury's Romanian Feteasca, Sauvignon/Reças
0 / 3 / 1   10/20

Nice try, JS. We like the idea of blending the native Feteasca with Sauvignon Blanc, but this old-fashioned, tarted-up white should have been put up against a wall with Mr and Mrs Ceausescu. A tasteless note, admittedly, but then the wine's pretty tasteless too.

Sainsbury's Romanian Chardonnay Cernavoda
0 / 3 / 1   11/20

Sweet, fat and lacking in acidity. One for the Black Sea sewage pipe.

SPAIN

*Sainsbury's Vino de la Tierra Blanco
££ / 2 / 1   13/20

Attractively priced Spanish white made in the international style by the peripatetic Australian winemaker, Peter Bright.

Sainsbury's Navarra Blanco
£ / 2 / 1   13/20

Pleasantly fragrant aromas, especially given the dullish grape (Viura) from which this wine is made, and plenty of soft, peachy fruit.

£3–5

ARGENTINA

Sainsbury's Tupungato Chenin/Chardonnay
£ / 2 / 1   14/20

A fresh, cool, high altitude Peter Bright blend made in conjunction with the Trapiche winery and hinting at the potential of Argentina's better vineyards. Like many Pampas whites, this one could do with a little extra concentration.

AUSTRALIA

*Sainsbury's Australian Chardonnay
££ / 3 / ▮   14/20

A ripe, tropical-fruity Aussie Chardonnay with lots of flavour and oak character. It shows exactly why Australian Chardonnay has become so popular in Britain.

1994 Hunter Valley Chardonnay, Denman Estate
£££ / 2 / ▮   16/20

Even more tropically fruity than the straight Australian Chardonnay, this Hunter Valley white is a full-bodied, pineapple chunk and buttered toast special with refreshing acidity.

*1994 Penfolds Koonunga Hill Chardonnay, South Australia
££ / 2 / ▮   15/20

From the ever-reliable Penfolds stable (or should that be ranch, given the weight of American oak on this and most other Pennie's wines?), this is a rich, smoky Aussie white with tropical sweetness and balancing acidity.

BULGARIA

1994 Rousse Chardonnay, Special Reserve
£££ / 2 / ▮   15/20

Like the same winery's Rikat white, this new-style Bulgarian Chardonnay is an encouraging development for Eastern Europe. Soft, ripe, boiled sweets fruitiness at a very good price.

CHILE

*Sainsbury's Chilean White Wine
££ / 2 / ▮   14/20

Made by Peter Bright at the Curicó co-operative in Chile's Central Valley, this is an excellent value, zesty dry white with crisp, grapefruit elegance.

Sainsbury's Chilean Chardonnay/Semillon, Curicó
£££ / 2 / ▮   15/20

Proof that Chile is now a serious contender in the value-for-money white wine stakes, this exuberantly fruity, crisp Chardonnay/Semillon blend is a real find.

FRANCE

1994 Enclos des Lilas Blanc, Vin de Pays de l'Aude
£ / 2 / ¾   13/20

A neutral, cool-fermented southern French white with a smidgeon of nutmeg spiciness to keep you from falling asleep.

1993 Château les Bouhets, Bordeaux Blanc Sec
££ / 2 / ¾   15/20

Crisp, expressive Sauvignon made by Christophe Olivier with attractively grassy fruitiness. It's encouraging to see Bordeaux responding to the New World challenge.

*1993 Muscadet de Sèvre-et-Maine Sur Lie, La Goelette
££ / 1 / ¾   15/20

With its fresh, bone-dry, carbon-dioxide prickle and creamy *sur lie* character, this well-made Muscadet is the sort of wine to restore the *appellation*'s flagging fortunes and your tired and thirsty palate.

Sainsbury's Alsace Pinot Blanc
££ / 2 / ¾   15/20

Fattish, perfumed, full-bodied Alsace white from the Bennwihr co-operative. Textbook Vosges Mountains dry white.

Sainsbury's Bordeaux Blanc, Cuvée Prestige
£ / 2 / ¾   14/20

Still a little closed when we tasted this as a cask sample in May, but it showed promising Sauvignon Blanc herbaceousness and zest.

*1994 Chais Baumière Sauvignon Blanc, Vin de Pays d'Oc
££ / 2 / ¾   15/20

Made by Australian Nigel Snead, resident winemaker at BRL-Hardy's southern French outpost in the Languedoc, this is one of a number of highly drinkable, excellent value wines from Chais Baumière.

*1993 Chais Baumière Chardonnay, Vin de Pays d'Oc
££ / 2 / ¾   15/20

This is another. The Chardonnay is fresh and citrusy with well-judged oak influence, combining New World fruitiness with crisp French elegance.

*Sainsbury's White Burgundy, Chardonnay
£ / 2 / 1   13/20

A botched attempt at a New World style Chardonnay by normally reliable *négociant*, Antonin Rodet. There's nothing wrong with this faintly buttery, innocuous Chardonnay, but we couldn't see the link with Burgundy's much-vaunted *terroir*, or vineyard character.

GERMANY

1983 Erdener Treppchen, Riesling Spätlese, Moselland
£££ / 4 / 1   16/20

Presumably Sainsbury's discovered this mature Riesling hidden away in a corner of the substantial Moselland co-operative. You certainly don't see many 13-year-old wines of this quality on the market at under a fiver. It's fresh and remarkably lively with attractive nut, ripe apple and lime overtones.

ITALY

1994 Bianco di Custoza, Geoff Merrill
££ / 2 / 1   15/20

One of a collection of fine Italian whites tailor-made for Sainsbury's by moustachioed, ebullient Australian winemaker Geoff Merrill and producer GIV. Fragrant, lemony quaffer with a refreshing bitter twist.

Sainsbury's Sicilian Inzolia/Chardonnay
££ / 3 / 1   14/20

Made by Peter Bright, Sainsbury's other regular commission, this is a cleanly made, nutty blend of the native Sicilian Inzolia grape and the ubiquitous Chardonnay.

1994 Sainsbury's Pinot Grigio, Atesino
£££ / 2 / 1   16/20

One of the best of an outstanding value-for-money Italian range, Geoff Merrill's zippy, fresh, peachy Pinot Grigio provides unbeatable value at under £3.50.

*Sainsbury's Orvieto Classico Secco
££ / 2 / ½   15/20
Fragrant, typical Umbrian dry white with clean, honeyed freshness.
Another Merrill/GIV hit with a local twang.

*Sainsbury's Chardonnay delle Tre Venezie
£££ / 2 / ½   16/20
With Chardonnay, Geoff Merrill is almost on home turf. Showing his
sure-footedness, he has produced a crisp, unoaked, intensely fruity
Chardonnay with a cool, northern Italian, lemony bite.

Sainsbury's Grechetto dell'Umbria
£££ / 2 / ½   15/20
The most Italian of Geoff Merrill's Sainsbury's whites, showing lots of
nutty, tangy, pear-like fruit and a blade of crisp acidity. Even better with
food.

Sainsbury's Frascati Secco Superiore
£££ / 2 / ½   16/20
This Malvasia and Trebbiano blend is ripe and on the buttery side for
Frascati. Purists might raise their eyebrows at such an international-
tasting Frascati, but we raise our glasses to Mr Merrill. Come back next
vintage, Geoff.

*Sainsbury's Sauvignon Blanc delle Tre Venezie
££ / 2 / ½   15/20
Another New World-influenced style, showing the melon-like aromatics
of an Australian Sauvignon Blanc and clean varietal fruit character.

***1994 Chardonnay Atesino, Barrique Aged, Geoff Merrill, Vino da
Tavola**
£££ / 2 / ½   16/20
The most recognisably Australian in style of Geoff Merrill's Italian
collezione, this is a rich, butterscotchy, oaky Chardonnay with lots of
body and flavour. Italians probably wouldn't like it, but then this is a
triumph of content over style.

NEW ZEALAND

*1994 Timara Dry White
££ / 2 / ♦   14/20

A floral blend of Chenin Blanc and Müller-Thurgau that could almost be
a Sauvignon Blanc. Montana's bottom-of-the-range Kiwi quaffer is fresh,
crisp and characteristically well made.

PORTUGAL

Sainsbury's Ribatejo Sauvignon Blanc
£ / 2 / ♦   13/20

A soft, overblown Sauvignon Blanc from southern Portugal which lacks
freshness and characteristic Sauvignon zest. We'd rather taste something
from a local grape variety.

Sainsbury's Ribatejo Chardonnay
£ / 3 / ♦   13/20

Sweetish, rather confected southern Portuguese Chardonnay. Our
comments about indigenous grapes apply here too.

SOUTH AFRICA

1994 Danie de Wet Grey Label Chardonnay, Robertson
££ / 2 / ♦   15/20

Made by the Chardonnay king of South Africa, Danie de Wet, this is a
subtly oaked, pungently fruity dry white with citrusy undertones.

SPAIN

Sainsbury's Valdeorras Blanco
££ / 2 / ♦   15/20

Made from the little-known Godello grape, this is exactly the sort of
thing we hope to see more of from the Iberian peninsula. Showing fresh
lime and orange-peel zest flavours, this distinctive dry white is a good
antidote to ubiquitous Chardonnay and Sauvignon styles.

1994 Sainsbury's Extremadura Viura/Chardonnay

££ / 2 / ⅓   14/20

From Spain's western border with Portugal, this a soft banana- and lemon-scented white made by Australian winemaker Peter Bright.

UNITED STATES

Sainsbury's California White

0 / 3 / ⅓   10/20

Made with grapes from California's bakingly hot fruitbowl, the San Joaquin Valley, this is a dull, confected white for Coca-Cola drinkers. The real thing? Definitely not.

South Bay Vineyards California Chardonnay

£ / 2 / ⅓   13/20

Blended by wheeler-dealer Jason Korman, a former East Coast fine wine merchant, this is a fat, heavy, ripely fruity, oaky West Coast Chardonnay that could do with a bit more elegance.

£5–8

AUSTRALIA

*1994 Rosemount Estate, Chardonnay/Semillon, South Eastern Australia

£££ / 2 / ⅓   16/20

From Chardonnay specialists Rosemount Estate, this complex, yeasty, barrel-fermented blend is full of toasty, almost Burgundian flavours. Great value at just over a fiver.

1990 Geoff Merrill Chardonnay, South Australia

£ / 2 / ⅓   14/20

Made at Geoff Merrill's home base in Australia's McLaren Vale, this is an old-fashioned, heavily oaked Chardonnay that's a bit long in the dental department.

CHILE

1994 Santa Rita Estate Reserve Chardonnay, Maipo
£££ / 2 / ⌐   17/20
After a couple of indifferent vintages, Santa Rita appears to be right back on form with this vibrantly flavoured, attractively oaked, grapefruit-zesty Maipo Chardonnay. A stunning wine at a knockout price.

FRANCE

1993 Four Terroirs Chardonnay, Vin de Pays d'Oc
££ / 1 / ⌐   16/20
One of a number of brilliantly made, barrel-fermented Chardonnays from the Aude's Limoux co-operative, this crisp, toasty white displays its cool climate (for the Languedoc) origins with pride.

1993 Mâcon Chardonnay, Domaine Les Ecuyers
££ / 2 / ⌐   16/20
From the village of Chardonnay, which may or may not have given its name to the world's most popular grape variety, this is a spicy, full-bodied white with plenty of creamy oak and fresh acidity.

1993 Sainsbury's Sancerre, Domaine Henry Pellé
£££ / 1 / ⌐   16/20
Better known for its outstanding Menetou-Salon, the Pellé domaine has produced a fragrant Sancerre with clean-cut, minerally fruitiness and a soft texture. At under £7, this is sensibly priced for a Sancerre.

1993 Pouilly Fumé, Figeat
££ / 1 / ⌐   15/20
Flinty, tightly focused, youthful Sauvignon Blanc from nearby Pouilly Fumé in the eastern Loire, showing the *appellation*'s characteristic austerity. Should open out over the next six months.

*1993 Sainsbury's Chablis, Domaine Sainte Céline, Brocard
££ / 1 / ⌐   15/20
Unoaked, traditional Chablis showing crisp, tangy Chardonnay fruitiness with the typical creamy character of Yonne whites.

NEW ZEALAND

1994 Private Bin, Villa Maria Sauvignon Blanc, Marlborough
££ / 2 / 🌢   15/20

In price and style, this is halfway between Montana Sauvignon Blanc and the more exalted wines of Cloudy Bay and Jackson Estate. Refreshing, dry, zesty Sauvignon Blanc with plenty of elderflower cattiness.

1994 Matua Sauvignon Blanc, Hawkes Bay
£££ / 2 / 🌢   16/20

Hawkes Bay Sauvignon tends to be fuller but less crisply aromatic than the Marlborough benchmark. This grassy, plump example from Auckland winery, Matua Valley, has touches of cassis and green bean Sauvignon Blanc character.

1994 Grove Mill Sauvignon Blanc, Marlborough
££ / 2 / 🌢   16/20

Grassy, asparagusy Marlborough Sauvignon with rounded fruitiness, grapefruity acidity and gratifying length of flavour.

1994 Matua Chardonnay, Eastern Bays
£££ / 2 / 🌢   17/20

New Zealand's answer to Puligny Montrachet – albeit at half the price. Nutty, crisp and elegantly balanced North Island Chardonnay with spicy undertones and well-crafted oak. An outstanding Kiwi white. Even Tony Underwood could tackle this one.

SOUTH AFRICA

1994 Boschendal Estate Chardonnay, Paarl
£ / 2 / 🌢   15/20

From a large white wine dominated estate in Paarl owned by the Anglo-American conglomerate, this is a rich, rather old-fashioned Cape Chardonnay with heavy-handed oak treatment.

Over £8

FRANCE

1992 Puligny-Montrachet, Domaine Gérard Chavy
££ / 2 / ♪   16/20
As we commented last year, this is a finely crafted, well-made Puligny
from one of the best Burgundian white wine vintages of the last decade.
Intense vanilla-oak with a core of citrus fruit concentration. Delicious
stuff. Another five editions of *Grapevine*, and who knows, Sainsbury's
might have shifted their allocation.

Red

Under £3

ARGENTINA

Sainsbury's Mendoza Cabernet Sauvignon/Malbec
££ / MB / ♪   14/20
Chocolatey, charry Bordeaux-style blend made by Peter Bright wearing
his pampas-grass skirt.

CHILE

*Sainsbury's Chilean Red Wine
£ / MB / ♪   13/20
Plain, blackcurrant pastille flavoured red with rasping, rustic acidity.
We'd almost rather drink claret at this price.

GREECE

Kourtaki Vin de Pays de Crète Red
£ / MB / ♪   13/20
Baked, raisiny Greek plonk with a fancy (and we wonder if it's legal)
French *appellation*. It's Zorba time again.

ITALY

*Sainsbury's Sicilian Red
£ / MB / ↓   13/20
A plum and damson concoction from the sole (rather than the soul) of
Italy. A decent trattoria rosso.

*Sainsbury's Rosso di Verona
£ / MB / ↓   13/20
Light, northern Italian red with soft, juicy fruit and a touch of sweetness.
For some reason, this is one of Sainsbury's top ten best-sellers. Perhaps
the supine performance of the lira has something to do with it.

Sainsbury's Merlot/Corvina, Vino da Tavola del Veneto
£££ / MB / ↓   15/20
Supple, savoury, peppery Venetian red with plenty of succulent fruit
and a fresh, bitter almond twist. One of the best cheap Italians we've
come across.

1994 Sangiovese di Toscana, Cecchi
£££ / MB / ↓   15/20
Here's another. With its robust tannins and chunky, savoury fruitiness,
this is like a mini-Chianti Classico in a style that contrasts with the
Merlot/Corvina blend.

MOROCCO

Sainsbury's Moroccan Red
££ / MB / ↓   14/20
Deeply coloured, gluggable North African red with soft raspberry and
prune-like fruit made in the modern style. Promising stuff from Morocco.
Drink with fez on, as it were.

PORTUGAL

Sainsbury's Do Campo Tinto
££ / MB / ↓   14/20
Beefy, robust, southern Portuguese quaffer showing a touch of
sweetness, from Australian master blender Peter Bright.

ROMANIA

Sainsbury's Romanian Pinot Noir/Merlot, Dealul Mare
0 / MB / ♪   12/20
One of five Romanian red wines at Sainsbury's, this brambly rustic blend
of Bordeaux and Burgundy doesn't taste much like either.

*Sainsbury's Romanian Pinot Noir, Dealul Mare
0 / MB / ♪   11/20
Sweet, rustic and jammy with a dry, tannic finish. Why does anyone
want to buy, let alone drink, this sort of plonk?

Sainsbury's Romanian Cabernet Sauvignon/Merlot, Reças
£ / MB / ♪   13/20
Cleaner, more modern blackberry fruity blend with a bit more life and
zip. This is the one to go for at under £3.

SPAIN

*Sainsbury's Vino de la Tierra Tinto
££ / MB / ♪   14/20
An oaky, chunky blend of Spain's two best red grapes, Tempranillo and
Garnacha, showing lots of chocolatey, ripe fruit in a modern, Rioja-style
mould. Another Bright moment.

£3–5

AUSTRALIA

*Sainsbury's Australian Red Wine
0 / MB / ♪   12/20
Nothing like as good as Sainsbury's Australian white, this red version is
somewhat basic, dull and jammy.

1993 Rosemount Estate Shiraz, South Eastern Australia
££ / MB / ♪   15/20
A wine that encapsulates all that's good about Rosemount, one of

Australia's most consistent performers. Fresh, berry-fruitiness and sweet vanillin oak held in attractive balance.

BULGARIA

*1989 Bulgarian Reserve Cabernet Sauvignon, Lovico Suhindol Region
££ / MB / ▮   14/20

Raisiny, Rioja-style Bulgarian red with charry oak, fresh acidity and plenty of spice.

CHILE

Sainsbury's Chilean Cabernet Sauvignon/Merlot, Maule
£££ / MB / ▮   15/20

A fresh, modern-style Chilean red with plenty of juicy blackcurrant fruit and coconut sweetness, and a lot more concentration than many inexpensive Chilean reds.

FRANCE

*Sainsbury's Claret
£ / MB / ▮   13/20

Robust, tannic, traditional and on the expensive side for a basic claret. You can see why people are turning to the New World in droves.

*Sainsbury's Bordeaux Rouge
££ / MB / ▮   14/20

This is more like it – a modern, fruitier style with soft tannins and green pepper undertones. It's also cheaper.

Sainsbury's Cabernet Sauvignon/Syrah, Vin de Pays d'Oc
££ / MB / ▮   14/20

Another New World influenced French red, this time from the Languedoc-Roussillon's go-ahead Foncalieu co-operative. It's a fresh, juicy, liquoricey red with some chocolatey ripeness and a chunky finish.

1993 Château Notre Dame du Quatourze, Coteaux du Languedoc
£££ / MB / ❧   15/20
With its soft, demerara sugar nose and Mediterranean spice, this is an enjoyable Grenache-based red with an attractive hint of the farmyard. Eeeay-Eeeay-O!

1992 Domaine le Cazal, Minervois
£££ / MB / ❧   15/20
Another excellent value red from the South of France, this time showing pungent raspberryish aromatics and a twist of the pepper mill. Perfect mid-winter fare.

Sainsbury's Claret, Cuvée Prestige
£ / MB / ❧   14/20
Dense, tightly packed, deeply coloured claret made by Bordeaux-based Australian Mandy Jones. It was only a sample from the barrel when we tasted it, but this modern, tannic red should open out with time in bottle.

*1993 Chais Baumière Merlot, Vin de Pays d'Oc
££ / MB / ❧   15/20
True to the style of wines produced by BRL-Hardy's domaine near Béziers in the South of France, this is a supple, supremely drinkable varietal with just the right amount of oak influence.

*1993 Chais Baumière Cabernet Sauvignon, Vin de Pays d'Oc
£££ / MB / ❧   16/20
Another successful red from BRL-Hardy's French base at Domaine de la Baume, showing similar grassy softness of fruit, but with a touch more concentration and backbone.

1993 Chais Baumière Syrah, Vin de Pays d'Oc
££ / MB / ❧   15/20
Chunkier still, this southern French Syrah is packed with blackberry fruitiness and charry oak. Needs robust food to show in its best light.

1993 Sainsbury's Beaujolais Villages, Les Roches Grillées
£ / MB / ❧   13/20
Just about recognisable as being made from the Gamay grape, this

sweetish, slightly soupy red is not the finest advertisement for the Beaujolais Villages *appellation*.

*Sainsbury's Red Burgundy, Pinot Noir
£ / LB / ♪   14/20
Jammy, commercial red Burgundy from *négociant* house Antonin Rodet. Like many a cheap Pinot Noir from the region, it lacks charm and suppleness.

ITALY

Sainsbury's Sicilian Nero d'Avola/Merlot
£ / MB / ♪   14/20
Oak-chippy, chocolatey Mediterranean blend made by itinerant Australian Peter Bright in a modern, New World influenced vein.

Sainsbury's Teroldego Rotaliano, Geoff Merrill
££ / MB / ♪   15/20
As a rule, Geoff Merrill has done more exciting things with white wines than reds in Italy, but this deeply coloured, vibrantly juicy quaffer, influenced by northern Italy's coolish climate, should please all but the most exacting Italian purists.

*Sainsbury's Cabernet Sauvignon delle Tre Venezie, Geoff Merrill
££ / MB / ♪   15/20
Soft, elegant, grassy, cool climate Cabernet Sauvignon from the man with the outlandish moustache.

1993 Cabernet Sauvignon Atesino, Barrique Aged, Geoff Merrill
£££ / MB / ♪   16/20
Using the Australian trick of finishing a red wine's fermentation in the barrel (as distinct from the tank), Geoff Merrill has produced a polished, richly oaked northern Italian Cabernet Sauvignon with plenty of zip and smoky concentration.

PORTUGAL

Sainsbury's Ribatejo Cabernet Sauvignon
£££ / MB / ⁵   15/20
Surprisingly for southern Portugal's warm Ribatejo region, this tastes like
a cool climate Cabernet Sauvignon with fresh acidity and lots of green
pepper notes. Perhaps Peter Bright asked for the grapes to be picked a
little early to retain acidity and freshness.

ROMANIA

1994 River Route Romanian Pinot Noir, Reças
£ / MB / ⁵   13/20
Basic, tannic Pinot Noir slouching towards the 20th century. Unlike
Count Dracula, we're still waiting to taste the first really exciting red
from Romania.

1994 River Route Romanian Merlot Cernavoda
££ / MB / ⁵   14/20
This soft, plummy Merlot-based red offers more to get your fangs into.

SPAIN

1994 Sainsbury's Extremadura Cabernet Sauvignon
££ / MB / ⁵   14/20
From a sparsely populated area not usually associated with wine
production, this juicy, modern Cabernet shows overtones of banana and
blackcurrant, and firm, punchy tannins.

UNITED STATES

*Sainsbury's California Red
0 / MB / ⁵   11/20
Confected, over-mellow West Coast plonk. We wouldn't brave the San
Andreas fault to get our hands on this.

South Bay Vineyards California Zinfandel
£ / FB / ⁵   13/20
Not the greatest example of California's adopted grape variety. This is
somewhat overoaked and charmless.

*South Bay Vineyards California Pinot Noir
££ / MB / ♪   15/20
Easily the best Pinot Noir under £5 we've come across from the New
World this year, showing California's potential with the variety. Broker
Jason Korman has sourced a highly aromatic, soft red fruits scented Pinot
balanced by a judicious splash of spicy oak.

£5–8

AUSTRALIA

1994 Rosemount Estate Cabernet/Shiraz, South Eastern Australia
£ / MB / ♪   14/20
Not as vibrant and well-balanced as the same estate's Shiraz reviewed
above, this simple Aussie red nonetheless has hints of cherry fruit and
pepper.

*1992 St Hallett Cabernet Sauvignon/Franc/Merlot, Barossa Valley
££ / FB / ♪   16/20
From a winery best known for its award-winning Old Block Shiraz, this
is an extremely ripe, fruity Bordeaux blend which displays its Barossa
Valley origins by trading full flavour for subtlety.

CHILE

1993 Santa Carolina Merlot Gran Reserva, San Fernando
£ / MB / ♪   13/20
Chile's red wines have been largely overtaken by its whites in the last
two vintages. This austere and hefty red does little to redress the
balance.

1991 Santa Carolina Cabernet Sauvignon, Reserva, Maipo
£ / MB / ♪   14/20
Considerably more attractive in the aroma department, but still showing
some astringency on the palate.

FRANCE

*1994 Fleurie, La Madone
£ / MB / 🍷   15/20
From the most famous of the ten Beaujolais crus – a fact which has as
much to do with its easy-to-pronounce name as the quality of its wines –
this is a fresh, light, juicy Gamay with some of the charm we expect from
the *appellation*. If only it were closer to £5 than £7 in price.

1991 Chassagne-Montrachet, Côte de Beaune
££ / MB / 🍷   15/20
Modern, overtly oaky Pinot Noir from Michel Picard with some
appealing, raspberryish Pinot fruitiness. At the moment, it's still on the
hefty side, but it should soften with another year in bottle – if you can
contain yourself.

1990 Château Fournas Bernadotte, Haut-Médoc, Cru Bourgeois
££ / MB / 🍷   15/20
Nicely mature, farmyardy claret from the classic 1990 vintage. Lots of
oak and fruit concentration make this something of a Christmas cracker.

*1992 Château la Vieille Cure, Fronsac
£££ / MB / 🍷   16/20
Sainsbury's plans to reverse the vintage order on this stalwart of its claret
range by replacing the lighter 1992 with the 1990. If the succulent,
oaky, elegant 1992 is anything to go by, the 1990 should be a treat.

SPAIN

1988 Orobio Reserva, Rioja Alavesa
££ / MB / 🍷   15/20
From the best of Rioja's three sub-regions, this old-fashioned, massively
oaked Spanish red has the savoury softness one would expect of a
Reserva aged for at least three years in American oak.

Over £8

AUSTRALIA

1992 Reynolds, Cabernet/Merlot, New South Wales
££ / FB / ➤   16/20
Nothing to do with the man whose toupée has graced many a
Hollywood adventure film, this Bordeaux blend of Cabernet Sauvignon,
Merlot and Cabernet Franc, aged for 20 months in oak, is a concentrated
Aussie red with bulging muscles. On second thoughts, maybe Burt did
have something to do with it.

FRANCE

*1990 Château Haut Faugères, Grand Cru, St-Emilion
£££ / MB / ➤   16/20
The best of Sainsbury's up-market claret range, and fortunately the most
widely available, this is a classically voluptuous Right Bank Merlot, with
intense, textured flavours and chocolatey richness.

*1989 Vosne Romanée, Georges Noëllat
£££ / MB / ▌   16/20
It's encouraging to see a supermarket taking a punt on a mature, serious
red Burgundy. From a comparatively forward vintage, best suited to early
drinking, this is a gamey, characterful, sweetly ripe Pinot Noir.

Rosé

Under £3

ITALY

Sainsbury's Sicilian Rosé
£££ / 2 / ▌   15/20
Surprisingly good at the price, this is a crisply fruity, delicate pink with
a refreshing, savoury bite.

PORTUGAL

1994 Alta Mesa Rosé, Estremadura
0 / 3 / 1   12/20
Soft, sweet, rather innocuous Mateus Rosé clone. At least the bottle can double as a candle holder.

£3–5

AUSTRALIA

*1994 Mount Hurtle Grenache Rosé, McLaren Vale
££ / 3 / 1   15/20
This day-glo pink from the exuberant Geoff Merrill has so much strawberry fruitiness and texture that it could almost be a red wine. Definitely not for wimps.

FRANCE

1994 Domaine de la Tuilerie, Merlot Rosé, Ryman
££ / 2 / 1   14/20
Made by Englishman Hugh Ryman in the Languedoc, this is another rosé with plenty of flavour. Drier than the Mount Hurtle, it's a fresh, exuberant style in which the grassiness of the Merlot grape is attractively apparent.

HUNGARY

Hungarian Cabernet Sauvignon Rosé, Nagyrede Region
££ / 2 / 1   14/20
Fresh, light, commercial rosé made by flying winemaker Kym Milne at Hungary's Nagyrede co-operative. Here too, the raw material gives the wine a green pepper twist.

Sparkling

£3–5

SPAIN

*Sainsbury's Cava
££ / 2 / ♪   **15/20**
One of the best Cavas we've tasted in 1995, this is a dry, yeasty, well-made Spanish fizz at an affordable price.

£5–8

AUSTRALIA

Cockatoo Ridge Sparkling Wine
££ / 3 / ♪   **15/20**
Attractive pink-tinged fizz from Geoff Merrill's base near Adelaide, showing soft strawberry fruitiness and lively, crisp acidity.

SOUTH AFRICA

Madeba Brut, Robertson
0 / 2 / ♪   **13/20**
From a swanky new winery in the Robertson district of South Africa's Western Cape, this is a coarse and rather obvious bubbly with broad, buttery flavours. Dramatically overpriced.

Over £8

FRANCE

*Sainsbury's Blanc de Noirs Champagne
£££ / 2 / ♪   **16/20**
The best and the cheapest of Sainsbury's regular Champagnes, this all-red grape blend is fresh, up-front and brimming with the strawberry fruitiness of the Pinot Noir and Pinot Meunier grapes.

Sainsbury's Champagne Demi-Sec, NV
££ / 4 / 🍷   15/20
Creamy, sweetish Champagne, reviving the old-fashioned preference for
fizz with an added dose of sugar.

*Sainsbury's Champagne Extra Dry
£ / 2 / 🍷   14/20
Youthful, yeasty, crisply assertive Champagne, which could have done
with a few months extra in the bottle before release. We're hoping for
better things from the next batch.

Fortified

Under £3

SPAIN

Sainsbury's Pale Dry Manzanilla 37.5cl
£££ / 1 / 🍷   16/20
Fresh, aromatic, salty Manzanilla from leading Sherry house Barbadillo.
Look out for the drink-by date on the back of the bottle, and consume
within a few days of opening.

£3–5

SPAIN

Sainsbury's Pale Dry Fino Sherry
£ / 1 / 🍷   14/20
A nuttier, dry style from Croft, which lacks the freshness and bite of the
Manzanilla.

SOMERFIELD (GATEWAY) **(*)

Head Office: Somerfield House, Hawkfield Business Park, Whitchurch Lane, Bristol BS14 0TJ

Telephone: 0117 9359359

Number of branches: 618 and 26 Food Giant

Credit cards accepted: All

Hours of opening: Varies from store to store, but generally Monday to Saturday 8.30am to 6.30pm and Sunday 10.00am to 4.00pm

By-the-case sales: No

Glass loan: No

Home delivery: No

Clubs: No

Discounts: No, but regular promotions

In-store tastings: Monthly, day-long tastings in top 100 stores

Top ten best-selling wines: Liebfraumilch; Lambrusco Bianco; Hock; Valencia Medium Sweet; Bulgarian Cabernet Sauvignon; Valencia Red; Bulgarian Country Red; Valencia Sweet; Muscadet; Valencia Dry

Range: GOOD: French country wines, Italian red, Australia
AVERAGE: Bordeaux, Burgundy, Rhône, Portugal, Italian white, South Africa, South America, England, Champagne and sparkling wines, New Zealand
POOR: Germany, Spain, Eastern Europe, United States

'Scum of the earth' is perhaps a dubious accolade, but Angela Mount seemed delighted with the description, apparently applied by a rival supermarket buyer. 'It's got them rattled,' she grinned. What was it that was getting up her rivals' noses? The stick was for Somerfield's aggressive monthly £1.99 promotions, which had reached a peak – or nadir, depending on your point of view – of £1.39 in April 1995.

A handful of wine critics had even gone out of their way to condemn the product in question as nasty, but as far as Mount was concerned, it was greater power to the elbow she's been sharpening in her battle with the Big Four ever since she took over the buying at Somerfield (fifth in the market share league after Sainsbury's, Tesco, Safeway and Asda). 'Five years ago, who would have taken Gateway, as it was then, seriously as a place to buy wine?' she asks.

Which raises another, related question: who takes Somerfield, as it now is, seriously as a place to buy wine? Certainly customers seem to like the idea. According to Mount, Price Check, as the promotion is called, is bringing in an extra one million customers a week, and she has had a lot of letters of support from loyal customers who keep coming back for top-ups of those £1.99 bottles.

But isn't the whole thing dragging the market down to the lowest common denominator? If customers are happy with the £1.99 bottle, why should they bother to try something more interesting? And doesn't it all mean squeezing suppliers till the grape pips squeak?

'Promotions, supported with leaflets, play a very important role,' responds Mount. 'When we price promote, we work on the blend and we've had more success with more interesting wines than, say, Liebfraumilch, Hock or Lambrusco. When we do promotions, you might expect sales of other products to dip, but it's increased volume. It's not taking away from the rest of the business.

'People who buy £1.99 continue to buy when the price goes back up to £2.99. Customers can broaden their repertoire by trying new wines at minimal risk to their pockets. The effect is that we're bringing in a lot more people who previously wouldn't have thought of shopping at Somerfield.' Mount doesn't agree with the notion that she is effectively giving away wine at £1.99 simply to gain market share over her rivals. 'If we were giving away wine to prop up the business, sales wouldn't be showing a healthy increase.'

Certainly the overall fortunes of Somerfield have improved since David Simons took over as chief executive in 1993. Already, half the ugly old Gateways have been turned into swan-like Somerfields, with another 100 conversions planned by the end of the year. Transforming down-at-heel Gateway into Somerfield, with its bigger fresh food, dairy products and meat sections, has improved the group's overall performance.

Nevertheless, there is evidence, as the competition between the big supermarket chains hots up, that the price cutting route is not necessarily the most effective way forward. Somerfield as a group has found itself struggling. Profits on the £3.2 billion turnover of its 618 outlets are clingfilm-thin. It's the more up-market Somerfields which are bringing home the goodies.

The wine range now stands at 380 wines. Last year's focus on the Languedoc-Roussillon brought in a number of good value Mediterranean reds from the large merchants Val d'Orbieu, Domaines Virginie and Jeanjean. The southern stuff has accounted, almost singlehandedly, for big increases in French wine sales and an equally huge jump in red wine drinking – up 22 per cent according to Mount, compared to 12 per cent generally.

But exchange rates have conspired against France, and Germany has been hit by a double whammy: a strong mark and declining consumption of Liebfraumilch. 'Pricing French and German wines is getting that much harder. The £2.99 Côtes du Rhône and claret have drifted over £3 for the first time in ages.' Why not stick at £2.99 and buy cheaper from her suppliers? 'There would be a risk of unripe fruit in what should be the standard-bearers for the range,' says Mount.

The weakness of the pound sterling against the French and German currencies and its relative strength against the Italian lire have inspired thoughts of Italy in Mount. 'And knowing we were weak in Italy made me focus on it. I refuse to accept the commonly held view that Italian wine is dull.' A foray into Italy has produced an array of good value Italians such as the keenly priced Araldica wines, Sicily's I Grilli di Villa Thalia, an attractive Valpolicella and, from Italy's heel, the characterful Taurino Salice Salentino. It's not surprising that Italian sales – representing 16 per cent of the business – are strong.

Somewhat belatedly perhaps, given the current grape shortage and price scare, Somerfield customers have taken Australia to heart. But now that they have started to embrace the New World, Mount's new mission will be to add to where the value is, notably South Africa and Chile. 'South Africa has a lot of potential and will do well this year,' says Mount, who has added seven new wines to the range. 'Chile also is suddenly getting its act together. It's exciting stuff.' Eastern Europe, admits Mount, needs more attention.

There is a fine wine section in roughly 100 Somerfield stores, which

Mount says she is 'reviewing'. Unless you're a Waitrose or M&S, the cachet their presence gives the range is usually outweighed by the clutter they create if they don't sell. And with customers eyeing up the £1.99 with such fondness, it's hardly surprising if the over-£5 bottles become wallflowers.

All in all, then, it's been a challenging year for the former Smirnoff brand manager, who, together with computer whizz-kid and product manager Lewis Morton, has worked tirelessly both at improving existing blends and, by keeping her nose to the ground, adding to the range where she finds good value. Somerfield may not yet be everyone's alternative wine destination, but you can be sure that 'scum of the earth' Mount is working on it.

White

Under £3

FRANCE

1994 Muscadet de Sèvre et Maine, J Beauquin
0 / 2 / ∤   12/20
Gluey, tart, basic Muscadet which we suspect has sacrificed flavour on the altar of price.

Somerfield Vin de Pays des Côtes de Gascogne, Grassa
£ / 3 / ∤   13/20
Appley, slightly sweet, cool-fermented Gascon white with commendable freshness. An example of why basic Muscadet has lost out.

GERMANY

Somerfield Liebfraumilch, Rheinberg Kellerei
0 / 6 / ∤   11/20
Liebfraumilch mustn't be too assertive in character, according to Somerfield wine buyer Angela Mount. This sweet but dilute sticky lives down to expectations.

ITALY

1994 Bianco del Monferrato, Araldica
£££ / 2 / 1   14/20

A spritzy, freshly bottled, appley Piemonte white from the Araldica co-operative. Crunchy, zesty fruit flavours.

Montereale Sicilian White Vino da Tavola
££ / 3 / 1   13/20

Baked, slightly sweet Mediterranean quaffer with weighty, full-bodied fruit flavours and a zip of added acidity.

Somerfield Lambrusco Bianco, Casa Vinicola Donelli
0 / 5 / 1   10/20

Lambrusco needs to be as fresh as possible to approach drinkability. This sweet, stale example fails on both counts.

SPAIN

1994 Santara Dry White, Conca de Barbera
££ / 2 / 1   14/20

Made in Catalonia by itinerant winemaker Hugh Ryman, this blend of Macabeo and the local Parellada grapes is a crisply refreshing, lemony party wine. Viña Sol for the 1990s.

Somerfield Medium White Vicente Gandia
0 / 5 / 1   11/20

Selected for what wine buyer Angela Mount calls 'that element of our customer base which hasn't changed its habits', this gluey, medium-sweet white is Spain's answer to Liebfraumilch made from the local Merseguera grape.

£3-5

AUSTRALIA

Somerfield Australian Chardonnay, Penfolds
££ / 3 / 1   14/20

A ripe, pineappley, commercial Australian Chardonnay with a hint of oak character and added acidity for balance and freshness. It's a sign of the times that even basic Australian whites like this are now selling at £4 a bottle.

1994 Berri Estates Unwooded Chardonnay
££ / 2 / ⚑   14/20
As its name suggests, this is an unoaked Australian Chardonnay made from grapes grown in the warm, irrigated Riverland region. As such, its a timely fruit-steered break with the old-fashioned styles previously produced at Berri.

1994 Rawsons Retreat Penfolds Bin 21 Semillon/Chardonnay
£££ / 2 / ⚑   15/20
A good example of the new-style Penfolds whites. With its spicy vanilla oak, herby Semillon and Chardonnay richness, these two grapes combine harmoniously to produce a sundae of vanilla ice cream and lemony fruit.

1994 Lindemans Bin 65 Chardonnay
££ / 3 / ⚑   14/20
By comparison, this sweeter, oakier Aussie white tastes a little clumsy and old-fashioned. It's still a good benchmark for under-£5 Chardonnays from Down Under, however.

CHILE

1994 Sauvignon Blanc, Caliterra
£££ / 2 / ⚑   16/20
Crisp, zesty, engagingly aromatic Chilean Sauvignon made by the passionate Ignacio Recabarren. This is midway between the elegance of Sancerre and the pungency of a Marlborough Sauvignon Blanc, showing flavours of grapefruit and melon, and tremendous concentration for a wine at under £4.

FRANCE

1994 Domaine de la Tuilerie, Vin de Pays d'Oc
££ / 2 / ⚑   14/20
Peachy, ripe, New World influenced Chardonnay from Hugh 'Grant' Ryman, showing typically smoky oak chip characters and melony richness. A good buy at under £4.

1993 Domaine de Rivoyre Chardonnay, Vin de Pays d'Oc
££ / 2 / ⚑   **15/20**

We found this a little fuller than the excellent 1992, but Hugh 'Guru' Ryman has once again produced one of the best value Chardonnays in the South of France. The wine combines the ripe, tropical fruit of the New World with some well-judged French elegance.

1994 Chardonnay, James Herrick, Vin de Pays d'Oc
££ / 2 / ⚑   **15/20**

Probably the best release yet from Englishman James Herrick's extensive Chardonnay plantings near Narbonne, this is a peachy, lightly oaked white with hints of butter and greengage, and an RSJ of supporting acidity.

1994 Gewürztraminer d'Alsace, Cave de Turckheim
££ / 2 / ⚑   **15/20**

On the unoily side for an Alsace Gewürztraminer, but none the worse for that, this is a fresh, lychee-like white with supporting acidity and definition. Well-priced at under £5.

1990 Château Haut-Theulet, Monbazillac, 50cl
££ / 7 / ⚑   **14/20**

A raisin and honey-like dessert white from the Bergerac region of southwestern France in a handy half-litre bottle. Poor person's Sauternes, which just limbos under the £5 barrier.

GERMANY

1990 Scharzhofberger Riesling Kabinett, R Müller
££ / 4 / ⚑   **14/20**

A well-priced, medium sweet Riesling with some of the green apple and petrol characters of good Mosel whites. Attractive enough, if a little lacking in concentration.

ITALY

1994 Soave Classico, Vigneti di Montegrande, Pasqua
££££ / 2 / ♪   15/20

An excellent value, textbook Soave showing soft, well-rounded flavours of ripe pears and almond. Carbon dioxide and natural acidity give the wine an extra fillip.

1994 Somerfield Frascati Superiore, Pallavicini
££ / 2 / ♪   14/20

Made at the Pallavicini estate from a blend of 60 per cent Trebbiano Toscano and 40 per cent Malvasia di Candia, this is a crisp, banana-like Roman white with appealing citrus-fruit freshness and good weight.

1994 Chardonnay del Piemonte, Araldica
££££ / 2 / ♪   15/20

A superfresh, unoaked, crisply fruity northwestern Italian Chardonnay with attractive peachy flavours and buttery softness. One of a series of well-made whites we've had this year from Piemonte's Araldica co-operative.

PORTUGAL

1994 Bairrada Branco, Caves Aliança
££ / 2 / ♪   14/20

A lemony, modern Portuguese white made from a blend of the local, lesser-spotted Bical, Maria Gomes, Sercial and Rabo d'Ovelha grapes. It's a clean, fresh, appley white with a touch of attractive spice and white pepper.

£5–8

AUSTRALIA

1993 Penfolds Organic Sauvignon/Chardonnay, Clare Valley
££ / 2 / ♪   15/20

Crisp, elegant, almost Graves-style white from Penfolds' pioneering organic vineyard in South Australia's Clare Valley. Toasty, fresh and restrained, this is one of the New World's best organic whites.

Red

Under £3

BULGARIA

Somerfield Bulgarian Country Red, Merlot/Pinot Noir, Sliven
££ / MB / ↓   13/20
A chunky, leafy attempt at a modern style by one of the better co-operatives in Bulgaria. You wouldn't necessarily guess that this rustic, blackcurrant pastille red included Pinot Noir in its blend, but it's still a good value quaffer at under £3.

FRANCE

1994 Vin de Pays des Côtes de Gascogne, Yvon Mau
£££ / MB / ↓   14/20
A fresh, softly grassy claret-style blend of Tannat and Cabernet Sauvignon, made by Bordeaux *négociant* Yvon Mau. It's unusual to find red Côtes de Gascogne wines in the UK, although some allegedly find their way onto British shelves labelled as claret.

ITALY

1994 Castelvero Rosso del Monferrato, Araldica
£££ / MB / ↓   14/20
A savoury, youthful blend of cherryish Dolcetto and spicy, lively Barbera from Piemonte's Monferrato hills. The Araldica co-operative does this sort of trattoria glugger as well as anyone in Italy.

PORTUGAL

Leziria Vinho Tinto, Almeirim
£ / MB / ↓   13/20
Light, peppery, slightly sweetened-up Portuguese quaffer which has lost some of its beefy concentration in the last two vintages.

£3–5

AUSTRALIA

Somerfield Cabernet Sauvignon, Penfolds
£ / MB / ⁅   13/20

A dry, rather basic, confected Australian red which ought to provide a lot more flavour and complexity than this at over £4.

1993 Penfolds Rawsons Retreat Bin 35
££ / MB / ⁅   15/20

In typical Penfolds mould, this Cabernet Sauvignon/Shiraz blend has masses of sweet plum and blackberry fruit overlaid by a forest of spicy American oak. But don't tell Greenpeace.

CHILE

Somerfield Chilean Cabernet Sauvignon, Segu Olle
££ / MB / ⁅   14/20

Juicy, sweetly ripe Cabernet Sauvignon from the highly respected winemaker Aurelio Montes. It's a deeply coloured, and, for Chile, relatively soft and supple style.

FRANCE

1994 Somerfield Syrah, Vin de Pays d'Oc, Jeanjean
£ / FB / ⁅   13/20

A chunkily aromatic Languedoc Syrah from one of the Midi's largest exporters. The perfume is more enticing than the wine's dry, robust tannins.

1994 Somerfield Côtes du Roussillon, Jeanjean
££ / FB / ⁅   14/20

Firm, broad-shouldered Roussillon blend of Syrah, Carignan and Grenache from the same supplier, with some scented Mediterranean spice and tarry tannins.

Somerfield Fitou, Cuvée Roches d'Embrée, Cave du Mont Tauch
££ / FB / ⅃   14/20
Soft, chocolatey, peppery Carignan and Grenache-based red made by the
well-run Mont Tauch co-operative in the heart of Cathar country.

Somerfield Cabernet Sauvignon, Vin de Pays d'Oc, Val d'Orbieu
£ / MB / ⅃   13/20
Dry, dour, blackcurranty Cabernet Sauvignon from southern France's
largest producer, Val d'Orbieu. We found previous releases of this wine
a good deal more supple.

1991 Château de Caraguilhès, Corbières
££ / FB / ⅃   15/20
With its stylish embossed label and complex aromas of thyme and
rosemary, this deeply coloured organic Corbières is a robustly
structured, well-made red.

1994 Château Carbonel, Côtes du Rhône
£££ / FB / ⅃   15/20
A modern, juicy, supple Côtes du Rhône with aromatic raspberry
fruitiness and good length of flavour based on the Grenache grape. Well-
priced at under £4.

ITALY

Somerfield Valpolicella, Pasqua
££ / MB / ⅃   13/20
A pleasant, light, cherryish quaffing Valpol with attractive, gluggable
fruitiness and a nip of tannin.

1993 Lazio Rosso, Casale San Giglio
£ / MB / ⅃   13/20
There's no truth in the rumour, as far as we're aware, that Somerfield is
about to launch a Rangers Cuvée following the departure of peroxide-
blonde Paul Gascoigne from Lazio, but this old-fashioned leafy blend of
Merlot and Sangiovese is apparently available for a free transfer.

1993 I Grilli di Villa Thalia, Calatrasi
£££ / FB / 🍾   15/20
A soft, tobaccoey, unoaked Sicilian blend of Nero d'Avola, Cabernet
Sauvignon, Sangiovese and Syrah. With its fresh acidity and baked,
slightly spearminty Mediterranean fruitiness, this unusual red is brilliant
value at around £3.70.

1993 Chianti Classico, Montecchio
££ / MB / 🍾   14/20
Made by the much-fêted consultant oenologist Franco Bernabei, this is
an oaky, concentrated, youthful Chianti with the robust chewiness of
the Sangiovese grape and good concentration.

PORTUGAL

1991 Cabernet Sauvignon, Quinta de Pancas
££ / MB / 🍾   15/20
A fluent Portuguese attempt at a modern, international style of Cabernet
Sauvignon. We enjoyed this soft, spicy, elegantly oaked red, and so, we
trust, will you.

1991 Foral Tinto, Caves Aliança
££ / FB / 🍾   14/20
Spicy, aromatic, sweety oaked, modern Portuguese red from the Douro
region with encouraging suppleness of fruit and balance.

1992 Tempranillo, Rioja Berberana
£££ / MB / 🍾   16/20
A wine which combines the best of traditional and modern-style
Rioja. It's got the succulent oak sweetness of the former and the
structured Tempranillo fruitiness of the latter. It all adds up to a soft,
attractively balanced red with plenty of strawberry fruit and vanilla
complexity.

UNITED STATES

Somerfield Californian Dry Red, Sebastiani
££ / MB / 🍷   14/20
Ripe, deeply coloured, softly commercial blend of Cabernet Sauvignon
and Petite Sirah from a winery which is leading the value-for-money
charge in America.

£5–8

FRANCE

1990 Margaux, Peter Sichel
£ / MB / 🍷   14/20
Apparently made from declassified Château Palmer grapes, this £7 claret
is elegant and oaky but a little lacking in stuffing, considering its
pedigree and vintage.

1990 Châteauneuf-du-Pape, Domaine de la Solitude
£££ / FB / �`   16/20
From the same harvest as the claret, this is a heady, modern, Grenache-
based Châteauneuf-du-Pape with a comparatively high percentage of
Syrah and Mourvèdre and a small amount of new oak ageing. It's a rich,
chocolatey, supple red with masses of fruit concentration and ripe
tannins.

ITALY

1990 Salice Salentino Riserva, Taurino
££ / FB / 🍷   15/20
A spicy, herby Mediterranean classic with savoury, bitter almond
characters and big, ripe, tarry tannins. It's a demanding Puglian red,
which gives you plenty of alcohol and flavour for your money at just
over £5. One of a line-up of excellent Italian reds at Somerfield.

Sparkling

£3-5

ITALY

Somerfield Asti Spumante, Araldica
££ / 5 / ⚑   14/20
An attractively grapey, fresh fizz in which Muscat sweetness and
sherbety, appley acidity are nicely balanced.

Over £8

FRANCE

Prince William Blanc de Blancs Brut Champagne, Michel Gonet
£ / 3 / ⚑   13/20
A homage to William Windsor rather than England rugby captain Will
Carling, we presume. This is a faintly toasty, basic Champagne which is
long on sweetness and short on finesse. One for the Tower.

Fortified

£3-5

SPAIN

Somerfield Manzanilla, Gonzalez Byass
£££ / 1 / ⚑   15/20
A salty, crisply dry, well-made Manzanilla from the respected house of
Gonzalez Byass, best known for its Tio Pepe Fino. Chill well and drink
with a bowl of olives for maximum enjoyment.

SPAR **

Head Office: Spar Landmark Ltd, 32–40 Headstone Drive, Harrow, Middlesex HA3 5QT

Telephone: 0181 863 5511

Number of branches: 2,400 stores of which 1,930 are licensed

Credit cards accepted: At individual retailer's discretion

Hours of opening: Varies. Average of 91 hours a week per store

By-the-case sales: At individual retailer's discretion

Glass loan: Yes, in some branches

Home delivery: No

Clubs: Not for consumers, but 480 retailers belong to the Spar Wine Club

Discounts: At individual retailer's discretion

In-store tastings: Yes

Top ten best-selling wines: Lambrusco; Liebfraumilch; Bulgarian Red; Valencia Red; Valencia Medium White; French Country Red; Claret; Bulgarian White; Soave; Jacob's Creek Shiraz/Cabernet

Range: GOOD: Regional France
AVERAGE: Italy, Bordeaux, white Burgundy, Germany, South Africa, Spain, Hungary, Bulgaria, Australia
POOR: Sparkling wines, Portugal, California, Chile

Before leaving at the end of 1994, Master of Wine Philippa Carr had, in seven years, taken Spar from an organisation with a couple of dozen dreary wines to a fighting force of 140-odd well-selected bottles. The good news is that Liz Aked, Carr's partner for half that time, has taken over the baton and is running with it. Running rather fast actually, because 75 Landmark cash and carry depots and their old-fashioned wine ranges have also been dumped in her lap.

Spar was founded in Holland in 1932 and now boasts a worldwide organisation of 25,000 shops in 25 countries, all sporting the familiar Christmas tree logo. The 2,400 shops in Britain – 1,930 of which are licenced – make Spar the country's second-largest (in pure numbers) off-licence chain after the Co-op. Branches, most of which are independently owned, are especially strong in outlying regions of the country, less so within the M25.

Spar means thrift in Dutch, the name being the key to what Spar is about; essentially a top-up shop, open long hours (50 stores are open 24 hours a day in city centres), and serving a local community in which the zimmer frame is an everyday sight. In the black and white world of marketing, where a wine shop is either a convenience or destination store, Spar is the epitome of the former. Customers will not go out of their way to try the Spar Don Darias or the Spar Rosenlieb, but they will pick up a bottle or two while buying their daily bread and *Daily Mail*.

It's hardly surprising, then, that Spar still ranks Germany as its biggest supplier, closely followed by Italy. France is in third place, while the New World trails several lengths behind. Nor will it stun you to learn that a good two-thirds of the Spar range is in the £2.99 to £3.99 price band. Despite the strong Lieb and Lambrusco orientation, though, both are on the wane, thanks to the gradual development of a wider range of better quality wines, in particular from southern France and Eastern Europe.

Though Liz Aked recognises that Spar does not have the image of, say, a Marks & Spencer, she is determined to ensure that she can at least offer a distinctive wine range, giving value for money at the right price. She must have been doing something right, because in an increasingly tough market, wine sales went up 26 per cent in volume over the past year without Aked having to resort to the £1.99 promotions on which the major supermarkets have focused so strongly.

'The retail trade is under strong pressure to maintain the £1.99 bottle, but they have to be careful they don't turn the £2.99 customer into a £1.99 one,' says Aked. Focusing instead on promoting two wines for a fiver, normally including six products at around the £2.99 mark, has resulted in a noticeable uptake of the promoted wines.

Why do Spar bother with wine? 'Wine is probably the most important product category in terms of changing people's perceptions,' says Aked. Baked beans are baked beans are baked beans, but 'wine can make a statement. Spar has used wine to try to elevate the perception of what it has to offer.' This involves a fine balancing act between bringing in a handful of exciting flying winemakers and New World wines and avoiding alienating the traditional Spar shopper.

Aked is working on a project with Australian flying winemaker Kym Milne to bring in some of his Italian wines, and aims to expand the Spar own-label range in the New World because 'brands in the New World areas don't offer the best value to consumers'. In stark contrast to the rest of the range, only one of Spar's 23 New World wines is priced at under £3.99, so it's quite an achievement to have got through 20,000 cases of Australia's Jacob's Creek at over £4 a bottle.

All the more so when the majority of Spar customers are pretty conservative and the shops themselves, many with only limited shelf space, are free to stock their wines from any source. (Most of them are independently owned.) Yet, despite these limitations and the lack of a strong wine image at Spar, Aked has a good opportunity this year to expand the horizons of Spar's customers by developing new labels in California, South Africa and Australia in 1996. We're looking forward to the changes.

White

Under £3

BULGARIA

Spar Bulgarian Country Muskat/Ugni Blanc, Slaviantzi
££ / 3 / ▌   13/20
Clean, fresh, grapey Bulgarian blend in which the aromas of the Muskat grape predominate. A good Liebfraumilch substitute.

HUNGARY

Spar Hungarian Danube White
££ / 3 / ≬   14/20
From the Kiskoros region, this is a curranty, peachy blend of the
Szürkebarat and Riesling grapes in an attractively off-dry, modern style.
Will Szürkebarat replace Chardonnay as the world's favourite grape? We
might have to learn how to pronounce it first.

ITALY

Spar Lambrusco 5%
0 / 6 / ≬   12/20
Baked, lemonady Lambrusco which has lost some of its freshness and
spark.

SPAIN

Spar Valencia, Gandia
0 / 4 / ≬   12/20
A baked, overripe, sweetened-up white made from the undistinguished
Merseguera grape. A picador short of a bullfight.

£3-5

AUSTRALIA

1993 Lindemans Coonawarra Colombard/Chardonnay
£ / 2 / ≬   13/20
Smoky oak and light, pineappley fruitiness make this a pleasant, if
slightly dilute, introduction to Australia.

1994 Jacob's Creek Riesling
£ / 3 / ≬   14/20
Crisp, lemony Riesling made by Orlando, one of Australia's most
successful exporters. An agreeable quaffer.

CZECH REPUBLIC

Spar Moravian Vineyards
£££ / 2 / ▌   15/20

Made from Olasz Riesling and Müller-Thurgau grapes, this is a soft,
modern, slightly peppery white which reminded us of an Austrian
Grüner Veltliner. Great value at just over £3.

FRANCE

Spar Chardonnay, Vin de Pays d'Oc, Cuxac
££ / 3 / ▌   14/20

A New World-influenced banana and boiled sweets-like Chardonnay
from the Languedoc's quality-conscious Cuxac co-operative.

1993 Spar Chardonnay, Domaine du Rivage, Cuxac
££ / 2 / ▌   15/20

From the same source, this is the identical wine aged in oak, which gives
it a sheen of vanilla sweetness.

1993 Vouvray, Donatien Bahuaud
£ / 4 / ▌   14/20

Well-made, well-priced, off-dry Chenin Blanc with green apple crispness
and balancing honeyed fruitiness from Loire *négociant* Donatien
Bahuaud (pronounced 'bow-wow').

Spar Vin de Pays de Côtes Catalanes
£ / 2 / ▌   13/20

A blend of the Catalan grape Macabeo with Grenache Blanc and Muscat,
this is a fresh, zesty, aromatic white from the Rivesaltes co-operative in
the Roussillon region.

Oaked Chasan, Vin de Pays d'Oc
0 / 2 / ▌   13/20

Oak-chippy, coarse, slightly spicy white from Domaines Virginie, an
operation which seems to have lost its sureness of touch.

1994 Chardonnay, James Herrick, Vin de Pays d'Oc
££ / 2 / ♪   15/20
Probably the best release yet from Englishman James Herrick's extensive
Chardonnay plantings near Narbonne, this is a peachy, lightly oaked
white with hints of butter and greengage, and an RSJ of supporting
acidity.

GERMANY

Spar Liebfraumilch
£ / 4 / ♪   13/20
One of the better and drier styles of high street Lieb (although it does
cost over £3), this is fresh and floral with soft, grapey fruitiness.

1993 Mainzer Domherr Spätlese, Rudolf Müller
£ / 4 / ♪   13/20
A soft, sweetish blend of Müller-Thurgau, Silvaner and Riesling. A step
up from Liebfraumilch. Well, a short one anyway.

HUNGARY

1993 Dunavar Prestige Chardonnay
££ / 2 / ♪   15/20
Made in Hungary's southern Szekszard region by the Italian firm of
Antinori, this is a really well-made, peachy, unoaked Chardonnay with
lots of richness and balance in a stylish Burgundy bottle.

ITALY

1994 Bianco di Custoza, Boscaini
0 / 2 / ♪   12/20
Great package, but the wine tastes bitter, old-fashioned, austere and out
of kilter.

PORTUGAL

1992 Duque de Viseu, Dão, Sogrape
£ / 2 / ♪   14/20
An unusual Iberian white with limey, Rhine Riesling-like aromas, spicy

freshness and a touch of oak from Sogrape (the people you can blame for Mateus Rosé).

Spar Portuguese White, Doña Elena
££££ / 3 / 🍷   15/20
Made by Paolo Negra at the Benfica co-operative, this is a blend of mainly local grapes with 10 per cent Muscat for added aromatic complexity. It's weighty and fresh with attractive lemony crsipness.

£5–8

FRANCE

1993 Spar Viognier, Vin de Pays d'Oc
£ / 2 / 🍷   14/20
Soft, apricoty Viognier from the hand of Serge Dubois at the Cuxac co-operative. A little overworked and lacking in acidity, but pleasant enough.

GERMANY

1992 Piesporter Goldtröpfchen Riesling, Grans Fassian
£££ / 4 / ⌐   16/20
One of the most expensive white wines on Spar's shelves, but it's still worth paying nearly £6 for this beautifully fresh, mouthwatering Mosel, with its featherweight elegance, faintly keroseney character and definition. One of the best German wines on the market at this price.

Red

Under £3

BULGARIA

Spar Bulgarian Country Red, Cabernet/Cinsault, Russe
££ / MB / 🍷   14/20
Soft, chocolatey, well-made red from one of the more reliable wineries

in Bulgaria. It's thanks to affordable, modern-style wines like this that Bulgaria is making a comeback in the UK.

HUNGARY

Spar Hungarian Danube Red
0 / LB / ♪   12/20
A light, rather rasping attempt at a Beaujolais-style red, using the local Kekfrankos and Kadarka grapes. An anaemic Bull's Blood.

SPAIN

Spar Valdepeñas, Felix Solis
0 / FB / ♪   11/20
Rooty, raisiny, old-fashioned Spanish tinto best used for greasing windmills.

Spar Valencia Red, Gandia
0 / MB / ♪   11/20
Another raisiny, tart Spanish plonk. And we thought Spain had moved into the 20th century . . .

£3–5

AUSTRALIA

1993 Jacob's Creek Shiraz/Cabernet
£ / MB / ♪   14/20
Tarry sweet oak and toffee-fudge flavours predominate here. The blackcurrant pastille fruit doesn't quite cope with the strong-armed combination.

BULGARIA

1993 Bulgarian Merlot/Gamay, Russe
£ / FB / ♪   13/20
Leathery, chunky Bulgarian red infused with American oak chip character, which adds complicating rusticity and dryness to what ought to be a fresher wine.

CZECH REPUBLIC

Spar Moravian Vineyards Czech Red
££ / MB / ⅜   14/20

Like its white counterpart, this red blend of Frankovka and Vavrinecke is an excellent calling card for Vaclav Havel's Czech Republic, which has yet to be recognised as a bona fide wine producing country. A juicy, peppery, strawberry-fresh red made by Australian Nick Butler.

FRANCE

1994 Hautes Terres, Coteaux du Tricastin
£ / MB / ⅜   13/20

A green, chewy, heftily rustic blend of Syrah, Cinsault and, mainly, the workhorse Carignan grape. *Basses* rather than *Hautes* Terres, we suggest.

1994 Spar Merlot, Vin de Pays d'Oc
££ / MB / ⅜   14/20

Fresh, grassy aromas give way to firm, oaky flavours in this decent, smartly packaged Languedoc red from the Cuxac co-operative.

1993 Château Bories Azeau, Corbières, Val d'Orbieu
££ / MB / ⅜   15/20

Soft, juicy, gingery, carbonic maceration style red with sandalwood spice and an appealingly dry, bitter twist.

Spar Vin de Pays des Côtes Catalanes
£ / MB / ⅜   13/20

Chunky, *garrigue*-like, unoaked Roussillon red tinged with pistachio spiciness and robust tannins.

1992 Faugères, Domaine du Moulin
0 / FB / ⅜   12/20

Another disappointing red from Domaines Virginie, in which some rather basic grapes have too much oak character. The result is a bitter and rather charry mishmash.

Spar French Country Red, Vin de Pays de l'Hérault, 1 litre
0 / MB / 🍷   12/20

Soft, deeply coloured southern plonk with a rustic bite.

1993 Spar Claret, Dulong
££ / MB / 🍷   14/20

A smooth, pleasantly grassy, modern-style claret from the house of Dulong, which shows that paying an extra 50 pence a bottle in Bordeaux is often worthwhile.

ITALY

1994 Spar Montepulciano d'Abruzzo, Cantina Tollo
££ / MB / 🍷   14/20

Cherried, attractive Marche red showing a hint of commercial sweetness and an Italianate nip of refreshing acidity.

PORTUGAL

Spar Portuguese Red, Doña Elena
££ / MB / 🍷   14/20

Originally labelled as Doña Maria, this bright, savoury, characterful red from the Benfica co-operative was forced to change its name to the equally snappy Doña Elena, when the Wine Standards Board discovered that Doña Maria was the name of a local grape variety. Good to know they're spending their time on such vital matters.

SOUTH AFRICA

1994 Table Mountain Pinot Noir, Stellenbosch
£ / MB / 🍷   13/20

Jammy, morello cherry style red with a sweet touch of Pinot Noir character.

£5-8

AUSTRALIA

1992 Bankside Shiraz, South Eastern Australia
££ / FB / ⏵-   **16/20**
Very rich, very minty, very spicy Aussie red from BRL-Hardy. It's a concentrated, charry style that could only come from Down Under. Francophiles may find the flavours a little too obvious for their subtle palates.

1994 Lindemans Cawarra Shiraz/Cabernet
£ / MB / ⏵   **15/20**
Sweet, soft, toffeed Aussie red with plenty of colour and succulence. Good stuff, but a little on the pricey side at nearly £6.

FRANCE

1992 Lussac St-Emilion, Dulong
£ / MB / ⏵   **14/20**
Decent, if a teeny bit pricey, Merlot-based claret from one of St-Emilion's many outlying satellite districts, which shows the lightness of the 1992 vintage.

1990 Château Clos l'Église, Côtes de Castillon
££ / MB / ⏵   **15/20**
Another Merlot-based Right Bank claret, from the hills of Castillon. The superior 1990 vintage shines through on this ripe, fleshy claret with its soft-leather finish.

ITALY

1991 Monastero di Nostra Signora Pinot Nero, Boscaini
££ / MB / ⏵   **15/20**
Unoaked, concentrated Pinot Noir in which Burgundian suppleness meets Italian spice. A big, dry Alto Adige version of a Bourgogne Rouge.

PORTUGAL

1991 Vinha do Monte, Alentejo
££ / FB / 🍷 **15/20**
From the baking-hot plains of southern Portugal's Alentejo region, this is a peppery, tarry, prune-like red with a core of minty, mature fruitiness and high acidity. A welcome curiosity.

Rosé

£3–5

FRANCE

1994 Spar Rosé de Syrah, Vin de Pays d'Oc
££ / 3 / 🍷 **14/20**
A sweetish, bubblegummy pink quaffer in which the blackberry fruitiness of the Syrah grape adds interest and a degree of complexity.

Sparkling

£3–5

AUSTRALIA

Great Western Brut, Seppelt
££ / 3 / 🍷 **14/20**
Frothy, soft, grapey fizz from Australia with the emphasis on quaffability and sherbety, tangy fruitiness.

Over £8

FRANCE

Spar Champagne, Marquis de Prevel, Marne et Champagne
££ / 2 / ▮   15/20
Youthful, malty Champagne with big, toad's-eye bubbles and strawberry
jam fruitiness. Good, basic, fresh, yeasty fizz at under £13.

Fortified

£3–5

FRANCE

Muscat de Saint Jean de Minervois, Val d'Orbieu, half-bottle
£££ / 8 / ▮   15/20
From the hills of the Languedoc, this perfumed, fortified Muscat has a
lightness and freshness that often eludes Mediterranean stickies.
Honeyed, dried-fruits flavours and fresh acidity make this a good value
alternative to the better-known Muscat-de-Beaumes-de-Venise.

£5–8

PORTUGAL

1988 Spar Old Cellar LBV Port
££ / FB / ▮   15/20
Fiery, plummy, spicy, Christmas pudding like Port with plenty of
chunky, Douro tannins and chocolatey sweetness. From the Symington-
owned Smith Woodhouse operation.

TESCO ***(*)

Head Office: Old Tesco House, Delamare Road, Cheshunt, Herts EN8 9SL

Telephone: 01992 632222

Number of branches: 521 (including former William Low stores and the Cité de l'Europe development)

Credit cards accepted: Access, Visa, Switch

Hours of opening: Monday to Thursday 9.00am to 8.00pm; Friday 9.00 am to 9.00pm; Saturday 8.00am to 8.00pm; Sunday 10.00am to 4.00pm

By-the-case sales: Contact Head Office for details. Tesco wine club offers case sales.

Glass loan: Available in larger stores

Home delivery: Through wine club; Tesco Wine Select

Clubs: Tesco Wine Select. Contact Freephone 0800 403 403

Discounts: Contact Head Office for details

In-store tastings: In selected stores. Permanent tasting area in larger stores

Top ten best-selling wines: Tesco Liebfraumilch; Tesco Hock; Tesco Lambrusco Bianco; Tesco French Red; Tesco Australian Red; Tesco Muscadet; Jacob's Creek Dry Red; Tesco Sicilian Red; Tesco Niersteiner Gutes Domtal; Tesco Bulgarian Country Red

Range: GOOD: Australia, Champagne, New Zealand, South Africa, Italy
AVERAGE: Bordeaux, Spain, Rhône, United States, Fortified, Canada, Eastern Europe, Burgundy white, Germany, regional France
POOR: Alsace, Burgundy red, Loire

Even by the cosmopolitan standards of British supermarkets, Tesco takes a globetrotting approach to wine buying. Its list is freighted with bottles from all sorts of strange places – Brazil and Canada are this year's additions to a range which spans 29 countries and 775 wines. Tesco customers do not want for variety and breadth of choice.

Naturally, some of these wines sell better than others. You can't, for instance, imagine queues forming around the block for a Canadian blend of Gamay and Baco Noir. But Tesco insists that it's not interested in stocking weird wines for the sake of it. 'A lot of our wines are small volume lines,' says wine buying controller Ann-Marie Bostock, 'but they still turn over a case or so a week. We're part of a supermarket and to keep our share of space we have to use it to good effect.'

Trading manager Stephen Clarke is proud of the fact that his team of buyers – Bostock, Judith Candy, Janet Lee, Sara Marsay, Daniel Quinn, Alistair Short and Pippa Rogers – spends more time travelling than any of its competitors. The line-up of buyers is more extensive than ever, the range continues to expand and everyone at Tesco seems pretty happy with developments over the last 12 months. The fact that Tesco officially overtook Sainsbury's as the UK's leading retailer in 1995 also helped raise spirits skywards.

As one of the highest profile departments within the chain, the wine team is anxious to remain competitive. 'A lot of our success can be put down to the quality of what we list and the fact that we keep innovating,' says wine buying controller Lee. Innovation there certainly has been. The last year has seen Tesco launch Tesco Wine Select (a mail order service for customers), open its largest ever wine store inside Calais' Cité de l'Europe, convert the Scottish William Low chain into Tesco supermarkets and hold a first-ever Wine Fair in May and June.

All this sounds terribly positive, but we feel that there have been a number of jarring notes. It began just before Christmas, with a party to unveil Wine Select at Madame Tussaud's. Surrounded by waxwork celebrities, it was hard to avoid the reflection that some of the dummies were more lively than the wines on the tasting table. The selection from France was particularly snoozeworthy.

The launch of the May Wine Fair was another disappointment. Many of the wines appeared to show an unhealthy obsession with price and scant regard for quality. Sancerre at £4.99 is all very well, but not when it tastes thin and charmless. The higher priced wines weren't necessarily any better – a Beaune Premier Cru at £12.99 was particularly rooty and rustic. Only the New World range – a round of applause for wines from Caliterra, De Wetshof, Rosemount and Yalumba – brought some much-needed interest to the proceedings.

So we approached this year's *Grapevine* tasting with mixed feelings. On the one hand, Tesco's enormous range was bound to provide us with some surprises; on the other, the average quality of many of its own-label wines – the stuff that accounts for 40 per cent of the list and sells in the biggest volumes – was worrying.

As it turned out, we enjoyed the tasting more than we thought we would. Apart from the chain's more prominent strengths, such as Australian wines over £6, and wines from Italy and Champagne, the basic range was a huge improvement on the May Wine Fair selection. There were still a lot of dull wines – the Sancerre, basic Muscadet, Chablis, Hock, Lambrusco, red Burgundy, claret and Australian red could all do with a visit to the nearest flying winemaker, or possibly plastic surgeon – but these were balanced by exciting wines from Chile, New Zealand, Spain and southern France.

How is a Tesco customer expected to pick his or her way between so many different wines? The answer is in-store advisers, first introduced two years ago and now being rolled out (as they say in marketing speak) to a total of 24 stores. 'It's all about increasing customer service,' says Bostock. 'It helps to have someone who is knowledgeable and can make customers feel comfortable.' Bad luck if you happen to live near one of the 500-odd stores which cannot draw on the services of a wine adviser.

Tesco Wine Select is part of the same consumer-friendly project, according to Bostock. For shoppers too busy or too lazy to lift themselves from the three-piece suite in the front room, Dudley Moore's favourite chain offers a range of pre-selected cases and an à la carte list of 80 wines. As we've indicated, most of the wines would encourage us to lead a more active life. Even Lee admits that selling wine by mail order 'is very different to selling wine in-store; it's a steep learning curve.'

Back with the main range, Tesco continues to work with two flying winemakers – Kym Milne and John Worontschak – though it has not gone airborne to the same extent as Sainsbury's. Mr Worontschak has been given some particularly difficult tasks. Any rational oenologist confronted with the prevailing winemaking conditions in Brazil would surely be tempted to take up another career.

Brazil included, the New World is still growing apace at Tesco.

Australia alone represents 10 per cent of sales; add Chile, South Africa, New Zealand and California and we're talking 20 per cent. Alongside Oddbins, Tesco is the country's biggest retailer of Aussie wines. 'We invested in it before it really took off,' says Bostock, 'and we're starting to see the benefits now.'

This is true enough. It's great to see wines from producers such as Chapel Hill, Tim Adams and Delatite featured, and apparently selling, on supermarket shelves. In fact, the New World range as a whole remains the most exciting area of Tesco's sprawling list. Nevertheless, some of the better Australian estates are in limited distribution only.

This is the problem at Tesco. When the range is good, it's very good; when it's poor, it's very poor indeed. Wacky, out-of-the-way bottles are all fine and dandy, but the wines that really matter are the everyday, generic own-labels. If your local Tesco stocks no more than the basic range, you could be distinctly underwhelmed by what you find. Perhaps Tesco's wine buyers should spend a little less time worrying about Canada, Brazil, and Outer Mongolia and a little more time tasting in Beaujolais, Burgundy, Germany, Bordeaux and the Loire.

White

Under £3

AUSTRALIA

Tesco Australian White
£££ / 3 / **}**   14/20
We suspect that sub-£3 Australian wine is an endangered species, so enjoy this grapey, lime-like, off-dry Rhine Riesling before economic realities catch up with it.

BULGARIA

1994 Bear Ridge Aligoté
£££ / 3 / **}**   15/20
It's unusual to find the Aligoté grape, better known for its supporting rôle in Kir, outside Burgundy. This is a racy, peachy, full-bodied white

from travelling winemaker Kym Milne. The modern face of Bulgarian white-winemaking – we hope.

GERMANY

Tesco Hock
0 / 6 / 1   **12/20**
Grapey, cheap and clean with lots of sugar and a faintly bitter aftertaste.

Tesco Liebfraumilch
0 / 5 / 1   **11/20**
A little less gaggingly sweet than the Hock, this has a whiff of almond kernel about it, which may or may not be something in its favour.

ITALY

Tesco Lambrusco Bianco
£ / 7 / 1   **12/20**
At 7.5 per cent alcohol, this lemonade-sweet fizz from Giacobazzi has a bit more character and freshness than the sweet Germans.

SPAIN

Tesco Marqués de Chivé White
0 / 2 / 1   **12/20**
From the denomination of Utiel-Requena close to Spain's eastern seaboard, this is an austere, sawdusty, extremely basic plonk with a rather sour note to it.

£3–5

AUSTRALIA

1994 Tesco Clare Valley Riesling
£ / 3 / 1   **14/20**
A little disappointing, given the high and normally justified reputation that the producer Mitchell's enjoys for its cool Clare Valley Rieslings. We found this pleasantly aromatic, if a little flat on the palate.

1993 Tesco Hunter Semillon
0 / 2 / 1   13/20

From the Upper Hunter Valley's Rosemount Estate, this oatmealy Semillon is in a dull phase at the moment.

1993 Tesco Western Australian Chenin Blanc
££ / 3 / 1   15/20

From Houghton, the Swan Valley's largest winery, this wine is also available elsewhere under the Moondah Brook label. Consistently one of Australia's most enjoyable whites, it offers flavours of smoky oak, tropical melon and ripe pears.

AUSTRIA

1994 Lenz Moser Grüner Veltliner
£££ / 2 / 1   15/20

Crisp, inexpensive Austrian white, made from the widely planted native Grüner Veltliner grape by one of Central Europe's best known producers, and showing white pepper aromas and fresh, lemony fruitiness. Great value at around £3.50.

BRAZIL

Tesco Brazilian Chardonnay/Semillon
0 / 2 / 1   12/20

From the Rio Grande do Sul region of Brazil (we didn't know they grew grapes there either), this dull, fruitless 1994 white is approaching the end of its natural life. The fresher 1995 follow-on vintage should be on the shelves by January 1996.

BULGARIA

1994 Bear Ridge White Cabernet Sauvignon
0 / 3 / 1   12/20

A Bulgarian curiosity made from red grapes. Neutral, mawkish and rather bitter. Some people will do anything to get the words Cabernet Sauvignon on a label.

CANADA

Tesco Canadian Wine
££ / 2 / ⅟   14/20
Tesco sent English-based Australian winemaker John Worontschak to a
vineyard near Niagara Falls to produce this grapey, toasty, cool climate
white made from the hybrid Vidal grape with a smidgeon of
Chardonnay. The EU forbids the mention of hybrid grapes on the label,
so we're delighted to share this privileged information with you.

CHILE

1993 Canepa Oak Aged Chardonnay
£££ / 2 / ⅟   16/20
An indication of the kind of exciting, value-for-money whites coming out
of Chile. Made by Canepa winemaker Andres Ilabaca, this is a fresh,
citrus-like white with an overlay of sweet, aromatic oak. Brilliant value
for money at under £5.

1994 Caliterra Casablanca Chardonnay
£££ / 2 / ⅟   17/20
**Star winemaker Ignacio Recabarren has produced a brilliant
value Chardonnay from Chile's most exciting white wine area,
the Casablanca Valley, halfway between Santiago and the port of
Valparaiso. Fresh, clean-cut, citrus-fruit flavours with a
grapefruity tang and a touch of oak.**

FRANCE

1993 Domaine Lapiarre, Côtes de Duras
£££ / 2 / ⅟   15/20
The Côtes de Duras is a diminutive appellation between Bordeaux and
Bergerac, producing good value Sauvignon Blanc like this grapefruity,
minerally dry white, halfway in style between a Graves and a good
Sauvignon de Touraine.

GERMANY

1993 Bereich Johannisberg Riesling, Kabinett Krayer
0 / 4 / ▮   13/20
Lots of sulphur and not much Riesling character in evidence here.

Tesco Bernkasteler Riesling Kurfürstlay, Mosel Saar Ruwer
£ / 5 / ▮   13/20
A sweet, faintly floral Riesling, once more swimming in sulphur dioxide.

Tesco Steinweiler Kloster, Liebfrauenberg Kabinett
£ / 5 / ▮   13/20
Fine if you like wines that smell of pine resin and coconut. One to
soothe your lumbago with.

Tesco Steinweiler Kloster, Liebfrauenberg Spätlese
£ / 6 / ▮   14/20
With its attractive apricot and honey-scented aromas, this sweeter
German white has a bit more concentration and peppery freshness.

Tesco Steinweiler Kloster Liebfrauenberg Auslese
££ / 7 / ▮   15/20
Sweeter still, but this is the best of Tesco's sub-£5 German range, a
spicily aromatic Riesling with good concentration and a refreshing
grapefruity tang to balance the richness.

ITALY

Tesco Italian White Wine, Vino da Tavola del Veneto
££ / 2 / ▮   14/20
Aficionados may remember this as Tesco's Italian White Merlot, but
thanks to EU red tape, the Merlot in the name has been dropped because
the wine is less than 100 per cent Merlot. It's a pleasant, stone-fruity
curiosity with a touch of green pepper Merlot character.

Tesco Nuragus di Cagliari
£ / 2 / ▮   13/20
Fresh, clean, aromatic Mediterranean white from Sardinia. The aftertaste
is a little baked and austere.

Tesco Pinot Grigio del Veneto, Pasqua
£ / 2 / ♪   13/20
The almondy character of this northern Italian white reminded us more of southern Italy's Frascati than the Veneto's Soave. A decent, if unexciting, dry white.

Tesco Prosecco del Veneto, Vino da Tavola del Veneto
££ / 1 / ♪   14/20
The name Prosecco usually suggests refreshing sparkling wine, preferably drunk while lying in a gondola on Venice's Grand Canal. This is an unsparkling version, showing lemon-crisp flavours and an attractive bitter twist. Just one Prosecco . . .

Tesco Sauvignon Blanc del Veneto
££ / 2 / ♪   14/20
For readers who like restrained Sauvignon Blanc, this faintly grassy example shows enough varietal character to be worth a punt at just over £3.

NEW ZEALAND

Tesco New Zealand Dry White
££ / 3 / ♪   14/20
With its characteristically fresh Kiwi acidity, this soft, peachy blend of Müller-Thurgau and a touch of Gewürztraminer is one of the few New Zealand whites on the British market available at under £4. If you've never tried a New Zealand white before, this is an undemanding place to start.

Tesco New Zealand Chardonnay, Cooper's Creek, Gisborne
££ / 2 / ♪   14/20
As you'd expect from New Zealand's Gisborne region on the east coast of North Island, this rich Chardonnay, with its bold electric-blue and yellow label, shows plenty of tropical fruit and an intriguing streak of cassis.

PORTUGAL

1993 João Pires Moscato
£ / 2 / ♪   13/20
A grapey, lime-like Portuguese white that has lost a bit of its zip and

concentration since the brand was sold to a multinational a few years ago.

SOUTH AFRICA

1990 Fleur du Cap Late Harvest, Bergkelder, 50cl
£ / 7 / ₤   13/20
A rich, ripe, almost oversweet Cape, sticky with candied orange peel flavours from the sprawling Bergkelder operation.

1995 Goiya Kgeisje
£ / 3 / ₤   13/20
Always among the first wines to arrive on British shores, thanks to early harvest conditions in the Western Cape, this is South Africa's (white) answer to Beaujolais Nouveau. A blend of Sauvignon Blanc and Chardonnay in equal parts from the Vredendal co-operative, this almost off-dry white shows simple banana and boiled sweet flavours. Not a wine to keep.

1994 Oak Village South African Sauvignon Blanc
0 / 2 / ₤   12/20
Bitter, confected Cape white which could be made from almost anything. Not one of the Vinfruco group's better efforts.

1994 Tesco Robertson Chardonnay
££ / 2 / ₤   15/20
From Danie de Wet, the Chardonnay king of Robertson, and one of the best producers in South Africa, this is a well-priced, lightly oaked, elegant white, with complex vanilla, melon and pineapple fruitiness.

Tesco South African Chardonnay/Colombard
£££ / 2 / ₤   15/20
A weightier, oakier Cape blend made at the Madeba winery by peripatetic Australian winemaker John Worontschak (and try saying that after you've had a few). Fantastic value at under £4.

SPAIN

1994 Marqués de Griñon Sauvignon Blanc, Vino de Mesa de Valladolid
££ / 2 / ⅛   15/20

As well as being one of Spain's great socialites – frequent appearances in ¡Hola! magazine would seem to confirm this – the Marqués de Griñon produces some of Spain's best red and white wines. This fresh, aromatic, piercingly citrusy Sauvignon Blanc with its melony concentration would cause a stir at any society bash.

Tesco White Rioja, Viña Mara
0 / 2 / ⅛   12/20

Old-fashioned, oak-chip-style white with too much oak character and too little fruit.

£5–8

AUSTRALIA

1994 Cape Mentelle Semillon/Sauvignon
£££ / 2 / ⅛   17/20

David Hohnen's Western Australian base is less famous than Cloudy Bay, his New Zealand offspring. But the wines can be just as good. This fresh, zippy, Bordeaux-style blend with its subtle oak and tropical melon and grapefruit flavours is one of Australia's most exciting and underrated white wines.

1993 Tesco McLaren Vale Chardonnay
££ / 2 / ⅛   15/20

Rich, ripe, almost old-fashioned Australian Chardonnay from Ryecroft in the McLaren Vale region south of Adelaide, this reeks of smoky oak and peachy fruit.

1992 Tesco Noble Semillon, 37.5cl
££ / 7 / ⅛   16/20

A luscious, extremely complex Aussie sticky made in the Riverina region by the little-known (certainly as far as we're concerned) Wilton Estate. Good weight and concentration and lots of botrytis-derived, honeyed intensity.

1994 The Antipodean
£££ / 2 / ⚊   16/20
An unusual blend of Sauvignon Blanc, Semillon and Viognier, produced
by the family firm of Yalumba, this has a hint of honey and plenty of
tropical citrus fruit flavours. The smart Italian bottle enhances the wine's
striking effect.

FRANCE

Château Liot, Sauternes, 37.5cl
0 / 6 / ⚊   13/20
Tesco blends across different vintages for its Château Liot Sauternes,
presumably in an attempt to produce a consistent style of wine. We
found this rather bitter, however, and lacking in richness. Stick with the
sticky from Oz.

1994 Domaine St James Viognier
0 / 2/ ⚊   13/20
Made by Henri Gualco, normally one of the best producers in the
Corbières region of southern France, this gluey, vulgar Viognier is a big
letdown. It just shows that the fashionable Viognier name doesn't
automatically guarantee quality.

1991 Montagny Premier Cru, Cuvée Spéciale
£ / 2 / ⚊   14/20
The Buxy co-operative produces a large chunk of the Côte Chalonnaise
Burgundies we see in this country. This toast and burnt butter flavoured
Chardonnay is tasty enough, but a little over-oaked and overpriced.

1994 Pouilly Fumé Cuvée Jules, Fouassier Père et Fils
££ / 2 / ⚊   15/20
On the ripe side for a Pouilly Fumé, this is a crisp, minerally Sauvignon
Blanc with plenty of flavour.

1993 Tesco Chablis, Cuvée Claude Dominique, Labouré-Roi
0 / 1 / ⚊   13/20
From the Nuits St Georges firm of Labouré-Roi, this rather austere
Chablis is a reflection of a cool, lean, white Burgundy vintage.

1994 Tesco Sancerre
0 / 1 / 🍾   13/20
Far less good than Tesco's Pouilly Fumé, this light, acidic Sancerre is
more like an inferior Sauvignon de Touraine.

GERMANY

1992 Trittenheimer Apotheke Riesling Kabinett
££ / 4 / ⬇   15/20
A refreshingly appley, typically crisp Mosel Riesling with the capacity
to age for a while yet.

NEW ZEALAND

1993 Coopers Creek Chardonnay, Hawkes Bay
££ / 2 / 🍾   16/20
One of a growing number of top-class Chardonnays emerging from New
Zealand, this Hawkes Bay classic made by Kim Crawford is richly
concentrated, with notes of butterscotch and toffee fudge underpinned
by fresh acidity.

Over £8

AUSTRALIA

1993 Kingston Estate Chardonnay
£ / 2 / 🍾   14/20
This is the first attempt at a premium Chardonnay we've come across
from the Riverland, Australia's Chardonnay hosepipe. It's a rich,
cinnamon-spice and pineapple-fruity white made by Bill Monlaradellis of
Kingston-on-Murray (as distinct from Kingston-upon-Thames). If only it
were half the price.

1993 Tim Adams Semillon, Clare Valley
££ / 1 / ⬇   16/20
Now established as one of the best winemakers in Australia's Clare
Valley, north of Adelaide, Tim Adams produces an award-winning range
of red and white wines. This creamy, vanilla-oak and citrus-flavoured
Semillon is consistently one of his top wines.

Red

Under £3

AUSTRALIA

Tesco Australian Red
£ / MB / ♪   13/20
A blend of Shiraz and Cabernet Sauvignon grapes made by Australia's largest winery, Penfolds. Companies Down Under have to work pretty hard to keep prices below £3, and on this light, and somewhat confected red, it shows.

FRANCE

Tesco Grenache, Vin de Pays d'Oc, Jeanjean
£££ / MB / ♪   14/20
You'd be far better off in fact with this fresh, supple, easy-drinking Grenache made using the carbonic maceration technique for maximum juiciness.

PORTUGAL

1991 Tesco Dão, Sogrape
£ / MB / ♪   13/20
Comparatively modern for a Dão, this dry, robust red has some soft, sweet raisined fruitiness lurking beneath its tannic surface.

SPAIN

Tesco Marqués de Chivé
0 / MB / ♪   12/20
Did someone say Marqués de Chippy? We certainly didn't find much fruit in this light, all-Tempranillo plonk from Utiel-Requena's Gandia winery.

£3-5

AUSTRALIA

Tesco Australian Mataro
0 / MB / 🍷   11/20
Browning, leathery, old-fashioned red from the Murray Valley. Perhaps
someone should tip it into the river of the same name.

CANADA

1994 Tesco Canadian Red
£ / MB / 🍷   13/20
You can't quarrel with Tesco's desire to innovate. Not many
supermarkets would list a Canadian red wine made mainly from the
hybrid Baco grape. This smoky, beetrooty, high-acid red is fine if you're
looking for something unusual, but be warned – its foxy flavours are
highly idiosyncratic.

CHILE

Tesco Chilean Cabernet Sauvignon, Canepa
£££ / MB / 🍷   15/20
Massively coloured, minty, juicy, concentrated Cabernet from one of
Chile's most dependable wineries. Brilliant value at under £4.

1992 Canepa Oak Aged Cabernet Sauvignon
£ / MB / 🍷   14/20
Drier and less fruity than the unoaked version.

1994 Errázuriz Merlot
££ / MB / 🍷   15/20
Consistently one of the best value Chilean reds, this soft, pungent, green
pepper Merlot blended by Kiwi Brian Bicknell at the unpronounceable
Errázuriz Panquehue winery is up to the standard of previous vintages.

FRANCE

Château Les Valentines Bergerac, Vignerons de Sigoulès
££ / MB / ∮   14/20

Chewy, chunky, oaky blend of Merlot, Cabernet Franc and Cabernet Sauvignon from southwestern France's Bergerac region. A solid co-operative red.

Tesco Claret, Yvon Mau
£ / LB / ∮   13/20

With its faint sweetness and green tannic edge, this basic claret is so light it could almost be mistaken for a cheap Anjou Rouge.

Tesco Beaujolais
£ / LB / ∮   13/20

A light, youthful, raspberry and bubblegum-style Beaujolais from the Cave de Bully. Drinkable enough, but plenty of other places provide better value than this at £3.99.

1992 Tesco Domaine des Baumelles, Côtes du Lubéron
££ / MB / ∮   15/20

A juicy blend of three-fifths Grenache and two-fifths Syrah, all the more remarkable given the weather conditions which washed away half the region in 1992.

1994 Tesco Domaine de la Source Syrah, Vin de Pays de l'Hérault
£ / LB / ∮   13/20

Sweet and savoury, easy-drinking red from the South of France. A little short of stuffing.

1992 Tesco Les Domaines, Domaine Beaulieu St Sauveur, Côtes du Marmandais
££ / MB / ∮   14/20

Well-made, claret-like blend from the Languedoc hinterland, showing plenty of soft, raspberry fruit and a nip of dry tannin.

Tesco St-Emilion, Dirovyre Diprovin
££ / MB / ∄   15/20

One of a number of supermarket St-Emilions to have crept under the £5
barrier, this deeply coloured, oaky Merlot-based red has plenty of
richness and fruitcake spice.

1992 Tesco Vintage Claret, Yvon Mau
£ / MB / ∄   13/20

Hard, green and tannic, showing too much oak for its rather lightweight
fruit.

ITALY

1993 Casale Giglio Shiraz
£ / MB / ∄   13/20

An Australian-influenced southern Italian red – even down to the name
of the grape on the label. It's chunky, robust and still rather closed at
the moment.

1991 Copertino Rosso, Francesco Colucci
£££ / FB / ∄   15/20

A powerful, traditional Mediterranean red, showing masses of liquorice
and thyme-scented fruit with lots of sweet alcohol and a raisiny finish.

1993 Tesco Chianti Colli Senesi, Grevepesa
£££ / MB / ∄   15/20

Hard to find better value Chianti than this youthful, savoury, almond and
bitter chocolate red from the Grevepesa co-operative.

Tesco Monica di Sardegna
£ / MB / ∄   13/20

A basic, baked Sardinian red at a basic price. Fine for barbecued sardines.

MEXICO

1990 Tesco Mexican Cabernet Sauvignon, LA Cetto
£ / FB / ∄   13/20

Full-bodied, foursquare Cabernet from Mexico's Baja California
peninsula. This dry, tannic red may have been suffering from a dodgy
cork. We've certainly liked it better in the past.

NEW ZEALAND

1992 Tesco New Zealand Cabernet/Merlot, Gisborne, Corbans
£ / MB / ⅃   13/20

Very much a cool climate red blend, showing the light greenness and lack of stuffing that goes with the absence of sunshine in a washout vintage.

Tesco New Zealand Cabernet Sauvignon, Huapai
££ / MB / ⅃   15/20

Also from New Zealand's cool climate, this richer, fuller red from the Cooper's Creek winery shows attractive, sweetly perfumed cassis fruit and medium-weight tannins.

PORTUGAL

1991 Tesco Bairrada, Cavas Primavera
0 / MB / ⅃   12/20

Old-fashioned, tannic, chewy Portuguese red. Useful in hand-to-hand combat, but not a lot of fun to drink.

SOUTH AFRICA

1992 Tesco Cape Pinotage
££ / FB / ⅃   14/20

With its rustic, baked-banana nose and full-bodied chunky fruitiness, this Cape red from the KWV is exactly what you'd expect from the Pinotage grape.

SPAIN

1992 Tesco Viña Mara Crianza, Rioja
£££ / MB / ⅃   15/20

A modern-style, savoury Crianza Rioja, in which the Tempranillo grape provides a good weight and depth of fruit by way of a counterpoint to the American oak. Berberana consistently produces good value reds such as this one.

£5–8

AUSTRALIA

1992 Chapel Hill Shiraz

££ / MB / ☛   16/20

Made by Pam Dunsford, one of Australia's growing band of women winemakers, this McLaren Vale red is typical of the Chapel Hill style, with soft tannins and concentrated minty fruitiness. Needs a few more years in bottle to develop its full potential.

1992 Delatite Devils River Cabernet/Merlot

£££ / MB / ☛   16/20

Another state (Victoria), another woman winemaker – Ros Ritchie. But a very different style of wine. Here, Victoria's cool climate has resulted in a spearminty, ginger-flavoured blend, with an unmistakeable aroma and refreshing liveliness and zip.

1989 Temple Bruer Shiraz/Malbec, Langhorne Creek

££ / MB / ⌇   15/20

A gold star for Tesco's Australian buyer, Ann-Marie Bostock, for unearthing this unusual aged blend from the Langhorne Creek region. A rich, supple and spicy red, which proves that Australian wines can improve with age.

1993 Yalumba Bush Vine Grenache

£££ / MB / ⌇   17/20

A smoky, opulent Grenache from old Barossa Valley vines, matured in French oak for extra flavour. This peppery, spicy, full-bodied red from the Yalumba winery is everything you'd expect, but seldom receive, from a good southern Rhône red.

1990 Bleasdale Malbec, Langhorne Creek

£££ / MB / ⌇   16/20

Malbec is a pretty rare grape in Shiraz and Cabernet-dominated Australia, but if this leathery, chocolatey, beautifully proportioned drop of the Black Stuff is a sign of what the variety can do down under, we'd like to see a few more producers sticking it in the ground. They could always pull out the Doradillo.

FRANCE

1992 Châteauneuf-du-Pape, Les Arnevels, J. Quiot
0 / FB / ⸖   13/20

From one of the least distinguished of recent southern Rhône vintages, this browning, alcoholic Châteauneuf is showing premature wrinkles.

1993 Clos de Chenôves, Bourgogne Rouge, Cave de Buxy
0 / MB / ⸖   13/20

An over-oaked red Burgundy in which sawdustiness and tart acidity mask what little Pinot Noir character the wine exhibits.

1990 Tesco Pauillac, Borie-Manoux
0 / MB / ⸖   12/20

A claret which has seen better days. Lots of them.

Tesco Red Burgundy, Labouré-Roi
0 / MB / ⸖   13/20

Rooty, heavy, excessively alcoholic red Burgundy from Nuits-St-Georges *négociant* Labouré-Roi.

ITALY

1990 Tesco Chianti Classico Riserva, Grevepesa
£££ / MB / ⸖   16/20

A Chianti Classico which lives up to its denomination, with well-judged oak, spicy fruit and considerable backbone. At just over £5, it's one of the best Italian reds in the high street. A Tuscan star.

1991 Villa Pigna, Cabernasco, Vino da Tavola Rosso
££ / MB / ⸖   15/20

With its chunky designer bottle and smoky mocha oak, this Cabernet-based red from the Italian Marches region is another find. A rich, dense, powerfully fruity mouthful that will repay patience.

SOUTH AFRICA

1992 Fairview Merlot Reserve
£££ / MB / ⚑   16/20
One of the stars of Tesco's South African range, this fresh, minty, succulent, strawberry-jam-like Merlot from Charles Back is almost impossible to dislike. Go on, make our day!

1993 Kanonkop Pinotage
££ / FB / ⚑   16/20
Possibly a little lighter than it has been in previous vintages, South Africa's leading Pinotage is still one hell of a mouthful, packed with plum, blackberry and liquorice flavours and substantial tannins.

1991 Rustenberg Pinot Noir
0 / MB / ⚑   11/20
Rustenberg is one of the Cape's most famous estates. So what happened here with this dried-out, Romanian-style Pinot Noir?

SPAIN

1988 Tesco Viña Mara Rioja Reserva, Berberana
£ / MB / ⚑   14/20
More traditional in style than the same bodega's Crianza red, also available at Tesco, this mature Rioja is starting to show its age. Drink up.

Over £8

AUSTRALIA

1991 Chapel Hill Cabernet Sauvignon
££ / MB / ⚬   16/20
A deeply coloured, concentrated, oaky red from leading winemaker Pam Dunsford, this South Australian Cabernet Sauvignon is chock full of soft, lush tannins and sweet eucalyptusy fruit. Needs three-plus years to open out.

1991 Mick Morris Durif
£ / FB / ←   **14/20**
At 15 per cent alcohol, this inky, raisiny, palate-busting brute made from
Durif grapes – planted by Mick Morris's grandfather in 1920 – is halfway
to a port. Best kept on a short lead.

Rosé

£3–5

FRANCE

1994 Domaine de la Done Syrah
££ / 2 / ♪   **15/20**
A modern coral-pink rosé made from the Syrah grape in a fresh, clean,
up-front fruity style. Good with food.

SOUTH AFRICA

1995 Van Loveren Blanc de Noir Red Muscadel
£ / 4 / ♪   **13/20**
Pale pink, slightly confected Cape Blush for the sweeter of tooth. Chill
well or freeze and serve as an ice lolly.

Sparkling

£5–8

FRANCE

Tesco Blanquette de Limoux
£££ / 2 / ♪   **16/20**
The excellent Limoux co-operative has produced a Mauzac-based fizz
with a biscuity, close-to-Champagne character. For the price, this
southern French fizz is one of the best sparkling wines around.

1990 Tesco Crémant de Bourgogne
£ / 2 / ᵻ   13/20

From Burgundy's Cave de Viré, this tart and rather eggy fizz is disappointing, especially at a pound more than the Blanquette de Limoux.

SPAIN

Tesco Cava, Castellblanch
£ / 2 / ᵻ   13/20

Basic, inexpensive fizz with large toad's-eye bubbles and an earthy bite.

1991 Tesco Vintage Cava, Marqués de Monistrol
0 / 1 / ᵻ   13/20

Dry, austere bottle-aged Spanish sparkling wine. A botched attempt at a Champagne taste-alike.

Over £8

FRANCE

Tesco Blanc de Blancs Brut Champagne, Duval-Leroy
££ / 2 / ᵻ   15/20

From the improving house of Duval-Leroy, this is a yeasty, tangy, all-Chardonnay Champagne, which would go down a treat as an apéritif.

Tesco Champagne Premier Cru Brut NV
£££ / 2 / ᵻ   16/20

Consistently among the best value supermarket Champagnes, this is a crisp, youthful, full-flavoured fizz from the Avize co-operative. Good house fizz, which will benefit from a few extra months under the stairs.

1985 Tesco Vintage Champagne
£££ / 2 / ᵻ   17/20

A first-rate successor to the 1982 Vintage Champagne, also from the Chouilly co-operative. In fact, we actually prefer this rich, toasty Pinot Noir dominated style from one of the smallest but best of Champagne's recent vintages. A wine which combines power with freshness.

Fortified

Under £3

SPAIN

Tesco Superior Manzanilla, Sanchez Romate, 37.5cl
££ / 1 / ¾   15/20
Dry, salty, pungently tangy Manzanilla Sherry with a cleansing, dry aftertaste.

Tesco Superior Oloroso Seco, Sanchez Romate, 37.5cl
£££ / 2 / ¾   16/20
Nutty, amber-coloured, traditional dry Oloroso with crème caramel and toffeed concentration.

£3–5

SPAIN

Tesco Superior Palo Cortado, Sanchez Romate, 37.5cl
££ / 2 / ¾   15/20
A shade sweeter in style, this spicy, fudge-like Sherry retains plenty of bite and acidity. Superior stuff.

£5–8

AUSTRALIA

Tesco Australian Tawny Liqueur Wine, Rosemount
££ / MB / ¾   15/20
A catch-all blend of Shiraz, Grenache, Cabernet Sauvignon and Semillon from McLaren Vale and the Hunter Valley. It's a massively sweet, concentrated, youthful Aussie fortified wine that made us think of Christmas pudding.

Yalumba Show Reserve Muscat
££ / 8 /]   16/20

Mature, fragrant orange peel and rose petal scented Muscat, dripping with candied fruit sweetness and concentration, and yet with enough acidity to prevent it from sticking to the tongue.

PORTUGAL

Tesco LBV Port, Smith Woodhouse
££ / MB /]   15/20

Young, fiery Late Bottled Vintage Port from the Symington-owned Smith Woodhouse company. Solid, well-balanced and extremely sweet.

Tesco Tawny Port, Royal Oporto
0 / MB /]   12/20

Rather young for a tawny, this sweet, spirity Port reminded us of a bistrot ruby.

Tesco Finest Madeira, Madeira Wine Company
££ / 7 / ↝   15/20

Finest might not mean much on a wine label, but this baked, raisiny, caramel-sweet, tangy, Malmsey-style Madeira is pretty good stuff at just under £7.50.

Over £8

PORTUGAL

Tesco 10 Year Old Tawny Port, Smith Woodhouse
££ / MB /]   15/20

A delicate, pruney tawny with lots of spice and a finish that intensifies on the palate. Delicious chilled as an apéritif.

THE THRESHER GROUP
THRESHER ***(*)
WINE RACK ****
BOTTOMS UP ****(*)

Head Office: The Thresher Group, Sefton House, 42 Church Road, Welwyn Garden City, Herts AL8 6PJ

Telephone: 01707 328244

Number of branches: 75 Bottoms Up; 118 Wine Rack; 1,410 Thresher (divided between 838 Thresher Wine Shops, 439 Drinks Stores, 131 Food and Drinks Stores and 2 Home Runs)

Credit cards accepted: Access, Visa, American Express, Switch

Hours of opening: Monday to Saturday 9.00am to 10.30pm; Sunday 11.00am to 4.00pm and 7.00pm to 10.00pm. Food and Drinks Stores the same except open from 8.00am.

By-the-case sales: Yes. Bottoms Up also offers a price guarantee: buy any wine cheaper by the case within seven days of purchase, and it will refund the difference and add a free bottle of the same wine.

Glass loan: Yes

Home delivery: Yes. Free locally. Free nationally where quantities justify it

Clubs: Cellar Key and Exclusively Alsace (Wine Rack); Imbibers (Bottoms Up); Wine with Food Club (Thresher Wine Shops)

Discounts: On cases of table wine (including sparkling wine) under £120: 10 per cent at Bottoms Up, 5 per cent at Wine Rack and Thresher Wine Shops. On cases of table wine (including sparkling wine) over £120: 10 per cent at Bottoms Up, Wine Rack and Thresher Wine Shops. On mixed cases of Champagne: 15 per cent (10 per cent off six if under £120) at Bottoms Up and seven for the price of six at Wine Rack. Generally, there are also special discounts for club members.

In-store tastings: Every Friday and Saturday at Bottoms Up and Wine Rack; occasionally at Thresher Wine Shops

Other services: The Wine Buyer's Guarantee available in Thresher Wine Shops (if you don't like a wine you've purchased, you can take it back and replace it with something else). Drinks Direct Gifting Service (any bottle of wine delivered next day within mainland UK for £9.99 plus standard store price; £5.99 within two days)

Top ten best-selling wines:

Thresher Wine Shops: Liebfraumilch Regional Classics; Jacob's Creek Red; Tollana Dry White; Albor Rioja Tinto; Lambrusco Bianco, Regional Classics; Tollana Red; Mâcon-Villages Blanc, Regional Classics; Figaro Vin de Pays de l'Hérault Red; Hock, Regional Classics; Russe Country Red, Cabernet Cinsault

Range: GOOD: Champagne and sparkling wines, Alsace, Italy, Spain, Australia, Bordeaux, New Zealand, regional France (especially Languedoc-Roussillon), California, Chile
AVERAGE: Burgundy, Beaujolais, Loire, Portugal, Eastern Europe, South Africa
POOR: Germany, Rhône

Wine Rack: Domaine du Tariquet; Albor Rioja Tinto; Tollana Dry White; Figaro Vin de Pays de l'Hérault Red; Jacob's Creek Red; Mâcon-Villages Blanc, Regional Classics; Etchart Torrontes; Gyöngyös Chardonnay; Jacob's Creek Dry White; Val de Torgan

Range: GOOD: Alsace, Champagne and sparkling wines, England, regional France (especially Languedoc-Roussillon), Bordeaux, Burgundy, Italy, Spain, Portugal, Australia, New Zealand, Fortified wines, California, Chile
AVERAGE: Beaujolais, Loire, Eastern Europe, South Africa, Germany
POOR: Rhône

Bottoms Up: Jacob's Creek Red; Jacob's Creek White; Tollana Dry White; Mâcon-Villages Blanc, Regional Classics; Domaine du Tariquet; Etchart Torrontes; Albor Rioja Tinto; Gyöngyös Chardonnay; Figaro Vin de Pays de l'Hérault Red; Tollana Red

Range: GOOD: Champagne and sparkling wines, regional France (especially Languedoc-Roussillon), Bordeaux, Burgundy, Italy, Spain, Portugal, Australia, New Zealand, England, Fortified wines, California, Chile, Alsace

AVERAGE: Beaujolais, Loire, Eastern Europe, South Africa, Rhône
POOR: Germany

Fifteen minutes talking to Tim Waters, Thresher's marketing controller, about 'signage', 'brand equity', 'gifting' and the 'evangelism of the product' would leave your average wine drinker groping for the nearest *Collins English Dictionary*. Like some latter-day retail Sphinx, Mr Waters speaks in riddles.

The jargon may be complicated, but then it probably has to be to convey the workings of Britain's largest off-licence chain. The Thresher Group now runs to a total of 1,603 stores, divided up between six different, er, brands. At the top of the pile there's Bottoms Up, which carries the entire 700-strong wine list. Then, in descending order of importance as far as wine is concerned come Wine Rack (650 wines), Thresher Wine Shops (up to 550 wines), Home Run (250 wines), Drinks Stores from Thresher (150 wines) and Food and Drinks Stores from Thresher (also 150 wines).

Why so many different chains? Wouldn't it be easier to call them all Thresher and concentrate on the one name? Apparently not, according to Waters. 'Our segmentation policy has been in place for five years now. Its aim is to maximise our opportunities in every locality.' In other words, not everyone wants to buy their wine from a Drinks Store, or a Bottoms Up for that matter.

Nevertheless, further changes are at hand. Drinks Stores and Food and Drinks Stores are about to be renamed. The words 'from Thresher' will be dropped because, explains Waters, 'we can't build the brand equity of Thresher Wine Shops if other retail brands can be confused with it.'

It's easy to giggle at all this marketing, but it's been effective where it matters most – on the high street shop floor. Thresher is such a powerful, well-run off-licence chain that its achievements are sometimes overlooked. In the past six years, it has done a great deal to revitalise the flagging prospects of the off-licence sector. Oddbins may have led the way, but without Thresher's efforts, there would have been no Wine Rack, no transformed Bottoms Up and arguably no Victoria Wine Cellars or Greenalls Wine Cellar.

So what's what? Well, Home Run, Drinks Stores and Food and Drinks Stores are essentially convenience off-licences (the first sells Pizza Hut pizzas and rents videos; the second two are community stores); Thresher Wine Shops are the core of the business (as their name suggests, wine-orientated off-licences); and Bottoms Up and Wine Rack are Thresher's upmarket responses to Majestic and Oddbins.

Not all of these names are performing equally well. Bottoms Up, with only 75 stores, is leading the way. Once part of the now-defunct Peter Dominic off-licence chain, Bottoms Up has been given a detox, a work-out programme and a blood transfusion since Thresher took over in 1990. Other parts of the business have fared less well. Our guess is that Master of Wine Jo Standen's move from buying to managing Wine Rack is an attempt to give the chain a bit more excitement and improve its performance. And down at the other end of the business, Drinks Stores and Food and Drinks Stores have almost certainly been hit by supermarket price-cutting. The former are, in any case, slowly being converted into the latter.

The problem with all this 'segmentation' is that the range of bottles on the shelves can vary from 150 basic lines to Bottoms Up's full house of 700 well-chosen wines. This is a shame, because the selection of wines has never been better. And the wine buying team of supremo Kim Tidy, Julian Twaites and John 'Goatee' Woodriffe has been further strengthened this year by the arrival of the rugby-playing Lucy Warner from Victoria Wine.

Each of the quartet has a different approach to wine buying. 'We don't buy by committee,' says Tidy. 'It's vital that the personality of the buyer comes through onto the shelf.' In the past, this has resulted in some rather wayward enthusiasms. 'We did list too many New Zealand Sauvignon Blancs and too many Alsace wines in the past,' he admits, 'but we've learnt from our overenthusiasms.' They sure have. Asked if she'd pruned the Alsace range, Lucy Warner replied, 'You could say it was a hatchet job.'

These days the passions of the buying team are far better channelled. John Woodriffe has come up with super new wines from Chile and California (a weak area in the past) from Duxoup, Morgan and Firestone; Lucy Warner has been busy in South Africa, where the Bush Vine project has turned out a couple of stunners; Julian Twaites has unearthed exciting things in the Loire, Germany, Bordeaux and especially Champagne; and Kim Tidy has continued his there-must-be-more-to-life-than-oaked-Chardonnay crusade in Australia with his Samuels Bay range and listings from The Willows, Heritage and Tim Adams. The result is one of the best-chosen lists in the country, with very few perceivable weaknesses. Only the Rhône, sadly, has been cut back this year, apparently because the higher priced wines weren't selling.

The most significant improvements this year have come from California. 'Producers were always able to make good wine, but they weren't interested in doing it at the right price,' according to Kim Tidy. 'You need a few entry point wines at £3 to £5.' This is the rationale behind the King's Canyon range, produced in partnership with Englishman Hugh Ryman and the Central Valley's Arciero winery, and the Prosperity Red and White from Firestone Vineyards.

The encouraging thing about most of the wines is that they're selling way above the £2.99 threshold. Sixty per cent of Thresher's sales are above £3.50, according to Tim Waters. 'Our biggest growth this year has come between £3 and £4.99,' he says. 'We're not interested in commodities. If you sell purely on price, the pressure is on you to cut costs and buy the cheapest job lot available.'

The chain which has benefited most from all these new signings is Bottoms Up, which has taken over from Wine Rack as Thresher's flagship brand. Bottoms Up is showing 20 per cent annual sales growth and numbers 'far and away our largest turnover shops' confirms Waters. Nevertheless, he denies that Wine Rack has been underperforming. 'It's not formal or off-putting, as you seem to think it is. In fact, we did a survey of core Wine Rack customers and they're still in love with it. We're quite confident that Wine Rack is reaching its target audience.' This may be true, but Bottoms Up is still a livelier place to buy wine as far as we're concerned. Perhaps we're too young at heart to qualify as 'core Wine Rack customers'.

The new wines may be the most visible sign of change at Thresher, but a lot of effort has also been put into something far less glamorous this year – staff training. It was a concern of ours in the past that the quality of the shop managers, especially in Thresher Wine Shops, was not high enough to sell esoteric and more expensive wines. The sight of older vintages of New Zealand reds and Alsace whites on the shelves appeared to point to a significant proportion of dust-gatherers. The large number of employees who have taken and passed Wine & Spirit Education Trust exams is no guarantee of sales, but the more knowledge a manager has, the better the advice he or she can offer the wine drinker.

Another way to sell more expensive wines, Waters believes, is to take the risk out of buying them. This is where the Thresher Wine Buyer's

Guarantee comes in. Launched in May 1995, this initiative is designed to make 'customers feel more comfortable about experimenting'. The deal is simple – if you don't like the wine, you can bring it back and exchange it for something else. The rumours that Oddbins shop managers have been seen loitering outside branches of Thresher Wine Shops with half-finished bottles of 1982 Bollinger RD Champagne are apparently groundless. 'We've only had a couple of cases of abuse,' says Waters. 'The whole thing has been an enormous success.'

Thresher runs lots of other clubs and schemes: Wine Rack has Cellar Key and Exclusively Alsace, Bottoms Up has Imbibers and Thresher Wine Shops have a Wine with Food Club. A recent favourite of ours is the Drinks Direct Gifting Service, invented by (who else?) Tim 'Segmentation' Waters. It also offers a wide range of discounts, especially at Bottoms Up, where the sharpest deals are to be found.

So, all in all, it's been another year of progress at Thresher. Competitors may carp that lottery ticket sales have done a lot to boost profitability, but as long as parent company and brewer Whitbread continues to invest in Wine Rack, Bottoms Up and Thresher Wine Shops, the high street will remain an exciting place to buy wine. 'The biggest threat to our business,' says Tim Waters, 'is consumers who are satisfied by supermarket offerings. Our mission is to change their minds.'

All wines are available from Thresher Wine Shops, Bottoms Up and Wine Rack, except where otherwise indicated.

White

Under £3

BULGARIA

1994 Yantra Valley Dry White, Aligoté/Dimiat
££ / 3 / 1   13/20
An aromatic, off-dry, boiled sweets blend of Aligoté and the local Dimiat grape made by Australian flying winemaker Kym Milne.

£3–5

AUSTRALIA

1994 Tollana Dry White, South East Australia
££ / 3 / ⅟   14/20

An inexpensive Riesling-based Aussie white with what buyer Kim Tidy
accurately describes as a fruit salad of Chenin Blanc, Sauvignon Blanc
and anything else they had to hand. It's a floral, sweetish, ginger spicy
style with a hint of the confectioners.

1994 Rawsons Retreat Penfolds Bin 21 Semillon/Chardonnay
£££ / 2 / ⅟   15/20

A good example of the new-style Penfolds whites. With its spicy vanilla
oak, herby Semillon and Chardonnay richness, these two grapes
combine harmoniously to produce a sundae of vanilla ice cream and
lemony fruit.

1995 Red Cliffs Estate Riesling/Traminer
£££ / 3 / ⅟   15/20

With 25 per cent Traminer (or Gewürztraminer to you and us) for extra
aroma, this is a crisp, clean, fresh, off-dry, tobaccoey white blend from
irrigated vineyards in Victoria.

1994 Red Cliffs Estate Chardonnay
££ / 2 / ⅟   15/20

From the same source, this is a citrusy, subtly oaked and delightfully
fresh style of Chardonnay, which would have left us looking forward to
a second and third glass if we hadn't been on the wagon at the time.

1994 Bridgewater Mill Riesling, Clare Valley
££ / 3 / ⅟   15/20

From Petaluma's extensive plantings in South Australia's Clare Valley,
this is an aromatic lemon and lime scented Riesling with good breadth
of flavour and some appealing grape sweetness.

AUSTRIA

1994 Lenz Moser Grüner Veltliner
£££ / 2 / ⚱   15/20

Crisp, inexpensive Austrian white, made from the widely planted native
Grüner Veltliner grape by one of Central Europe's best known
producers, and showing white pepper aromas and fresh, lemony
fruitiness. Great value at around £3.50.

BULGARIA

1994 Yantra Valley Riesling, Kym Milne
££ / 3 / ⚱   14/20

A limey, grape-scented Bulgarian Riesling made in an off-dry, New World
influenced style by the talented Kym Milne.

CHILE

1994 Las Colinas Riesling, Lontue, Jacques Lurton
£££ / 3 / ⚱   15/20

Made by Frenchman Jacques Lurton at the San Pedro winery from grapes
grown in the Lontue Valley, this is an aromatic, zesty, lime marmalade-
like Rhine Riesling, which shows the Frenchman at his unchauvinistic
best.

1994 Las Colinas Semillon/Sauvignon, Maipo
££ / 2 / ⚱   14/20

A fifty–fifty Maipo Valley blend of Semillon and Sauvignon which is more
exciting than the basic Las Colinas Chilean white, and well worth the
extra 30 pence. It's lively, grapefruity, fresh and piquantly perfumed.

1994 Santa Carolina Chenin Blanc, Casablanca
£££ / 2 / ⚱   15/20

The Casablanca in question is Santa Carolina's brand name, not to be
confused with Chile's most exciting new white wine region of the same
name. This is a richly aromatic, appley white with zip, concentration
and attractive balance. If you find Chenin Blanc from the Loire a
challenging proposition, try this fruitier style instead.

1995 Villa Montes Sauvignon Blanc, Curicó

£££ / 2 / ♦   15/20

Made by local winemaker Aurelio Montes and Englishman Hugh 'Grant' Ryman, this is a crisp, almost austere Sauvignon Blanc from the Curicó district of Chile's Central Valley. It's a nettley style with plenty of grapefruity intensity. Long may the partnership flourish.

1995 Santa Carolina Special Reserve Sauvignon Blanc, Maipo

£££ / 2 / ♦   16/20

With 15 per cent barrel-fermented Sauvignon for extra complexity, this is the richest and most tropically fruity of Thresher's substantial line-up of Chilean white wines. It's a soft, rich, melony style with balancing fruit zest and a lingering aftertaste. An excellent wine from Santa Carolina.

1995 Villa Montes Chardonnay, Curicó

£££ / 2 / ♦ (WR/BU only)   16/20

More appealing than the previous vintage's effort, which tasted like a rather undistinguished Sauvignon Blanc, this is a crisp, delicately oaked style with tropical fruit flavours and zingy acidity.

1994 Caliterra Casablanca Chardonnay

£££ / 2 / ♦   17/20

Star winemaker Ignacio Recabarren has produced a brilliant value Chardonnay from Chile's most exciting white wine area, the Casablanca Valley, halfway between Santiago and the port of Valparaiso. Fresh, clean-cut, citrus-fruit flavours with a grapefruity tang and a touch of oak.

FRANCE

1994 Domaine du Tariquet, Vin de Pays des Côtes de Gascogne, Yves Grassa

0 / 3 / ♦   13/20

A blend of Ugni Blanc and Colombard made by modernist Yves Grassa. This is a rather undistinguished, apple-core-flavoured white with cosmetic sweetness.

1994 Laperouse, Vin de Pays d'Oc
££ / 2 / 1   15/20

The offspring of a joint venture between Penfolds of Australia and France's largest wine company, Val d'Orbieu, this unoaked blend of Chardonnay, Marsanne, Grenache and Colombard is like fresh pears spiced with aniseed. A very promising start.

1994 Muscadet, Côtes de Grandlieu Sur Lie, Vignerons Noëlle
£££ / 2 / 1   16/20

From a new Muscadet *appellation*, this is the best of three good Côtes de Grandlieu whites at Thresher, showing more softness than you'd expect from a Melon de Bourgogne white, and enlivened by a prickle of *sur lie* character.

GERMANY

1994 Niersteiner Pettenthal Scheurebe, Rheinhessen QbA, Weingut Rappenhof
££ / 4 / 1   14/20

From a winery that sounds like a new style of music from Jamaica, this is a good example of the Scheurebe grape, with its combination of grapefruit and white pepper aromas. Pleasant enough at under £5 without the excitement of the best examples from the Rheinpfalz.

HUNGARY

1994 Cool Ridge, Unoaked Chardonnay, Nagyrede
£££ / 2 / 1   15/20

One of a pair of Cool Ridge Chardonnays at Thresher (we preferred the unoaked Chardonnay to the more expensive oaked version), this is a rich, buttery, modern style made by Mike Gadd at the Nagyrede winery under Kym Milne's supervision.

1993 Disznoko Furmint, Tokaji
££ / 1 / 1   15/20

Named after the immoveable rock in the middle of the vineyards, Disznoko, as you probably know already, means pig of a rock in Hungarian. This is a characterful dry white with flavours of raisin, toffee and tea-leaf. It also shows the austere side of Tokaji's Furmint grape. A promising first vintage for this French-owned estate.

ITALY

1994 Pinot Grigio, Fiordaliso, Vino da Tavola
££ / 2 / 🍷   15/20
Blended at Gruppo Italiano Vini by English Master of Wine Angela Muir, this is an attractively peachy, unoaked northern Italian white with a fresh tang of acidity. It's easy to see why the wine's so popular with Thresher's customers.

1994 Cortese del Piemonte, Alasia
££ / 1 / 🍷 (WR/BU only)   15/20
One of a series of wines made at the Araldica co-operative by the original flying winemaker, Australian Martin Shaw, this uses the native Cortese grape to create a distinctively Italian style, with angelica spice and green olive characters and a characteristic nip of acidity.

1994 Muscaté Sec, Alasia, Vino da Tavola
££ / 2 / 🍷   15/20
From the same team working in Piemonte's Monferrato hills, this is an aromatic ginger and grapefruit-like dry white with excellent weight and length of flavour.

1994 Newlands White, Bianco di Monferrato
££ / 2 / 🍷   14/20
Not a reference to the stadium in which the Springboks won the Rugby World Cup, as far as we know, especially since this wine was made by Australian Martin Shaw at the Araldica co-operative in Piemonte. It's a peachy, gooseberry-like white which owes more to the New World than northwestern Italy.

NEW ZEALAND

1994 Kapua Springs Dry White, Gisborne, Villa Maria
£ / 3 / 🍷   14/20
It says Dry on the label, largely to distinguish it from the Medium Dry style also stocked by Thresher, but this is a grapey, commercial, off-dry Kiwi Müller-Thurgau from the North Island's Gisborne region.

1993 Stoneleigh Vineyard Riesling, Marlborough
££ / 3 / ⅃   15/20

From a wet, cool vintage in the South Island, this is a honeyed and
characterful Riesling made in a dryish style by the highly rated Alan
McCorkindale, with citrusy, perfumed fruitiness and zing.

SOUTH AFRICA

1995 Winelands Bush Vine Chenin Blanc, Stellenbosch, Kym Milne
£££ / 2 / ⅃   16/20

A ripe, concentrated, oatmealy Chenin Blanc which makes the most of
old vines to extract a surprising amount of character from a grape that
covers a third of South Africa's extensive vineyards. This may well be the
best white wine Kym Milne has made outside New Zealand.

SPAIN

1994 Viña Calera, Sauvignon Blanc, Rueda
£££ / 2 / ⅃   16/20

Another wine which proves that flying winemakers can produce more
than basic styles, this is a beautifully fresh lemon, gooseberry and melon
scented Sauvignon Blanc made in Rueda by Hugh Ryman in conjunction
with Rioja's Marqués de Riscal.

UNITED STATES

1994 King's Canyon Black Label Californian Chardonnay
£ / 3 / ⅃   14/20

A charry, smoky, punchily alcoholic white, which is one of a range of
King's Canyon wines produced by the ubiquitous Hugh Ryman at the
Arciero winery in California's Central Valley. Our favourite was the
Sauvignon Blanc, but so was everyone else's, so you probably won't find
it on Thresher's shelves by the time the 1996 edition of *Grapevine*
surfaces.

£5-8

AUSTRALIA

1994 Samuels Bay Chardonnay, Barossa Valley
£££ / 2 / ⅃ (WR/BU only)   16/20
Samuels Bay is a venture created by Kim Tidy of Thresher and Australia's
Adam Wynn as a way of proving that white and reds from Down Under
don't have to be oaked to be exciting. This is a rich, yeasty, pineappley
style, whose clarity of fruit we preferred to the more expensive
Mountadam Chardonnay, Adam Wynn's flagship white wine.

1994 Samuels Bay Riesling, South East Australia
£££ / 2 / ⅃ (WR/BU only)   16/20
After appearing at a ludicrously inflated price last year, Samuels Bay
Riesling is now available at a more reasonable £6 a bottle. Not that there
was ever anything wrong with the wine, as this follow-on vintage
demonstrates. It's an aromatic, almost cassis-scented, refreshing style
made from a blend of Coonawarra and Eden Valley grapes.

1994 Chapel Hill Riesling, Eden Valley
£££ / 2 / ⅃ (BU only)   16/20
Another superb Aussie Riesling, the previous vintage of which was a
former *Grapevine* wine of the year. Now repackaged in a more
commercial Burgundy bottle, Pam Dunsford's zesty, lime and guava
scented Riesling is shot through with an almost Mosel-like crispness of
acidity and elegance.

1993 The Willows Vineyard Semillon
£££ / 2 / ⌐ (WR/BU only)   17/20
Wow! Made at Peter Scholz's Barossa Valley home base – he also
helps to make the wine at Peter Lehmann – this is possibly the
best Australian Semillon on the UK market. It's a rich, yeasty,
herbal style with subtle oak toastiness and concentrated flavours
of lemon and lime marmalade.

1994 Katnook Estate, Sauvignon Blanc, Coonawarra
££ / 2 / ⅃ (WR/BU only)   16/20
One of a handful of Australian Sauvignon Blancs which can compete

with New Zealand for concentration and depth of aroma and varietal flavour, this is a juicy, tropically fruity Coonawarra white with notes of asparagus and lemon zest.

CHILE

1994 Caliterra Reserve Chardonnay
£££ / 2 / ▌   16/20

Another first-rate South American white, this time from Chile's excellent 1994 vintage. It's an oaky, grapefruity, richly complex Maipo Valley white made by Ignacio Recabarren. Wonderful value at under £6.

FRANCE

1994 Turckheim, Alsace Tradition
££ / 2 / ▌ (WR/BU only)   15/20

This is a basic, traditional Edelzwicker blend spiced up – and that's the word – with a dollop of Gewürztraminer. The result is a fresh, aromatic introduction to Alsace at just over £5.

1994 Pouilly-Fumé, Les Duchesses, Cave de la Cresle
££ / 1 / ►   16/20

Pungently scented, classically crisp Pouilly-Fumé with citrus fruit flavour, good length and a minerally, almost flinty, undertone. It should soften with a few months in bottle.

GERMANY

1992 Durckheimer Nonnengarten Riesling Spätlese, Castel Vollmer, Rheinpfalz
££ / 4 / ▌ (WR only)   15/20

A well-made, ripe, grapefruit and honey style Riesling in which the sweetness is nicely balanced by zesty acidity.

1994 Ruppertsberger Linsenbusch Riesling Spätlese Rheinpfalz
££ / 4 / ▌   15/20

From the same relatively warm region, this is a more appley, almost petrolly style of Riesling with the sort of fresh acidity you're more likely to come across in the Mosel Valley.

1991 Friedelsheimer Kreuz Gewürztraminer Spätlese Rheinpfalz, Castel Vollmer

£££ / 4 / ▮ 16/20

An indication of the travails facing fine German wines, this soft, fragrant, elegantly spiced Gewürztraminer was an Augustus Barnett listing two years ago before the now defunct 1960s chain hitched its wagon to the Victoria Wine cause. Let's hope Thresher can do better with this ripe, rose-petal-scented white, because it deserves a wider audience.

NEW ZEALAND

1994 Private Bin, Villa Maria Sauvignon Blanc, Marlborough

££ / 2 / ▮ 15/20

In price and style, this is halfway between Montana Sauvignon Blanc and the more exalted wines of Cloudy Bay and Jackson Estate. Refreshing, dry, zesty Sauvignon Blanc with plenty of elderflower cattiness.

1994 Villa Maria Chardonnay, Lightly Oaked

££ / 2 / ▮ 15/20

As the name suggests, this is a delicately oaked Villa Maria Chardonnay blend which combines the tropical fruitiness of Gisborne Chardonnay with 15 per cent of the crisper Marlborough style made to wine buyer Kim Tidy's specifications.

1993 Selaks Riesling, Marlborough

£££ / 2 / ▮ 16/20

A crisp, nicely focused, aromatic Riesling in which grapefruity flavours are reminiscent of a Sauvignon Blanc. The lime zest aftertaste brings you back to Riesling base.

SOUTH AFRICA

1995 Villiera Riesling

£££ / 2 / ▮ (WR/BU only) 16/20

Made by Jeff Grier, who specialises in aromatic white and sparkling wine styles, this is a crisp, off-dry, intensely citrusy Riesling with plenty of grapey, juicy fruit character. The best Cape Riesling we've tasted this year.

1995 De Wetshof Chardonnay d'Honneur, Robertson
£££ / 2 / ⅓ (WR/BU only)   16/20
The most Burgundian of Danie de Wet's extensive range of Robertson Chardonnays, this is a Puligny-like white with toasty, lemony fruit flavours and a rich, caramel fudge aftertaste. It's hard to believe you can get this sort of elegance from grapes grown in such a hot climate. Maybe he learnt a trick or two at Geisenheim University in Germany.

UNITED STATES

1992 Newtonian Chardonnay, Napa Valley
£££ / 2 / ⅓ (WR/BU only)   16/20
Another Côte de Beaune style Chardonnay, this time from grapes grown in the cool climate of Carneros on San Pablo Bay. It's a leesy, complex, judiciously oaked style, which has developed into something really delicious after three years in barrel and bottle.

Over £8

AUSTRALIA

1993 Tim Adams Semillon
££ / 1 / ⌐   16/20
Now established as one of the best winemakers in Australia's Clare Valley, north of Adelaide, Tim Adams produces an award-winning range of red and white wines. This creamy, vanilla-oak and citrus-flavoured Semillon is consistently one of his best wines.

1993 Petaluma Chardonnay, South Australia
£££ / 2 / ⌐   17/20
A wine which has a strong claim to being one of the top dozen Chardonnays produced in the New World, Brian Croser's Petaluma is a toasty, flavoursome, concentrated white, which, though powerful, has the fresh acidity and balance to age beautifully.

FRANCE

1993 Trimbach Muscat Réserve
££ / 2 / ⅟   **15/20**

A subtle, fragrant, rose-petal-scented Muscat from an Alsace family firm whose wines are never oily or over-unctuous. True to the Trimbach style, this is sophisticatedly dry and well-made.

1992 Rully Les Saint Jacques, Laborbe Juillot
£££ / 2 / ⅟ (WR/BU only)   **16/20**

From a spectacular white Burgundy vintage, this is a Côte Chalonnaise Chardonnay with unusual richness, balance and complexity. It's on the oaky side, but there's more than enough fruit to support the staves.

1991 Chablis, Vieilles Vignes, Daniel Defaix
££ / 2 / ⅟   **16/20**

A traditional, unoaked Chablis in which old vines have lent richness and concentration to the wine. It's just starting to mature into something nutty, minerally and very typically Chablis-like.

1988 Chablis Premier Cru, Vaillons, Daniel Defaix
£££ / 2 / ⅟ (WR/BU only)   **17/20**

From the same traditional grower, this is a fascinatingly mature Chablis, which proves that the best Chardonnays from the Yonne have the freshness and structure to age into smoky maturity for 10 years or more.

1993 St-Aubin, Premier Cru, Gérard Thomas
£££ / 1 / ⌐ (WR/BU only)   **16/20**

Situated in the hills behind Chassagne and Puligny Montrachet, St-Aubin produces some of the Côte de Beaune's best value white. This minerally, finely balanced Chardonnay with its leesy weight and refreshing acidity is a case in point.

1993 Zind-Humbrecht, Pinot Gris, Vieilles Vignes
££ / 3 / ⅟   **16/20**

French Master of Wine Olivier Humbrecht makes ripely textured Alsace whites across a full spectrum of grape varieties. This old vine Pinot Gris is typically rich and honeyed with exotic mango and botrytis lusciousness. Make sure that there are six of you around the dinner table, because one glass of this heady liquid is enough.

1989 Trimbach, Riesling, Cuveé Frédéric Emile
££ / 2 / ⅟ (WR only)   16/20

A mature, toasty, aromatic Riesling from a ripe vintage, the Frédéric Emile Cuveé is produced solely from *grand cru* vineyards owned by the Trimbach family.

NEW ZEALAND

1994 Hunter's Sauvignon, Marlborough
££ / 2 / ⅟   16/20

An intense, tropical fruit Sauvignon Blanc from Jane Hunter, OBE. As ever, it's fresh, grapefruity, concentrated and highly aromatic with flavours of passion fruit and melon. We slightly preferred the previous vintage, but this is still a super wine.

1993 Neudorf Sauvignon Blanc, Nelson
££ / 2 / ⅟ (WR only)   16/20

Steely but ripe, green bean and gooseberry style Sauvignon Blanc made by Tim Finn in Nelson on South Island. As with all his wine styles, Finn's Sauvignon Blanc is distinguished by its richness and depth of flavour.

1994 Palliser Estate Sauvignon Blanc, Martinborough
£££ / 2 / ⅟ (WR/BU only)   17/20

From a winery which has rapidly established itself in the front rank of New Zealand producers, this is a melony, powerfully aromatic Sauvignon Blanc from North Island's Martinborough, which produces marginally subtler styles than those of its South Island competitor, Marlborough. Kim Tidy thinks this is the best Sauvignon Blanc in New Zealand, and, on the evidence of the 1994, we wouldn't disagree.

1993 Martinborough Vineyards Chardonnay, Martinborough
££ / 2 / ⅟ (WR/BU only)   16/20

Made by the solidly built Australian, Larry McKenna, who employs Burgundian techniques to produce his highly praised Chardonnay and Pinot Noir, this is a rich, alcoholic but complex style, with smoky bacon oak and fine balancing acidity.

1994 Elston Chardonnay, Hawkes Bay, Te Mata
£££ / 2 / ⌣ (WR/BU only)   17/20
John Buck's Te Mata Estate is best known for its long-lived
Bordeaux-style reds, but Elston frequently belongs in the same
exalted company. This is an elegant, toasty, toffee and citrus fruit
style with sweet pipe-tobacco oak adding a sheen of complexity.
Well worth its £13 price tag.

UNITED STATES

1993 Morgan Chardonnay, Monterey County
£££ / 2 / ⌡ (BU only)   17/20
From a so-called warehouse winery situated in the middle of an
industrial estate on California's Central Coast, this is a complex
Puligny-Montrachet-style Chardonnay, with lots of classy French
oak and citrus fruit elegance.

Red

Under £3

BULGARIA

1994 Vintage Première, Merlot, Iambol Region
£££ / MB / ⌡   14/20
A plummy, modern red with robust but juicy fruit concentration and
attractive ginger spice. Excellent value.

1994 Vintage Première, Cabernet Sauvignon, Iambol Region
£££ / MB / ⌡   15/20
Another similarly exuberant Bulgarian red with chunky, fresh,
blackcurrant fruit flavours unencumbered by the sort of drying oak that
often mars the more old-fashioned style of Eastern European red. Even
better value than the Merlot.

PORTUGAL

JP Vinhos Tinto, Vinho da Mesa
£££ / MB / ◗   14/20

Made in similar style to the previous wine but from native Portuguese varieties, this is sweet, soft and juicy with robust, peppery, almost Rhône-like acidity and tannin.

SPAIN

Copa Real Tinto, Cosecheros y Criadores
£££ / MB / ◗   14/20

A light, cassis and strawberry scented, unoaked red dominated by the Tempranillo grape with a dollop of Garnacha. Good tapas bar quaffer.

£3–5

AUSTRALIA

1992 Tollana Black Label Shiraz
£ / FB / ◗   13/20

Tarry, spicy, foursquare Shiraz with plenty of American oak sweetness from the Penfolds stable. You can bet we don't drink much of this particular Black Label.

1993 Red Cliffs, Cabernet Sauvignon, Coonawarra
££ / MB / ◗   15/20

From Australia's Wingara group, this is a well-made blackcurrant and cassis flavoured alternative to claret with nicely integrated oak flavours and grassy, cool climate fruitiness.

AUSTRIA

1994 Blaufränkisch, Lenz Moser
££ / LB / ◗   15/20

Austrian reds are as rare as Kurt Waldheim celebration medals in Jerusalem. So it's good to see Thresher listing this peppery, fresh, lightly juicy red made from the Austro-Hungarian Blaufränkisch grape. It was also one of the Kaiser's favourites, according to English historian Giles MacDonogh's seminal work on the subject.

CHILE

1994 Las Colinas Cabernet Sauvignon, Chimbarongo
££ / MB / 🍷   14/20
Made by American winemaker Ed Flaherty at the Cono Sur winery, this
is a well-priced, minty, medium-bodied Chilean Cabernet with the
emphasis on up-front, juicy fruit rather than oak-aged complexity.

1994 Errázuriz, Merlot, Maule
££ / MB / 🍷   15/20
Consistently one of the best Merlots in Chile, this grassily aromatic style
blended by Kiwi winemaker Brian Bicknell is a sweet and savoury
delight, with youthfully vibrant blackcurrant fruit flavours and a nip of
tannin.

1990 Santa Carolina, Special Reserve Cabernet Sauvignon, Los Toros Vineyard, Maipo
£££ / MB / 🍷   16/20
Proof that Chile's red wines are not necessarily the poor cousins of its
whites, this is a soft, spearminty, herby red with well-judged oak and
attractive, bottle-aged maturity.

FRANCE

1994 Côtes du Ventoux, 'La Mission'
0 / LB / 🍷   11/20
After two vintages of this southern French plonk made by Kiwi Mark
Robertson, we feel it's high time the mission was aborted.

1994 Domaine de Rivoyre, Vin de Pays d'Oc, Cabernet Sauvignon
£££ / MB / 🍷   15/20
An elegant, green pepper and spicy American oak flavoured Cabernet
Sauvignon made from relatively cool climate grapes at Hugh 'Grant'
Ryman's home base near Limoux, affectionately known as 'The Dump'.

ITALY

1994 Newlands Rosso di Monferrato

££ / MB / 🍷   14/20

A blend of Barbera and Dolcetto made by Australian Martin Shaw at the Araldica winery in Piemonte. Chocolatey, spicy, savoury style with youthful, plummy fruitiness and plenty of character.

1994 Dolcetto d'Asti, Alasia

££ / MB / 🍷   14/20

Fresh, summery fruitiness and an attractively soft texture make this Martin Shaw red from the Araldica co-operative a good sub-£5 pasta basher. Another order for Pizza Express, please.

PORTUGAL

1992 Bright Bros Douro Red

££ / FB / ➥   15/20

An inky, Australian-style blend of Cabernet Sauvignon and the native Portuguese Maria Gomes and Trincadeira. It's a liquoricey, tarry, minty style with a rough Portuguese edge made by Australian Peter Bright, a pioneer of native Portuguese varieties.

1994 Alandra, Herdade do Esporão

££ / LB / 🍷   14/20

Made by David Baverstock, the only other Australian winemaker we know to have made his home in Portugal, this is a peppery-fresh, juicy, soft red produced in a Beaujolais style.

1994 Quinta de Lamelas, Douro

£ / FB / 🍷   13/20

A dusty, old-fashioned, green-edged Douro red with a rustic snarl of tannin and acidity.

SOUTH AFRICA

Boschendal Estate Red, 'Le Pavillon', Paarl

£ / MB / 🍷   14/20

Made by Hilko Hegewisch, Le Pavillon is a 1992/1993 vintage blend of

Merlot, Pinot Noir plus a bit of Cabernet Sauvignon, Shiraz and Ruby Cabernet for good measure. It's a minty, herby, chewily tannic red with all the elegance of a Springbok forward's gumshield.

SPAIN

1994 Albor Rioja, Campo Viejo
£££ / MB / 🍷   15/20
An innovative, unoaked Rioja made entirely from the Tempranillo grape variety and showing fresh cherry fruit and a soft carbonic maceration style texture.

1994 Tempranillo, Jacques Lurton
££ / MB / 🍷   14/20
This is a similar style from flying winemaker Jacques Lurton, with juicy strawberry fruit and a rasp of acidity.

1990 Agramont, Navarra
££ / MB / 🍷   15/20
A modern, smoky blend of Tempranillo and Cabernet Sauvignon made in a Rioja style at a leading winery in neighbouring Navarra. Minty, fresh and attractively oaked.

UNITED STATES

1994 Prosperity Red, Santa Ynez Valley
££ / MB / 🍷   15/20
Considerably better than the Santa Ynez white, this is a ripe, full-flavoured unoaked Cabernet Sauvignon from the Firestone winery in the Santa Ynez Valley on the Central Coast of California. It's highly encouraging to see wines of this quality emerging from an often overpriced area.

£5–8

AUSTRALIA

1994 Rosemount Estate, Cabernet Sauvignon, South Australia
££ / MB / ⚑   15/20
Perfumed, sweetly minty, tobacco-pouch-style Cabernet Sauvignon with voluptuous, liquoricey tannins and nice length of flavour.

1994 Samuels Bay Grenache, Barossa Valley
££ / FB / ⚑ (WR/BU only)   15/20
Soft, juicily alcoholic Barossa Valley Grenache with sweet raspberry fruitiness and the peppery spice of a southern Rhône red.

1994 Samuels Bay Malbec, Padthaway
£££ / FB / ➦ (WR/BU only)   16/20
With its sagey, herby aromas and piercingly ripe, sweetly balanced fruit, this is an attractive alternative to the plethora of Australian Shiraz, Cabernet, Cabernet/Shiraz and Shiraz/Cabernet styles.

1993 St Hallett Shiraz, Barossa
£££ / FB / ➦   17/20
Back on planet Shiraz, this is becoming a Barossa classic. It's every bit as good as Old Block, St Hallett's cult red, but retails at £2 less. It's a thick, spicy, eucalyptus-scented red with masses of sweet, dark chocolatey fruit and ripe, accessible tannins.

1992 Heritage Cabernet/Malbec, Steve Hoff
££ / MB / ➦ (BU only)   16/20
Made by the grizzly-bear-like Steve Hoff, this is even better than his off-the-wall, but acclaimed, Cabernet Franc. It's a supple, succulent, spicy, easy-drinking red, which is more complex then it seems on first acquaintance.

1992 Chapel Hill Shiraz, McLaren Vale
££ / MB / ➦ (WR/BU only)   16/20
Made by Pam Dunsford, one of Australia's growing band of women winemakers, this McLaren Vale red is typical of the Chapel Hill style, with soft tannins and concentrated minty fruitiness. Needs a few more years in bottle to develop its full potential.

CHILE

1992 Caliterra Reserva, Cabernet Sauvignon, Maipo
£££ / MB / 🍷   16/20

One of the few Chilean reds we've had this year that doesn't taste splintery and dry, this Maipo Valley Cabernet is fresh, elegant and almost claret-like in texture and blackcurrant flavour.

1994 Santa Carolina Reserva, Pinot Noir
££ / MB / 🍷   15/20

This is not quite up to the very high standard of some of the Pinot Noirs we've tasted in the past from Cono Sur, but at just over £5, Santa Carolina's savoury, strawberry-like red is still elegantly fruity and well-priced. Lovers of red Burgundy should give it an outing.

1994 Valdivieso Pinot Noir, Lontue
£££ / MB / 🍷   16/20

This is a vibrant, weighty, spicily oaked, voluptuous Chilean Pinot Noir, made from grapes previously destined for Valdivieso's sparkling wine production. But Australia-trained winemaker Luis Simian was given the opportunity to produce a limited amount of Chardonnay and Pinot Noir. This 1994 is an attractively made, worthy successor to the first vintage.

FRANCE

1993 Château Mercier, Côtes de Bourg (Unoaked)
££ / MB / 🍷   15/20

This is one of a number of interesting clarets sourced by wine buyer Julian Twaites on his long and lonely passage through the Gironde in the winter of 1994. It's a youthful, lively, equal parts unoaked blend of Merlot and Cabernet Sauvignon with farmyardy notes and rustic tannins.

1990 Château Suau, Premières Côtes de Bordeaux (Oak Aged)
£££ / MB / 🍷   16/20

From a superior vintage, this is a more succulent, Merlot-based claret from the hillside vineyards of the Premières Côtes overlooking the city of Bordeaux. There's plenty of new oak and rich fruit, but they're balanced by firm tannins and a whiff of the pig-pen.

1990 Château Mercier, Côtes de Bourg (Oak Aged)
£££ / MB / ➡   17/20
The best of Julian Twaites' Bordeaux discoveries, this is a
succulently fruity, chocolatey, Merlot-inspired claret with classy
oak and a St-Julien-like finesse.

1992 Château de la Rivière, Fronsac
££ / MB / ⌁   16/20
Another fine Merlot-led claret with far more weight and concentration
than many 1992 red Bordeaux. It's soft, attractively aromatic and full of
fruit and vanilla spice.

1993 Château du Grand Prebois, Côtes du Rhône
££ / FB / ⌁   15/20
Chunky, leafy, rather rustic Côtes du Rhône made in a traditional style
with little concession to finesse.

1991 Domaine Gauby, Côtes du Roussillon, Elevé en Fûts de Chêne
££ / FB / ➡ (WR/BU only)   16/20
Another wine with no time for wimps, this is a broad-shouldered, spicily
concentrated Roussillon red with masses of dry vanilla oak and *garrigue*-
like aromas. Gérard Gauby is fast emerging as one of the best red wine
producers in the Roussillon region.

NEW ZEALAND

1994 Delegat's Cabernet Sauvignon/Merlot, Hawkes Bay
££ / MB / ⌁   15/20
Made by Brent Marris, Delegat's talented young winemaker, this is a
grassy, blackberryish Hawkes Bay blend with a hint of the herbaceous
greenness which is the hallmark of many New Zealand red wines.

SPAIN

1991 Conde de Valdemar, Rioja Crianza, Martinez Bujanda
£££ / MB / ➡   16/20
The best of the large number of Martinez Bujanda Riojas at Thresher, this is
a modern, strawberry-fruity, elegantly oaked blend of mainly Tempranillo
with 10 per cent of the rare Mazuelo grape. Well-priced at around £5.50.

Over £8

AUSTRALIA

1994 The Fergus, Clare Valley, Tim Adams
££ / FB / ↳ (WR/BU only)   16/20

With its massively charry oak nose and knee-weakening alcohol, this Grenache-based Clare Valley red is a huge mouthful of wine and wood with a barbecue of hickory smokiness and meaty tannins. Drink with fire extinguisher to hand.

1992 St Hallett Old Block Shiraz
£££ / FB / ↳   17/20

With its stylish new label designed by the Barossa's resident artist, Rod Schubert (no relation to Max or Franz, as far as we're aware), the new vintage of Old Block is, as ever, deceptively seductive to drink in its youth with coffee bean spice and rich, liquoricey fruit flavours. We still think it's worth squirreling this strapping cult red away for a few years yet.

1992 Petaluma Coonawarra Red
££ / MB / ↳ (WR/BU only)   16/20

After the strong-arm embrace of the Barossa's Old Block, this seems like a peck on the cheek from the much cooler Coonawarra region of South Australia. It's closed and a little shy at the moment, but Brian Croser's elegant blend of Cabernet Sauvignon with 25 per cent Merlot usually takes a little time to get into its stride.

FRANCE

1992 Givry Premier Cru, Clos Marceaux, Laborbe-Juillot
£££ / MB / ↥ (WR/BU only)   16/20

From one of the best domaines in the often overlooked Côte Chalonnaise, this is a well-balanced, oaky Pinot Noir with considerable stuffing and a core of sweet strawberry fruitiness.

1992 Chorey lès Beaune, Tollot-Beaut
££ / MB / ↥   16/20

Produced in the typically accessible Tollot-Beaut style, this little beaut is elegant, delicate and seductively oaked. A good luncheon Burgundy to sip with your pork luncheon meat.

1992 Châteauneuf-du-Pape, Domaine Font de Michelle, Gonnet
££ / MB / 🍷   16/20

Even in modest vintages such as the rain-drenched 1992, the Gonnet brothers manage to produce Châteauneuf reds with character and attractive fruitiness. This leafy, Grenache-based red is fresh, minty and not unlike a Pinot Noir in texture.

ITALY

1988 Amarone Classico, Recioto della Valpolicella, Zenato
££ / FB / 🍷   15/20

A rustic, alcoholic, full-bodied, aged Amarone made from dried Valpolicella grapes, with plenty of savoury fruitiness and refreshing acidity. Amarone is an acquired taste, but this aged example is worth a try at £10 a bottle if you're feeling adventurous.

NEW ZEALAND

1993 Martinborough Vineyards, Pinot Noir, Martinborough
££ / MB / 🍷 (WR/BU only)   15/20

A mild disappointment after the superlative Martinborough Pinots of recent years, this is still a fresh-faced, aromatic Pinot Noir with faintly drying tannins on the aftertaste.

UNITED STATES

1993 Firestone Merlot, Santa Ynez Valley
£ / MB / 🍷 (BU only)   15/20

A robust, tannic Merlot from the radial kings of the Santa Ynez Valley. Merlot is a 'hot' grape in California, which is presumably why the price of this oaky, concentrated but dry example weighs in at £8.50.

1994 Voss Zinfandel, Alexander Valley
££ / FB / 🍷   15/20

Named, we presume, after the hero of Patrick White's epic novel (or possibly the equally heroic British wine writer of the same name), this is Australian winery Yalumba's attempt to go native in California. It's a sweetly oaky, extracted style with a powerful mule kick of alcohol.

1992 Morgan Pinot Noir, Monterey County
££ / MB / ♪ (BU only)   16/20
A dense, chocolatey, full-bodied Pinot Noir that you could almost mistake for a modern Côte de Nuits red. Morgan is starting to produce some of the best Chardonnays and Pinot Noirs on the Central Coast. A winery to follow closely.

1992 Duxoup Pinot Noir, Carneros, Napa Valley
£££ / MB / ♪ (BU only)   17/20
Made with grapes from coolish climate Carneros by the wacky Sonoma-based winery Duxoup, this is a rich, unfiltered, softly complex Pinot Noir in which new oak and subtle, ripe red fruits characters combine in a California-meets-Burgundy style.

1993 Duxoup Syrah, Dry Creek Valley
££ / FB / ↝ (BU only)   16/20
A peppery, southern Rhône-like red from Andy and Deb Cutter's amusing Sonoma circus – or should that be opera. This is a plummy, spicy Syrah with a sweet kernel of fruit and chunky tannins.

Sparkling

Over £8

AUSTRALIA

1992 Croser Brut
£££ / 2 / ♪ (WR/BU only)   16/20
Modestly named after the man who made it, Brian Croser's Adelaide Hills fizz is an intensely lemony, weighty blend of Pinot Noir and 30 per cent Chardonnay with an idiosyncratic, almost savoury, smoky bacon note. It's one of Australia's classiest sparkling wines – just as well Mr Croser didn't call it Brian.

FRANCE

Champagne de Praisac Brut, F. Bonnet
££ / 2 / ♪   15/20
Light, fresh, elegant Champagne with youthful fruitiness and an
appealing savoury note. A very good house Champagne.

Jean Louis Malard Champagne, Grand Cru, Chouilly
£££ / 2 / ♪ (BU only)   17/20
One of an excellent range of Grand Cru growers' Champagnes
sourced by buyer Julian Twaites, this is an aromatic, finely
balanced Chardonnay-based fizz, with a fresh, mouthfilling
mousse and lemony freshness. Very stylish stuff.

Jean Louis Malard Champagne, Grand Cru, Bouzy
£££ / 2 / ♪ (BU only)   17/20
A contrast in style, this Pinot-dominated fizz from the commune
of Bouzy is bigger and more powerful, with fine, soft, richly
flavoured bubbles and malty fruitiness. Another stunning
grower's Champagne in the Twaites line-up.

NEW ZEALAND

Deutz Marlborough Cuvée
£££ / 2 / ♪   16/20
A fine, elegantly crafted blend of Pinot Noir and Chardonnay made in
New Zealand using the southern hemisphere's only Coquard
Champagne press. The result of a fruitful partnership between
Champagne house Deutz and New Zealand's Montana, Marlborough
Cuvée has established itself as a complex, dry fizz of considerable tangy
complexity.

Fortified

£3–5

SPAIN

Manzanilla de Sanlúcar, Barbadillo
£££ / 2 / ▌(WR/BU only)   16/20
Superfresh, salty, delicate Manzanilla with savoury flor-yeast characters
and refreshing acidity. Just the thing for those Andalucian moments.

£5–8

SPAIN

Amontillado Fino de Jerez, Lustau, half-bottle
£££ / 1 / ▌(WR/BU only)   16/20
Made by the Jerez region's leading *almacenista*, or blender, this is a
Sherry lover's style with rich, dry, burnt toffee flavours shot through
with a nutty tang. Edgar Allan Poe would have enjoyed this one.

Don Zoilo Very Old Oloroso
£££ / 2 / ▬   16/20
Amber-hued with fudge and toffee-like aromas, this is another traditional
Sherry for those who like their Oloroso rich and at the same time dry on
the aftertaste.

UNWINS **(*)

Head Office: Birchwood House, Victoria Road, Dartford, Kent DA1 5AJ

Telephone: 01322 272711

Number of branches: 304

Credit cards accepted: Access, Delta, Switch, Visa, Master Card, American Express, Diners Club, Transax

Hours of opening: Monday to Saturday 9.00am to 10.00pm; Sunday 12.00pm to 3.00pm and 7.00pm to 10.00pm

By-the-case sales: Yes

Glass loan: Free

Home delivery: Most branches deliver free

Clubs: No

Discounts: Five per cent on 6 bottles of table and sparkling wines (may be mixed); 10 per cent on 12 bottles of table and sparkling wines (may be mixed); 12.5 per cent on 12 bottles of Champagne (not including Duchâtel); 12.5 per cent on all other orders over £200.

In-store tastings: Yes

Other facilities: Monthly accounts; mail order; gift vouchers

Top ten best-selling wines: La Mancha Red; La Mancha White; Frascati; White Burgundy; Stockman's Bridge Red; Liebfraumilch; Stockman's Bridge White; Mauregard White; Mauregard Red; Hock

Range: GOOD: Red Bordeaux
AVERAGE: Sparkling wines, Champagne, White Bordeaux, Burgundy, Rhône, Loire, Alsace, Italy, Spain, Portugal, Port, Australia, South Africa, England
POOR: Beaujolais, regional France, Germany, Bulgaria, Hungary, New Zealand, United States, Chile

'Uncork, unwind, Unwins', reads the slogan on the colourful T-shirts produced this year by the Dartford-based off-licence group. For a company which seems to regard the late 20th century with suspicion, this is revolutionary stuff. Unwins may still lag way behind the likes of Thresher, Victoria Wine and Oddbins in the innovation stakes, but 1995 has seen verifiable signs of a new approach.

As well as the sartorial introduction, Unwins announced a new series of wines with the Clint Eastwood style title 'Undiscovered'. Released every five or six weeks, these are parcels of wine sold at around £5 a bottle. So far the quality has been extremely mixed, but Unwins has been 'much more aggressive' in the way it advertises these promotions, according to purchasing and marketing director Bill Rolfe. Go on, make his day, punk.

Competitors, too, acknowledge that Unwins has dropped some of its more inflated prices, introduced some keen deals at the lower end of the market and generally become more competitive in the last 12 months. 'We have been more active,' says Rolfe. 'But we still want to do more on the marketing front.'

This is just as well. Improvements there have been, but Unwins is still far from an exciting retail operation. Part of the problem is that the shops look and feel old-fashioned. Unwins could do worse than spend some of its £100 million annual turnover on a few refits.

It also needs to improve its wine range dramatically. Outside the traditional areas of Bordeaux and Port, where Unwins can offer a strong range of older vintages, things are still far too safe, relying on British importers like D&F for Portuguese wines, the *négociant* Yvon Mau for Bordeaux, the KWV in South Africa and the likes of Bichot and Loron in Burgundy.

The split between whites and reds is also strangely biased in favour of reds - 231 out of 441 wines, compared with 52 sparkling and 158 white. It is also dominated by France (249 wines) to the detriment of Eastern Europe (18 wines), New Zealand (7), South Africa (10) and Chile (6).

This is not to say that the range has stood still over the last year. A lot of old clarets have been cleared out - presumably to the auction houses - and the Portuguese, Spanish, New Zealand and Australian ranges have all seen one or two interesting additions. There is even evidence of a bit of risk-taking in Canada and England - commendable, even if the gamble doesn't necessarily pay off.

The new strategy, such as it is, has proved popular with Unwins' long-standing (or should that be long-suffering?) customers. Wine sales, according to purchasing and marketing executive Jim Wilson, are up 16 per cent by value, with claret, French *vins de pays* and Australia among the strongest areas.

Another vibrant area of growth has been non-Spanish (ie British) Sherry, one of the nastiest drinks available in the UK. This highlights a fundamental problem at Unwins. However innovative Messrs Rolfe, Wilson and wine buyer Gerald Duff wish to be, many of their customers remain resolutely traditional and even downmarket. Why else would anyone want to drink British Sherry?

Rumours about Unwins' future continue to flutter in the Dartford air. Is Greenalls Cellars, in the oversized shape of Nader Haghighi, about to swoop? Will Unwins build a new nest with Fuller's or the revamped Davisons? Or will it continue on its lonesome? The third option seems the most likely.

If Unwins is for sale – and everything has its price – then the asking figure is almost certainly a deterrent. Unwins owns the freehold on two-thirds of its sites, and its mix of fags, snacks, spirits, beers, confectionery and wine is clearly popular with a certain type of shopper. In spite of commercial predators, Unwins goes on opening shops in places like East Grinstead, Chelmsford and Gerrard's Cross.

Unwins is not without strengths. Apart from its list of clarets, it has good and usually competent shop managers who enjoy being part of the local communities in which the majority of Unwins' southern-based stores are situated. The most enthusiastic of them regularly do well in Wine and Spirit Education Trust exams.

But if Unwins is to take advantage of its loyal staff and capitalise on the advances of the last year, it needs to put more money behind its shops and, more importantly, extend and improve its wine range. We have yet to meet Gerald Duff, the man who buys the majority of Unwins' wines. This is a mystery to the *Grapevine* team. A glance at his list would suggest that the man doesn't spend much time investigating the wine regions of the world for himself. Nor is he a regular presence on the London tasting circuit. So what does he do? Answers on a postcard to our publishers.

White

Under £3

GERMANY

1994 Liebfraumilch, R. Müller
£ / 5 / ₰   13/20
Fresh, sweet, grapey, floral Lieb at a higher price than many an example
of the style.

SPAIN

La Mancha, Verdier
0 / 3 / ₰   11/20
Strangely enough, given what a boring grape it is, Airén is the world's
most widely planted variety, most of it on the arid plain of La Mancha.
This is baked, basic, sweetish plonk.

£3–5

AUSTRALIA

Penfolds Stockman's Bridge
££ / 3 / ₰   14/20
A blend of mainly Semillon and Chardonnay from well-irrigated
vineyards in the Riverland region of Australia. Zesty, clean white with a
sheen of oak character. Good Aussie quaffer.

ENGLAND

Denbies Chardonnay
0 / 3 / ₰   12/20
One of the few commercially produced Chardonnays in England, this
sour, unripe example shows you why English growers steer clear of the
world's most popular grape variety.

FRANCE

1993 Mauregard Petit Château, Tour le Pin
£ / 2 / ⚊   13/20

A blend of Semillon and Sauvignon Blanc from Bordeaux *négociant* Yvon Mau, this is basic, faintly gooseberryish fare.

1993 Graves Special Reserve
0 / 2 / ⚊   10/20

Overoaked, grubby, coarse Graves, also from Yvon Mau. We don't see the point of wines like this.

ITALY

1994 Frascati Superiore, 'Tullio', San Marco
££ / 2 / ⚊   14/20

Malvasia-based Roman white with good weight and lime and baked banana character.

PORTUGAL

1994 Ramada White
£ / 3 / ⚊   13/20

Marred by excessive sulphur dioxide on the nose, this sweetish, baked, orange peel flavoured white is a decent Iberian quaffer.

SPAIN

Doña Isabella Navarra
££ / 2 / ⚊   14/20

A fresh, lemony, modern, unoaked white made from the Viura grape and showing the benefits of cool temperature fermentation.

£5-8

AUSTRALIA

1987 Lindemans Botrytis Semillon
£ / 7 / ⚑   14/20

This deep, golden, mature Semillon wine is rich in honey and barley sugar sweetness, but has lost the refreshing acidity it once had. Now that the European Union and Australia's winemakers have settled their differences over sweet wines, we are seeing better value stickies than this from Down Under.

1994 Rosemount Chardonnay
££ / 2 / ⚑   15/20

From the company which has done so much to popularise Australian Chardonnay in Britain, this is a vanilla-fudge and tropical fruit style white with more restraint than some of the more Dolly Partonesque examples from Down Under.

CANADA

1991 Calona Vineyard Pinot Blanc
0 / 3 / ⚑   12/20

A praiseworthy attempt by Unwins to take the odd risk, this strange Canadian white with its pungent aromas and sweetish fruit doesn't quite come off. One to blend with the Niagara Falls.

GERMANY

1992 Niersteiner Spiegelberg Kabinett, Guntrum
0 / 4 / ⚑   13/20

Ludicrously expensive for a basic Müller-Thurgau, this is a floral, slightly peppery white with grapey sweetness and no finesse.

NEW ZEALAND

1993 Grove Mill Chardonnay
££ / 2 / ⚑   15/20

Rich, pineapple and butterscotch flavoured Chardonnay with more weight and tropical fruit character than most Marlborough whites.

1992 Matua Valley Sauvignon Blanc
££ / 2 / 🍷   16/20

Mature Matua Sauvignon with plenty of ripe, gooseberry aromas and flavour in the classic Marlborough style.

SOUTH AFRICA

1993 Klein Constantia Chardonnay
£ / 2 / 🍷   15/20

A full, spicy, smoky Cape Chardonnay with masses of toasty oak and a buttery texture. You can buy the same wine for £1 less at Waitrose.

SPAIN

1989 Marqués de Murrieta, Rioja
££ / 1 / 🍷   15/20

Murrieta is one of the few Rioja wineries still producing traditional oaky whites such as this. It's not a terribly commercial style, but we rather like the combination of tea-leafy, Sherryish aromas, vanilla oak and bracing acidity. Must be drunk with food.

Over £8

FRANCE

1989 Vouvray Moelleux
£ / 6 / 🍷   14/20

Made in a brilliant vintage for sweet Loire Chenin Blanc, this co-operative Vouvray has some appley Chenin Blanc character and plenty of sweetness, but lacks a bit of concentration, given that 1989 was an *annus mirabilis* in the region.

Red

Under £3

SPAIN

La Mancha
£ / MB / ♪   12/20
A price-fighting carbonic maceration style Spanish red made from the
Cencibel grape. Light, soft and basic.

£3-5

AUSTRALIA

Penfolds Stockman's Bridge
£ / MB / ♪   14/20
Like its white counterpart, the Stockman's Bridge red is a good
introduction to the pleasures of Australian wine. Soft, ripe, mint and
blackcurrant style blend of Cabernet Sauvignon and Shiraz.

1993 Jacob's Creek Shiraz/Cabernet
£ / MB / ♪   14/20
Tarry, sweet oak and toffee-fudge flavours predominate here. The
blackcurrant pastille fruit doesn't quite cope with the strong-armed
combination.

FRANCE

1993 Mauregard Petit Château, Château du Bois Bousquet
£ / MB / ♪   14/20
Supple, grassy Merlot-dominated claret from ubiquitous (as far as
Unwins is concerned) Bordeaux *négociant*, Yvon Mau.

1993 Vin de Pays des Côtes de Gascogne Gamay, Yvon Mau
0 / MB / ♪   12/20
Did someone say Gamay? This rustic, rather tannic red tastes more like
the local Tannat.

1994 Vin de Pays des Côtes de Gascogne, Cabernet Sauvignon, Yvon Mau

£ / MB / 🍷   14/20

Chunky, blackcurrant-fruity Gascon red with an astringent, peasant-like bite to it.

ITALY

1993 Merlot del Veneto, Via Nova, Bartolomeo

££ / MB / 🍷   15/20

A juicy, grassy, well-made northern Italian red for easy drinking.

PORTUGAL

1994 Alta Mesa Estremadura

£ / MB / 🍷   13/20

A lightly peppery, soft, modern Portuguese glugger with a touch of jammy sweetness.

1994 Pedras do Monte

££ / MB / 🍷   14/20

Made from southern Portugal's widely planted Periquita grape, this is a chunky, mulberry and damson-fruit red for autumn and winter drinking.

1993 Terras do Xisto

£ / MB / 🍷   13/20

Savoury, rustic, tobaccoey red with a gutsy, chewy aftertaste. Traditional Portuguese fare.

1992 Quinta do Manjapão, Torres Vedras

££ / FB / 🍷   15/20

Another Periquita-based red, this time with the added structure derived from ageing in oak barrels. A leathery, full-throated style with bottle-aged complexity.

SPAIN

1994 Don Fabian
0 / FB / 🌓   11/20
Nothing terribly intellectual about this chunky, tarry, over-extracted
Spanish red. Perhaps the winemaker didn't consult his pamphlet.

£5–8

AUSTRALIA

1990 Wakefield Cabernet Sauvignon
££ / MB / 🌓   15/20
Made by a large Clare Valley estate which aims to release its wines with
a little bottle age, this is a mature, sweetly oaked, almost Rioja-like
Cabernet Sauvignon with coffee bean and vanilla character.

CANADA

1988 Calona Vineyards Rougeon
££ / MB / 🌓   15/20
It says Rougeon on the label, but we thought this Canadian curiosity
bore more than a fleeting resemblance to the Pinot Noir of Burgundy.
Swathed in smoky American oak, this hybrid variety is Canada's answer
to Bourgogne Rouge.

FRANCE

1991 Fitou, Château Ségure
£££ / FB / ►   16/20
The traditional flagship of the excellent Mont Tauch co-operative in
Fitou, made only in the best vintages, this is a deeply coloured, aromatic,
angostura bitters style red blend with plenty of sandalwood spice, dry
tannins and southern French bite.

1993 Bourgueil Couly-Dutheil
£££ / MB / 🌓   16/20
From Couly-Dutheil, one of the best *négociants* in the Loire Valley, this

is a classic Bourgueil, with fresh, raspberry and green pepper fruitiness and lively acidity.

1989 Madiran, Château de Crouseilles
£ / FB / 🌶   14/20

Robust, dark-chocolate-like, oaky, tannic Madiran from the Cave de Crouseilles. Solid stuff, but make sure you've got a toothbrush and dental floss to hand.

1994 Fleurie, Domaine des Carrières
£ / MB / 🌶   14/20

Attractively juicy, well-made Gamay from the reliable Beaujolais *négociant*, Loron. A little bit under-fruited for a cru wine.

SOUTH AFRICA

1992 Klein Constantia Shiraz
££ / FB / 🌶   15/20

Ripe, powerfully alcoholic Shiraz from one of the best estates in the Cape. It's heavily oaked with plenty of liquoricey, spicy fruit for balance.

SPAIN

1989 Torres Gran Sangredetoro
£ / MB / 🌶   14/20

A traditional blend of Garnacha and Cariñena, this is one of the most Mediterranean of Torres' large range. It's spicy and dry with a core of sweet blackcurrant fruit. If only it were under £5.

1990 Marqués de Murrieta, Rioja
££ / MB / 🍷   16/20

Tempranillo-based Rioja with lashings of sweet, spicy oak from a traditional bodega. This has the concentration and acidity to age for almost as long as you want it to.

Over £8

AUSTRALIA

1990 Lindemans Pyrus
££ / MB / ⌐   16/20

Another wine that would benefit from a prolonged spell in your cellar, this Bordeaux-style blend from Lindemans' Coonawarra winery is packed with coffee bean and vanilla oak flavours and smooth, succulent tannins.

1990 Orlando St Hugo
££ / MB / ⌐   16/20

Another Coonawarra classic, this time from the giant Orlando-Wyndham operation. It's more restrained in style than the Pyrus, with an elegance that reminded us of a St-Julien claret.

ITALY

1989 Brunello di Montalcino, Castelgiocondo
££ / FB / ⌐   16/20

From the aristocratic Marchese di Frescobaldi, this is one of the best reds on the Unwins list. A sweetly concentrated, powerful Sangiovese from Tuscany's Montalcino hills with a dry tannic backbone and a surprising degree of finesse.

Sparkling

£3-5

FRANCE

Chardonnay Blanc de Blancs, 'Le Baron', Brut
£ / 3 / ⌐   13/20

Frothy, soft fizz from an unspecified vineyard area somewhere in France.

£5–8

AUSTRALIA

Angas Brut Rosé
£ / 3 / ♪   14/20
A sweetish, copper-coloured Aussie fizz with big bubbles and gluggable strawberry fruit. Increased costs mean that this is no longer the bargain it once was, but it's still a good party fizz.

Yalumba Pinot Noir/Chardonnay
£££ / 2 / ♪   16/20
A rich, full-bodied, fruity blend of the Champagne grapes Pinot Noir and Chardonnay, showing some of Champagne's biscuity character and toasty maturity. Another winner from winemaker Brian Walsh.

Over £8

FRANCE

Duchâtel Champagne, Thiénot
£ / 3 / ♪   13/20
Unwins' house Champagne is a clean, appley fizz with some sweetness and too much tart acidity. Strictly for Bucks Fizz.

VICTORIA WINE ***(*)
VICTORIA WINE CELLARS ****

Head Office: The Victoria Wine Company, Dukes Court, Duke Street, Woking, Surrey GU21 5XL

Telephone: 01483 715066

Number of branches: 1,533, including 31 Victoria Wine Cellars (70 in total planned to be in place by Christmas 1995) and 178 Haddows in Scotland, plus Victoria Wine in Cité de l'Europe, Calais

Credit cards accepted: Access, Visa, Amex

Hours of opening: Varies by location. Majority of stores open 10.00am to 10.00pm Monday to Saturday. Hours on Sunday vary by location

By-the-case sales: Yes

Glass loan: Free with larger orders

Home delivery: On a local basis by arrangement

Clubs: No

Discounts: Five per cent discount on mixed cases of light and sparkling wine; 7 for the price of 6 on non-promoted Champagnes; 7 for 6 on sparkling wines over £5.99 at Victoria Wine Cellars

In-store tastings: In selected shops on an occasional basis – more frequently in Wine Shops and Victoria Wine Cellars

Top ten best-selling wines: Puerta de la Villa; Landema Falls Colombard Chardonnay; Liebfraumilch Victoria Wine; Soave Pasqua; Vin de Pays de l'Hérault Dry; Cooks Riesling Chenin (special purchase); Jacob's Creek Dry Red; Hardy's Stamp Series Semillon; Hardy's Stamp Series Shiraz; Chapel Hill Sauvignon Blanc. (The top ten varies across the segments and depends on the time of the year and the promotion, but the above shows a typical month and gives an indication of the countries/styles featured)

Range: GOOD: Germany, Spain, Champagne and sparkling wine, Eastern Europe, Chile, Australia, New Zealand, South Africa, Southern France, Bordeaux
AVERAGE: California, Portugal, Burgundy, Rhône
POOR: Loire, Alsace, Beaujolais, England

Now that the union with Augustus Barnett is finally complete, Victoria Wine, with its 1,533 branches, has become the fourth biggest take-home drinks retailer in the UK behind Sainsbury's, Tesco and Thresher. But if you thought that the curtain falling on Augustus Barnett was the cue for Vicky Wine to rest on its high street laurels, think again. The curtain is already rising on Act 2.

The *succès de scandale* of the past year has been the performance of Augustus and Victoria's débutante daughter, Victoria Wine Cellars. Masterminded to compete head-on with Thresher's Wine Rack by the sun-tanned, thong-sporting Adrian Lane before his return to the Costa del Sol, 'the success of Victoria Wine Cellars has surprised everyone', says wine buyer Thomas Woolrych. Sales were up a total of 10 per cent, with wine sales up 36 per cent and sparkling wines a whopping 49 per cent.

Targeting customers who the company's marketing men like to refer to as 'promiscuous', a Victoria Wine Cellars is bigger than the average Victoria Wine Shop, sits in a generally more salubrious location, and, with a choice of 500 to 550 wines, sells wines which the old faithful Victoria Wine customer wouldn't touch with a didgeridoo.

The New World, for instance, does well and Germany badly in Cellars, as they are known, while the reverse is true in the beer-fag-and-crisp Neighbourhood Drinks Stores and Haddows (the latter in Scotland only). So it's not hard to understand why Victoria's parent, Allied-Domecq, is anxious to capitalise on Vicky's success by pouring £4 million into increasing the number of flagship stores. The plan is for 70 Cellars by Christmas, with up to 120 by the end of 1997.

The convenience end – Neighbourhood Shops, Drinks and Food Stores and Haddows in Scotland, a total of 683 shops – will also get a facelift, to the tune of £2.6 million. To their credit, even in the corner-shop stores Victoria Wine has not gone the downmarket £1.99 route. 'The cheapest we do is a £2.69; £1.99 means compromising quality. We don't want to drag people downmarket,' says wine buyer Joanne

Convert. The neighbourhood off-licences carry around 250 wines, but less than 20 per cent of what they sell is wine.

The meat in the sandwich made by Victoria Wine Cellars and the Neighbourhood Drinks Stores, and most of the bread and butter too, is Victoria Wine's 810 Wine Shops. Bigger Wine Shops carry 400 to 500 wines, smaller ones under 400 wines. Drawing on the experience of setting up Cellars, Act 3 will consist of refitting 126 Wine Shops over the next 18 months at a cost of another £4 million, with £15 million in total to be spent on kitting out 395 Wine Shops in three years. Loadsamoney to be sure, but still £2 million less than its parent spent on promoting their whisky brand, Teachers, in 1995.

What's the point of all this investment? The stated aim is to make the shops more user-friendly by looking good and delivering better customer service via the winsomely named Who Cares Wins training programme. All new managers will have to take the Wine and Spirit Education Trust's Certificate, while more advanced courses will be available on self-study tapes. Former buyer Geraldine Jago has been appointed cheerleader-in-chief to chivvy the ranks of shop managers into appreciating the wines they're selling.

And the increasingly exciting range at Victoria Wine is well worth closer acquaintance. Some of the best work has been done by buyer Thomas Woolrych in South Africa with the addition of new wines from Kym Milne, including the vibrant 1995 White Ridge Sauvignon Blanc, the excellent Warwick Cabernet Sauvignon, wines from Australia's Orlando, and *Grapevine*'s very own winemaker of the year in 1995, Danie de Wet. Victoria Wine has also gone out on a limb with Achim von Arnim's Clos Cabrière Rosé, one of South Africa's best sparkling wines.

Chile has come up trumps with a handful of excellent value wines made by young Chilean winemaker Andres Ilabaca at the modern Canepa winery – in particular, an outstanding 1994 oak-aged Semillon, and the more old-fashioned styles of Concha y Toro. The plan is to build on the Chilean range and 'look at Argentina'. With 67 Australian wines, Oz is still a major force. Here, a new raft of wines bought through the importing arm of Bibendum – the extensive Deakin Estate, Basedow and Katnook range – has been hitched to the more familiar likes of Penfolds, Lindemans and Orlando's ubiquitous Jacob's Creek.

In California, buyer Joanne Convert's baby, Victoria Wine has done well to bring in characterful idiosyncrasies such as the 1993 Parducci Petite Sirah, 1993 Kenwood Mazzoni Zinfandel and 1991 Atlas Peak

Sangiovese. There is still rather too much Gallo for our taste and the Geyser Peak wines are pricey, but a planned own-label range at the £4.59 price level could be interesting.

Southern France and Bordeaux are the most impressive growth areas in the French portfolio. The full Vin de Pays d'Oc selection is second to none in the high street, with a thicket of good value wines such as Gabriel Meffre's modern Galet red and whites at the £3.99 mark, as well as Gilbert Alquier's classy Faugères. Welcome signs of a resurrected Bordeaux include a trio of whites – Château La Tuque Bel-Air, Haut-Bonfils and Château Terres Douces.

In Portugal, Victoria Wine have neatly combined elements of the new (Australia's Peter Bright providing the modern styles) with more traditional wines from the quality-conscious firms of J M da Fonseca and Sogrape. Similarly, in Spain, the buying team have introduced both good value, everyday quaffers at the £2.99 mark, and a handful of more expensive quality reds from Navarra and Rioja.

In the fine wine arena, the classic regions of France still have something to offer Victoria Wine's well-heeled customers. There are a number of classy new clarets such as Château Teyssier from St-Emilion, Carbonnieux in the Graves and the Haut-Médoc classified property Château La Tour Carnet. For sheer hedonistic pleasure, however, the 1991 Cornas from Allemand and Guigal's sumptuous 1990 Côte Rôtie Brune et Blonde are tough acts to follow.

In April, Victoria Wine opened a store in the new Cité de l'Europe carrying the full range, 'a first step which could lead to an international dimension to the business', according to managing director Michael Hammond. A rather limited international dimension, we suspect, if the Calais store is anything to go by. Not that there's anything wrong with it *per se*. But with a giant new Tesco just a few doors down the mall, and a fistful of French hypermarket cut-price goods in nearby Carrefour, Victoria Wine will have to pull out a few more stops if it is not to be squeezed out of cross-Channel contention.

Wines marked with an asterisk (*) are stocked in Victoria Wine Cellars only. The full range is available in Victoria Wine's Cité de l'Europe store.

White

Under £3

GERMANY

Liebfraumilch, Victoria Wine
£££ / 5 / 🍷   14/20
Blended by the firm of Kendermann, this is one of the best high street
Liebs we've had this year, with honeyed grapey flavours and a hint of
white pepper. Above all, it's fresh and well-balanced.

PORTUGAL

1994 Alta Mesa Dry, Estremadura
££ / 2 / 🍷   13/20
A blend of the indigenous and somewhat obscure Malvasia Rei, Vital,
Jampal and Rabo de Ovelha grapes produced at the Sao Mamede co-
operative. Cool fermentation techniques have produced a clean, full
lime-juicy white which could be a Portuguese Riesling.

£3–5

AUSTRALIA

1994 Rawsons Retreat Penfolds Bin 21 Semillon/Chardonnay
£££ / 2 / 🍷   15/20
A good example of the new-style Penfolds whites. With its spicy vanilla
oak, herby Semillon and Chardonnay richness, these two grapes
combine harmoniously to produce a sundae of vanilla ice cream and
lemony fruit.

1994 Deakin Estate Chardonnay
££ / 2 / 🍷   15/20
This is the best of the extensive range of Deakin Estate wines available
at Victoria Wine. It's a citrusy, subtly oaked and delightfully fresh style
of Chardonnay, which would have left us looking forward to a second
and third glass if we hadn't been on the wagon at the time.

1994 Hardy's Stamp Series Semillon/Chardonnay
£ / 3 / ❄   13/20

With its cuddly Koala label, this top ten best-selling blend is confected and a little short on flavour, even if a portion of the wine is enhanced by malolactic fermentation.

CHILE

1994 Canepa Oak Aged Semillon
£££ / 2 / ❄   16/20

One of winemaker Andres Ilabaca's most successful whites, this is a French oak-aged Semillon from Chile's Maipo Valley, showing oatmealy, full-bodied flavours of vanilla and lemon meringue. One of the best white wines we've tasted from Chile.

1994 Casillero del Diablo Sauvignon Blanc
££ / 2 / ❄   15/20

Another Maipo Valley white with some spicy American oak influence. With its lemongrass nose and rich, honeyed mouthfeel, this Concha y Toro white is fuller than most Chilean Sauvignon Blancs.

FRANCE

Vin de Pays de l'Hérault Dry
0 / 3 / ❄   12/20

Produced by Skalli Fortant de France from a kitchen sink of grape varieties including Ugni and Sauvignon Blanc, this is a dull, sweetish white with some appley fruitiness.

1994 Grenache Blanc, Vin de Pays d'Oc, Galet Vineyards
££ / 2 / ❄   14/20

Made by New World influenced French winemaker Thierry Boudinaud, this is a modern, perfumed, unoaked Languedoc white which extracts every ounce of flavour from the normally innocuous Grenache Blanc grape.

1994 Chardonnay, Vin de Pays d'Oc, Galet Vineyards
£££ / 2 / ❄   15/20

From the same cellar, this is a similarly well-made, unoaked Chardonnay with crisp, green malt notes and fresh, minerally fruitiness. Light, crisp and delightfully drinkable.

1994 Rolle, Vin de Pays d'Oc
£££ / 1 / ♪   15/20

From a single estate in the Coteaux du Languedoc, this is a fresh, unusual, unoaked white with the bracing acidity typical of the Mediterranean Rolle (or Vermentino) grape and some grip on the aftertaste.

1994 Big Frank's White
£££ / 2 / ♪   15/20

An eccentric but successful blend of Chardonnay, Marsanne and Viognier by an equally eccentric (but we're not sure how successful) Polish-American painter. It's peachy, soft and lightly oaked with appealing French elegance and seductive Viognier aromas.

1994 Château La Tuque, Bordeaux Blanc
£££ / 2 / ♪   15/20

Made by Calvet's Yves Barry, a French winemaker who has amassed valuable experience in Australia, this blend of Sauvignon Blanc and Muscadelle with a smidgeon of Semillon is an unoaked delight, with some creamy, fermentation lees-derived softness and zesty, grapefruity flavours. If only more Bordeaux Blanc tasted like this.

1994 Château Haut Bonfils, Bordeaux Blanc
££ / 2 / ♪   15/20

A different style of white Bordeaux made entirely from Sauvignon Blanc, half of which was fermented in American oak barrels, according to its producer, Hugh 'Grant' Ryman. A smoky, grassy white with a grapefruity tang.

HUNGARY

1994 Chapel Hill Sauvignon Blanc
£ / 3 / ♪   13/20

A sweetish, slightly bitter Sauvignon Blanc made by Kym Milne at Hungary's Balatonboglar winery. The wine appears to have suffered from the rather wet and humid conditions in 1994.

ITALY

1994 Soave, Pasqua
££ / 2 / ⚱   14/20
A yeasty, beery, stainless steel fermented Soave made from 90 per cent
Garganega and 10 per cent Trebbiano. We're particularly keen on the
cheeky cherub's bottom label.

MOLDOVA

1994 Kirkwood Moldovan Chardonnay
£ / 3 / ⚱   13/20
An attempt to revamp the Hincesti Moldovan Chardonnay, this French-
bottled white is Hugh Ryman's best effort yet, but still tastes rather
confected, with boudoir aromas of talcum powder and a curious touch
of baked banana.

PORTUGAL

1994 Bright Brothers Fernão Pires/Chardonnay, Ribatejo
£££ / 2 / ⚱   15/20
The Fernão Pires grape variety is one of the most interesting of an
impressive array of indigenous grapes. Australia's Peter Bright has done
a great deal to popularise this undervalued variety. Here he combines it
nicely with the internationally acclaimed Chardonnay grape, adding a
touch of oak to create an intensely flavoured dry white with a note of
orange peel zest.

SOUTH AFRICA

1995 Firgrove Colombard/Chenin
£ / 2 / ⚱   13/20
Made at the winningly named Bovlei co-operative in Wellington, this is
typical of the peardrop and lemon sherbet school of technological
winemaking. It's sound, if a bit confected.

Landema Falls Colombard/Chardonnay, Sonop
££ / 2 / ⚱   14/20
A more interesting wine, even though it retails at the same price as the

Firgrove. It's fuller and better balanced with peach and pineapple fruitiness and a touch of oak character.

1995 Cape View Chenin/Sauvignon
£££ / 2 / 1   15/20
An extremely well-made and aromatic Stellenbosch blend from the much-travelled Kym Milne. It's grassy, zesty and fresh with none of the confected, boiled sweets character that mars so many cheap Cape whites.

1995 White Ridge Riesling
££ / 3 / 1   14/20
Another stylish white from crampon-wearing winemaker Kym Milne – not to be confused with Bear Ridge or Matra Mountains, two of his Eastern European labels. This is a fresh expression of the Riesling grape with tropical lemon and lime flavours.

1995 White Ridge Sauvignon Blanc
£££ / 2 / 1   16/20
Selected from cooler vineyards in the picturesque hills around Stellenbosch, this is a fresh, intensely flavoured Sauvignon Blanc with a pungent grapefruit and gooseberry zing. The best South African white we've had from Kym Milne this year.

SPAIN

1994 Santara Chardonnay, Conca de Barbera
££ / 2 / 1   14/20
From a recently elevated Spanish *denominación*, this ripe, rounded, melony Chardonnay made by Hugh Ryman at the Concavin winery is decently priced at under £4, but slightly affected by oak bitterness.

£5-8

AUSTRALIA

1993 Basedow Semillon
£ / 2 / 1   14/20
An old-fashioned, alcoholic, charry mouthful of Barossa Semillon which

is long on oak-smokiness and desperately short on finesse. We prefer the Basedow reds.

1992 Katnook Botrytised Chardonnay
£££ / 8 / ➟   16/20

One of a small number of botrytised Chardonnays produced in the world, this is an extremely rich but well-balanced sticky, with peachy, barley sugar and raisin complexity underpinned by fresh acidity.

CHILE

1994 Marqués de Casa Concha Chardonnay
££ / 2 /]   15/20

Rather old-fashioned Chilean Chardonnay made by French winemaker Gaetane Carron at the Concha y Toro winery, with lees-derived Burgundian characters and plenty of lemony fruit flavour.

FRANCE

1994 Mâcon Vinzelles, Cave de Vinzelles
£ / 2 /]   14/20

Produced at the Vinzelles co-operative by South African Jean-Luc Sweerts of the Avontuur Estate, this is a partially oak-aged, alcoholic, spicy Mâcon white with ripe fruit flavours and soft, buttery lees flavours. The wine pulls up a bit short.

*1994 Château Terres Douces, Cuvée Prestige
£££ / 2 /]   16/20

Made by the *négociant* house of Ginestet, this is closer to a Graves-style white Bordeaux, with toasty new oak flavours, plenty of Semillon weight and waxiness, and a crisp, lingering aftertaste.

*1993 L de Louvière, Pessac-Léognan
££ / 2 /]   16/20

There were apparently no fewer than five people involved in the making of this wine – oenologists Michel Gaillard and Vincent Cruego, and consultants Pascal Ribereau-Gayon, Denis Dubourdieu and Jacques Lurton. The result is a new-oak fermented Sauvignon Blanc-dominated blend with fresh spicy oak, crisp acidity and attractively grassy flavours. Many hands . . .

*1990 Château de Berbec, Premières Côtes de Bordeaux
££ / 6 / ♦   15/20
With its aromas of honey and Charentais melon, this is a fresh, nicely balanced, good value alternative to Sauternes with an elegant, clean finish.

1993 Montagny Premier Cru, Cave de Buxy
£ / 2 / ♦   14/20
From the Côte Chalonnaise's Buxy co-operative, this is a laudable attempt at a complex white Burgundy. As with the 1992, we felt that there was rather too much oak for the weight of fruit.

SOUTH AFRICA

1995 De Wetshof Lesca Chardonnay
£££ / 2 / ♦   16/20
Named after winemaker Danie de Wet's wife, this is a typically elegant, flavoursome Chardonnay from a Cape producer who's made the variety his speciality. It's fresh, zesty and lightly oaked, with a prickle of carbon dioxide and well-judged, fudge-like flavours.

SPAIN

1993 Monopole Barrel Fermented Rioja, CVNE
£ / 2 / ♦   14/20
A modern white Rioja in which the high acidity of the Viura grape is balanced by fruit concentration. The trouble is the new oak dominates to the detriment of the wine.

UNITED STATES

Geyser Peak Chardonnay
0 / 2 / ♦   14/20
Made by Australian Daryl Groom, this is heavier than many a California Chardonnay, with ripe, melon fruitiness, plenty of alcohol and barrel-loads of toasty oak. At over £7, this is risible value for money.

Over £8

FRANCE

*1990 Riesling Grand Cru Schoenenberg, Turckheim
££ / 2 / ▬   16/20
A complex, mature, minerally Alsace Riesling, which for once lives up
to the *grand cru* designation. Fresh lime-like and aniseedy, this has
considerable finesse and length of flavour. Worth its £9 plus price tag.

Red

Under £3

MOROCCO

Domaine Cigogne, Moroccan Red
££ / FB / ▌   14/20
From the Berkane region in eastern Morocco, this is a rustic, peppery,
baked blend of Cinsault, Grenache, Carignan, Syrah and Mourvèdre. Can
you tell Cigogne from Châteauneuf-du-Pape?

PORTUGAL

1994 Alta Mesa, Estremadura
££ / MB / ▌   13/20
You might be surprised to find this juicy, peppery, modern red at high
table, but it's the sort of thing cheapskate Oxbridge dons serve up in
decanters to deserving students.

SPAIN

1994 Ed's Red, La Mancha
££ / MB / ▌   14/20
American winemaker Ed Flaherty made this all-Tempranillo red at the
Bodegas Centro Españolas winery in La Mancha, using stainless steel
fermentation to produce a vibrantly fruity, soft plum and cherry red.

1994 Puerta de la Villa, Valdepeñas
£££ / MB / ⅟   15/20
Made from the same grape variety, known in southeastern Spain as
Cencibel, this is another soft, unoaked red with an even more
exuberantly juicy fruit character. An excellent value thirst-quencher at
under £3.

£3–5

AUSTRALIA

1993 Jacob's Creek Shiraz/Cabernet
£ / MB / ⅟   14/20
Tarry sweet oak and toffee-fudge flavours predominate here. The
blackcurrant pastille fruit doesn't quite cope with the strong-armed
combination.

1992 Hardy's Stamp Label Shiraz/Cabernet
££ / MB / ⅟   14/20
Sweetly oaked, deeply coloured Aussie blend which, at under £4,
deserves its berth in Victoria Wine's top ten best-selling wines.

1993 Deakin Estate Cabernet Sauvignon
££ / MB / ⅟   15/20
From Australia's Wingara group, this is a well-made blackcurrant and
cassis-flavoured alternative to claret, with nicely integrated oak flavours
and grassy, cool climate fruitiness.

CHILE

1994 Canepa Zinfandel
£££ / MB / ⅟   15/20
Zinfandel is normally associated with California rather than Chile, but
these vines have been planted at Canepa since 1980. Winemaker Andres
Ilabaca has used their maturity to produce a soft, tobaccoey red with full-
bodied peppery fruitiness and lots of colour.

1992 Casillero del Diablo Cabernet Sauvignon

£ / MB / ♪   14/20

A Cabernet Sauvignon which shows the minty, herby, sage-like aromas of old-fashioned Maipo Valley reds.

FRANCE

1994 Riverbed, Vin de Pays du Gard

£ / MB / ♪   13/20

A basic, fruity, orange peel scented red made by Thierry Boudinaud of Gabriel Meffre using Grenache, Carignan, Merlot and Syrah grapes. The plonk in the bottle doesn't live up to the brilliant psychedelic label.

1993 Domaine du Tauch, Corbières, Mont Tauch

0 / FB / ♪   13/20

A rustic, unyielding blend of Grenache and Carignan taken from 50-year-old vines in the Languedoc. The angostura bitters aromas are promising, but the dry tannins fail to deliver.

1992 Château de Léret, Cahors

£ / MB / ♪   14/20

A traditionally vinified blend of predominantly Cot with 10 per cent each of Merlot and Tannat, this is a tarry, mature red which is on the light, slightly green side for a Cahors.

1993 Coteaux Varois, Abbaye Saint Hilaire

££ / MB / ♪   14/20

An elegant, grassy, leafy red made by Domaine Listel in the Coteaux Varois area of southern Provence from Cabernet, Grenache and Syrah grapes. Drink up.

1994 Syrah, Galet Vineyards, Vin de Pays d'Oc

££ / MB / ♪   14/20

A wine which benefited from the comparatively rare technique of thermovinification to extract colour but little tannin, this is a juicy, Beaujolais-style Syrah with attractive smoky fruitiness.

1992 Domaine St-Hilaire, Cabernet Vin de Pays d'Oc
££ / MB / ♪   15/20

From a large estate in the Languedoc, this is rich, chocolatey, nicely balanced, unoaked Cabernet Sauvignon with a whiff of the southern farmyard.

1994 Costières de Nîmes, Celliers du Colombier
££ / FB / ♪   14/20

Soft, ripe, beefy southern blend of Carignan, Grenache, Cinsault and Syrah. Good, honest, old-fashioned drinking at just over £3.

1993 Château Mauléon, Côtes du Roussillon Villages
££ / FB / ♪   15/20

Another southern French red, with the accent this time on more modern carbonic maceration derived flavours, this blend of Grenache, Syrah and Carignan is fresh, aromatic and peppery with attractive juicy fruit flavours and a chunky bite.

1994 Big Frank's Red Minervois
££ / MB / ♪   14/20

Produced by eccentric Polish-American painter Frank Chludinski, this counterpart to Big Frank's White is a ripe, juicy, undemanding introduction to the Languedoc.

Victoria Wine Claret, Calvet
££ / MB / ♪   14/20

Reblended this year by Victoria Wine's buyers in conjunction with Yves Barry of *négociant* Calvet, this is a grassy, well-made, unoaked young claret with softer tannins than many a cheap red Bordeaux.

1994 Château la Jalgue, Bordeaux
££ / MB / ♪   14/20

Another strand in Victoria Wine's 'Back to Bordeaux' campaign, this is a concentrated, plummy claret with plenty of backbone and solid tannins.

ITALY

1993 Lambrusco Grasparossa
££ / LB / 🍷   14/20
Made by Anselmo Chiarli, this is a light, dry Lambrusco with plenty of
cherryade-like fizz and a refreshing tang. It's good to see an off-licence
taking a punt on a dry red Lambrusco.

*1990 Chianti Rufina Riserva, Fattoria di Galiga
££ / MB / 🍷   15/20
An almondy, leathery traditional Chianti from the Rufina hills near
Florence, showing a good core of cherried fruitiness, lively acidity and
dryish tannins.

1993 Le Trulle, Primitivo del Salento
£ / FB / 🍷   13/20
Despite the fact that this is made by Kym Milne from the local Primitivo
grape, we found that the oak chip sweetness rather got in the way of any
indigenous character. Chewy stuff.

PORTUGAL

1994 Bright Brothers Douro, Vinho Regional Trás Montes, Terras Duriensis
££ / MB / 🍷   14/20
A vibrantly coloured, plummy Douro red blend with peppery spiciness
and rasp of thirst-quenching acidity. A good, modern Portuguese quaffer
from Peter Bright, a dab Australian hand with native Portuguese grape
varieties.

1991 Grão Vasco, Dão
£££ / FB / 🍷   15/20
From a region which has only recently moved into the modern
winemaking world, this is an aromatic, peppery, modern Dão with
sweet, almost Grenache-like flavours, but in fact made from a line-up
which sounds like the Portuguese Davis Cup team – Touriga Nacional,
Jaen, Alfrocheiro Preto and Tina Pinheira.

1994 Ponte de Alcorce, Quinta da Gouxa, Ribatejo
£££ / MB / ⅓   15/20

Another modern Portuguese red, this time made entirely from the
southern Portuguese Periquita grape. Sage, ginger and spicy aromatics
are supported by fresh, juicy, punchy fruitiness.

1989 Quinta da Camarate, Fonseca
£££ / MB / ⅓   15/20

Not so long ago, José Maria da Fonseca was one of only three modern-
thinking producers in Portugal. And it was wines like this that inspired
the rest of Portugal to follow suit. This is a mature, claret-like blend of
Castelão Frances, Cabernet Sauvignon and Espadeiro with sweet, minty
fruitiness and a balance which comes with maturity. Rather like us, really.

SOUTH AFRICA

1994 Cape View Cinsault/Shiraz
££ / MB / ⅓   14/20

Exclusive to Victoria Wine, this Kym Milne blend is a deeply coloured,
aromatic, plum-jam scented red with lots of carbonic maceration
softness rounded out with a hint of oak chip.

1995 Firgrove Ruby Cabernet/Cinsault
£ / MB / ⅓   13/20

Cheaper by 50 pence, this is a more rustic Cape blend from the Bovlei
co-operative. Confected and faintly rubbery plonk.

SPAIN

1993 El Liso Barrel Aged Tempranillo
££ / MB / ⅓   14/20

Otherwise known as Fuente del Ritmo at Oddbins and Safeway, this
modern La Mancha red was made by American Ed Flaherty at the
Bodegas Centro Españolas. It's a chunky, youthful, prominently oaked
red which proves that La Mancha can make more than neutral white wines.

1990 Chivite Reserva, Navarra
£ / MB / ⅓   14/20

A blend of Tempranillo and Garnacha from one of the most forward-thinking bodegas in Navarra, this is a tobaccoey, sweetly oaked red which resembles a Rioja Crianza in style. Only a dry finish prevented us from giving it a higher mark.

£5–8

AUSTRALIA

1992 Basedow Cabernet Sauvignon
0 / MB / ⚑   13/20
Oak-fermented, oak-aged and oak-flavoured. That's still more than enough oak, thank you.

1992 Basedow Shiraz
££ / FB / ⚑   15/20
Quintessential Barossa Valley Shiraz with liquoricey, minty fruitiness and a copse, rather than a forest, of American oak. We enjoyed the wine a little more this year.

1992 Bankside Shiraz, Hardy's
££ / MB / ➠   16/20
Just as flavoursome and heavily oaked but with a little bit more elegance to it, this is a soft, nutmeg-spicy, medium-weight Shiraz from the BRL-Hardy conglomerate.

1983 Brown Brothers Shiraz/Cabernet
££ / MB / ⚑   15/20
When this wine was made, Australian wines weren't even a glint in wine buyers' eyes. Brown Brothers was one of Australia's pioneering exporters, so it's fitting that this mature, mint-toffee, red Victorian blend has turned up now, like an old timer at a party. Not quite time for the zimmer frame yet.

CHILE

1991 Marqués de Casa Concha Cabernet Sauvignon
£ / MB / ⚑   14/20
From the Maipo Valley's Puerto Alto vineyard, this Concha y Toro red is dry and on the green side.

1990 Cousiño Macul Antiguas Reservas Cabernet Sauvignon
££ / MB / ⌐   16/20
The showcase Cousiño Macul winery on the outskirts of Santiago is one
of Chile's most old-fashioned estates, producing wines which tread a
tightrope between success and failure.This particular vintage is a
success, with minty, fresh, aromatic and slightly rustic liquid essence of
blackcurrant flavours and spicy American oak.

FRANCE

1994 Gigondas, Les Perdrix, Cave de Gigondas
££ / MB / ⌐   15/20
Made by South African winemaker Jean-Luc Sweerts of the Avontuur
Estate, this is a modern, fruity Grenache-based red, of which 15 per cent
is aged in oak. It's well-made, but a little bit short of stuffing for a
Gigondas.

1993 La Cuvée Mythique, Vin de Pays d'Oc
££ / FB / ⌐   16/20
A southern French blend of Syrah, Mourvèdre, Carignan, Grenache and
Cabernet Sauvignon made from old vines by the go-ahead Val d'Orbieu
co-operative. This dense, oaky, complex red wine is oenologist Marc
Dubernet's homage to the Mediterranean's viticultural traditions.

1990 Château Laclaverie, Côtes de Francs
££ / MB / ⌐   15/20
An unfiltered Merlot-based Right Bank claret made by the family which
owns Vieux Château Certan and Le Pin, this is structured by rustic village
tannins which should soften with age.

*1989 Château Peyros, Madiran
££ / FB / ⌐   15/20
A typical southwestern blend of 60 per cent Tannat and 40 per cent
Cabernet Sauvignon, Cabernet Franc and Pinenc, this is an unoaked,
mature, claret-like Madiran with characteristically chunky tannins and
supple, underlying fruitiness.

*1992 Domaine de Larrivet, Graves
££ / MB / ⌡   15/20
A fresh, attractive, coffee bean/oak style Graves with chocolatey
sweetness and forward, easy-drinking fruit for early consumption.

*1993 Faugères, Gilbert Alquier
£££ / FB / ⌐   16/20
From one of the Languedoc's star red performers, this is a blend of Syrah,
Grenache, Mourvèdre and Carignan with densely packed, almost wild
flavours of rosemary and blackberry fruit. Concentrated, massively
characterful stuff from the most homogeneous *appellation* in the South
of France.

ITALY

*1993 Chianti Classico, Rocca delle Macie
0 / MB / ⌡   13/20
Made by the normally reliable firm of Rocca delle Macie, a winery
owned by an Italian film producer, this tasted rather stale when we saw
it in July, but it may be worth a retake – or should that be remake?

PORTUGAL

1992 Cabernet Sauvignon, Quinta de Pancas
££ / MB / ⌡   15/20
A fluent Portuguese attempt at a modern, international style of Cabernet
Sauvignon. We enjoyed this soft, spicy, elegantly oaked red, and so, we
trust, will you.

1993 Vinha do Monte, Sogrape, Alentejo
££ / FB / ⌡   15/20
Modelled on the style successfully pioneered by the Tinto Velho winery,
this is a rustic, tobaccoey, characterful southern Portuguese red with
refreshing acidity to cut through the tannic crust.

SOUTH AFRICA

*1991 Warwick Cabernet Sauvignon
£££ / MB / ⇌-   16/20

From one of South Africa's few world-class estates, this is a delightfully balanced, claret-like red made by Canadian owner Norma Ratcliffe. Mint, cassis and damson flavours mingle harmoniously in this elegant, ageworthy Cape red.

1988 Overgaauw Tria Corda
0 / FB / ♪   13/20

Overoaked, over-confected, overpriced, Overgaauw.

1994 Clos Malverne Pinotage Reserve
£££ / FB / ⇌-   16/20

A deeply coloured, richly juicy, aromatic Pinotage with the tarry blackcurrant and raspberry fruitiness of the grape and succulently ripe new oak characters.

SPAIN

1989 Campillo Crianza Rioja
££ / MB / ♪   15/20

The price may have crept over the magic £4.99 point, but this leafy, mature, almost red Burgundy-like Rioja, made entirely from the Tempranillo grape, is still a good buy at around £5.50.

1989 Campo Viejo Rioja Reserva
££ / MB / ♪   15/20

Lighter in body than the Campillo, this is an attractively perfumed, equally mature, gamey Rioja red.

UNITED STATES

1993 Parducci, Petite Sirah
£££ / FB / ⇌-   16/20

A rich, tarry, inky, aromatic California red made from the Petite Sirah, or Durif, grape with vibrant tobacco and blackberry fruitiness and little of the hard tannins often found on this sun-baked variety. Excellent value at just over £5.

Over £8

AUSTRALIA

1991 Katnook Merlot, Coonawarra
££ / MB / ➠   16/20
One of a number of excellent Katnook wines we've had this year from winemaker Wayne Stehbens, this is a lush, mint humbug, vanilla oaky red, which still needs a year or two yet to harmonise.

1991 Katnook Cabernet Sauvignon, Coonawarra
£££ / MB / ➠   17/20
Another wine for the long haul, this is a full-throated, attractively textured Cabernet with flavours of coffee bean, blackcurrant and green pepper, supported by fine-grained tannins. One of the best Australian reds we've seen this year.

FRANCE

1990 Château Teyssier, St-Emilion Grand Cru
££ / MB / ➠   16/20
From a British-owned property in St-Emilion, which has recently benefited from investment in new technology, this is a mature, medium-bodied red with plenty of colour and ripe, silky tannins.

1992 Château Carbonnieux, Graves
££ / MB / ↯   16/20
With its mocha oak character and lightish, green pepper fruitiness, this is a fresh, well-made claret for early drinking.

1990 Château La Tour Carnet, Haut-Médoc
££ / MB / ➠   16/20
Finely crafted, elegant Left Bank classified claret in which the ripeness of the vintage lends finesse and flavour to the new oak backdrop. Not cheap at nearly £15, but it's already drinking nicely and should develop further complexity over the next five years.

1989 Marsannay, Louis Jadot

££ / MB / 🍷   15/20

From the extreme north of Burgundy's Côte de Nuits, this is a ripe, mature, softly strawberryish Pinot Noir, attractively priced at under £10.

1991 Cornas, Thierry Allemand

£££ / FB / ⌐   17/20

Smoky, peppery, aromatic Syrah from one of the best growers in the tiny northern Rhône *appellation* of Cornas. Although £16 is a lot to pay for a red wine, when it's as good as this massively concentrated and spicy red, it's well worth it.

1990 Côte Rôtie, Guigal

£££ / MB / ⌐   18/20

A gloriously aromatic, stunning example of Côte Rôtie Syrah at its superb best, made by darling of the northern Rhône (and Robert Parker), Marcel Guigal. A silky, peppery, spicy red in which flavour, texture and tannins are in near-perfect harmony. In the northern Rhône, 1990 was a classic vintage. You could drink this now, but make sure you leave a few bottles to enjoy in the coming millennium.

SPAIN

1989 Contino Rioja Reserva

£££ / MB / ⌐   16/20

One of a growing number of single-estate Riojas, this CVNE-owned property produces densely fruity, concentrated wines, which have defined the style of modern Tempranillo-based reds in the region. True to form, this is youthful, oaky and built for the long haul.

UNITED STATES

1993 Kenwood Mazzoni Zinfandel

££ / FB / ⌐   16/20

The best of three Zinfandels sourced from Kenwood at Victoria Wine, this one comes from the Mazzoni vineyard near Geyserville in northern California's Sonoma County. It's an oaky, complex, tobacco-pouch style with intense raspberry fruit flavours, plenty of concentration and vivid acidity.

1991 Beringer Cabernet Sauvignon, Napa Valley
££ / MB / ▮   16/20
Unusually for a Napa Valley Cabernet Sauvignon, this juicy, deeply coloured style is not overstuffed with tannin and extracted macho bitterness. It's an elegant, mint and cigar-box style with supple, fine-grained tannins. And it's £1 cheaper at Majestic.

Rosé

£3-5

FRANCE

1994 Fortant de France, Syrah Rosé, Vin de Pays d'Oc
£ / 2 / ▮   13/20
There's a touch of peppery Syrah character in this well-packaged wine from pasta merchant Robert Skalli, but not enough to make the wine really exciting.

Sparkling

£5-8

SPAIN

1990 Torre del Gall, Cava
£ / 2 / ▮   15/20
From Champagne house Moët et Chandon's Spanish outpost, this is one of the better Cavas on the market, but we still found it a bit coarse and celery-like, not to mention overpriced. We're all for indigenous grapes when they're good, but feel it's about time Moët shipped a lorry-load of Chardonnay and Pinot Noir down to the Penedés.

Over £8

AUSTRALIA

1990 Green Point Rosé
££ / 2 / 1   16/20
A fizz that shows the benefits of using the classic Champagne grapes, Chardonnay and Pinot Noir. Moët et Chandon's Australian operation, based in the coolish climate of Victoria's Yarra Valley, is currently producing some of the best non-French sparkling wines of all. This delicate, onion skin-coloured rosé made by the multi-talented Dr Tony Jordan is a deliciously mature addition to the Green Point range.

1992 Croser Brut
£££ / 2 / 1   16/20
Modestly named after the man who made it, Brian Croser's Adelaide Hills fizz is an intensely lemony, weighty blend of Pinot Noir and 30 per cent Chardonnay with an idiosyncratic, almost savoury, smoky bacon note. It's one of Australia's classiest sparkling wines – just as well Mr Croser didn't call it Brian.

FRANCE

Pol Roger White Foil, Extra Dry
£££ / 2 / 1   17/20
An equal blend of Pinot Noir, Chardonnay and Pinot Meunier, Pol Roger's White Foil is consistently among the best non-vintage Champagnes. It's a soft, subtle, refreshingly elegant Champagne with delicate bubbles and biscuit and brioche notes. This was one of Winston Churchill's favourite Champagnes (Pol Roger have even named their top fizz after him), but that's no reason to raise two fingers to it.

1989 Victoria Wine Vintage Champagne
£ / 3 / 1   14/20
Made by the giant Marne et Champagne group, this is marred by the same sulphurous egginess we found on the 1986 last year. It also tastes young and oversweetened. There's consistency for you.

Deutz Marlborough Cuvée
£££ / 2 / ♪   16/20
A fine, elegantly crafted blend of Pinot Noir and Chardonnay made in
New Zealand using the southern hemisphere's only Coquard
Champagne press. The result of a fruitful partnership between
Champagne house Deutz and New Zealand's Montana, Marlborough
Cuvée has established itself as a complex, dry fizz of considerable tangy
complexity.

SOUTH AFRICA

Clos Cabrière, Cuvée Belle Rose
£££ / 2 / ♪   17/20
**Clos Cabrière produces most of the Cape's best fizz. Made by the
eccentric Achim von Arnim, a fellow who collects African
elephant droppings and has twice been voted South Africa's
worst-dressed man, this is a zippy, stylishly dry pink sparkling
wine made exclusively from Pinot Noir grapes.**

Fortified

£3–5

SPAIN

Victoria Wine Pedro Ximenez Sherry, 37.5cl
££ / 8 / ➤   16/20
Ginger biscuits, raisins and treacle come to mind when you taste this
supersweet, almost pruney Sherry from Sanchez Romate. It's delicious
stuff, but drink it in small doses.

Victoria Wine Palo Cortado Sherry
£££ / 2 / ♪   16/20
From the same supplier, this is a fresh, complex burnt almond style
Sherry, which is one step on from an Amontillado.

£5–8

ITALY

Pellegrino Marsala Superiore Dolce

£/6/⅟   14/20

Less exciting than the dry wine we enjoyed so much last year, this fortified Sicilian is deep, almost coffee-coloured, and sweet – like a compôte of dried Mediterranean fruits. We just found the aftertaste a bit baked and rustic.

SPAIN

La Ina, Pale Dry Sherry, Domecq

££/2/⅟   15/20

A Fino which is consistently among the most enjoyable dry Sherries on the market, this is a nutty, fresh, salty fortified white with a characteristic savoury bite.

Over £8

PORTUGAL

1990 Dow's Crusted Port

££ / FB / ⌐   16/20

Halfway to vintage port in style, Crusted Ports throw a deposit and need to be decanted. This wine could also do with a few more years in bottle. At the moment, it's sweet, massively concentrated and peppery, with a fiery Portuguese punch.

1985 Taylor's Vintage Port

££ / FB / ⌐   17/20

On the advanced side for a vintage Port, but this 1985 from one of the Douro's leading houses is a stunner – powerful, chocolatey and peppery with fruitcake spices and layer upon layer of flavour and complexity.

1983 Fonseca Vintage Port

£££ / FB / ⌐   17/20

Liquorice, toffee and raisin scented vintage Port showing the softness and spicy drinkability of the Fonseca style. Loaded with ripe plum and raspberry fruit sweetness, this is drinkable now, but will improve for a good 20 years yet.

WAITROSE ****

Head Office: Waitrose Ltd, Doncastle Road, Southern Industrial Area, Bracknell, Berkshire RG12 8YA

Telephone: 01344 424680

Number of branches: 111

Credit cards accepted: Switch, Visa, Delta

Hours of opening: Monday and Tuesday 8.30am to 6.00pm, Wednesday and Thursday 8.30am to 8.00pm, Friday 8.30am to 9.00pm, Saturday 8.30am to 6.00pm. Selected branches open Sunday 10.00am to 4.00pm

By-the-case sales: Yes

Glass loan: Free against returnable deposit of £5

Home delivery: No, but carry to car service at all Waitrose supermarkets

Mail order: Some Waitrose wines available through Findlater Mackie Todd, acquired by the John Lewis Partnership in 1993. Tel: 0181 543 0966

Clubs: No

Discounts: Wines of the month discount of 12 bottles for the price of 11 (without 5 per cent discount) or 5 per cent discount on a whole case of wine, including Champagne and fortified wines.

In-store tastings: Occasional customer tastings

Top ten best-selling wines: 1994 Winter Hill Vin de Pays de l'Aude; 1994 Masquerade Vin de Pays de l'Aude; 1994 Merlot del Veneto Vallade Vino da Tavola; 1994 Chardonnay Vin de Pays du Jardin de la France; 1994 Vin de Pays du Gers le Pujalet; Waitrose Liebfraumilch; Hock DTW; Waitrose Good Ordinary Claret; 1994 Waitrose Côtes du Rhône; 1994 Chardonnay Vino da Tavola delle Tre Venezie Vallade

Range: GOOD: Bordeaux, Burgundy, regional France, Australia, South
Africa, Champagne and sparkling wine, Eastern Europe
AVERAGE: Rhône, Spain (red), New Zealand, Chile, Germany,
England, Italy
POOR: Portugal, Spain (white), United States

In our comments last year about *The Gazette*, the in-house journal of the
John Lewis Partnership, we omitted to mention the joys of the readers'
letters page, through which the chairman and sundry chief honchos deal
with the questions and complaints of 'partners', as John Lewis staff are
known. Latest issues have raised a number of fascinating topics, from the
workings of the descriptive ticketing system to problems within the
Partnership's trend departments, whatever they might be.

As the contents of those letters suggests, the John Lewis Partnership
and its supermarket subsidiary, Waitrose, are a retail world apart. The
same sense of quirky eccentricity is apparent in the company's wine list.
'I'm wary of uniformity,' says tango-dancing Julian Brind, head of wines,
beers, spirits and soft drinks. 'We've always been courageous in taking
on new things. Some have been successful, and some we've had to delist
almost immediately.'

Armed with no fewer than five Masters of Wine, (Neil Sommerfelt,
Dee Blackstock, David Gill, David Grandorge and Brind himself),
Waitrose has amassed one of the most interesting supermarket wine
lists, with unusual bottles from almost every corner of the globe. With
just over 400 wines, it doesn't have the most extensive range in the
country, but Waitrose is still a good place to bump into something
unusual – a Grüner Veltliner from Slovakia, a Crouchen/Chardonnay
blend from Australia's Clare Valley or a barrel-fermented Merlot from
Chile.

This is not to say that Waitrose is equally strong in all winemaking
countries. Last year, we singled out Spain and Portugal as weak areas.
Even Julian Brind concedes that 'we're trying to develop Italy, Spain and
Portugal'. So far, Italy has received more attention than the Iberian
peninsula. 'We've cut two wines from our Italian range,' says Brind, 'and
taken on half a dozen.' Spain and Portugal are next. 'I'm very excited by
what's happening in places like Somontano,' adds Brind. 'We'll be listing
new things soon.'

While these countries still need attention, Waitrose can be forgiven for concentrating its firepower elsewhere. If the list is still packed with French wines (145 of them in all), this is for a good reason – Waitrose customers like it that way. Claret, Burgundy and Champagne have always been among the chain's strengths; more recently, Waitrose was among the first supermarkets to take seriously what was happening in the Languedoc-Roussillon.

Not that Waitrose is obsessed with French wines. Its Australian range is good – reflected in the fact that wines from Down Under stand second only to France in popularity with Waitrose shoppers – and the arrival of David Gill from Bulgarian Vintners a year ago has prompted a profitable foray into Eastern Europe. South Africa is well-represented, too. Even during the grim days of apartheid, Waitrose retained a touching loyalty to Cape wines. Now, free of consumer opposition, it's grabbed an armful of South African bottles from Delheim, Avontuur and Klein Constantia.

'The New World is very exciting,' says Dee Blackstock, 'and our sales are growing in all areas, especially Chile and South Africa. But we have to remember our more traditional customers who are happy to stick with Bordeaux and Burgundy.' Perhaps this loyalty explains the boom in red wine sales over the last year, described as 'astronomical' by Brind. While white and fortified wine sales have been flattish, red wines have been zooming out of the starting gates.

'We're pretty pleased with developments over the last year,' says Brind. 'Overall, we've increased sales by 18 per cent.' This puts his department third in *The Gazette*'s all-important performance league table. Such an increase has been achieved against the trend of supermarket price cutting. Waitrose currently lists 41 wines under £3, but has avoided £1.99 special deals. 'If someone could offer us a wine we like and we could make a margin on it, we'd do it,' says Brind.

The reality, of course, is that no one can. Brind and his department are great believers in encouraging customers to buy better wines. 'If half your list is under £3, then you'll sell a lot of wine under £3. It's as simple as that. We don't go any lower than £2.65, and I don't think our customers believe they're getting a poor deal as a result.'

But if things are going swimmingly at Waitrose, its mail order operation, Findlater Mackie Todd, appears to paddling against the tide. Managing director Jane Turner has left, to be replaced by Nick Roome, and sales are clearly not up to expectation. 'Mail order is a very difficult field,' says Brind euphemistically, 'and we're finding our way slowly.'

Part of the problem is that no one finds it easy to define a typical FMT customer. 'They should be a different set of people to Waitrose customers,' says Brind, 'but 50 per cent of them buy from us, too.' This isn't surprising, given that the FMT list is selected by the Waitrose wine team and that, while it contains a number of individual wines, draws heavily on the main Waitrose list.

Customers on the FMT mailing list receive two offers a year, but our impression is that, for the time being, not enough of them are buying what is placed before them to make the whole operation viable. In a company where trends and profitability are scrutinised weekly by partners in *The Gazette*, a sluggish performance will not be tolerated for long.

Wines also available from Findlater Mackie Todd are marked with an asterisk.

White

Under £3

FRANCE

*1994 Vin de Pays du Gers le Pujalet
0 / 3 / 1   11/20

A coarse, baked apple, confected white from the Armagnac region of southwestern France. Why didn't someone pour it into the nearest continuous distillation still?

GERMANY

*Hock DTW
0 / 5 / 1   10/20

Dull, flat, fruitless Germanic blend with a whiff of almond and Elastoplast. Patchy stuff.

*Waitrose Liebfraumilch
0 / 5 / 1   11/20

Marginally better.

HUNGARY

Deer Leap Dry White, Debró
££ / 3 / ⅓   13/20
Made by flying winemaker Nick Butler, this is a soft, slightly spicy,
Hungarian white made from the native Hárslevelü grape. It's encouraging to see the airborne division making the most of the local raw material.

ITALY

1994 Chardonnay Vino de Tavola delle Tre Venezie, Vallade
0 / 2 / ⅓   12/20
Dilute, snoozeworthy white from northeastern Italy. Did someone
mention the Chardonnay grape?

£3–5

AUSTRALIA

1995 Ridgewood Trebbiano, South East Australia
£££ / 3 / ⅓   15/20
An Australian curiosity made as a varietal wine from the Italian
Trebbiano grape. Perfumed, intensely floral with refreshingly zesty,
almost Riesling-like fruitiness.

1992 Wakefield Crouchen/Chardonnay Clare Valley
££ / 2 / ⅓   15/20
From one of the largest wineries in South Australia's Clare Valley, this is
another unusual Aussie white, produced from Chardonnay and what
Craig Smith of the Australian Wine Club in Berkshire likes to call Clare
Valley Riesling. Released deliberately with a degree of bottle-age, it's a
distinctive style reminiscent of cassis and a touch of tea-leaf.

1994 Moondah Brook Verdelho, Western Australia
££ / 3 / ⅓   15/20
Ripe, melon and mango flavoured tropical fruit cocktail from
Houghton's Moondah Brook operation in Western Australia. Yet one
more well-selected Waitrose white from Down Under, proving that
Australia is not a one-grape wonder.

CANADA

1994 Harrow Estates North Shore White
0 / 3 / ⚊   12/20

The shore in question, in case you wondered, belongs to Canada's half of Lake Erie. Not that we'd advise you to paddle your canoe in these rather muddy waters.

CHILE

1995 Caliterra Chardonnay, Curico
£££ / 2 / ⚊   15/20

Fresh, unoaked pineapply chunky Chardonnay from the southern end of Chile's vast, hot Central Valley. A crisp, fruity and attractively balanced example of the 1995 vintage.

ENGLAND

1991 Chiltern Valley Medium Dry, Oxfordshire
£ / 4 / ⚊   13/20

One of a number of English wines stocked by Waitrose, this is a sweetish, hedgerow white with some grapey, elderflower pungency. David Ealand's showpiece winery also makes its own beer if you're really thirsty.

FRANCE

1994 Waitrose Bordeaux Sauvignon Blanc
££ / 2 / ⚊   14/20

A crisp, nettley Bordeaux white that reminded us of a good Sauvignon de Touraine.

*1994 Château Darzac, Entre-Deux-Mers
£££ / 2 / ⚊   15/20

For an extra 70 pence, you get a white Bordeaux with more weight and the added complexity of the Semillon grape. A crisply defined, unoaked white with plenty of zesty acidity.

1994 Château Terres Douces, Cuvée Prestige
£££ / 2 / ❷   16/20
Made by the *négociant* house of Ginestet, this is closer to a Graves-style
white Bordeaux, with toasty new oak flavours, plenty of Semillon
weight and waxiness, and a crisp, lingering aftertaste.

1994 Tokay Pinot Gris d'Alsace, Cave de Beblenheim
££ / 2 / ❷   15/20
Understated, peachy Alsace white with smoky, rose-petal spice. A well-
balanced wine that works better with food than some of the more
obviously aromatic varieties.

1994 Chardonnay, Vin de Pays du Jardin de la France
0 / 2 / ❷   11/20
Heavy, coarse, sweetened-up white with an edge of grapeskin
bitterness. The Chardonnay name counts for little except marketing
here.

1994 Touraine Sauvignon, Domaine Gibault
££ / 1 / ❷   15/20
This Waitrose favourite may have edged over £4 in the last year, but it's
still a ripe, textured, honeyed Sauvignon Blanc with typically
gooseberryish fruit. A mini-Sancerre.

1994 Domaine Petit Château Chardonnay, Vin de Pays du Jardin de la France
££ / 2 / ❷   15/20
From the Couillaud brothers, who have uprooted Gros Plant in favour
of Chardonnay, this is one of the few really successful Loire examples of
the grape. Ripe for a cool climate Chardonnay, it's a lightly oaked,
melony style with good concentration.

1994 Domaine des Fontanelles Sauvignon, Vin de Pays d'Oc.
£££ / 2 / ❷   15/20
Made at the Languedoc's Foncalieu co-operative, this is a wine which
shows that even after their departure, flying winemakers can leave a
permanent stamp on local styles. This is aromatic, hyperfresh and
honeyed with characteristically grassy Sauvignon zing.

1994 Domaine de Raissac, Vermentino, Vin de Pays d'Oc, Jean-Luc Viennet
££ / 1 / ﬂ   15/20

Vermentino is one of the few Mediterranean white grapes with natural acidity. From an estate which until recently was better known for its porcelain *trompe-l'oeil* food than its wines, this is a well-made, if austere, nectarine and greengage scented Languedoc white. Flying winemaker Nick Butler's recent arrival at Raissac appears to have had a rejuvenating effect on the domaine's wines.

1994 La Fontaine Chardonnay, Vin de Pays d'Oc
£ / 2 / ﬂ   14/20

The sort of white wine the Languedoc-Roussillon is now producing with its eyes shut – buttery, peardroppy, unoaked Chardonnay with a New World bent.

1994 Chardonnay (matured in French oak), Vin de Pays d'Oc
££ / 2 / ﬂ   15/20

Apparently made by two Frenchmen, this prominently oaked, melon and peach style Chardonnay is so rich and up-front that it might have come from Australia's Hunter Valley. We've been wondering about that underwater pipeline from Sydney to Montpellier.

1994 Viognier, Vin de Pays d'Oc, Chais Cuxac
£ / 2 / ﬂ   14/20

Produced at the Cuxac co-operative, where winemaker Serge Dubois has established a solid reputation for his white wines, this is a plump, apricoty Viognier, which pulls up slightly short.

GERMANY

1994 Devil's Rock Riesling, QbA
£ / 3 / ﬂ   13/20

Another wine whose name, if not its contents, shows the influence of Australia on the UK market. It's a crisp, grapey Palatinate white from the St Ursula operation, with citrusy acidity.

1993 Bad Bergzaberner Kloster Liebfrauenberg Auslese Pfalz
££ / 5 / ♪   14/20
In this case, Bad doesn't necessarily imply undrinkability. Well-priced
for an Auslese, it's a sweet, juicy, honeyed white with a hint of aniseed
character.

1993 Kirchheimer Schwarzerde Beerenauslese Pfalz (half-bottle)
£££ / 7 / ⌐   16/20
Rich gold, botrytis-intense, luscious peach and apricot German sticky
with enough acidity to give balance to this excellent half-bottle.

HUNGARY

*1994 Lakeside Oak Chardonnay
££ / 2 / ♪   14/20
The lake is Balaton, the oak American, the Chardonnay Hungarian and
the winemaker, Australian. Lemony, lightly oaked white from the Kym
Milne school of aviation.

1994 Deer Leap Gewürztraminer
£££ / 2 / ♪   15/20
Fresh, brilliant-value Hungarian white from Australian winemaker Nick
Butler, with a softly fragrant, ginger biscuit nose, typical of Alsace's
Gewürztraminer, but at a giveaway price.

*1993 Disznoko Furmint, Tokaji
££ / 1 / ♪   15/20
Named after the immoveable rock in the middle of the vineyards,
Disznoko, as you probably know already, means pig of a rock in
Hungarian. This is a characterful dry white with flavours of raisin, toffee
and tea-leaf. It also shows the austere side of Tokaji's Furmint grape. A
promising first vintage for this French-owned estate.

ITALY

*1994 Orvieto Classico Secco, Cardeto
£££ / 2 / ♪   15/20
An unoaked blend of the local Procanico, Verdello and Grechetto
varieties, this comes from the largest producer of Orvieto Classico. A
nutty, bracingly fresh Umbrian white with a whiff of green olive.

1994 Soave Classico, Vigneto Colombara, Zenato
££ / 2 / 🌡   15/20
A handsomely packaged Garganega/Trebbiano blend with plenty of ripe,
peachy, concentrated fruit in an almost New World-like vein.

*1994 Lugana, Villa Flora, Zenato
££ / 2 / 🌡   15/20
More distinctively Italian in flavour, this is a nutty, peachy, weighty Lake
Garda white with a knife blade of fresh acidity and a bitter twist.

SLOVAKIA

*1993 Grüner Veltliner, Nitra Region
££ / 2 / 🌡   14/20
From vineyards near Bratislava, this is a commercial, well-made white
pepper style white using neighbouring Austria's most widely planted
white grape to good effect.

SOUTH AFRICA

1995 Culemborg Chenin Blanc, Paarl
££ / 2 / 🌡   14/20
Soft, aromatic, full-bodied, guava-like Chenin Blanc with plenty of fresh
fruit flavours for your money.

1995 Stellenzicht Sauvignon Blanc, Stellenbosch
£ / 2 / 🌡   14/20
Light, lemony Sauvignon Blanc with crisp acidity and a hint of
gooseberry character. There's a lot of Sauvignon planted in South Africa,
but with one or two exceptions, the heat seems to blunt the grape's
zesty edge.

UNITED STATES

Cartlidge and Browne Chardonnay
0 / 3 / 🌡   12/20
From a winery best known for its value-for-money Zinfandels, this is a

confected, burnt toffee style Chardonnay with pronounced oak bitterness.

£5–8

AUSTRALIA

*1992 Mitchelton Reserve Wood Matured Marsanne, Goulburn Valley, Victoria
£££ / 2 / �   16/20

One of two styles of Marsanne made at Mitchelton's distinctive Goulburn Valley winery. As its label informs you, this is the oak-aged one – a yeasty, toasty, waxy slab of a wine with oodles of concentrated, full-flavoured fruit and balancing, clean acidity.

1994 Ninth Island Chardonnay, Tasmania Wine Company
£ / 2 / ➊   15/20

Made by Dr Andrew Pirie, the thinking woman's winemaker, this is a crisp, grapefruit and melon style Chardonnay from Tasmania's picturesque, cool vineyards.

CHILE

1994 Valdivieso Barrel Fermented Chardonnay
£££ / 2 / ➊   16/20

Veteran winemaker Luis Simian's attempt to out-Burgundy the Côte d'Or, using all the traditional techniques of barrel fermentation and lees stirring, this is a super-rich, butterscotch and toffee style Chardonnay in a slightly more fruity style than the equally enjoyable 1993.

FRANCE

*1993 Château Carsin, Cuvée Prestige Bordeaux
£ / 2 / ➊   15/20

The latest release from Australian Mandy Jones, this is not as exciting as the brilliant 1992. Nevertheless, it's a well-made, grapefruity white Bordeaux with some toasty oak for added complexity.

1994 Pouilly Fumé, Masson-Blondelet
££ / 1 / ♪   15/20

From Jean-Michel Masson (no relation to California's Paul, we presume), this is a smoky, flinty, concentrated Loire Sauvignon with bracingly fresh acidity.

GERMANY

1989 Erdener Treppchen Riesling Spätlese
££ / 5 / ►   15/20

A mature Mosel white with lime-drop and apple fruitiness and a whiff of the garage forecourt. A well-priced Riesling that will probably age better than we will.

NEW ZEALAND

1994 Jackson Estate Sauvignon Blanc, Marlborough
££ / 2 / ♪   16/20

With its flavours of green malt, mango and asparagus, this richly grapefruity Marlborough Sauvignon Blanc is consistently one of New Zealand's finest examples of the variety.

SOUTH AFRICA

1993 Klein Constantia Chardonnay
££ / 2 / ♪   15/20

A full, spicy, smoky Cape Chardonnay with masses of toasty oak and a buttery texture. You can buy the same wine for £1 more at Unwins.

1994 Delheim Chardonnay, Stellenbosch
££ / 2 / ♪   15/20

A lighter, more elegant style of Cape Chardonnay, with lemony-fresh flavours and well-handled vanilla oak character.

Over £8

FRANCE

1993 Chablis Premier Cru, Beauroy
£ / 1 / ♪   14/20

Showing the high acidity of the vintage, this is a minerally, austere
Chablis that needs another year or two in bottle.

1993 Beaune, Edouard Delaunay
0 / 2 / ♪   13/20

Just to prove that five Masters of Wine don't always get it right, this is a
charry, underfruited white Burgundy from a *négociant* whose wines
disappoint more often than they delight.

Red

Under £3

BULGARIA

1994 Cabernet/Merlot Iambol
£££ / MB / ♪   14/20

The best of Waitrose's Bulgarian selection, this is a soft, chocolatey
blend, whose oak character and blackberry sweetness places it
somewhere between a claret and a Rioja in flavour.

FRANCE

1994 Winter Hill, Vin de Pays de l'Aude
0 / MB / ♪   11/20

'French wine made by Australians' reads the label. Why anybody would
bother travelling thousands of miles to make this rustic Carignan/Merlot
plonk is a mystery to the lads at *Grapevine* HQ.

1994 Domaine de la Rose Merlot/Syrah, Vin de Pays d'Oc
££ / MB / ♪   13/20

Not selected by Anthony Rose, in case you were thinking of returning the bottle, this is a boiled sweets and banana style red made using the carbonic maceration technique.

1994 Bergerac Rouge
£££ / MB / ♩   14/20

Easy-drinking, green pepper-fruity red from southwestern France, with a nip of chewy tannin. What basic claret ought to taste like, but often doesn't.

PORTUGAL

Ramada Tinto, Estremadura
£££ / FB / ♩   14/20

Baked banana and crushed black pepper red made in a modern style, but still showing robust Portuguese tannins.

ROMANIA

*1993 Simburesti Pinot Noir
££ / MB / ♩   14/20

A modern-style raspberry fruity Pinot Noir from southern Romania bottled by West Country wine merchant and brewer, Eldridge Pope. For Burgundy lovers struggling to pay the mortgage.

£3–5

AUSTRALIA

*1993 Oxford Landing Cabernet/Shiraz, South East Australia
££ / MB / ♩   15/20

An elegant, blackcurrant and coffee-bean Aussie blend with minty fruit flavours and appealing freshness. Another good value wine from Yalumba.

1994 Yaldara Whitmore Old Vineyard Grenache, South Australia
£ / FB / ♩   14/20

Rich, warm, peppery Grenache with tons of sweet, heady fruit, mirroring the styles produced in the southern Rhône Valley.

CANADA

Harrow Estates North Shore Red Ontario
0 / MB / ♪   10/20
A harrowing combination of the hybrid grapes Villard and Baco Noir.
Animal, fecal red with high acidity. Canada's revenge on the European
Union?

FRANCE

Waitrose Good Ordinary Claret, Ginestet
££ / MB / ♪   13/20
Unsurprisingly, given its customer profile, Waitrose numbers this basic
Bordeaux among its top ten best-sellers. It's an earthy, chunky, but well-
made, no-frills claret.

1994 Waitrose Côtes du Rhône
£ / MB / ♪   13/20
Another top ten fixture, this is a decent, if somewhat tannic, Rhône quaffer.

1994 Graves AC
££ / MB / ♪   15/20
An attractively fresh and concentrated claret with surprising softness of
texture and fruit and no obvious oaky character.

1993 Waitrose Special Reserve Claret, Bordeaux
££ / MB / ♪   15/20
As you'd expect from the Right Bank Côtes de Castillon *appellation*,
Merlot is the dominant grape variety in this juicy, supple everyday claret.
It's well worth paying around a fiver for the extra character you get from
Bordeaux at this level.

1993 Château Haut d'Allard, Côtes de Bourg
£££ / MB / ⬤–   16/20
Another illustration of exactly the same point, with rich savoury fruit, stylish
oak handling and a succulent texture. A serious wine with backbone and
complexity, which will repay a year or two in the wine rack.

1994 Morgon Georges Duboeuf (half-bottle)
££ / MB / ♪   15/20
From the man who bestrides the Beaujolais like the proverbial Colossus,

this is an aromatic, unmistakably juicy Gamay with red fruits flavours and gentle tannins in a convenient TV dinner format.

1994 Domaine de Cantemerle, Côtes du Rhône Villages
££ / MB / 🌶   15/20

Not to be confused with the classified Bordeaux château of the same name, this is a vibrantly fruity, gingery, southern French red with loads of soft, supple fruitiness.

1993 Château St-Maurice, Côtes du Rhône
££ / FB / �'   15/20

Chunkier than the Côtes du Rhône Villages, this is a highly aromatic, Grenache-dominated blend in the Gigondas style. It's peppery, warmly alcoholic and chunky.

1994 Masquerade, Vin de Pays de l'Aude
££ / 2 / 🌶   14/20

With its colourful carnival-style label based on the local Fécos parades, this is a justifiably popular southern French red with cinnamon spice and attractively soft, lush fruitiness made by the carbonic maceration method.

1994 Les Galets Syrah, Vin de Pays d'Oc
££ / MB / 🌶   14/20

Made by New World-influenced French winemaker Thierry Boudinaud this is a defiantly modern, juicy, gluggable red with an attractive pudding-stone label (hence Les Galets).

1994 Terrasses de Landoc, Grenache, Vin de Pays de l'Hérault
0 / MB / 🌶   12/20

A wine sourced by Aimé Guibert, the Languedoc's most famous proprietor thanks to the renown of his Mas de Daumas Gassac wines, this co-operative varietal is rooty, sweet and rather alcoholic.

1994 Cabernet Sauvignon, Vin de Pays de l'Aude, Foncalieu
££ / MB / 🌶   14/20

A firm, well-priced southern French Cabernet Sauvignon with attractive blackcurrant fruitiness from the increasingly impressive Foncalieu operation.

1993 Château de Nages, Costières de Nîmes
££ / MB / ♪   14/20
A blend of predominantly Grenache and Syrah. The winemakers have used carbonic maceration to produce a soft, easy-drinking style at an affordable price.

*1993 Cabernet Sauvignon, Vin de Pays d'Oc, Hugh Ryman
£££ / MB / ♪   15/20
From English winemaker Hugh Ryman's home base near Limoux, affectionately known as 'the Dump', this is smokily oaked Cabernet with the green pepper character of cool Atlantic-influenced vineyards.

HUNGARY
*1994 Sopron Cabernet Sauvignon
££ / MB / ♪   14/20
Fresh, light, cassis-style Cabernet with medium-weight tannins from Agi Deszneyi, the homegrown winemaker who works under the supervision of Australian Nick Butler.

ITALY

1993 Waitrose Chianti
££ / MB / ♪   14/20
Pleasantly perfumed, typically Tuscan red with the savoury, almondy aromas of the Sangiovese grape and accessible tannins. A top ten best-seller at Waitrose.

SOUTH AFRICA
1993 Culemborg Pinotage
££ / MB / ♪   14/20
A medium-weight example of South Africa's native Pinotage grape, this is a boiled sweets and banana style red with vibrant, gutsy fruitiness. A good way to make the grape's acquaintance.

1992 Stellenzicht Cabernet Sauvignon, Stellenbosch
££ / MB / ♪   14/20
A dry, minty, coffee-bean Cabernet with a sweet, plummy middle palate from one of the Cape's up-and-coming estates.

1994 Avontuur Pinotage, Stellenbosch
££ / FB / ⌘   15/20
Concentrated, exuberantly fruity, raspberry and cherry style Pinotage
with good depth of colour and none of the grape's harder edges.

SPAIN

*1991 Agramont, Navarra
££ / MB / ⌘   15/20
A blend of recently planted Tempranillo and Cabernet Sauvignon from a
co-operative which is now among the best producers in Spain's Navarra
region. It's an ultra-modern red dominated by smoky American oak, but
with sufficient weight of strawberry fruit to mop up the sawdust.

£5-8

AUSTRALIA

*1992 Château Reynella Shiraz McLaren Vale, South Australia
£ / MB / ⌐   14/20
Big, brash, excessively oaked Shiraz from BRL-Hardy with chewy tannins
and a touch of the pork scratchings about it.

1994 Brown's Shiraz/Malbec, Padthaway, South Australia
£££ / MB / ⌐   16/20
There are quite a number of Brown Brothers in Australia, but Donald,
Waitrose assures us, is not one of them. We're certainly glad to make his
acquaintance with this minty, elegant, finely honed, coolish climate
blend. Buy two bottles and stash one away for posterity.

1993 Peter Lehmann Cabernet Sauvignon, Barossa Valley, South Australia
££ / FB / ⌘   15/20
An unmistakably heartwarming red from Barossa character Peter
Lehmann. Minty, spicy, and sweetly oaked with no shortage of flavour
or alcohol.

CHILE

1994 Cono Sur Pinot Noir Reserve
£ / MB / ♪   14/20
From Concha y Toro's boutique winery, Cono Sur, this is the follow-up
to last year's highly successful first release. Spicy and structured, but
with a little too much oak for what's supposed to be a comparatively
delicate grape variety.

FRANCE

1993 Château Les Moulins de Calon, Montagne St-Emilion
££ / MB / ♪   15/20
Farmyardy, old-fashioned claret from the hills of St-Emilion. One for
fogeys and Simon Jenkins.

*1990 Hautes Côtes de Beaune, Tête de Cuvée, Caves des Hautes Côtes
£ / MB / ♪   14/20
The Hautes Côtes co-operative's attempt at an up-market *cuvée* is a
partially successful, modern, strawberry and cinnamon-oak style red
Burgundy with some varietal character.

1994 Domaine Sainte Lucie, Gigondas
£££ / FB / �María   16/20
Dense, richly upholstered Grenache-based red with ripe succulent fruit
flavours, a touch of cinnamon spice and the strong, peppery undertones
of the supporting Syrah grape.

ITALY

1992 Campo ai Sassi Rosso di Montalcino, Castelgiocondo
££ / MB / ♪   15/20
An attractively framed Tuscan Sangiovese, with leafy, chocolatey fruit
flavours unencumbered by oak interference. A good alternative to
Chianti at just over £5.

SOUTH AFRICA

1994 Fairview Shiraz Reserve, Paarl
££ / MB / ►   **15/20**

One of winemaker Charles Back's more expensive offerings, this is a fresh, minty, plum and spice scented Shiraz with considerably less oak than the charry 1991 vintage we saw last year.

1992 Delheim Cabernet Sauvignon, Stellenbosch
££ / MB / ▮   **15/20**

Another deeply coloured Cape red, this time making use of the new clones of Cabernet Sauvignon to produce a minty, cigar-box style with a nip of lively acidity.

1990 Klein Constantia Cabernet Sauvignon, Constantia
£££ / FB / ►   **16/20**

Made by chubbily cheerful winemaker Ross Gower, this is the most complex and concentrated of Waitrose's plentiful selection of South African reds. Although five years old, it's an intensely fruity Cabernet with fine, silky tannins.

1994 Clos Malverne Pinotage Reserve, Stellenbosch
££ / FB / ►   **15/20**

Closed, almost brutish Pinotage with masses of charry oak and firm, unyielding blackberry fruit and tannin. Come back in three years' time.

Over £8

FRANCE

1992 La Roseraie de Gruaud Larose, St-Julien
££ / MB / ▮   **16/20**

Light, cedary, forward third-label claret from the second growth St-Julien estate of Gruaud Larose. As you'd expect from this vintage, it's not packed with tannin or fruit, but it's surprisingly successful nonetheless, with soft, grassy flavours and spicy oak.

1990 Château Lestage-Simon, Haut-Médoc
££ / MB / ►   **16/20**

Spicily oaky, concentrated claret from a classic vintage with a whiff of the farmyard, this could happily be drunk at Christmas or tucked away for the next five years.

1993 Châteauneuf-du-Pape, Guy Mousset
££ / FB / ♪   15/20
Atypical for Châteauneuf, this ripe, almost Australian Shiraz-like red is overflowing with strapping liquorice and blackberry fruit sweetness.

ITALY

1991 Barolo, Vigneto Castelletto, Gigi Rosso
£ / FB / ♪   14/20
Truffley, dry, old-fashioned Barolo with undertones of the Nebbiolo grape's tarriness and big, chewy tannins.

Rosé

Under £3

FRANCE

1994 Domaine des Fontanelles Rosé de Syrah, Vin de Pays d'Oc
£££ / 2 / ♪   14/20
Another well-made wine from Foncalieu with dry, raspberry fruitiness at a good price.

£3–5

UNITES STATES

1994 Canyon Springs Pinot Noir Rosé
££ / 2 / ♪   14/20
Drier than it looks, this day-glo California rosé made from the Pinot Noir grape has an attractive rosehip syrup character to it.

Sparkling

£3–5

HUNGARY

BB Chardonnay Dry
£ / 2 / ♪   13/20
Possibly related to the BB Club Brut we spent most of last year trying to
prise the cork out of, this is fresh, lemony, light fizz with slightly raw
acidity.

£5–8

SOUTH AFRICA

1993 Krone Borealis Brut, Twee Jonge Gezellen
££ / 2 / ♪   15/20
Twee stands for two rather than kitsch and sweet in this context. Made
by the Méthode Cap Classique (Méthode Champenoise to you and us),
this is an appealing, full-flavoured fizz with some strawberry softness,
presumably derived from the Pinot Noir grape.

Over £8

FRANCE

Waitrose Brut Non Vintage Champagne, Blanc de Noirs
£££ / 2 / ♪   16//20
A *Grapevine* favourite, this all-Pinot Champagne from Les Riceys in the
Aube region is a ripe, malty fizz with plenty of strawberry fruitiness. Still
great value at under £13.

Waitrose Non Vintage Champagne, Blanc de Blancs
£££ / 2 / ♪   17/20
**Another excellent Waitrose Champagne, this time made entirely
from Chardonnay grapes. It's a rich, yeasty style with attractively
elegant, biscuity fruitiness.**

1989 Waitrose Brut Vintage Champagne

£ / 2 / ⅓   14/20

Hazelnutty and slightly sweet, this particular *cuvée* didn't live up to expectations. Maybe it could with another year or two in bottle.

Fortified

£5–8

ITALY

1993 Passito de Pantelleria, Pellegrino

£ / 8 / ⅓   14/20

A mouthful of Ps, this is like liquid brandy snaps and raisins with figs, dates and assorted dried fruits tossed in for good measure. Mitigate the hefty alcohol content by pouring over vanilla ice cream.

THE *GRAPEVINE* GUIDE TO INDEPENDENT WINE MERCHANTS

Introduction

The works of John Ruskin have been popular with British independent wine merchants this year. At least three of them quoted the great critic and social reformer in their lists. The essence of his views on price – a subject close to the heart of wine retailers of whatever stripe – is contained in the following sentence: 'There is hardly anything in the world that some man cannot make a little worse and sell a little cheaper, and the people who consider price only are that man's lawful prey.'

The continuing drift downmarket is turning Britain into a nation of cheap wine drinkers. There's nothing wrong with this *per se* – after all, there are plenty of drinkable and inexpensive bottles on the market and no shortage of over-priced dross. But the cause of Britain's independent wine merchants has suffered badly from an inability to match the economies of scale commanded by a Tesco or a Sainsbury's, not to mention cope with the better ranges stocked by the likes of Bottoms Up, Wine Rack, Oddbins and Victoria Wine Cellars.

It's easy to be over-sentimental about this. Many independents have gone to the firing squad wall in the last decade, some of them deservedly so. It's worth contrasting a list of today's most prominent independents with one of 10 years ago. RIP Sookias & Bertaut, The Upper Crust, The Barnes Wine Shop, Ostlers, The Fulham Road Wine Centre, Alex Findlater, Greens and Yorkshire Fine Wines. A company's independence (or not, in the case of IDV-owned J&B or brewery-backed Adnams), doesn't give it a divine right to buy good wines.

Nevertheless, the best independent wine merchants in this country are a unique source of expertise and experience. This is why we've decided to remedy an oversight from previous editions of this book by including a dozen such merchants in *Grapevine*.

We are aware that our choice is a personal one, but we've tried to mix specialists (The Australian Wine Club and Enotria Winecellars) with generalists (Lay & Wheeler, Averys and Tanners); traditionalists (Berry

Brothers and Justerini & Brooks) with modernists (Adnams and Bibendum); and the small (Lea & Sandeman) with the large (Thomas Peatling and Eldridge Pope). Our list is not immutable, but it's a start – a very important start, in our view.

Is there a future for the independent wine merchant?

Cassandras have been saying for years that the independent wine merchant has no future. This may be true in the mass market – that is, wines priced between £1.99 and £3.99 – but things are considerably rosier in the £4–6 range, according to David Gleave of Enotria Winecellars. 'On cheap wines, the independents can't do battle with the supermarkets and the cross-Channel retailers, but we can still compete on slightly more expensive bottles. Above £4 the cross-Channel duty savings are negligible and the supermarkets can't offer the same diversity as an independent.'

Diversity, range, quality and service

Unusual wines and personal service are the key to an independent's success. The supermarkets have tried to sell expensive clarets, Burgundies and Italian reds and largely failed. They've also experimented with in-store advisers to guide shoppers towards new wines, but this is expensive, requires trained staff and can frighten customers away. Some people actually enjoy the hypnotic anonymity of supermarket shopping.

The high street off-licences have done rather better in both these areas. The sums invested in education by Oddbins, Thresher, Unwins, Davisons, Fuller's and Victoria Wine have enabled them to sell higher priced wines. This, in turn, means that they can stock more individual bottles. The range of wines at Oddbins, Bottoms Up or Victoria Wine Cellars can even rival the independents in some areas.

Levels of service are not yet comparable, however. There's something rather reassuring about dealing with Charles Lea of Lea & Sandeman, Richard Tanner of Tanners, John Avery of Averys or Richard Wheeler of Lay & Wheeler, all people whose livelihoods depend on the quality of advice and service they provide.

Where the independents score in terms of range is by specialising. No high street retailer can match the Italian lists of Enotria Winecellars or Lea & Sandeman, the Australian wine selection of the Australian Wine Club, the Burgundies of Justerini & Brooks, the Rhônes of Yapp

Brothers, the Riojas of Moreno Wines or the clarets of Lay & Wheeler. Equally, the more traditional merchants carry stocks of older, ready-for-drinking vintages which you simply can't find in the high street.

This is crucial for maintaining a breadth of choice, which is more extensive in this country than anywhere. Many of the world's best wines are made in small quantities (and sold at comparatively high prices), so we need independents to source, nurture and sell them. As one of our country's best wine merchants once told us: 'What we're doing is hand-selling wine, getting involved from the vineyard to the shop floor.'

Traditionalists versus modernists

Although they may fall into one general category, independent wine merchants are by their nature individual to the point of quirkiness. There's an enormous difference between super-smooth, plummy Justerini & Brooks in St James' and the mail order operation of the Australian Wine Club, where prospective customers are treated, if that's the right word, to a blast of rough-edged Aussie banter.

The difference between these two extremes is an indication of the health and diversity of the independent sector. Traditional firms, some of which have been in business since before Barbara Cartland was a child, are still flourishing, as the fitness of Lay & Wheeler, Tanners, Berry Brothers, Justerini & Brooks and a revamped Averys demonstrates. But they've been joined in the last decade by a different style of independent wine merchant – quirkier, brasher and more focused.

Bibendum is typical of the modernists. Wine buyer Simon Farr is convinced that today's wine merchant has to offer traditional values ('one-to-one relationships with local and mail order customers') as well as 'first-hand experience'. Partnerships with growers and the new projects which grow out of them require an investment of time and money. 'It's not a four-day hit-and-run job,' he says, 'but if you don't do your own research, you're on a level playing surface with the likes of Thresher and Victoria Wine.'

'The only way the independent sector will survive is through evolution,' adds David Gleave of Enotria Winecellars. 'We have to be quicker off the mark because everyone else is these days. There has to be a flow of new ideas, new styles, new projects and new producers.' Selling the stuff is important too, as the traditionalists have been forced to acknowledge. 'It's not just a question of having good wines on your list,' says Gleave. 'You have to know how to run a business. In some ways, you could argue that the over-enthusiastic amateur represents a great danger to the image of the independents.'

The Hungerford syndrome

Enthusiasm doesn't get much more contagious than it did at the Hungerford Wine Company, a wacky, media-oriented business which dealt in unbottled en primeur claret, or Bordeaux futures, as they're known in America. When the company sank in 1993, holed below the plimsoll line by average-to-poor Bordeaux vintages in 1991 and 1992, it took a lot of customers' wines down with it. Much of the wine, it transpired, had never been paid for in Bordeaux. Instead, Nick Davies of the Hungerford Wine Company used the money to keep his business afloat.

Hungerford was not an isolated case, though given Mr Davies' love of publicity, it was not surprising that, even in adversity, he should attract the most coverage. Consumers also lost cases of wine, for various legal reasons, when Greens, Stapylton Fletcher and Ellis, Son & Vidler went belly-up.

This was a timely warning to those of us who hadn't bought wines from these companies. Namely, if you're going to hand over large sums of money to a merchant, especially if you don't expect to take delivery of your wines for another two years, choose extremely carefully. Anyone who is financially rocky or has a history of disappointing customers should be avoided like a bar room bore.

The Bunch

It was partly as a result of the Hungerford débâcle that a group of like-intentioned independent wine merchants set up something called The Bunch. The club's members are Lay & Wheeler, Adnams, John Armit, Corney & Barrow, Laytons, Tanners and Yapp Brothers. Each abides by a Code of Practice which includes the Bunch Guarantee (return a wine you don't like within a month of purchase and they'll refund your money) and sundry solemn rules about mail order, delivery and the identification and storage of customers' reserves.

Anything which soothes the anxieties of wine lovers considering a tryst with an independent wine merchant is a good thing. But this does not mean that non-Bunch members are in any way suspect. The likes of Lea & Sandeman, Averys, Justerini & Brooks, Berry Brothers, The Wine Society, Eldridge Pope, D. Byrne, Gauntleys of Nottingham, Haynes,

Hanson & Clark, Peter Green and Domaine Direct are no less trustworthy than, say, Laytons or John Armit.

Over to you

In conclusion, we'd like to quote another good merchant – Christopher Piper of Ottery St Mary, down in Coleridge country. The back page of Mr Piper's list contains the following quotation: 'Minds, like parachutes, only work when they're open.' This applies to wine as much as anything else. The familiar is always comforting. But is it any harder to pick up the phone and buy by mail order than push a trolleyful of wine round the aisles of a supermarket? We think not.

ADNAMS

Head Office: The Crown, High Street, Southwold, Suffolk IP18 6DP

Telephone: General enquiries, 01502 727220; Mail order, 01502 7272221

Hours of opening: Monday to Friday 9.00am to 5.00pm, Saturday 9.00am to 12.00pm for mail order

Mail order: Yes

Number of branches: 2

Also at: The Cellar and Kitchen Store, Victoria Street, Southwold, Suffolk IP18 6JW

Telephone: 01502 727220

Hours of opening: Monday to Saturday 10.00am to 6.30pm. Closed Sundays, Bank Holidays and for New Year stocktaking

And: The Grapevine, 109 Unthank Road, Norwich NR2 2PE

Telephone: 01603 613998

Hours of opening: Monday to Saturday 9.00am to 9.00pm. Closed Sundays, Bank Holidays and for New Year stocktaking

Credit cards accepted: Access, Visa

By-the-case sales: Minimum order is one case by mail order and at The Cellar & Kitchen Store

Bottle sales: Yes, at The Grapevine

Facilities and services: A party service including glasses and ice. Gift packs and dispatch service, corporate service, consultancy and wine search service

Home delivery: Yes. Free local delivery for orders of one case or more.

For the mail order service, see carriage terms

Discounts (excluding mail order service): Yes. A £3 discount per case

In-store tastings: Yes. Also arrange lectures and tutored tastings on request

Special offers: En primeur and bin-end sales

Top ten best-selling wines: Colombard Côtes de Gascogne; Adnams Champagne Cuvée Special Brut; Adnams Sparkling Chardonnay; Jean des Vignes; Côtes du St Mont Producteurs Plaimont; Figaro Vin de Pays de l'Hérault; Château du Grand Moulas; Ozidoc Sauvignon; Adnams' Claret; Domaine de Rieux

The most recent copy of Adnams' award-winning list features a grainy photograph of The Crown in Southwold, with employees hanging from the windows and draped around the front of the building. The two most visible presences are that of Alastair Marshall, posed Samson-like in the entrance between two pillars, and stripey-blazered Simon Loftus standing on top of the portico like the captain of a pirate ship.

They are not the only people who work at Adnams, but Loftus and his henchman Marshall have had a lot to do with its success over the last decade. Recently strengthened by the acquisition of Houghton Fine Wines, which added a list of prestigious agencies such as Mas de Daumas Gassac, Newton and Mountadam, Adnams is established as one of the best independent wine merchants in the country.

Adnams is all about enthusiasm – that of Loftus, now chairman of the entire Adnams caboodle, his employees and his customers. The hyperbole can sound a little silly at times (the words 'delectable', 'delightful', 'sublime' and 'outstanding' seem to crop up in the list rather a lot), but at Adnams you always get the sense that people are passionate about wine. You also get some extremely well-written offers, especially from the pen of Loftus himself. The author of *Anatomy of the Wine Trade* and *Puligny-Montrachet* is a pleasure to read. We just wish he'd employ someone else to take the photographs.

Loftus has done a great deal to extend the range of wines we see in this country. He was an early enthusiast for Italian fine wines, Barossa Valley reds and whites, saw what was happening in the South of France before many of his competitors, and is now championing the underloved Riesling grape and the even less appreciated wines of Portugal. His latest discovery is a £12 sparkling Recioto from the Veneto.

Not everything at Adnams is well selected. Indeed, we felt that some of the basic wines submitted for our tasting were rather disappointing. But that's the thing about Adnams – you love some wines, you dislike others, but you know that new curiosities will appear on the next list: things you'd never heard of, things you hoped you'd never taste, things you've always wanted a British wine merchant to import. As long as Loftus and his team can sustain their frenetic sense of enthusiasm, Adnams will remain in the front rank of independents. It also turns out some rather good ales.

White

£3–5

FRANCE

1994 Jean des Vignes, Vin de Pays du Gers, Blanc Sec
0 / 3 / ½   12/20

Cardboardy, slightly sweetened-up Gascon blend of Colombard and Ugni Blanc with tart acidity and apple-core bitterness.

1994 Domaine Sablayrolles, Chasan Vin de Pays d'Oc
£ / 2 / ½   14/20

Faintly oaky, fresh, pear-like Languedoc white with crisp lemony acidity, made at Domaines Virginie from the unusual Chasan, a crossing of Chardonnay and Listan.

1994 Domaine de Perches Mauzac, Vin de Pays des Côtes du Tarn
£ / 2 / ½   14/20

From Nicholas and Charlotte Fraser's domaine in southwestern France, this is a clean, fresh, neutral white made from a grape which is best known for its contribution to Blanquette de Limoux. We struggled to find the greengage character trumpeted by the Adnams list.

1994 Domaines Virginie Marsanne, Vin de Pays d'Oc
££ / 2 / ⌐   15/20

A well-made, oak-influenced, weighty Marsanne from Domaines Virginie with almost Chardonnay-like texture and a zip of carbon dioxide for freshness.

HUNGARY

1994 Château Pajzos Tokaji Muscat
££ / 1 / ⌐   15/20

A full, aromatic, well-made Muscat from Frenchman Jean-Michel Arcaute's winery in the Tokaji region of northeastern Hungary, this is spicy, elegantly dry and showing a tea-leafy bite of tannin and acidity.

£5–8

CHILE

1994 Valdivieso Barrel Fermented Chardonnay
£££ / 2 / ⌐   16/20

Veteran winemaker Luis Simian's attempt to out-Burgundy the Côte d'Or, using all the traditional techniques of barrel fermentation and lees-stirring, this is a super-rich, butterscotch and toffee Chardonnay in a slightly more fruity style than the equally enjoyable 1993.

FRANCE

1992 Domaine des Aubuisières Cuvée Victor, Vouvray Sec, Bernard Fouquet
£££ / 2 / ⌐   17/20

A brilliant Loire oddball from a mediocre vintage made by the youthful Bernard Fouquet from Domaine des Aubuisières. Dry Chenin Blanc can taste raspingly austere, but this aniseed and dry honey-like white shows the benefit of low yields in the vineyard and an experienced hand in the cellar.

1993 Château Le Chec Graves
£ / 2 / 1   14/20

A bizarre, celery and vanilla scented, barrel-fermented Graves with some sandalwood spice from barrel fermentation, tart acidity and a dry finish.

1994 Menetou-Salon Morogues, Clos des Blanchais, Domaine Henry Pellé
££ / 2 / 1   16/20

A good alternative to Sancerre, this wine from a lesser-known eastern Loire *appellation* is zippy and modern with elderflower and grapefruit characters from the Sauvignon Blanc grape.

Over £8

GERMANY

1992 Maximin Grunhauser Abtsberg Kabinett
££ / 4 /   16/20

Fresh, featherweight Mosel Riesling from the excellent 1992 vintage with minerally, grapefruity notes, a hint of white pepper, and delicately balanced sweet and sour acidity.

Red

£3–5

AUSTRALIA

1993 David Wynn Red South Eastern Australia
££ / MB / 1   15/20

An intriguing blend of Shiraz and Pinot Noir blended by the roly-poly Adam Wynn at the Mountadam winery, his Eden Valley base, showing leafy, cinnamon-tinged, sweetly ripe wild strawberry fruitiness.

FRANCE

Jean des Vignes, Vin de Table
£ / FB / ⚫   13/20

An honest wine bar red made at the Villeveyrac co-operative in the Languedoc from Carignan, Cinsault and Grenache. It's soft, sweetish and plummy on the palate with a dry, rasping, hot climate finish.

1993 Domaine du Belvezet, Côtes du Vivarais VDQS
£ / MB / ⚫   13/20

Alcoholic, Grenache-like red apparently based on the Syrah grape variety. Time for a new vintage.

1993 Château Pech-Celeyran La Clape, Coteaux du Languedoc
££ / FB / ⚫   15/20

Jacques de Saint-Exupéry makes characterful, deeply concentrated reds on the hill of La Clape near Narbonne. This is a typical example, with a youthful, chewy texture, spicy flavours of thyme and blackberry and a dry, robust finish.

1994 Domaine Michel, Vin de Pays de Vaucluse
££ / MB / ⚫   14/20

Provence's answer to Beaujolais, this is a juicy, softly fruity, cherried, carbonic maceration red with a giveaway tannic aftertaste.

ITALY

1991 Chianti Rufina, Villa di Vetrice
££ / MB / ⚫   15/20

A highly aromatic, almondy, tangy dry red with the appealing, rustic edge which distinguishes the wines of Villa di Vetrice, situated not a million miles from the current home of Nick Belfrage, author of *Life Beyond Lambrusco*.

SPAIN

1994 Baso Navarra Garnacho
£££ / MB / ⚫   15/20

Made at the Remelluri winery in Rioja from the Garnacha grape variety, known for reasons best known to winemaker Telmo Rodriguez as Garnacho, this is a modern raspberry and cherry-fruit red, with the emphasis on gluggability.

£5–8

CHILE

1994 Valdivieso Pinot Noir, Lontue
£££ / MB / ♪   16/20
This is a vibrant, weighty, spicily oaked, voluptuous Chilean Pinot Noir, made from grapes previously destined for Valdivieso's sparkling wine production. But Australia-trained winemaker Luis Simian was given the opportunity to produce a limited amount of Chardonnay and Pinot Noir and he took it with both hands. This 1994 is an attractively made, worthy successor to the first vintage.

FRANCE

1993 Carignanissime de Centeilles, Minervois
£££ / FB / ♪   16/20
A complex, unfiltered, pistachio-scented Languedoc red made by John Lennon-lookalike Daniel Domergue. The name of the wine is an *appellation* rule-bending reference to the fact that it's illegal to mention the Carignan grape on the label. Aged in barrel to round out the southern tannins, this 100 per cent Carignan red is a spicy delight discovered by the retiring Simon Loftus.

1990 Bourgogne Côte Chalonnaise Mont Avril, Michel Goubard
£ / MB / ♪   14/20
Rustic, rasping red Burgundy from the Côte Chalonnaise, this Pinot Noir has a rooty, red fruits character with a drying aftertaste.

1994 Château du Grand Moulas, Côtes du Rhône Villages, Marc Ryckwaert
£££ / FB / �   16/20
Rich, vibrant, heady southern Rhône red with plenty of spice and chocolatey concentration. Marc Ryckwaert's famously low-yielding

vines have produced a Côtes du Rhône Villages of great power and finesse.

ITALY

1993 Fattoria Le Terrazze, Rosso Conero
£ / FB / ♩   14/20
A full, deeply coloured, if one-dimensional, red from the Marche region, with plum and cherry fruitiness, dark chocolatey, grainy tannins and an alcoholic bite.

UNITED STATES

1993 Madrona Zinfandel Sonoma Conty
££ / FB / ♩   16/20
Madrona is a label used by Adnams for wines picked up by barrel-broker Mel Knox from distressed wineries on the American market. This youthful, tobacco and raspberry fruity Zinfandel from Sonoma County is attractively fresh and manages to conceal its alcoholic punch beneath the fruit.

Rosé

£3–5

FRANCE

1994 Domaine de Limbardie Rosé, Vin de Pays des Coteaux de Murviel
££ / 2 / ♩   15/20
A fruity, ripe, bubblegummy blend of Grenache and Syrah grapes made in a refreshingly modern, thirst-quenching style. A wine that would taste as good on a rainy day in Southwold as under the azure skies of the Mediterranean.

THE AUSTRALIAN WINE CLUB

Address: Freepost (WC5500), Slough, Berks SL3 9BH

Telephone: Freephone credit card orderline, 0800 716893. Other enquiries, 01753 544546

Hours of opening: 24-hour answerphone: 0800 716893. Office open Monday to Friday 9.00am to 6.00pm, Saturday 9.00am to 2.00pm.

Number of branches: None (sadly, the owners are debarred from holding a retail licence)

Credit cards accepted: Visa, Access, American Express

By-the-case-sales: Minimum order 1 dozen (which can be mixed – very mixed indeed)

Glass loan: Contact lenses only

Home delivery: Free delivery anywhere in mainland UK

Clubs: Isn't one enough?

Discounts: You're getting free delivery, what else do you want, service? Because you won't get it with this bunch

In-store tastings: Fortunately not. But the AWC holds an annual Great Australian Wine Tasting in London attended by sundry visiting Australian winemakers, including Bob 'El Gordo' McLean and the Mayor of Marananga

Top ten best-selling wines: White – St Hallett Poacher's Blend; Laraghy's Semillon Chardonnay; Tim Adams Semillon; Allandale Chardonnay; Chapel Hill Unwooded Chardonnay. Red – Tim Adams 'The Fergus'; St Hallett Barossa Shiraz; Heritage Cabernet Franc; Water Wheel Shiraz; Chapel Hill Cabernet Sauvignon

At the back end of 1994, following the closure of the Australian Wine Centre on health and safety grounds, Craig 'Cooper's' Smith, Phil 'W'

Reedman and Mark 'Glugger' Manson repaired to a back room in Windsor, where it was assumed they would be less of a menace to the public. However, the resourceful team set up the Australian Wine Club, which, since they all have nothing better to do, has since deluged unsuspecting members of the public, trade and press with incomprehensible monthly newsletters.

The Australian Wine Club is 'probably the worst wine merchant in Great Britain', according to its owner. But why stop at probably? Gratuitous press comment has hoodwinked the British public into thinking that the Australian Wine Club are actually a fine bunch of Cooper's-swigging fellows with an interesting range of wines, but the truth is rather different. Not only are their wines a sad reflection of what Australia has to offer, but the people who run – if that's the right word – the Club, are an equally sad bunch of losers.

Perhaps even more amazing is that such no-hopers have conned some of the supermarkets and high street merchants into selling wines like their El Gordo's St Hallett range, the dreadfully thin wines of Chapel Hill and, more amazing still, absurdly alcoholic concoctions from the dubious likes of Steve Hoff, Peter Scholz and Tim Adams. When *Grapevine* eventually goes pictorial, we will be able to warn readers about Craig Smith, Mark Manson and Phil Reedman. In the absence of pictures, all we can do is advise you to give Windsor a wide berth.

White

£5–8

AUSTRALIA

1994 Henschke Eden Valley/Barossa Valley Dry Muscat
£££ / 3 / 1   16/20
From 30-year-old Muscat à Petits Grains vines planted in the Eden and Barossa Valleys by Cyril Henschke, father of Stephen, the current owner, this is a superfresh, delightfully aromatic, full-bodied style with intense floral, grapey fruitiness tapering to an elegant dry finish. It's hard to find a bad wine at Henschke.

1994 Chapel Hill Unwooded Chardonnay

£££ / 2 / ♪   16/20

There's often so much oak cladding on Australian Chardonnay that it's hard to get through to the essence of the grape variety. But when the wine's as concentrated and expresses Chardonnay's flavours as well as this McLaren Vale, Padthaway and Barossa blend, the less oak the better. It's a fresh, melon and fig flavoured dry white with cleansing acidity.

1994 St Hallett Barossa Valley Chardonnay

££ / 2 / ♪   15/20

More elegant than previous releases of St Hallett Chardonnay, this is a ripe, but restrained, Barossa style, with Rioja-like smoky bacon American oak and attractive, fresh pineapple fruitiness.

1994 Allandale Hunter Valley Chardonnay

£ / 2 / ♪   14/20

A broad, charry-oaky, vanilla fudge and lemon curd-like mouthful of Hunter Valley Chardonnay in which the constituent parts of alcohol, acidity and oak are not yet pulling in the same direction.

1994 Willows Barossa Valley Semillon

£££ / 2 / ►   17/20

Peter Scholz's boutique-size operation has quickly established itself as one of the finest Semillon producers in Australia. We enjoyed the superb 1993, available at Bottoms Up, and the herby, lemony, attractive ice cream soda perfumed 1994 is a worthy successor.

1994 Tim Adams Clare Valley Semillon

££ / 2 / ♪   16/20

Made by Tim 'Bonecrusher' Adams, one of the best producers in the Clare Valley, this is a creamy, vanilla-scented, toasty Semillon with good weight and depth and a refreshing tang of acidity, giving the wine considerable backbone.

1994 David Traeger Verdelho

£££ / 2 / ♪   16/20

An unusual, almost Condrieu-like, barrel-aged white from David Traeger's Goulburn Valley vineyard. Its sweetly ripe, lime and apricot fruitiness is nicely offset by a refreshing, lees-derived prickle of carbon dioxide.

1994 Tim Adams Clare Valley Riesling
£££ / 2 / ↝   **17/20**
Tim Adams thinks this is the best Clare Valley Riesling he's produced yet, and who are we to disagree? With its delightfully fresh, fragrant aromas, this is a toasty, herby, melon and lime flavoured Riesling with superb balance and a lingering dry aftertaste.

1993 Heritage Clare Valley Riesling
££ / 2 / ↝   **15/20**
Using grapes from some of the oldest vineyards in the Clare Valley, Barossa-based Steve Hoff has produced a ripe, full-bodied, lime-scented Riesling, which is starting to develop some toasty, bottle-matured flavours and aromas.

1994 Tim Adams Botrytis Semillon, half-bottle
£ / 6 / ↝   **15/20**
A light, peachy, elegant dessert Semillon with muted botrytis undertones and notes of stem ginger sweetness. With its dried apricot acidity, it should age well for a few years yet.

Red

£3–5

AUSTRALIA

1994 Laraghy's Kapunda Road Shiraz/Grenache/Cabernet Franc
£ / MB / ↑   **14/20**
An unusual, if rather basic blend of Shiraz, Grenache and Cabernet Franc, with spicy-oaky, slightly confected, blackberry pastille fruit flavours and a rasp of acidity on the aftertaste. The sort of thing they serve in economy class on Qantas.

£5–8

AUSTRALIA

1990 Ashton Hills Pinot Noir
£ / MB / ♪   13/20

Craig Smith of the Australian Wine Club is also President of the Australian Pinot Noir Why-do-they-bother Society. This dry, heavily oaked example from the cool climate of the Adelaide Hills is light and lacking true Pinot Noir charm. Why does he bother?

1990 Ashton Hills Merlot/Cabernet
£ / MB / ♪   14/20

Cool climate, green bean scented Bordeaux blend from Piccadilly in the Adelaide Hills, Stephen George's Merlot/Cabernet reminded us of a vegetal, unripe New Zealand in an overcool vintage.

1993 St Hallett Cabernet Sauvignon/Cabernet Franc/Merlot
££ / MB / ►   15/20

In a completely different style, this is a ripe, sweetly oaked, mint and blackcurrant flavoured Bordeaux-style blend with dryish tannins from the warm Barossa Valley. Still youthful.

1994 St Hallett Gamekeeper's Reserve
££ / 2 / ♪   15/20

A sweet, ripe, raspberry-hued Barossa blend of Grenache, Touriga, Shiraz and Mourvèdre, this is a light, vibrant, raspberry-fruity Australian-style Côtes du Rhône, rounded out with well-handled American oak.

1994 Blaxland Barossa Valley Mourvèdre/Grenache
££ / MB / ♪   15/20

Fleshy, soft, almost Zinfandel-like blend of Mourvèdre and Grenache with spicy, liquorice and tobacco-pouch tannins, vanilla oak, black pepper fruitiness and a fresh, nicely balanced aftertaste.

1993 Water Wheels Bendigo Shiraz
£££ / MB / ►   16/20

Classically Victorian, cool climate Shiraz with crushed black pepper and ginger aromas, and fleshy raspberry fruitiness. An elegant, well-priced, characterful red from Peter Cumming, which should age for another three to five years with no difficulty.

1992 Primo Estate Shiraz
££ / FB / ⬛▬   **16/20**
A rich, oaky, concentrated, wild blackberry Shiraz fermented in open vats, and made in a traditional style by the talented Joe Grilli from vineyards on Adelaide Plains. Rich, chewy, characterful stuff which needs another five years in bottle.

1993 Tim Adams Clare Valley Shiraz
£££ / FB / ▬⬛   **16/20**
Fresh, minty, full-bodied Clare Valley Shiraz with abundant cassis and plum fruit flavours, creamy vanilla oak, and the fresh acidity which characterises Tim Adams' well-crafted wines.

1994 Blaxland Barossa Valley Shiraz/Mourvèdre Pressings
£££ / FB / ▬⬛   **16/20**
Well-structured, concentrated, oaky red made from the grape pressings left behind after the free-fun juice has been removed for the main label. With its tarry, grapeskin aromas and thick coating of sweet tannins, this is a macho wine that will repay patience.

1993 Heritage Barossa Valley Shiraz
£££ / FB / ▬⬛   **16/20**
A big, rich, hefty, chewy mouthful of concentrated Shiraz fruit from Peter Scholz's Barossa Valley operation. Walking a flimsy tightrope between massive oak and richly concentrated liquoricey fruit, it's the sort of wine that ought to have a long beard and shotgun with a wimps-keep-out warning label.

1991 Willows Barossa Valley Shiraz
0 / FB / ⬛   **13/20**
Cooked, extracted, overoaked, macaroon-sweet red from a winemaker whose Semillon and Cabernet/Merlot blends are considerably more exciting.

Over £8

AUSTRALIA

1993 Chapel Hill Cabernet Sauvignon

££ / FB / ↩   16/20

Youthful, profoundly oaked, deeply concentrated Cabernet Sauvignon from McLaren Vale and Coonawarra. Pam Dunsford's previous release was a multi-award winner in Australia, and this powerful, structured, showy, chocolatey red should also win a few prizes.

1993 Tim Adams, The Aberfeldy

££ / FB / ↩   17/20

A rich, chewy, tannic, minty Shiraz made from old vines in the Clare Valley. It's a big, extracted style with lashings of spicy American oak, which needs at least another five years to soften, but we reckon it's one of the best reds we've had yet from Tim Adams.

AVERYS OF BRISTOL

Head Office: Averys of Bristol, Orchard House, Southfield Road, Nailsea, Bristol BS19 1JD

Telephone: 01275 811100

Mail order: Yes

Number of branches: 2

Also at: The Averys Shop, 11 Park Street, Bristol

Telephone: 0117 921 4145

Hours of opening: Monday to Saturday 10.00am to 6.00pm

And: The Averys Wine Cellar, Culver Street, Bristol

Telephone: 0117 921 4146

Hours of opening: 10.00am to 7.00pm

Credit cards accepted: Access, Visa

By-the-case sales: Exclusively for mail order and through the The Averys Wine Cellar, although cases may be mixed

Bottle sales: From The Averys Shop

Facilities and services: Free glass loan in the Bristol area to customers buying wines for special occasions (contact The Averys Wine Cellar for details). Sale or return for parties. Glasses and bar tools may be purchased from The Averys Shop and Wine Cellar. Mail order customers receive a monthly newsletter. Advice on cellaring and disposing of wines surplus to customers' requirements. Gift vouchers

Cellarage: Yes: £5.36 per case per annum for wines purchased at Averys. Customers' reserves marked with owner's name

Home delivery: Delivered free nationwide (minimum two cases outside

Bristol, one case in Bristol). Delivery of one case or less outside the Bristol area costs £5.50

Discounts: Through the Averys Bin Club, which gives 10 per cent discounts to members, and on monthly newsletter special offers

In-store tastings: On a regular basis in Averys Wine Cellars

Special offers: En primeur and bin-end offers.

Top ten best-selling wines: Avery's Special Cuvée Champagne; Cabernet Sauvignon, Vin de Pays d'Oc, Chenet; Averys Fine White Burgundy; Averys Fine Claret; Undurraga Cabernet Sauvignon; Tyrrells Long Flat Red; Averys Clochemerle Red; Nobilo Marlborough Sauvignon Blanc; Tyrrells Long Flat Chardonnay/Semillon; Averys Club Red

Averys is to Bristol what Lay & Wheeler is to Colchester or Tanners to Shrewsbury – an established wine merchant with a long history. Averys was created in 1793, the year of Louis XVI's execution, and in the course of the last two centuries has helped generations of Bristoleans to drink better wines.

The revolutionary coincidence is appropriate. Master of Wine John Avery was one of the first wine merchants to list new (and in those days, highly innovative) things from Australia and New Zealand. That was nearly 20 years ago, but the New World connection continues to this day. Averys has a good line-up of southern hemisphere agencies in Tyrrells of Australia, Nobilo of New Zealand and Klein Constantia of South Africa, as well as Swanson, Sonoma Cutrer, Far Niente and Inniskillin in North America.

Not so long ago, the New World connection was even closer, when the company was owned by American multimillionaire Clarke Swanson. Swanson sold out to Hallgarten in 1994, but John Avery's tastes are still influenced by modern winemaking styles. His other great passion is Burgundy – an Averys specialism which, despite the firm's long-standing connection with the dull *négociant* house of Remoissenet, remains reasonably strong.

The change of ownership appears to have endowed Averys with a renewed sense of dynamism. It has opened a Wine Cellar in Culver Street to house a retail selection from its 1,000-strong list (complete with bottles open for tasting and other 20th century innovations) and moved its warehouse from the old Culver Street location to modern premises on the edge of Bristol. The Head Office went with it, leaving Park Street after 120 years. This, says John Avery, will 'give even better service to all our customers, including the many who entrust the secure, long-term storage of their reserves to us'.

Averys has an extensive mailing list of loyal customers built up over the centuries. This is both a strength and a weakness. It's always nice to have people who buy your wines, but if they lack a critical edge, it can stop you developing and refining your range. Avery's cosy relationship with some of its suppliers occasionally leads to lazy buying. Rustenberg, which seems to have hit a dull patch, and Remoissenet are obvious examples.

Still, after the big-dipper-style changes of the last eight years, Averys is a better-run company than it has been for ages. It is perfectly capable of finding exciting new wines, such as those from Enate in Spain's Somontano region, and its new cellaring and mail order facilities are efficient and reasonably priced. Here's to the next 200 years.

White

£3–5

NEW ZEALAND

1994 Nobilo White Cloud, Gisborne
££ / 3 / ¶   14/20

A soft, sweetish, highly commercial Kiwi blend of Müller-Thurgau with a dash of Sauvignon Blanc for aromatic lift. Asparagus, lime and tinned pea notes with the freshness we've come to expect from New Zealand whites.

£5–8

CANADA

1993 Inniskillin Chardonnay, Niagara Peninsula
££ / 2 / ¶   15/20

Numbered among Canada's few drinkable wines, this is a fresh, Chablis-like Chardonnay with crisp, cold climate acidity and medium weight and body.

FRANCE

1994 Domaines Virginie Chardonnay, Vin de Pays d'Oc
£ / 2 / ₤   14/20

One of an extensive array of Domaines Virginie whites, this is a lightly oak-chipped, boiled sweets style Chardonnay made from vineyards around Béziers. A little expensive at over £5.

1993 Averys Fine White Burgundy, Mâcon-Péronne, Cave de Lugny
0 / 2 / ₤   13/20

Gluey, rather old-fashioned unoaked white Burgundy from the Lugny co-operative in the southern Mâconnais. Averys prides itself on its ability to select 'fine' white Burgundies, so it really ought to be able to come up with something more substantial than this at around £6.

NEW ZEALAND

1994 Nobilo Sauvignon Blanc, Marlborough
££ / 2 / ₤   15/20

With its asparagus and grapefruity characters, this is a soft, juicy, tropically ripe Sauvignon which could only come from the South Island's Marlborough region.

1994 Nobilo Poverty Bay Chardonnay, Gisborne
££ / 2 / ₤   15/20

If you've taken a British Airways flight in the last year or so, you may have come across this wine in handy economy-class sized bottles. It's proved extremely popular with BA fliers – sorry, customers – and you can see why. Softly ripe, unoaked Chardonnay with flavours of melon and citrus fruit acidity.

SOUTH AFRICA

1994 Klein Constantia Estate Chardonnay
£££ / 2 / ₤   16/20

Less stridently oaked than the 1993, which is available at Waitrose, this is a rich, structured Chardonnay from the coolish hills behind the Cape's famous Table Mountain. The best-balanced Chardonnay we've had from the talented Ross Gower.

SPAIN

1993 Enate Chardonnay, Somontano
£££ / 2 / 1   16/20

With its appealing, child-like scrawl of a label, this is a stylish, barrel-fermented white from the Somontano region of northern Spain. Eight months of ageing in cask on its fermentation lees have given the wine extra richness and an almost Burgundian full, buttery texture.

Over £8

FRANCE

1994 Sancerre Domaine La Moussière
££ / 1 / 1   16/20

Flinty, dry, complex Sancerre made by the eccentric Alphonse Mellot. The coolness of the vintage has resulted in a wine which brings out the character of the local terrain more than the grape variety. Just what *appellation contrôlée* should be all about.

1992 Puligny-Montrachet, Remoissenet Père et Fils
£ / 2 / 1   16/20

A super-ripe, honeyed, old-fashioned white Burgundy from the Beaune-based *négociant* Remoissenet, which Averys have been dealing with for aeons. It's full and fat with some botrytis-derived complexity. One for drinking rather than tucking away.

GERMANY

1992 Niersteiner Pettenthal Riesling Spätlese, Rheinhessen, Georg Albrecht Schneider
£££ / 5 / 1   17/20

Exotic, concentrated Rheinhessen Riesling with rich grapefruit and mango fruit leavened by white pepper spiciness and refreshing carbon dioxide gas and acidity. It may sound like an oxymoron, but this is exciting stuff from the Rheinhessen.

UNITED STATES

1992 Swanson Chardonnay, Carneros, Napa Valley
£££ / 2 / ⌐   18/20
From former Averys owner Clarke Swanson's Napa Valley estate, this is a rich, powerful but beautifully balanced California Chardonnay with well-judged oak, toffee-fudge fruit and piquant acidity, giving it the structure to age well. Even at £14 a bottle, this puts most village white Burgundy in the shade.

Red

£3–5

FRANCE

1994 Cabernet Sauvignon, François Dulac, Vin de Pays d'Oc
££ / MB / ⌐   14/20
Soft, light, unoaked southern French Cabernet Sauvignon with the accent on juicy blackberry fruit and slightly rustic tannins.

SPAIN

1993 Enate Tinto, Somontano
££ / MB / ⌐   15/20
A youthful, attractively fruity, elegant blend of Cabernet Sauvignon, Tempranillo and Morestell. Fresh cherry fruit with a nip of damsony acidity make this a lively, decently priced red.

£5–8

SOUTH AFRICA

1993 Rustenberg Merlot/Cabernet Sauvignon
0 / FB / ⅟   13/20

Mousy, baked, old-fashioned Cape red with rasping acidity and dry tannins. There's some fruit there struggling to get out, but it's so far down we couldn't get at it.

1990 Klein Constantia Marlbrook
£ / MB / ⅟   15/20

Promisingly minty aromas are succeeded by fresh cassis fruitiness, marked oak and a slightly green edge.

SPAIN

1992 Enate Crianza, Somontano
£££ / MB / ⅟   16/20

A youthful, charrily oaked, yet still vibrantly fruity Aragón red from the excellent Enate winery, which has applied modern winemaking expertise to produce this stylish, concentrated blend of Tempranillo and Cabernet Sauvignon.

UNITED STATES

1992 Paul Thomas Cabernet/Merlot, Columbia Valley
££ / MB / ⅟   15/20

A light, elegant cool climate blend of Cabernet Sauvignon and Merlot from Washington State's Columbia Valley, this is a toffeed red with minty, raspberry fruitiness and a nip of fresh acidity and tannin.

Over £8

FRANCE

1990 Averys Fine Red Burgundy
0 / MB / ⅟   13/20

A rather soupy, old-fashioned red Burgundy from an unidentified *négociant-éleveur*. At over £10 a bottle, you can buy seriously good red Burgundy, so why bother with Bourgogne Rouge? Did someone say 'fined'? Maybe it should be.

1990 Givry, Remoissenet Père et Fils
£ / MB / 1   15/20

For £1 less than Averys 'Fine' red Burgundy, this is a solid, better balanced red in which the Côte Chalonnaise Pinot Noir character is at least evident.

1990 Aloxe-Corton, Diamond Jubilée, Remoissenet Père et Fils
0 / MB / 1   14/20

Sweet and alcoholic, this is another souped up Remoissenet Burgundy from an excellent vintage, which really shouldn't need such heavy-handed treatment. *Spectator* readers and Julie Burchill may still enjoy this sort of ultra-conservative, old-fashioned red Burgundy, but they're in a rapidly dwindling minority.

1990 Château Cantelaude, Margaux
0 / MB / 1   14/20

Well-made, if not exactly well-priced, Cru Bourgeois from a property which borders on Château Giscours. We were a little disconcerted here by a faintly medicinal character on the nose and dry tannins on the aftertaste. If, as Averys claims, this if of *cru classé* quality, then it's time to give Bordeaux a miss.

SOUTH AFRICA

1990 Rustenberg Gold, Estate Wine
£ / MB / 1   15/20

Rustenberg's flagship red, apparently made from a combination of Cabernet Sauvignon, Cabernet Franc and Merlot, is much more concentrated and supple than the 1993 estate blend. Spicy oak with plum and blackcurrant notes and robust, chewy tannins.

UNITED STATES

1990 Far Niente Cabernet Sauvignon, Napa Valley

££ / MB / ┅-   **17/20**

Deeply coloured, extremely well-made California Cabernet from one of the Napa Valley's most historic estates. The £25 price tag may make you lift an eyebrow, but winemaker Dirk Hampson has produced a concentrated, powerfully aromatic Cabernet Sauvignon with cedarwood spice and surprising balance and elegance.

1992 Swanson Napa Valley Merlot

££ / MB /┅-   **16/20**

A youthful, chewy, concentrated California Merlot which is still in short trousers at the moment. It's intensely blackcurranty, American-oaky stuff, which needs at least five years for the toughish tannins to soften.

BERRY BROTHERS & RUDD

Head Office: 3 St James's Street, London SW1A 1EG

Telephone: 0171 396 9669/9600

Fax: 0171 396 9611

Hours of opening: Monday to Friday 9.00am to 5.30pm

Number of branches: 3

Also at: Berry's Wine Warehouse, Houndmills, Basingstoke, Hampshire RG21 6YB

Telephone: 01256 23566

Hours of opening: Tuesday and Wednesday 10.00am to 5.00pm, Thursday and Friday 10.00am to 8.00pm, Saturday 10.00am to 4.00pm

And: Terminal Three Departures Lounge, Heathrow Airport

Telephone: 0181 563 8361/3

Hours of opening: Seven days a week, 6.00am to 10.00pm

Credit cards accepted: All major cards

By-the-case sales: Yes

Bottle sales: Yes

Facilities and services: Discounts, wine tastings, wine broking, wine by subscription, gifts service/vouchers, wines for parties, glass hire

Cellarage: Yes. Customers' private reserves cellared at a charge of £4.80 per year

Home delivery: Free delivery for one case or more on UK mainland

Discounts: On more than two cases (mixed if required)

In-store tastings: Six regular annual wine tastings in London and Basingstoke

Special offers: En primeur, seasonal offers, bin-end sales, etc.

Top ten best-selling wines: Berrys' Good Ordinary Claret, AC Bordeaux; Berrys' House White, Vin de Table; Berrys' House Red, Vin de Table; Berrys' Sauvignon Sec, AC Bordeaux; Berry Bros UKC Champagne; Berrys' White Burgundy, AC Bourgogne; Berrys' Extra Dry Sparkling Wine, Méthode Champenoise; Veuve Lorin Champagne; Berrys' Australian Chardonnay, Barossa Valley, South Australia; Berrys' French Country White Wine, Vin de Pays des Côtes de Gascogne

From the 17th-century façade to the ancient uneven floorboards, everything about Number Three St James's Street wears a carefully nurtured air of anachronistic fogeyishness. But don't be fooled. If customers like the image to be traditional, they want their wines and services to be a little more up-to-date. And it is. The engine room of Berry Brothers & Rudd, its modern, mail order business, is based at a purpose-built warehouse in Basingstoke.

Over three-quarters of Berrys' business is mail order, with the information-packed list sent out to some 35,000 names, the majority private customers aged 35 to 65. As you might expect at Berrys', two-thirds of sales are of French wines. French country wines are increasingly gaining on the classics, while Australia (there's even an Australian Chardonnay in Berrys' top ten) and the New World are also catching up.

Berry Brothers stopped bottling its own wines only in 1993. Thanks to Cutty Sark, the Scotch whisky, which subsidises the wine side, the company can still afford to buy and stock young wine and hold it until it's ready to be released for drinking. In an effort to bring in a younger clientèle, Berry Bros recently took on a new Master of Wine, David Roberts, to bolster the growers' side of the list.

A new scheme, Like Clockwork, in which customers receive a selected case quarterly on payment of a £25 monthly subscription, is working, er, like clockwork, and a new Duty Free shop at Heathrow's Terminal Three has resulted in door-to-door deliveries in Japan and the United States. The main drawback with Berrys' is that the wines don't come cheap, but at least you get a nice engraving of the 1922 frontage on the house wine label.

White

£3–5

CHILE

1994 Errázuriz Sauvignon Blanc, Maule Valley
££ / 2 / 1   15/20
Typical of the emerging quality of Chile's white wines, this is a crisp,
attractively proportioned, grapefruity Sauvignon Blanc with flavours of
honeydew melon.

FRANCE

**Berrys' French Country White Wine, Vin de Pays des Côtes de
Gascogne**
£ / 3 / 1   14/20
A soft, appley Gascon quaffer with tangy acidity to keep it fresh.

£5–8

AUSTRALIA

Berrys' Australian Chardonnay
£ / 3 / 1   14/20
A well-made, smoky bacon and pineapple-fruity Chardonnay from the
self-styled Baron of the Barossa, Peter Lehmann.

FRANCE

1993 Reuilly, Domaine Aujard-Mabillot
£££ / 2 / 1   16/20
Extremely well-made, concentrated, nettley Sauvignon Blanc, which
could easily be mistaken for a top Sancerre. It's fresh and crisp on the
palate, with a lingering aftertaste.

Berrys' White Burgundy, Chardonnay
££ / 2 / ▸   15/20

Made by Antonin Rodet, the leading *négociant* in the Côte Chalonnaise,
this is a rich, buttery, well-crafted house white Burgundy with the
emphasis on fresh fruit rather than oak.

Berrys' Vin d'Alsace, Kuentz-Bas
££ / 2 / ▸   15/20

Lanolin-scented, full-bodied Alsace white with floral fruitiness and
refreshing acidity to prevent the wine from cloying. A good, reasonably
priced introduction to the region.

GERMANY

1992 Brauneberger Juffer, Riesling Kabinett, Weingut Max Ferdinand Richter
£££ / 4 / ▸   16/20

A crunchy aniseed and petrol scented Riesling with apple and cassis
juiciness, showing the delicacy of touch which is the hallmark of Dirk
Richter's Mosel estate.

Over £8

AUSTRALIA

1992 Mitchelton Reserve Wood Matured Marsanne, Goulburn Valley, Victoria
££ / 2 / ▸   16/20

One of two styles of Marsanne made at Mitchelton's distinctive
Goulburn Valley winery. As its label informs you, this is the oak-aged one
– a yeasty, toasty, waxy slab of a wine with oodles of concentrated, full-
flavoured fruit and balancing, clean acidity.

FRANCE

1993 Pouilly-Fuissé, Les Crays, M. Forest
£ / 2 / ▸   16/20

Aromatic, slightly smoky Pouilly-Fuissé, which is still youthful at the moment. The impression of immaturity is enhanced by the slight austerity of the 1993 vintage. This is an extremely good, almost Chablis-like Chardonnay, which needs another two to three years in bottle.

1992 Chassagne-Montrachet, En Remilly, Domaine Michel Colin-Deleger
££ / 2 / ﹏   17/20
A hazelnutty, complex, richly textured white Burgundy from one of the best producers in Chassagne-Montrachet. This is modern in style and carefully crafted, using barrel fermentation and lees stirring for extra weight and malolactic fermentation for added complexity.

UNITED STATES

1992 Iron Horse Chardonnay, Green Valley, Sonoma County
££ / 2 / ﹏   16/20
A California oddball made in Sonoma County's cool Green Valley by a winery better known for its sparkling wines. This is an elegant, Chablis-style Chardonnay, which relies on neither sweetness nor abundant oak for its effect. Stylish and subtle.

Red

£3–5

FRANCE

Berrys' French Country Syrah, Vin de Pays d'Oc
£ / MB / ﻝ   14/20
Light, funky, faintly farmyardy southern French Syrah with sweet fruit flavours and a plonky finish.

1994 Domaine Castan, Merlot, Vin de Pays d'Oc
££ / MB / ﻝ   14/20
A softly juicy, grassy Merlot from the Languedoc, which demonstrates why it's often better to buy Bordeaux-style reds from the Languedoc than from Bordeaux itself.

£5–8

AUSTRALIA

1992 Goundrey Langton Cabernet/Merlot, Mount Barker, Western Australia
£ / MB / ♪   15/20

A simple, raspberry fruity and attractively oaked, juicy Cabernet Merlot blend from one of Mount Barker's largest producers.

FRANCE

Berrys' Own Selection Margaux
££ / MB / ♪   15/20

An elegant, finely balanced young Margaux, which we suspect has been declassified from something rather grander. Cherry and cassis fruitiness and lively acidity rather than oak are the dominant characteristics here.

ITALY

1990 Barco Reale di Carmignano, Tenuta di Capezzana
££ / MB / ♪   15/20

A tarry, tannic, still youthful red blend of Sangiovese and Cabernet Sauvignon with a dry finish from Count Ugo Bonacossi's estate in the Carmignano hills.

SPAIN

1989 Buena Cepa, Bodegas Felix Callejo, Ribero del Duero
££ / FB / ⬤   16/20

An old-fashioned expression of Ribera del Duero's Tinto Fino, or Tempranillo grape, this is a dry and rather demanding red with lots of sweet, charry American oak and damson fruit flavours. Time for that rack of lamb.

Over £8

AUSTRALIA

1991 Hollick Estate Coonawarra Red
£££ / MB / ⌐   17/20
You will need to decant this distinguished Coonawarra blend of
Cabernet Sauvignon and Merlot from one of the smaller, quality-
conscious estates in South Australia's finest red wine region. It's
a super-elegant wine with supple berry flavours, a trace of mint,
beautifully judged oak and the finesse of a classified claret.

FRANCE

1990 Château Fontenil, Fronsac
££ / MB / ⌐   16/20
A firm, tannic 1990 Right Bank claret made by the guru of Libourne,
oenologist Michel Rolland. It's not quite as fleshy as some Rolland reds,
but it does have characteristic new oak smokiness and plenty of
extracted concentration. The tannins need another five years to soften.

1989 Hermitage, M. Chapoutier
£££ / FB / ⌐   17/20
Packaged with a label made to look like a French country wine,
this is in fact a concentrated, characterful red from one of
France's best red wine *appellations*. Berrys' were able to bottle it
themselves because of their long-standing relationship with the
Chapoutier family in Hermitage. It's tannic, spicy and full of
blackberry Syrah fruitiness. It's also pretty good value, especially
by the arm-and-a-pin-striped-leg standards of St James's.

1989 Volnay, Clos des Santenots, Domaine Jacques Prieur
£ / MB / ⌐   16/20
Made by the Antonin Rodet-owned Jacques Prieur, this is a heftily oaked,
ripe Pinot Noir made with Heathrow's Terminal Three customer in
mind. Which is to say, it's showy, with all the soul of a transit lounge
seat.

1985 Château Léoville-Lascases, St-Julien
££ / MB / ⌐   18/20
An aromatic, beautifully weighted St-Julien supersecond, which is
only just out of the starting blocks. Acidity, fine-grained tannins
and smoky, cedary blackcurrant fruit are all bedded down for a
long life.

ITALY

1988 Amarone Classico, Vigna Monte S. Urbano, Speri
£ / FB / ▯   15/20
A powerful, full-bodied, liquorice and sage like, single vineyard Amarone
with a dry, almondy finish, made from dried Valpolicella grapes at the
Speri domaine.

Sparkling

Over £8

FRANCE

Berry Bros UKC Champagne, Binet et Fils
£ / 3 / ▯   14/20
A youthful, fresh, strawberry-fruity fizz, which is rounded out with a
touch of sweetness. UKC stands for United Kingdom Cuvée, presumably
to distinguish it from the stuff that remains in France.

BIBENDUM

Address: Bibendum Wine Limited, 113 Regents Park Road, London NW1 8UR

Telephone: 0171 722 5577

Number of branches: 1

Hours of opening: Monday to Thursday 10.00am to 6.30pm; Friday 10.00am to 8.00pm; Saturday 9.30am to 5.00pm

Credit cards accepted: Access, Visa, American Express

By-the-case sales: Minimum order one case, but can be mixed

Facilities and services: A comprehensive party service is available, including advice, supplies of glasses, ice and chilling bins. Sale or return applies. Newsletters are sent out to customers three times a year

Cellarage: Yes. Further details supplied on request

Home delivery: Free delivery in mainland England: orders received by 11.00am can be delivered on the same day to London postal districts and within three days elsewhere in mainland England; free delivery in Scotland and Wales with orders of five cases or more, otherwise the delivery charge is £10

Discounts: No

In-store tastings: Yes. Also tutored tastings once a month

Special offers: En primeur offers, bin-end sales, special offers about once a month

Top ten best-selling wines: La Serre Sauvignon Blanc; La Serre Chardonnay; La Croix Rouge; Red Cliffs Colombard/Chardonnay; Red Cliffs Cabernet Sauvignon; Palazzino La Rosa Bianca Red; Gavi Tenuta La Raia; Basedows Shiraz; Chablis Bernard Legland; Champagne Veuve Delaroy

'Bibendum and The Great Crusade' is the title of the Primrose Hill based wine merchant's rather overdesigned new list. The crusade in question is buyer Simon Farr's one-man mission to track down wines with regional or preferably local character. In search of the unusual, he probably travels more than any other independent wine merchant. Recent trips have taken him, broadsword in hand, to Chile and Argentina, South Africa, Australia and New Zealand, as well as to the more familiar areas of France and Italy.

Created in 1981 with the aim of offering a middle way between the traditional merchants of the City and St James' and what Farr calls the 'stack it high boys', Bibendum is typical of a new breed of wine merchant: pro-active, dynamic and swift on its toes.

It's also accessible, though clearly not accessible enough for the crook who drove a dumper truck through the front door last Christmas. Farr and sidekick William 'Svensson' Lebus run amusing and informative tasting evenings where members of the public get the chance to brush shoulderpads with the glitterati of the wine world. 'We want,' says Farr, 'to provide an environment where customers can talk to the people who make, buy and sell the stuff.'

The emphasis at Bibendum is on shifting wine, however. A large part of the business is selling agency wines to high street off-licences and supermarkets. Indeed, successful brands such as La Serre and Red Cliffs Estate are Bibendum creations.

This is Bibendum's bread and butter. The marmalade, as it were, is provided by the higher priced wines from the New and Old Worlds. Farr is a Francophile (or possibly Italophile) at heart, as his range of domaine-sourced wines from France and Italy aptly demonstrates, but it's the wines he sources from California and the southern hemisphere which get the most coverage.

Catena in Argentina, Lawson's in New Zealand, Grangehurst in South Africa, Duxoup and Acacia in California and Yeringberg and Katnook in Australia are among Farr's best discoveries. Misplaced enthusiasm has resulted in a few less impressive listings, too – the new vintages of Waimarama and the overoaked whites from Basedows should have been left in the Pacific. But Bibendum is still an exciting and original place to buy wine. Long may the crusade continue.

White

£3–5

ARGENTINA

1993 Alamos Ridge Chardonnay, Mendoza
££ / 2 / 1   15/20
Smoky oak, lemon and lime juicy Chardonnay with some buttery lees
character, nicely integrated oak and lots of alcohol. Surprisingly fresh
and well-made given the body and weight of the wine. Good value at
under £5.

FRANCE

1994 Domaine de l'Espérance Colombard, Vin de Pays de Terroir Landais
£ / 2 / 1   13/20
This is a domaine-bottled Colombard from the sands of France's Atlantic
coast. Old-fashioned, nettley aromas reminiscent of Sauvignon Blanc are
followed by crisp, lemony, elderflower characters and underpinned by
austere appley acidity.

£5–8

FRANCE

1994 Sancerre, Domaine Thomas
££ / 2 / 1   16/20
Perfumed, softly grassy Sancerre in a modern, carbon dioxide enhanced
style. It's fresh, with some attractively grapefruity flavours, and not
bitingly austere as some Sancerre can be. Lovely clean fruit flavour,
intensity and good length.

ITALY

1993 Malvira Roero Arneis
£££ / 1 / ♪   16/20

A fresh, unusual Piedmontese white made from the native Arneis grape variety. With its fragrant green olive aromas, this is bracingly crisp for a two-year-old white and shows a hint of banana-like fruit on the aftertaste. Italy's answer to Chablis?

Over £8

AUSTRALIA

1993 Yeringberg Marsanne/Roussanne, Yarra Valley
££ / 2 /   17/20

From a beautiful and historic estate in the picturesque Yarra Valley north of Melbourne, this is an unusual blend (for Australia) of the northern Rhône grape varieties that go into white Hermitage. It's a rich, barrel-fermented oatmeal, pear and cinnamon-like white with crisp cool climate elegance and acidity.

FRANCE

1993 Chablis, Domaine des Marronniers, Bernard Legland
££ / 1 / ♪   15/20

The acidity on this 1993 straight Chablis may be a little austere but there's plenty of underlying weight, concentration and attractive lemony aromas too. It's still somewhat closed, as you'd expect from the vintage, but we think the wine should develop nicely over the coming year.

GERMANY

1991 Piesporter Domherr Kabinett Riesling, Reinhold Haart
£ / 4 / ♪   15/20

An aromatic, petrol, kerosene and lemon barley water style Mosel Riesling, but not for the spare tank. It's fresh for its age, with crisp acidity, well-balanced sweetness and delicate fruit flavours. Thinking person's Piesporter.

NEW ZEALAND

1994 Te Kairanga Sauvignon Blanc, Martinborough
££ / 3 / ♪   15/20

This Martinborough Sauvignon Blanc is redolent of gooseberry and elderflower, if less assertively so than examples from Marlborough. It's ripe, honeyed and a little sweet, with soft melon notes underpinned by fine acidity on the finish. The naff bunch-of-grapes label could do with a visit from Terence Conran.

Red

£3-5

ARGENTINA

1993 Alamos Ridge, Cabernet Sauvignon
££ / MB / ♪   15/20

An Argentinian red from the promising Catena winery, with coffee bean oak, plenty of juicy, blackcurrant fruit and none of the bitterness neighbouring Chile often seems to produce in its Cabernets.

FRANCE

1994 La Serre Merlot, Vin de Pays d'Oc
££ / MB / ♪   14/20

A deeply coloured, vibrant, modern carbonic maceration style red, this is a grassy Languedoc Merlot with smoky oak influence, fresh blackcurranty fruit and dry tannins.

ITALY

1993 Sangiovese dell'Umbria, Brogal Vini
££ / MB / ♪   14/20

A youthful, deeply coloured, plummy, succulent Montepulciano d'Abruzzo style red with the emphasis on fruit and drinkability. Well made, with a hint of tobacco on the finish and robust tannins.

£5–8

AUSTRALIA

1994 Basedow Bush Vine Grenache
££ / MB / ♪   15/20
Fresher and fruitier than many examples of Barossa Valley Grenache, this
is a smoky, chocolatey Grenache in which the American oak is nicely
integrated and the alcohol well proportioned.

FRANCE

1992 Château Cascadais, Corbières
££ / FB / ➡   15/20
A peppery, concentrated, chunky Corbières with a strong dose of toasty
new oak and a core of elegant fruitiness. Our only concern is that the
splinters might last longer than the wine.

1993 Domaine des Tours, Vin de Pays de Vaucluse
££ / FB / ♪   15/20
Made by Emmanuel Reynaud, nephew of the absent-minded eccentric
Jacques Reynaud of Château Rayas in Châteauneuf-du-Pape, this is a
spicy, angostura bitters style Provençal red with soft, Grenache-based
raspberry fruitiness and firm cigar-box tannins. Ideal if you're picnic or
barbecue bound.

ITALY

1991 Vigneto Antanel, Valpolicella Classico
£ / MB / ♪   13/20
On the ancient side for a Valpolicella, but this almond and cherry skin
red is well made and a bit of a curiosity. Dry and almost Mediterranean
in style with a baked fruitiness that reminds us more of Puglia than the
Veneto. Drink up before it pegs out.

NEW ZEALAND

1993 Undercliffe Hawkes Bay Cabernet/Merlot
0 / MB / 🔥   12/20
Underripe Hawkes Bay Cabernet/Merlot?

SOUTH AFRICA

1993 Grangehurst Pinotage
££ / FB / ➤   15/20
Made at Jeremy Walker's family winery on Helderberg Mountain, this is
a chunky, tannic, modern Pinotage with lots of American oak and
chewy, full-bodied fruit. The wine may soften with time in bottle. One
of a range of Grangehurst wines worth looking out for at Bibendum.

Over £8

AUSTRALIA

1991 Katnook Cabernet Sauvignon, Coonawarra
£££ / MB / ➤   17/20
**Another wine for the long haul, this is a full-throated, attractively
textured Cabernet with flavours of coffee bean, blackcurrant and
green pepper, supported by fine-grained tannins. One of the best
Australian reds we've seen this year. More Katnooks, including
this one, can be found at Victoria Wine Cellars.**

FRANCE

1992 Château Tour Haut-Caussan, Cru Bourgeois
££ / MB / 🔥   15/20
Typical of a well-made 1992 Médoc, this is an oaky, seductively
aromatic and forward organic claret with the distinct green edge of
the lean 1992 vintage.

1993 St-Amour, Domaine de Mongrin
££ / MB / 🔥   15/20
A fresh, well-made Gamay with a touch of Pinot Noir like strawberry
fruitiness, hefty alcohol and refreshing acidity.

UNITED STATES

1993 Acacia Pinot Noir
£££ / MB / ⊷   17/20
A toasty, densely fruity, concentrated young Carneros Pinot Noir
with lots of chocolate and supple strawberry characters made in
a more Burgundian style than most California examples. Thanks
to its attractively balanced fresh acidity, it should age for a good
three years plus. One of America's finest Pinot Noirs.

Rosé

£3–5

FRANCE

1994 Côtes de Provence, Château Saint Baillon, Hervé Goudard
££ / 2 / ▮   15/20
Pale bronze and dry on the palate, this subtle raspberry-perfumed
Provençal rosé, with its zip of carbon dioxide gas, attractive
concentration and nip of tannin, is more elusive and complex than you
might expect.

Sparkling

Over £8

FRANCE

Champagne Albert Beerens, Brut Reserve
££ / 2 / ▮   15/20
This grower's Champagne from Bar-sur-Aube has proved highly popular
with Bibendum customers and not only because it's reasonably priced.
Seductive, strawberry Pinot aromas give way to frothy bubbles and
youthful acidity. It should benefit from a bit more bottle age.

Fortified

Over £8

PORTUGAL

1990 Niepoort LBV
£££ / FB / ➼   **16/20**

A sweet, rustic, but attractively individual style from the under-rated Portuguese house of Niepoort. It's distinctively Portuguese in perfume and flavour with a peppery alcoholic bite and plenty of spicy plum and bitter chocolate characters.

ELDRIDGE POPE

Head Office: Weymouth Avenue, Dorchester, Dorset DT1 1QT

Telephone: 01305 251251; telesales freephone, 0800 378581

Number of branches: 8 wine shops in Dorchester, Shaftesbury, Sherborne, Wareham, Westbourne, Weymouth, Wincanton and Winchester, plus 4 'Wine Libraries', in Pimlico and Trinity Square, London, Exeter and Bristol

Hours of opening: Monday to Saturday 9.00am to 5.30pm, with some regional variations

Credit cards accepted: Visa, Access

By-the-case sales: Yes

Bottle sales: Yes

Facilities and services: Wine search, cellar valuations, free glass loan, recommend caterers and suppliers of marquees, chill wine for parties, gift packs. Organise the Dorset Wine Society lectures and tastings

Cellarage: Yes. Further details on request

Home delivery: Yes

Discounts: Yes. 5 per cent case discount

In-store tastings: Yes. Also hold regular tutored tastings at the Wine Libraries

Special offers: En primeur, bin-end sales and various special offers throughout the year

Top ten best-selling wines: Not supplied

If you live in the West Country and you enjoy a drop of beer or wine, there's only one Dorchester, and it's not in Park Lane. The Dorchester in question is the Dorset-based home of Royal Oak, Hardy County and sundry other ales brewed by the pub owner, retailer and wine merchant Eldridge Pope.

Only a third of Eldridge Pope's total turnover is in wine, but the list is one of the most interesting, not to mention informative, in the country. One reason is the enthusiasm generated by Eldridge Pope chairman, Christopher Pope, the inspiration behind the Chairman's Selection range of wines. With their labels drawn by Sir Hugh Casson, all are extremely well chosen examples of their kind, especially the Chairman's Claret and the extravagantly named Chairman's Exuberantly Fruitful New World Sauvignon.

Credit for the bulk of the range must go to Master of Wine Joe Naughalty, who, in 12 years with the company since arriving from neighbouring Averys, has been responsible for filling the list with a mixture of reliable stalwarts and fascinating growers' wines.

Naughalty, who retires this year, leaves his French-accented legacy to his successor, Robin Kinahan, also a Master of Wine, who will be buying the wines with Sue Longman. Kinahan plans to build on Naughalty's list by expanding the New World section.

Apart from its eight West Country shops, Eldridge Pope runs four 'Wine Libraries'. These are basically little bistrots where you can snack on cheese and pâté with a bottle from the Eldridge Pope list at its retail price. It's a brilliant idea. If only they'd change the rather silly name – you can hardly borrow the wine and take it back, after all – and bring in some bright spark to do something about the basic fare, the Wine Libraries could be the talk of Bristol, Exeter and London.

White

£3–5

FRANCE

1993 Domaine de la Renière Saumur

£££ / 2 / ➥   16/20

From the Loire estate of René Hugues Gay, this is a ripe, full-bodied

Chenin Blanc with rich apple and pear fruitiness, just the right amount of refreshing grapefruity acidity and excellent length of flavour.

1994 Jurançon Sec Grain Sauvage, Cave des Producteurs de Jurançon
£££ / 2 / ⅟   16/20
From the Jurançon co-operative in southwestern France, this is a classic example of the unusual white wines of the *appellation*. Exotic, guava-like aromas followed by fresh, citrus-fruit acidity and a crunchy dry tang.

1993 Domaine de Maubet, Cuvée Coup de Coeur, Gros Manseng
£££ / 2 / ⅟   16/20
An ambitious Gascon white from Jean-Claude Fontan, showing the ripe, honey and apricot characters of the southwest's Gros Manseng grape as well as its zesty, refreshing acidity. Concentrated and tangy.

1994 Chardonnay, Vin de Pays d'Oc
££ / 2 / ⅟   15/20
A banana-fruity, buttery, cool-fermented southern French Chardonnay produced by Mâcon-based *négociant* Mommessin, with good weight and flavour. Like a mini-Mâcon in style.

£5–8

FRANCE

1992 Domaines du Château de Riquewihr Gewürztraminer, 'Les Sorcières', Dopff & Irion
££ / 2 / ⅟   16/20
A well-balanced, Turkish Delight scented single vineyard Gewürztraminer, which is delicately flavoured but at the same time richly textured. Gewürztraminer can be a one-glass grape, but we'd be happy to scoff the whole bottle here.

1993 The Chairman's White Burgundy, Vieilles Vignes
££ / 2 / ⅟   15/20
From the Côte Chalonnaise-based house of Antonin Rodet, the chairman has selected a buttery, soft Chardonnay with some lees-enhanced

richness and attractive weight. Another well-priced white at just over £6.

1993 Vouvray, Château Gaudrelle
££ / 3 / ⚑   16/20
With its baked apple fruitiness, fresh acidity and honeyed texture, this is a classic Vouvray with restrained, rounded fruit sweetness. The estate owner, Alexandre Monmousseau, is a producer to watch.

1993 Savennières, Clos du Papillon, Domaine des Baumard
£££ / 1 / ⬤   17/20
The more than acceptable face of Chenin Blanc is often epitomised by the small Loire Valley *appellation* of Savennières. This is a rich and delicately dry white pepper style Chenin Blanc, with a steely, life-enhancing backbone of acidity. It should age well for a good five years.

GERMANY

1988 Schloss Vollrads Rheingau Riesling Kabinett Blaugold
£££ / 4 / ⚑   16/20
Made by Graf Matuschka-Greiffenclau, a man whose name sounds like a truck changing gear, this is a well-priced, delicate Rheingau Riesling from the excellent 1988 vintage. Matuschka's great crusade is to demonstrate that German wines are at their best with food. This soft, grapefruity, mature Riesling proves his point.

NEW ZEALAND

1994 The Chairman's New World Sauvignon, Nelson
£££ / 2 / ⚑   16/20
Via his messenger, wine buyer and Master of Wine Joe Naughalty, the chairman, Christopher Pope, has again chosen well. This gooseberry-scented Sauvignon Blanc, made at the Seifried family's Redwood Valley Estate in South Island's Nelson region is fresh, grapefruity, complex and attractively dry. The chairman should be happy with this one.

Over £8

FRANCE

1992 Meursault, Domaine Prieur-Brunet Chevaliers
£££ / 2 / ▮   17/20
A richly oaked, golden Meursault from the excellent 1992 vintage,
in which toasty oak flavours marry beautifully with full-bodied,
concentrated, fudge and butter fruitiness and highly refreshing
acidity.

UNITED STATES

1992 Gundlach Bundschu, Sonoma Valley Chardonnay
£ / 2 / ▮   14/20
The appealingly named Gundlach Bundschu estate was founded by a
German immigrant in the 1850s and remains one of the oldest operative
wineries in California. There's plenty of coconut oak in evidence here,
but we found the acidity on the harsh side, especially for a California
Chardonnay. Could it be the Germanic touch?

Red

£3–5

FRANCE

1993 Merlot Vin de Pays d'Oc
££ / MB / ▮   14/20
Soft, jammy, faintly rustic Merlot made by the Burgundian house of
Mommessin. We'd rather drink this than most cheap red Burgundy.

1994 Anjou Rouge, 'Logis de la Giraudière', Domaine des Baumard
0 / MB / ▮   13/20
A souped-up, prematurely aged Cabernet Franc from a difficult vintage
in the Loire Valley, this is dry and leafy with insufficient fruit.

1993 Abbaye de Valmagne, Gaudert d'Allaines, Coteaux du Languedoc
£££ / FB / ⌐   16/20

An equal blend of Syrah, Grenache and Mourvèdre, this is a vibrantly juicy, highly aromatic Languedoc red with refreshing acidity, spicy cherry fruit and chunky southern tannins.

£5–8

AUSTRALIA

1992 Peter Lehmann Clancy's, Barossa Valley, South Australia
£££ / FB / ⌐   16/20

From the Baron of the Barossa, Peter Lehmann, this is a typically heart-warming, minty blend of Carbernet Sauvignon, Cabernet Franc, Shiraz and Merlot. Lehmann pooh-poohs elegance in favour of wines with richness and density of flavour and texture.

FRANCE

1989 The Chairman's Claret, Haut-Médoc
£££ / MB / ↓   16/20

Selected by the chairman's representative on earth, Master of Wine Joe Naughalty, from the highly rated 1989 vintage, this claret from Château Beaumont's second label, Moulin d'Arvigny, is composty, rich and characterful, with spicy oak, supple cassis fruitiness and mature, farmyardy tannins.

1993 Côte de Brouilly, Clos du Calvaire
££ / MB / ↓   15/20

From a vineyard which sounds like a Station of the Cross, this is a fresh, strawberry-fruity Gamay with clean acidity and little of the concentration and complexity you'd normally expect from a Beaujolais cru.

1992 The Chairman's Red Burgundy
££ / 2 / ↓   15/20

Selected from the extensive cellars of Nuits St-Georges *négociant* Labouré-Roi, this is an honest, strawberry and chocolate-like Pinot Noir with suitably rustic tannins.

1992 Bourgogne Domaine Prieur-Brunet
££ / 2 / ↕   15/20
A different style at a similar price, this is an oaked, mature Pinot Noir
from a grower based in the Côte de Beaune village of Santenay, with
tomato-skin notes and dry tannins.

Over £8

FRANCE

1990 Château Caronne Ste-Gemme, Haut-Médoc
££ / MB / ⌐   16/20
Fragrant Merlot-like aromas make this youthful, refreshing Cru Bourgeois
with its spicy oak and cassis fruit a good buy at under £10.

1992 Gevrey-Chambertin Domaine Armand Rousseau
£££ / MB / ⌐   17/20
A savoury, spicy, youthful, village red Burgundy from one of the
leading domaines in Gevrey-Chambertin. It's a toasty, aromatic,
funky but beautifully expressed red-fruits-flavoured Pinot Noir.

**1992 Châteauneuf-du-Pape Domaine de Monpertuis, 'Cuvée
Classique', Paul Jeune**
££ / FB / ⌐   16/20
1992 was such a difficult vintage in Châteauneuf that it's a pleasure to
come across Grenache-based wines with this much weight, tannin and
alcohol. It's a heady, but still youthfully robust, southern Rhône red
which should develop over the next three to five years.

UNITED STATES

1992 Gundlach Bundschu Sonoma Valley Merlot
£ / FB / ⌐   15/20
Sweetish, punch-in-the-mouth, extracted Sonoma Merlot, made with the
California market in mind. The Right Bank of the Gironde offers better
value than this at £11 a bottle.

ENOTRIA WINECELLARS

Head Office: 48 Chandos Park Estate, Chandos Road, London NW10

Head Office Retail: 153–155 Wandsworth High Street, London SW18 4JB

Telephone: 0181 871 2668

Fax: 0181 874 8380

Number of branches: 1

Hours of opening: Monday to Saturday 10.00am to 7.00pm

Credit cards accepted: American Express, Access, Visa, Switch

By-the-case sales: Yes

Bottle sales: Yes

Facilities and services: Mail-outs throughout the year with case offers, tutored tastings and special offers. Anniversary Fair to take place on 11 November with many wines available to taste. Free glass hire for orders over a case in London only

Home delivery: Free for one case or more inside the M25 or two cases and more for the rest of the UK mainland; otherwise £5

Discounts: Case discounts available if collecting your wines from the shop

Top ten best-selling wines: Not supplied

A shaft of Italian sunshine appeared in 1985 with the opening of Winecellars, a brand new kind of Italian wine specialist. Co-founded by Colin Loxley, Jamie Pickford and Nick Belfrage, the author of *Life Beyond Lambrusco*, they were soon joined by David Gleave, also an authority on fine Italian wines, as his Salamander series book, *The Wines of Italy*, testified. With Italian wines in the UK dominated by a handful of big Italian importers, Winecellars illuminated the obscure arcana of native Italian grape varieties and fine Italian wines as never before.

So it was with trepidation that we heard, at the end of 1993, that one of the big Italian importers, Enotria, headed by the Ferrari and white truffle loving Remo Nardone, had taken more than a passing interest in Winecellars. We were reassured that Winecellars would be allowed to continue to plough its fine wine retailing furrow, while Enotria got on with the bread and butter – or should that be the spagbol Valpol – trade end of the business.

After a brief flirtation in which Winecellars managed to keep the attentions of the macho Enotria at arm's length, the high-class Italian specialist finally succumbed to Nardone's advances. Nardone, whose main agencies include Gruppo Italiano Vini (which includes Fontana Candida and Bigi), Umani Ronchi, Fontanafredda, Anselmi, Jermann, Ricasoli and, until recently, Rocca delle Macie, took over Winecellars in 1994. Most of the Wandsworth staff transferred to Head Office or left the company, although at the time of writing the Wandsworth shop is still intact.

Combining the two lists has given Enotria Winecellars the most powerful pair of Italian biceps in the country, accounting for 34 per cent of the quality wine market in the UK. Tuscany, Piemonte and the Veneto, and the south, all of which Belfrage and Gleave did so much to build up, offer a coruscating array of growers' and merchants' wines. The merger has also brought Australia, South Africa and Hungary to Enotria, while for its part, Enotria has hitched the quality Italian firm of GIV, not to mention an excellent French range, to the Winecellars bandwagon.

Are we being oversentimental in lamenting the departure of some of the Winecellars soul and an understanding of independent retailing from the merger? It would jeopardise much that Winecellars developed if the list were no longer so readily available to the wine drinking public. All the more so since Enotria Winecellars remains the best place in the country to seek out quality Italian wines, from Araldica and GIV at the basic level to some of the most interesting and unusual wines around. Maybe there's no place for sentimentality in business.

White

£3-5

HUNGARY

1994 Furmint, Château Megyer
££ / 1 / ♪   15/20
The first dry white from Jean-Michel Arcaute's Hungarian venture, this
is a fascinating tea-leaf and angelica spice-scented Furmint with the
native grape's characteristic refreshing acidity. A welcome change from
Sauvignon Blanc.

ITALY

1994 Chardonnay del Piemonte, Alasia
£ / 2 / ♪   14/20
A new venture combining the talents of Martin Shaw, the original
Australian flying winemaker, and the excellent Araldica co-operative in
northwestern Italy's Piemonte region. This rich, full-fruited, unoaked
Chardonnay marries the best of the New and Old Worlds. Our only
worry is that it seems to be ageing quickly.

1994 Muscaté Sec, Alasia, Vino da Tavola
££ / 2 / ♪   15/20
From the same team working in Piemonte's Monferrato hills, this is an
aromatic ginger and grapefruit-like dry white with excellent weight and
length of flavour.

£5-8

AUSTRALIA

1994 Chardonnay/Semillon, Salisbury Estate
£ / 2 / ♪   14/20
Made at the Alambie Wine Company in Victoria, this is a fresh, melony,
lightly spiced blend with well-handled oak character. Price increases in
Australia have regrettably taken this over the £5 barrier.

1994 Chardonnay, Salisbury Estate

£ / 2 / ≹   14/20

A ripe, golden-hued Victorian Chardonnay with soft, tropical fruit flavours and a faintly bitter, oak-derived aftertaste.

FRANCE

1994 Château Le Payral, Bergerac Blanc Sec

£££ / 2 / ≹   16/20

Ultra-fresh, tangy, grapefruity Sauvignon Blanc made by Thierry Daulhiac and showing excellent richness and concentration. So zingy it's halfway to New Zealand.

ITALY

1994 Casal di Serra, Verdicchio dei Castelli di Jesi, Umani Ronchi

££ / 2 / ≹   15/20

A single-vineyard Verdicchio with rounded, full-bodied, unoaked fruit and a nutty, refreshing tang. A wine which almost tastes as if it's been blended with Chardonnay.

1994 Soave Classico Superiore, Pieropan

£££ / 2 / ≹   16/20

From some of the steepest vineyards in Soave's Classico zone, this is an attractively fragrant white with soft, delicate apricot fruitiness and zingy acidity enhanced by a prickle of carbon dioxide. Leonildo Pieropan is one of Soave's top producers, and in this instance, *superiore* means what it says.

SOUTH AFRICA

1995 Sauvignon Blanc, Thelema

££ / 2 / ≹   16/20

Delicate, grassy Stellenbosch Sauvignon made by Gyles Webb, one of South Africa's most engaging and enlightened winemakers. It's an elegant, subtle style, closer to Sancerre than Marlborough in flavour, with added carbon dioxide for extra freshness.

Over £8

AUSTRALIA

1993 Reserve Chardonnay, Shaw and Smith
££ / 2 / ▮   16/20

Winemaker Martin Shaw's successful attempt at a Burgundian style Down Under using fruit from the cool Adelaide Hills to produce a rich, toasty, grapefruity Chardonnay, which combines power with finesse.

FRANCE

1993 Mâcon-Charnay, Vieilles Vignes, Domaine Manciat-Poncet
££ / 2 / ▮   16/20

Rich, concentrated grower's southern white Burgundy with flavours of aniseed, honey and coconut, underpinned by the typical fresh acidity of the vintage. If only a few more Mâcons were like this.

1992 Puligny-Montrachet, Premier Cru, Hameau de Blagny, Domaine Jean-Luc Pascal
££ / 2 / ↳   17/20

Leesy, rich, old-fashioned but full-flavoured white Burgundy from Puligny grower Jean-Luc Pascal, with the crisp acidity we expect from the relatively high vineyards of Blagny overlooking the Côte de Beaune.

HUNGARY

1988 Tokaji Aszu 5 Puttonyos, Château Megyer, 50cl
££ / 6 / ▮   16/20

With its aromas of raisin and marmalade, this amber-hued, sweetly mature, faintly mushroomy Tokaji is an old-fashioned product of the former Communist regime, subsequently bought in barrel and bottled by Jean-Michel Arcaute. Not perhaps a wine for anyone of politically correct sensibilities.

Red

£3–5

ITALY

1993 Montepulciano d'Abruzzo, Umani Ronchi
££ / MB / ⚑   14/20
Deeply coloured, aromatic Montepulciano whose rough plum-skin edge
has been planed down with a touch of sweetness. The sort of central
Italian rosso you'd be delighted to come across at Pizza Express – but all
too rarely do.

1994 Dolcetto d'Asti, Alasia
££ / MB / ⚑   14/20
Fresh, summery fruitiness and an attractively soft texture make this
Martin Shaw red from the Araladica co-operative a good sub-£5 pasta
basher. Another order for Pizza Express, please.

£5–8

AUSTRALIA

1993 Salisbury Cabernet Sauvignon
£ / MB / ⚑   14/20
From Victoria's Alambie winery, this red has plenty of sweet raspberry,
mint and cassis fruitiness with some coarse tannins poking through on
the aftertaste. A pity it isn't under a fiver.

FRANCE

1994 Beaujolais, Domaine du Vissoux, Cuvée Traditionnelle
££ / MB / ⚑   15/20
Priced at the same level as a Beaujolais cru, this pure, old-vine Gamay is
a fresh, juicy, attractively made red with a gluggable red fruits character
the region often fails to deliver.

1993 Château Mourgues du Grès, 'Terre d'Argence', Costières de Nîmes

£££ / FB / ⇝   17/20

A remarkable find from southern France made predominantly from 25-year-old vines, this is a deeply coloured, highly aromatic, beautifully balanced liquorice and blackberry like red, which could easily be mistaken for a top northern Rhône Syrah.

ITALY

1990 Villa di Vetrice, Chianti Rufina, Riserva

£££ / MB / ♪   15/20

Chocolatey, old-fashioned, robust Chianti Riserva from the Grati estate in the Rufina hills not a million miles from the current home of Winecellars founder Nick Belfrage. Good, honest Sangiovese with few rough edges at an exceptional price for a Riserva.

1994 Barco Reale di Carmignano, Tenuta di Capezzana

££ / MB / ♪   15/20

A damson, raspberry and tobacco-like red with a dry finish, made from a blend of Sangiovese and Cabernet Sauvignon. It reminded us of a rather elegant Zinfandel.

Over £8

AUSTRALIA

1992 Langi Shiraz, Mount Langi Ghiran

££ / MB / ⇝   15/20

An aromatic, cool climate Shiraz from producer Trevor Mast with a sage and mint-like perfume, underpinned by oak spiciness, fresh acidity and firm tannins.

FRANCE

1990 Château Merville, Cru Bourgeois, St-Estèphe

££ / MB / ⇝   15/20

A robustly fruity, farmyardy claret with sweet, ripe mint and liquorice flavours and well-judged oak bound in a tight fist of tannin.

ITALY

1993 Rosso di Montalcino, Argiano
£££ / MB / 🍷   16/20
From the historic estate of Argiano in Montalcino, this is a soft, leafy
Sangiovese with refreshing acidity and delicate, sweet fruit
concentration. If the Rosso's this good, you can imagine what the
Brunello must be like.

1990 Chianti Rufina Riserva, 'Bucerchiale', Selvapiana
££ / FB / ➧   16/20
From the eccentric Francesco Giuntini's best Rufina vineyard, this is an
almondy, concentrated cherry and damson-skin Chianti Riserva with a
sheen of new oak and a coating of dry, robust tannins. One to put away.

JUSTERINI & BROOKS

Head Office: Justerini & Brooks Ltd, 61 St James's Street, London SW1A 1LZ

Telephone: 0171 493 8721

Fax: 0171 499 4653

Hours of opening: Monday to Friday 9.00am to 5.30pm

Mail order: Yes

Number of branches: 2

Also at: 45 George Street, Edinburgh

Telephone: 0131 226 4202

Fax: 0131 225 2351

Hours of opening: Monday to Friday 9.00am to 6.00pm, Saturday 10.00am to 5.00pm

Credit cards accepted: All major cards

By-the-case sales: Yes

Bottle sales: Yes

Facilities and services: Glass loan/accessories/cellaring advice

Home delivery: Carriage charges per delivery to one address in mainland UK and Northern Ireland as follows: 1 to 23 bottles: £9.00 per delivery; 24 bottles and over: free delivery. Carriage to other offshore UK destinations will be charged at £15.00 per dozen bottles

Discounts: Yes: 2 to 4 cases, £1.00 per case discount; 5–7 cases, £2.00; 8 cases and over, £3.00

In-store tastings: Yes

Special offers: En primeur, seasonal offers, bin-end sales

Top ten best-selling wines: Sarcey, Private Cuvée, Justerini & Brooks, Brut Champagne; 1992 Mâcon-Uchizy, Domaine Talmard; 1992 Pouilly-Fumé, Domaine Serge Dagueneau; 1992 Chablis, Domaine Ste-Clair, Jean-Marc Brocard; 1992 Chardonnay, Scotchman's Hill 1993, Geelong; 1992 Côtes du Rhône, Cuvée des Capucines, Domaine Vieux Chêne; Justerini & Brooks Claret; 1992 Bourgogne, Domaine Robert Chevillon; 1993 Pinot Noir, Scotchman's Hill; 1989 Chianti Classico, Castello di Querceto

For traditional wine lovers, Bordeaux divides between the Left and the Right Bank. For the same group of people, St James's is split between Berry Bros & Rudd on the east side and Justerini & Brooks on the west. Since comparisons are generally odious, we would only add that both 18th-century merchants are strongly French-orientated and both umbilically linked to famous whiskies – Cutty Sark in the case of Berry Bros and J & B Rare in Justerini's.

Justerini's buyer, Hew Blair, justifiably prides himself on the fact that J & B's list is based on growers' wines. 'We adopted a principle of buying from growers where possible. The wines are more interesting and customers appreciate them.' Anyone – well, almost anyone – can buy claret, but the real skill comes in finding excellent growers in the more bewildering areas of Burgundy, Loire and the Rhône. On that basis, J & B's list is star-studded with some of the best growers from all three regions. The German list is pretty spectacular too.

J & B's business is mainly mail order to private customers, 'a mixture of aristos, pop stars and people with money in the City', according to Hew Blair, a mixture, in other words, of people with two things in common: the enjoyment of fine wine and the possession of substantial amounts of spare cash. A lot of customers call into the St James's shop and, if you're in the area and a little peckish, you'll more than likely find a J & B wine on the list of one of the fancier local hostelries such as The Square and The Coast. In Edinburgh, by contrast, only a quarter of the business is with private customers, while the rest is with country house hotels.

In case all this leads you to think that J & B is the exclusive preserve of the posh and the snobbish, think again. Hew Blair has been developing the more affordable southern French and country wine range since 1983. Domaine du Vieux Chêne alone sells 5,000 cases. He's also been busy sniffing out new things from Australia (Scotchman's Hill, Pauletts), Chile (Montes), California (Saintsbury, Calera) and to a lesser extent, South Africa, although even here he's managed to stock the wines of Charles Back, one of South Africa's best producers. We wouldn't go as far as to say that you'll never find a bad wine at J & B, but you might have a job trying.

White

£3–5

FRANCE

1993 Sauvignon, Domaine Gourg de Laval, Vin de Pays de l'Hérault
££ / 2 / ⅟   15/20
Nicely weighted Languedoc Sauvignon with melon and grapefruit characters and refreshing acidity. Just the sort of thing the Midi ought to be able to do in its sleep.

1993 Domaine du Vieux Chêne, Vin de Pays de Vaucluse
££ / 2 / ⅟   15/20
An extra dash of Viognier has added some peachy aromas to this soft, well-rounded Provençal white. A very full-bodied style with considerable buttery weight.

1993 Domaine Boyer, Vin de Pays des Côtes de Thongue
£ / 2 / ⅟   14/20
An unusual, aniseedy white from the Languedoc-Roussillon region, this is made from the Chasan grape, a Listan/Chardonnay crossing, which has given this baked apple style varietal a zip of balancing acidity.

£5–8

FRANCE

1993 Mâcon-Uchizy, Domaine Talmard
£££ / 2 / ▮   16/20
A full-bodied, vibrantly tangy, unoaked Mâcon-Villages from Paul and Philibert Talmard with ripe, spicy flavours of melon and pineapple chunks. Hardly surprising that this excellent southern white Burgundy is Justerini & Brooks' best-selling white wine.

GERMANY

1991 Riesling QbA, Fritz Haag
£££ / 3 / ▮   16/20
A light, delicate Mosel Riesling with fragrant, green apple aromas and crunchy acidity from Fritz Haag, one of Germany's top producers – a man with a bone-shuddering handshake making incongruously elegant wines.

Over £8

AUSTRALIA

1993 Scotchman's Hill Chardonnay
££ / 2 / ▮   16/20
A sweetish, richly alcoholic Chardonnay from the cool Geelong district opposite Victoria's Mornington Peninsula. With its blockbuster flavours of butterscotch, barley sugar and honey, this barrel-fermented white will appeal to fans of top-class Australian Chardonnay.

FRANCE

1993 Chablis, Domaine Ste-Clair, Jean-Marc Brocard
££ / 2 / ▮   16/20
Chablis produced some excellent wines in 1993 and this rich domaine-bottled example abundantly proves the point. It's full-bodied, pungently aromatic, but dry and crisp with a lot of minerally character.

1992 Meursault, Domaine Albert Grivault
£££ / 2 / 🍷   18/20

This powerful village Meursault is so packed with flavour and concentration that it's hard to believe it's not a Premier Cru. Buttery, nutty and richly textured Chardonnay, but with a halter of acidity which keeps the wine's plumper curves in check. Outstanding quality and value at around £16.50.

1993 Crozes-Hermitage, Château Curson
£££ / 2 / 🍷   16/20

Etienne Pochon's red and white Crozes are part of the *appellation*'s exciting new wave. This rich, attractively oaked blend of Marsanne and Roussanne is like a cross between a Condrieu and a white Hermitage at a fraction of the price. Fresh, lightly toasty and beautifully balanced. If only all white Crozes tasted like this.

1993 Gewürztraminer, Cuvée Théo, Domaine Weinbach
££ / 3 / 🍷   16/20

Super-ripe, unctuous, rose-petal Gewürztraminer from one of Alsace's best domaines, showing weight, concentrated fruit, plenty of spice and enough acidity to prevent the wine from sticking to the roof of your palate.

NEW ZEALAND

1994 Sauvignon, Dry River, Martinborough
£££ / 2 / 🍷   17/20

More restrained than the untamed Marlborough style, this Martinborough Sauvignon Blanc from Neil McCallum's tiny but excellent estate can compete with the best in New Zealand. It's a fragrant, grapefruity, nettley, full-bodied style with a minerally note and the acidity of a top Sancerre.

UNITED STATES

1992 Chalk Hill Chardonnay, Sonoma County
££ / 2 / 🍷   16/20

Midway between Burgundy and Australia in style, California produces some of the best Chardonnay in the world. This Sonoma County example made by acclaimed oenologist Dave Remy is powerfully alcoholic and packed with flavours of caramel fudge, butter and cinnamon toast. Retiring palates may find the 14 per cent alcohol a little over the top.

Red

£3-5

FRANCE

1993 Cuvée de l'Arjolle, Vin de Pays des Côtes de Thongue, Teisserenc

££ / FB / ▮   15/20

An aromatic, attractively structured Languedoc blend of Cabernet Sauvignon and Merlot, with some chunky, mildly astringent tannins. Like the excellent 1992, available at Tanners, it shows that the South of France can compete on price and quality with Bordeaux.

1990 Côtes du Rhône, La Haie aux Grives, Domaine du Vieux Chêne

££ / FB / ▮   15/20

An aromatic, lead-pencil-scented southern Rhône red from a fine vintage, showing the robust tannins of the Syrah grape, which adds aroma and character to the tea-leafy Grenache base.

£5-8

AUSTRALIA

1992 Cabernet/Merlot, Neil Paulett, Clare Valley

£££ / MB / ▬   16/20

Attractively drinkable Clare Valley Bordeaux blend with elegant tannins and fresh, berry fruitiness. The oak flavours are well-integrated on this youthful, accessible Australian red.

FRANCE

1993 Morgon, Château de Raousset
£££ / MB / ♪   16/20

Robust, peppery, honest Gamay from one of the best Beaujolais crus, this is a juicy, concentrated red with some spicy oak, thirst-quenching acidity and firm tannins.

1993 Crozes-Hermitage, Domaine Pochon
£££ / MB / ♪   16/20

Gorgeously aromatic, blackberryish Syrah from the talented Etienne Pochon, this is all the more impressive, given the vicissitudes of the 1993 vintage in the northern Rhône.

1992 Bourgogne Rouge, Domaine Robert Chevillon
£££ / MB / ♪   16/20

Delightfully fruity, fresh red Burgundy which shows the strawberry fruit of the Pinot Noir grape at its immediate best. Nuits-St-Georges grower Robert Chevillon has produced an excellent Bourgogne Rouge, which is well worth its £8 price tag.

Over £8

FRANCE

1990 Marsannay, Les Longeroies, Domaine Bruno Clair
£££ / MB / ♪   17/20

From the obsessive Bruno Clair's extensive cellars in Marsannay, this is just the kind of wine to turn you on to red Burgundy. It's well-priced at under £9, and full of juicy, chocolatey, wild strawberry-like Pinot Noir fruit, with an imprint of village tannins for added structure.

1990 Chinon, Cuvée des Varennes du Grand Clos, Charles Joguet
£££ / MB / ►   18/20

Magnificent, concentrated, elegant Cabernet Franc from sculptor and star winemaker Charles Joguet, with pure, ripe cassis and black-berry sweetness and refreshing acidity. It would be hard to find a better expression of Cabernet Franc anywhere in the world.

1990 Château Fourcas-Loubaney, Cru Bourgeois, Listrac-Médoc
££ / MB / ⊷   16/20
Youthful, substantially oaked Cru Bourgeois claret from the excellent
1990 vintage with attractively ripe blackcurrant fruit flavours and the
characteristic hardness of the Listrac *appellation* for backbone.

**1989 Château Beauséjour-Duffau-Lagarrosse, Premier Grand Cru
Classé, St-Emilion**
£ / MB / ⊷   16/20
Powerful, extracted, deeply coloured St-Emilion from the much-
acclaimed bicentenary vintage. It's still a baby at the moment, but this
£30 blockbuster will almost certainly improve as the tannins soften and
melt into the cassis-like, leafy Right Bank claret. Oh, well, we may have
to taste it again next year.

1991 Côte-Rôtiè, René Rostaing
£££ / FB / ⊷   18/20
**Powerfully aromatic, superbly elegant Syrah from an underrated
vintage in the northern Rhône. It's drinkable now, but this
stunningly rich and smoky, blackberry-fruity Côte Rôtie will age
for another 10 years.**

ITALY

**1990 Cignale, Castello di Querceto, Vino da Tavola dei Colli della
Toscana Centrale**
£ / FB / ⊷   16/20
Massively oaked, all-Cabernet Supertuscan with high acidity, rustic,
drying tannins and a hefty £20 price tag. Good concentrated fruit quality
and richness, but it's not immediately apparent at this stage that the fruit
will beat the tannins to the finishing line.

LAY & WHEELER

Head Office: 6 Culver Street West, Colchester, Essex CO1 1JA

Telephone: 01206 764446

Hours of opening: Monday to Saturday 8.30am to 5.30pm. Mail order Monday to Friday 8.00am to 6.00pm; Saturday 8.00am to 5.30pm

Mail order: Yes

Number of branches: 3

Also at: Wine Market, Gosbecks Road, Shrub End, Colchester, Essex CO2 9JT

Telephone: 01206 764446 (evenings 01206 762944)

Hours of opening: Monday to Saturday 9.00am to 7.00pm

And: Mackeanston House, Doune, Perthshire FK16 6AX

Telephone: 01786 850414

Hours of opening: Monday to Friday 8.30am to 5.30pm

Credit cards accepted: American Express, Visa, Access, Mastercard, Switch

By-the-case sales: Yes

Bottle sales: Yes

Facilities and services: Ex-cellar and under bond purchases available, wine racks, sale or return, free glass loan, ice, additional party equipment (ice buckets, punchbowls, etc.), waiters, waitresses and food for cocktail parties, gift vouchers

Cellarage: Yes. Further details supplied on request

Home delivery: Yes

Discounts: Yes. Case discount of 30 pence per bottle

In-store tastings: Yes. There is a regular programme throughout the year

Special offers: En primeur, bin-end sales, bi-monthly customer newsletter

Top ten best-selling wines: Not supplied

Lay & Wheeler is most people's idea of a traditional wine merchant – reliable, friendly and well-run, with a comprehensive wine range covering almost everything from the Mosel to Madeira. It's also family-owned. Open the thickly bound list to the page marked 'personnel' and the first three faces to greet the eye are director and cricket lover John Wheeler, chairman Richard Wheeler and personnel director Sue Wheeler.

In and around Colchester, Lay & Wheeler is a much-loved institution. It's nominally based in Essex, but it would be hard to imagine a company which caters less for the tastes and predilections of modern Essex Man. There's nothing flashy about Lay & Wheeler. It's a solid independent with strong local roots and an awareness of tradition.

If all this makes Lay & Wheeler sound a little boring, it shouldn't do. There's nothing wrong with developing long-term relationships with suppliers if they're the right suppliers. And, in Lay & Wheeler's case, most of them are. Henschke in Australia, Gilles Noblet in Pouilly-Fuissé, Paul Thomas in Sancerre, Heinrich in Austria, Michel Tête in Beaujolais, René Rostaing in Côte-Rôtie and Schramsberg and Peter Michael in California are all outstanding producers.

The Lay & Wheeler list is long on information and terse on waffle and gush. Packed with more than 1,000 lines, it covers all of the major bases, often with some style. For a traditional merchant grounded in Bordeaux, Burgundy and fortified wine styles, Lay & Wheeler has always taken the trouble to seek out interesting bottles from the New World and the South of France. Only in southern Italy has it been a little sluggish.

Service and staff training are important at Lay & Wheeler. The belief here is that wine merchants are moulded by years of experience and hard work. This means that Lay & Wheeler's customer tastings are some of the best in the country, tutored by knowledgeable members of the Lay & Wheeler team or, often, high-profile visiting winemakers. No wonder they're happy to make the journey to Colchester.

White

£5-8

FRANCE

1994 Viognier Vin de Pays d'Oc, Eugène Pontier
£££ / 2 / ♦   16/20
From the Cellier des Samsons in Beaujolais, this is an extremely tasty
Viognier with the intense flavours of a ripe peach and attractively
refreshing acidity for balance.

1993 Picpoul de Pinet, Fûts de Chêne, Cuvée Prestige, Hugues de Beauvignac
££ / 2 / ♦   16/20
It's unusual to find a white wine made from the Picpoul grape in this
country, never mind one that's been fermented in new oak barrels. This
appealing curiosity with its smoky concentration and spicy, pear-like
fruitiness is well worth a try at just over £7.

1994 Château Pierrail, Bordeaux
£££ / 2 / ♦   16/20
From Jacques Demonchaux, a stalwart of the Lay & Wheeler list, this is
an attractive, full-bodied, nettley Bordeaux blend of Semillon and
Sauvignon with excellent lemony freshness and fruit concentration.

SOUTH AFRICA

1994 Rosenburg Grand Vin Blanc, Stellenbosch
£ / 2 / ♦   14/20
A well-made Stellenbosch blend of Sauvignon and Chardonnay, a pairing
which is becoming something of a Cape speciality, produced at
Uiterwyk. The wine shows full body and alcohol with crisp, appley
acidity, but it's a little short on fruit.

Over £8

AUSTRALIA

1993 Semillon, Eden Valley, Henschke
£££ / 2 / ⊷   17/20
Stephen and Prue Henschke's Eden Valley winery is one of
Australia's truly great domaines, producing red and white wines
of outstanding quality. This oatmealy, lemony Semillon with its
sheen of new oak is just starting to open out. A beautifully
balanced, superbly crafted wine.

FRANCE

1993 Saint Véran, Domaine de la Collonge, Gilles Noblet
££ / 2 / ⊷   16/20
Gilles Noblet is one of the best young producers in the southern
Mâconnais, as this subtly spicy and delicately oaked white Burgundy
demonstrates. Fresh, crisp and concentrated with a lean streak of
acidity.

1994 Bourgogne Aligoté, Bouzeron, de Villaine
££ / 2 / ⅃   16/20
Made by Aubert de Villaine, the self-styled co-president of Vosne
Romanée's world-renowned Domaine de la Romanée-Conti, this is a
white made from the comparatively humble Aligoté grape in the Côte
Chalonnaise *appellation* of Bouzeron. Mind you, this is no ordinary
Aligoté. Instead of the grape's characteristic tartness, this example is
rich, weighty, aniseedy and refreshingly dry.

1992 Meursault Premier Cru Les Genevrières, Boisson-Vadot
£££ / 2 / ⊷   18/20
Twenty pounds may sound like an awful lot to pay for a white
wine, but when Meursault is as classy as this zesty, intensely
concentrated, nutty, complex Premier Cru, even Scrooge would
scrabble under the floorboards to find the necessary readies.

1993 Sancerre Les Comtesses, Paul Thomas, Chavignol
£££ / 2 / ♪   17/20
Made by an excellent grower based in the Sancerre commune of
Chavignol, where the famous Crottin goat's cheese hails from,
this is one of the best Loire whites we've had this year. Powerfully
scented, ripe, minerally Sauvignon Blanc of near perfect balance
and weight.

UNITED STATES

1993 Chardonnay, Clos du Ciel, Howell Mountain, Peter Michael
££ / 2 / ⌐   16/20
From Englishman and Classic FM shareholder Sir Peter Michael's isolated
Howell Mountain eyrie, this is a super-rich, toffee fudge and burnt butter
style Chardonnay with masses of oak, alcohol and flavour. Well made,
but evidently priced for the California market at £15.50 a bottle.

Red

£3–5

FRANCE

1994 Côtes du Rhône, A. Dépagneux, Marquis de Richevigne
££ / MB / ♪   14/20
From Beaujolais *négociant* Dépagneux, this is an ultra-soft, quaffing
Côtes du Rhône with appealing raspberry fruitiness and a grind or two
of the pepper mill.

1993 Domaine du Barrès Syrah, Vin de Pays d'Oc
£££ / 2 / ♪   15/20
Produced at a domaine situated in the hills above Carcassonne, this is a
deeply coloured, smokily aromatic, blackberryish Syrah with a dryish
aftertaste.

£5–8

AUSTRALIA

1994 Shiraz/Grenache, 'Christa/Rolf', Veritas Winery
££ / FB / ♪   15/20

Made by the brother-and-sister team of Rolf and Christa Binder, this is a well-priced, aromatic Midi-style blend from the Barossa Valley, with supple mint and blackberry fruit and a hefty whack of alcohol.

FRANCE

1993 Lay & Wheeler Claret
££ / MB / ♪   15/20

Well-made, fleshy, Merlot-based claret from Right Bank *négociant* Jean-Pierre Moueix. Château Pétrus it isn't, but at just over £5, this pleasantly cherryish, succulent red Bordeaux is a good buy.

Over £8

AUSTRIA

1991 Gabarinza, Heinrich
£££ / MB / ☛   17/20

An exciting blend of the Central European Blaufränkisch, Zweigelt and Saint Laurent grapes made by Gernot Heinrich in his family winery at Gols in eastern Austria's Burgenland region. This is an oaky, yet elegant, plum and raspberry fruity red with spicy concentration and supple tannins. It's good to see a wine merchant giving Austria's best producers the prominence they deserve. One of Austria's top wines.

FRANCE

1989 Château Mazeris-Bellevue, Canon-Fronsac
£££ / MB / ♪   16/20

From vineyards on the bluff overlooking the town of Libourne, this is a softly ripe, attractively oaked, Merlot-based claret, which is drinking exceptionally well at the moment.

1994 Juliénas, Domaine du Clos du Fief, Michel Tête
£££ / MB / ➜ **17/20**
One of a number of first rate Beaujolais crus at Lay & Wheeler, this reminds you what really good Gamay should taste like. Made by the ruddy-faced Michel Tête, it's an exuberant but well-proportioned Juliénas with just the right amount of tannin and acidity to lend backbone to the pure raspberry fruitiness of the wine.

1993 Gevrey-Chambertin, Vieilles Vignes, Domaine Marchand-Grillot
£££ / MB / ➜ **17/20**
From the excellent 1993 vintage for red Burgundy, this old-vine Pinot Noir is fragrant and comparatively forward. It's supple, beautifully oaked and extremely concentrated for a village-level Côte de Nuits red. You can happily imbibe this now, but the tannins on the finish suggest a long life.

1991 Volnay Premier Cru Clos de la Bousse d'Or, Domaine de la Pousse d'Or
£££ / MB / ➜ **18/20**
We wouldn't normally give three stars for value to a £30 wine, but Gérard Potel's vineyard produced a stunning wine in 1991. It's a big, rich, intense, traditional Pinot Noir with masses of stuffing, flavour and structure. If only all Premier Cru red Burgundy could match the thrill of a wine like this.

1992 Côte-Rôtie, René Rostaing
££ / MB / 🍷 **17/20**
From the lightish 1992 vintage, this is an alluringly aromatic, elegant Côte-Rôtie with crushed black pepper and ginger spice notes adding complexity to the blackberry fruitiness of the Syrah grape.

1992 Châteauneuf-du-Pape, Domaine La Roquette
££ / FB / 🍷 **16/20**
The southern Rhône suffered even more than the north in 1992. But you wouldn't know it from this powerfully aromatic, well-structured blend

of Grenache, Syrah and Mourvèdre, which comes from the same stable as the world-famous Domaine du Vieux Télégraphe.

SOUTH AFRICA

1992 Wellington Red, Claridge
££ / FB / ━━   16/20

Made by Englishman Roger Jorgensen, who prospects for diamonds in his spare moments, this is a 70/30 blend of Cabernet Sauvignon and Merlot aged in French oak for that extra Bordeaux-like touch. It's a concentrated, broad-shouldered Cape red with powerful tannins and a core of red fruits flavours.

Rosé

£5–8

FRANCE

1994 Domaine La Fadèze, Grenache Vin de Pays de l'Hérault
££ / 2 / ⸙   15/20

From a beautifully situated vineyard on the shores of the oyster-rich Bassin de Thau, this is a full-bodied, dry, herb and strawberry like rosé made from the Grenache grape, which needs food to show at its best.

Sparkling

Over £8

UNITED STATES

1987 Blanc de Noirs Schramsberg
£££ / 2 / ⸙   16/20

Jack and Jamie Davis, the Ronald and Nancy Reagan of the Napa Valley, are dedicated to producing the best, and in the case of their J. Schram

Cuvée, one of the highest-priced Champagne-method sparkling wines in California they have succeeded. This blend of Pinot Noir and Pinot Meunier is considerably cheaper, and shows attractive, strawberry fruitiness, a fine mouthfilling mousse and elegant acidity. A better buy at under £14 than most Champagne.

LEA & SANDEMAN

Address: 301 Fulham Road, London SW10 9QH

Telephone: 0171 376 4767

Hours of opening: For all branches, Monday to Friday 9.00am to 8.30pm; Saturday 10.00am to 8.30pm.

Mail order: Yes

Number of branches: 3

Also at: 211 Kensington Church Street, London W8 7LX

Telephone: 0171 221 1982

And: 51 High Street, Barnes, London SW13 9LN

Telephone: 0181 878 8643

Credit cards accepted: Visa, Access, Switch, American Express

By-the-case sales: Yes

Bottle sales: Yes

Facilities and services: Full party service, including delivery on the night with wine in tubs on ice (£1.25 per 5lb bag). Glasses loaned free of charge with wine orders. Breakages £1 each.

Home delivery: Yes. Free on a case in central London (or close to the Barnes outlet) for a case or more, and on any order over £150 anywhere else in mainland Britain south of Perth. Elsewhere or in smaller quantities by arrangement (usually deliver free to the Isles of Scilly)

Discounts: Sell by the bottle at one price, and have a discounted price (no strict percentage, but usually over 10 per cent) for any volume over 9 litres (ie 12 bottles, 24 halves or 6 magnums) in any combination

In-store tastings: Individual bottles open on Saturdays. Several major tastings a year open to all customers

Special offers: En primeur claret; 1990 Supertuscans; southern French reds; Viognier; 1990 Tuscan DOC wines; new estates in Tuscany; 1993 red Burgundy; and Rhône red. Tend not to make bin-end offers, but have done so occasionally

Top ten best-selling wines: Not supplied

'Size isn't everything in the wine business, you know,' says Charles Lea, the taller half of the dynamic Lea and Sandeman duo. Lea and motorcycling Patrick Sandeman set up their first Fulham Road shop in November 1988 and, with the recent acquisition of the former Barnes Wine Shop, have now extended their west and southwest London empire to three elegant dark blue and cream hued stores.

Their buying policy is simple. 'We only buy things that we'd both drink to the bottom of the bottle,' says Lea. Both are unashamed aficionados of French and Italian wines. (Lea admits that he doesn't like Australian wine, although his list includes a few wines from cooler areas Down Under, as well as wines from Chile, New Zealand and South Africa.)

The Old World is certainly the stronger area of the list. Lea spends much of his time in France, while Sandeman concentrates on Italy. This has resulted in a superb range of domaine-bottled reds and whites, many of them exclusive to Lea and Sandeman, such as Domaine Capmartin in Madiran and Tenuta del Terriccio in Tuscany.

'Most of these domaines wouldn't have enough wine to sell to the high street,' says Lea. 'We're small enough to be able to buy in 25-case parcels.' The approach is clearly popular with customers who visit the shops, as well as with the two-thirds who purchase by mail order. Recent, highly popular offers have included Viognier, 1990 Tuscans and southern French reds.

Lea & Sandeman may not be the cheapest wine merchant in London, but it offers slightly old-fashioned, pin-striped shirt and apron-style service and a range of very well-chosen bottles. Any merchant that chooses to set up premises opposite a busy Oddbins doesn't lack self-confidence. And that confidence is justified. Lea & Sandeman is one of the few really successful independents to have emerged in the last decade, specialising in hand-picked wines between £5 and £12 and proving, as Lea himself would no doubt agree, that small can also be best.

White

£5–8

FRANCE

1994 Château Tour de Gendres, Bergerac Blanc Sec, Cuvée Sur Lie
££ / 2 / ♪   15/20
A crisp, aromatic, early-bottled white Bordeaux-style blend from Luc de
Conti, with attractive, nettley aromas, crisp acidity and the weight you'd
expect from the addition of 40 per cent Semillon.

**1992 Domaine de Jöy, Cuvée Spéciale, Elevé en Fûts de Chêne, Vin
de Pays des Côtes de Gascogne**
££ / 2 / ♪   16/20
Made mainly from Gros Manseng, a grape native to southwestern France,
with the balance made up of Ugni Blanc and Colombard, this is an
ambitiously rich, partially barrel-fermented white with exotic grapefruit
characters, spicy oak and tangy acidity.

**1994 Viognier Domaine La Condamine l'Evèque, Vin de Pays des
Côtes de Thongue**
£££ / 2 / ♪   16/20
Made from young Viognier vines by consultant winemaker Guy Bascou
at his home base in the Languedoc, this tank-fermented white is rich in
ripe apricot aromas dusted with herby aniseed notes.

**1994 Château de Belle Coste Viognier, Cuvée Saint Marc, Costières
de Nîmes Blanc**
££ / 2 / ♪   15/20
It says Viognier on the label, but this is a blend of Viognier with 20 per
cent Roussanne. It's an abundantly perfumed, appley style showing full-
bodied fruit and plenty of alcoholic weight with a nip of tart acidity on
the aftertaste.

ITALY

1994 Vigneto Le Contessine Bianco Vermentino, Le Macchiole, Bolgheri
£££ / 2 / ▮   16/20
A perfumed, complex Tuscan blend from the Livornian coast of 85 per cent Vermentino with 15 per cent Chardonnay. Ripe, rounded and concentrated with lemon and green olive characters, this signs off with a sophisticated dry tang of acidity.

Over £8

FRANCE

1992 Mâcon Viré Domaine Emilian Gillet, Thévenet
£££ / 3 / ▮   17/20
An unusual, exotic Chardonnay from the Mâcon region of southern Burgundy, made by the wiry Jean Thévenet in a deliberately off-dry style. Thévenet believes that, in the past, many Mâconnais whites contained a degree of residual sugar, and claims that his wines reflect this tradition. Whatever the historical truth, the resulting wines can be spectacular. This super-ripe, botrytis-affected, honey and mango-like cuvée makes the point fluently.

1994 Chablis, Adhémar and Francis Boudin
££ / 2 / ▮   16/20
Ignore the old-fashioned parchment scroll label and pull the cork on this delightfully pure unoaked Chardonnay with its delicious, almost flinty complexity and an underlying milky sweetness. More expensive than most basic Chablis, but well worth its £11 price tag.

1993 Pouilly-Fuissé Vieilles Vignes, Domaine Daniel Barraud
£££ / 2 / ➤   17/20
Beautifully oaked, concentrated Pouilly-Fuissé, which has the elegance and length of flavour of a Puligny-Montrachet Premier Cru. It's modern, crisp and attractively poised with the structure to age for a further five years.

1992 Riesling Bergheim Engelgarten, Domaine Marcel Deiss
££ / 2 / ⮌   **16/20**

Marcel Deiss is one of the stars of the Lea & Sandeman French selection. This dry Alsace Riesling has more weight than most German examples, but retains the petrolly complexity of the grape variety at its best. Pure, minerally and profoundly flavoured, its refreshing prickle of gas adds extra balance and zip.

ITALY

1994 Rondinaia, Tenuta del Terriccio
££ / 2 / ♪   **16/20**

Another Tuscan find from biker Patrick Sandeman, this is an adventurous, cool-fermented blend of Chardonnay, Sauvignon and Gewürztraminer, the only such blend we've ever encountered. It's an al fresco style with a pot-pourri of rose petal fragrance, fresh acidity and lychee and green bean fruitiness. You'll never taste its like again – at least until next year's vintage.

Red

£3–5

FRANCE

1994 Merlot, Domaine de Terre Megère, Vin de Pays d'Oc
£ / MB / ♪   **14/20**

Made by Michel Moreau, this is a plummy, chocolatey, unoaked Languedoc Merlot with honest, robust fruitiness. A bit basic at nearly £5 a bottle. You can buy Moreau's wines a good deal cheaper at the Grape Shop in Boulogne.

£5–8

FRANCE

1991 Madiran Tradition, Domaine Capmartin
£££ / FB / ♪   16/20

It may not be as famous as Alain Brumont's overhyped Château Montus, but this soft, attractively proportioned, traditional Madiran is one of the best reds we've tasted from the southwestern French *appellation*. A blend of the local Tannat with 55 per cent Cabernet Sauvignon, it's a deeply coloured, chunky, succulent red with masses of flavour and complexity.

1992 Faugères, 'Cuvée Fleur de la Passion', Syrah, Domaine du Fraisse
££ / FB / ♪   15/20

A perfumed, lightly oaked Languedoc Syrah made by the softening carbonic maceration technique for early drinking. Chocolatey, supple and full of vibrantly textured blackberry fruitiness.

1992 Domaine du Deffends, Clos de la Truffière, Coteaux Varois
£££ / MB / ↝   16/20

Made at a domaine owned by a Marseilles University law professor, this is an elegant blend of Syrah and Cabernet Sauvignon modelled on Domaine de Trévallon in the Côteaux des Baux de Provence. As the name suggests, it's truffley and aromatic with some black pepper Syrah notes to leaven the structured tannins of the Cabernet Sauvignon.

ITALY

1993 Vigneto Le Contessine Rosso, Le Macchiole, Bolgheri
£££ / MB / ↝   16/20

A Supertuscan red blend of Sangiovese with 10 per cent Cabernet Sauvignon, this is a chunky, flavoursome, savoury, sweetly oaked red with masses of colour and ripe, plum and cassis fruitiness. At £7 a bottle, it's comparatively cheap for a Tuscan heavyweight.

Over £8

FRANCE

1993 Givry Premier Cru, Clos Jus, Domaine François Lumpp
£ / MB / ▮   15/20
A modern, attractively fruity, oaky Côte Chalonnaise Pinot Noir with masses of vibrant colour and some of the tannic structure of the vintage. All the same, we found this berry-fruity red a little simple for a wine at £12.50 a bottle.

1988 Château Haut-Beychevelle Gloria, St-Julien
££ / MB / ▬▬   16/20
If you've been hanging around bistrots in Antwerp, Brussels or Amsterdam, you may have come across Château Gloria, relabelled for the Benelux market as Château Haut-Beychevelle Gloria. This is a funky, farmyardy, terroir-influenced St-Julien with the rich, but elegant tannins of the classic 1988 vintage.

1992 Châteauneuf-du-Pape, Domaine de la Mordorée
£££ / FB / ▬▬   17/20
From a domaine based in nearby Tavel, Delorme's Châteauneuf is a Grenache-dominated style with oodles of colour and rich, chocolate and brown sugar fruitiness. This is just the sort of heady concoction we expect to find in Châteauneuf. Sadly, in a wet year like 1992, such wines are rare.

1991 Côte-Rôtie, Domaine Clusel-Roch
££ / FB / ▬▬   16/20
With its curious Sydney Opera House-style label, this is a fresh, judiciously oaked northern Rhône Syrah from an underrated vintage. It still needs time for the wine's smoky, blackberry-fruity core to fuse with the new oak.

ITALY

1992 Chianti Colli Senesi, Villa Santa Anna
£££ / MB / ▮   16/20
Made at a small, family-run 7-hectare estate in the Colli Senesi's

Montepulciano district, this is a savoury, traditional Sangiovese, with nutmeg spice and orange peel notes and relatively fine tannins for a medium-priced Chianti.

1990 Chianti Classico Riserva, Querciabella
£££ / FB / ⤴   17/20
An oakier, more modern style of Chianti with tarry, richly concentrated tannins, lashings of spice and the structure of a riserva from a fine vintage. This should age well for 5 to 10 years.

1993 Tassinaia, Tenuta del Terriccio
£ / FB / ⤴   15/20
A mint and pine resin scented Tuscan blend of Cabernet Sauvignon with a touch of Merlot, this is an oaky, stylish red with herbal flavours, ripe concentration and a tea-chest of dry tannins.

Sparkling

Over £8

FRANCE

Legras Grand Cru Blanc de Blancs Brut
£ / 2 / ▌   15/20
A Grand Cru all-Chardonnay Champagne from the house of Legras in the village of Chouilly, this is a light, lemony, biscuity Champagne with appealing delicacy of fruit and a fine, soft mousse.

Fortified

£5–8

SPAIN

Inocente Fino, Valdespino
£££ / 1 / 1   16/20
Made by the celebrated Miguel Valdespino, this is a clean, fresh, savoury,
flor-yeasty dry Sherry with zest, freshness and length of flavour. One of
the best Finos on the market.

TANNERS

Head Office: 26 Wyle Cop, Shrewsbury, Shropshire SY1 1XD

Telephone: 01743 232400

Fax: 01743 344401

Hours of opening: Monday to Saturday 9.00am to 6.00pm

Number of branches: 4

Also at: 4 St Peter's Square, Hereford HR1 2PG

Telephone: 01432 272044

And: The Old Brewery, Brook Street, Welshpool SY21 7LF

Telephone: 01938 552542

And: 36 High Street, Bridgnorth WV16 4DB

Telephone: 01746 763148

Hours of opening: For Hereford and Bridgnorth, Monday to Saturday 9.00am to 5.30pm. For Welshpool, Monday to Friday 9.00am to 5.30pm; Saturday 9.00am to 12.00pm

Credit cards accepted: All major credit cards (but not Diners Club)

By-the-case sales: Yes

Bottle sales: Yes

Facilities and services: Glass loan with drink order, party and wedding service including waiter, range of accessories, free estimates on cellar value in area, newsletter, monthly payment cellar scheme.

Home delivery: Local delivery is free for 12 bottles or more. National delivery is free for £75 worth of goods or more

Discounts: Yes: 3 dozen, 2 per cent discount; 5 dozen, 5 per cent discount; 10 dozen, 7 per cent discount

In-store tastings: One large tasting is held in the spring for private customers and trade customers. Various local tastings for customers including tutored tastings.

Special offers: En primeur claret offer, January Sale, Spring Sale and special offers through the year with newsletter

Top ten best-selling wines: Tanners Claret; Tanners Brut Extra Réserve; Rowlands Brook Semillon/Chardonnay; Chantarel Medium; Rowlands Brook Shiraz/Cabernet; Tanners Cava; Chantarel Red; Domaine de Rieux; Choix du Roy Red; Choix du Roy Medium

As you amble along Wyle Cop on one of the horseshoe bends in the Severn, what first strikes you as the Old Curiosity Shop in fact turns out to be the antiquated premises of Tanners' shopfront. Behind it lies an equally Dickensian office and cellar complex, practically unchanged in 153 years of business. Just in case there were any lingering doubts that you were in Tanners country, the numerous pictures of prize-winning Shropshire sheep on the office walls testify to the Tanners lineage – gentleman farmers and wine merchants to Middle England since 1842.

Family-owned and independent, Tanners embodies the solid virtues of the English country wine merchant: personal service with a friendly smile and an extensive list of well-chosen, quality wines bought by a team of five – Richard Haydon, Stephen Crosland, Mark Motley and of course Richard Tanner and his son James. The list is mailed to 12,000 customers nationwide – with a strong presence in the West Country, the Midlands and Wales – while two-thirds of the company's sales are to hotels and restaurants.

If 26 Wyle Cop is the old-fashioned façade, Tanners' informative list, which runs to over 100 mouthwatering pages, supplemented by a regular chatty newsletter appropriately called *Talking Tanners*, is the modern shop window for the company's wares. No stone, pebble or slate is left unturned in the effort to cover a range of wines from as many interesting estates in as many regions and countries as possible. Tanners house wines are reliable and good value, as is the broad selection of over 60 'Recommended Wines for Everyday Drinking'.

Like the family solicitor, who covers everything from drink-driving to divorce, Tanners, too, aims to supply all wines to all people, making it one of the most catholic wine merchant specialists in the country. The claret list, which goes back as far as 1961, is as vertical as it's broad, Rhônes include the best of Domaine du Vieux Télégraphe, Château de Beaucastel and Ryckwaert, while the Burgundy list is liberally sprinkled with growers of the calibre of the Dauvissat-Camus, Thévenet, Henri Germain and Etienne Sauzet.

Germany is a strong feature of the list; England is present too, as might be expected; and there are several top-class growers from Italy, notably Allegrini, Aldo Conterno and Sandrone. The New World is well-represented, with a particularly strong Australia section which includes Jim Barry, Shaw & Smith, Cape Mentelle, Coriole, Rockford, Bowen Estate and Tim Adams. If you're having sleepless nights, keep the Tanners list by your bedside. If nothing else, it might inspire you to count sheep.

White

£3–5

FRANCE

Tanners Chardonnay, Vin de Pays d'Oc
££ / 2 / 1   15/20
Fresh, fruity, unoaked, well-crafted Chardonnay selected by Tanners from Domaines Virginie's extensive array of whites. The emphasis here is on clean, lemony crispness with some southern French weight rather than oak.

Tanners White Bordeaux, Sauvignon Sec, Anthony Sarjeant
££ / 2 / 1   15/20
Zesty, clean, nettley Sauvignon Blanc with good weight and concentration for a wine under £5. As with the Chardonnay, the attraction lies in the refreshingly unoaked, fruity style. Very moreish stuff.

1994 Les Vignes d'Hauressat, Vin de Pays des Côtes de Gascogne, Bernard et Jean-Marc Sarran

££ / 2 / ▌ 15/20

A traditional, attractively weighted Gascon white in which pear and crisp apple fruitiness are flecked with flavours of aniseed and white pepper. Pretty complex for a basic Gascon white.

£5-8

AUSTRALIA

1993 Jim Barry Watervale Rhine Riesling, Clare Valley

£££ / 2 / ▌ 16/20

Rich, oily, aged Clare Valley Riesling made by the eccentric Barry family. Complex, lime-scented and dry, it's the sort of wine which should continue to mature nicely for another few years yet – one of the well-kept secrets of fine Clare Valley Riesling.

FRANCE

1994 Apremont, Les Rocailles, Pierre Boniface, Vin de Savoie

£££ / 2 / ▌ 16/20

A rich, spicy, complex Alpine white which may be familiar to anyone well-heeled enough to have taken a skiing holiday in Val d'Isère. Although it's relatively light in alcohol at 11.5 per cent, its flavours are so concentrated that it tastes considerably weightier. An intriguing and unusual wine.

1994 Muscadet de Sèvre-et-Maine sur lie, Fief de la Brie, Auguste Bonhomme

££ / 2 / ▌ 15/20

Priced at just over £5, Auguste Bonhomme's traditional Muscadet is ripe, weighty, concentrated and very well made, showing some lemony, *sur lie* grip and attractive length of flavour. When Muscadet is as good as this, it makes you realise how pleasant unoaked wines can be.

Over £8

FRANCE

1992 Corton Blanc Grand Cru, Domaine Chandon de Briailles
£££ / 2 / ➧   19/20
A wine which reminds you that when it's great, white Burgundy
is incomparable. This is a rich, subtle, multi-faceted Côte de
Beaune Grand Cru white with powerfully toasty, fresh butter
aromas, leesy, unfiltered complexity and a steel girder of acidity
underpinning the lemony fruit concentration. Stunning stuff,
even at over £30.

GERMANY

1989 Riesling Auslese Trocken, Weingut Schales, Rheinhessen
£££ / 3 / ➧   16/20
Softly mature, full-bodied, honeyed Riesling from a family-owned estate
in Flörsheim-Dalsheim, which can trace its roots – the family rather than
the vines, that it – back to the late 18th century. It's unusual to find
dryish Auslese in England, a style which is more common in fancy
German restaurants.

Red

£3–5

FRANCE

Tanners Claret, Peter A. Sichel
£££ / 2 / ➧   15/20
Soft, ripe, aromatic, juicy young claret showing plenty of the Merlot
grape's lush fruitiness. Peter Sichel obviously reserves some of his best
vats for faithful old customer Tanners.

£5–8

ARGENTINA

1992 Gauchos Lurton Cabernet Sauvignon, Mendoza

££ / 2 / ⚱   15/20

A rich, spicy American oaked style of Cabernet Sauvignon made by France's
most widely travelled winemaker, Jacques Lurton. It's still youthful, but this
attractive, well-structured red has softened nicely with age.

FRANCE

1994 Château du Grand Moulas, Côtes du Rhône-Villages, Marc Ryckwaert

£££ / FB / ➴   16/20

Rich, vibrant, heady southern Rhône red with plenty of spice and
chocolatey concentration. Marc Ryckwaert's famously low-yielding
vines have produced a Côtes du Rhône-Villages of great power and
finesse.

1992 Cuvée de l'Arjolle, Vin de Pays des Côtes de Thongue, Teisserenc

£££ / 2 / ⚱   16/20

A ripe, fleshy, attractively structured Languedoc blend of Cabernet
Sauvignon and Merlot, which proves that the South of France can
compete on price and quality with Bordeaux. It's a supple, grassy,
almost Right Bank style, which should appeal to lovers of St-Emilion.

1989 Château Abiet, Médoc, P. Vialard

£ / MB / ⚱   14/20

A traditionalist's claret showing plenty of tannins and mature, farmyardy
notes. We found the aftertaste a little dry and rustic. Ready to drink now.

1990 Château La Grande Maye, Côtes de Castillon

£££ / MB / ⚱   16/20

Soft, beautifully oaked, Merlot-based claret from the Right Bank
appellation of Côtes de Castillon, showing the ripeness and richness of
the 1990 vintage. This classic petit château is excellent value at just over
£6.50 a bottle.

ITALY

1993 Dolcetto d'Alba, Sandrone
££££ / MB / ♪   17/20
Lively, exuberant Dolcetto from one of Piemonte's best exponents of the style with masses of damson and berry-fruit characters and considerable length of flavour. Why anyone would want to drink a Beaujolais cru when they can buy something as joyously juicy as this is a mystery to us.

SPAIN

1990 Lar de Barros Tinto Reserva, Bodegas Inviosa
££ / FB / ♪   15/20
An old-fashioned Rioja-like blend of Tempranillo, Garnacha and Graciano from the southwestern Spanish region of Extremadura. This is a tannic, spicily oaked red with lots of robust extraction and supple underlying raspberry fruitiness.

Over £8

AUSTRALIA

1992 Bowen Estate Coonawarra Cabernet Sauvignon
££ / FB / ◞   16/20
An aromatic, minty Cabernet Sauvignon from Jim Bowen, one of Coonawarra's relatively small producers, with fine silky tannins and a deceptive elegance, given that the wine weighs in at a bruising 15 per cent alcohol by volume.

FRANCE

1992 Auxey-Duresses, Michel Prunier
££ / MB / ♪   15/20
Light, appealing, honestly fruity Côte d'Or Pinot Noir with a rustic bite. It's a fragrant grower's red, which could only come from Burgundy.

1991 Cornas La Geynale, Robert Michel
££ / FB / ⌐   16/20

Attractively tarry, fresh Syrah with good cassis fruit concentration and
hefty, drying tannins for added backbone.

Rosé

£3–5

FRANCE

**1994 Domaine de Limbardie Rosé, Vin de Pays des Coteaux de
Murviel**
££ / 2 / ⌐   15/20

A fruity, ripe, bubblegummy blend of Grenache and Syrah grapes made
in a refreshingly modern, thirst-quenching style. A wine that would taste
as good on a rainy day in Shrewsbury as under the azure skies of the
Mediterranean.

Sparkling

£5–8

SPAIN

Tanners Cava
£££ / 2 / ⌐   15/20

Creamy, surprisingly elegant Cava made by Conde de Caralt with some
toasty, lemony fruit, and showing none of the characteristic bitterness
of Spain's leading sparkling wine.

Fortified

£5–8

SPAIN

Tanners Mariscal Manzanilla

£££ / 2 / ¦   16/20

Salty, light, superfresh Manzanilla from Hidalgo, one of Sanlúcar's best bodegas. A tangy, aromatic, softly textured dry Sherry.

Tanners Very Fine Old Sanlúcar Amontillado

£££ / 2 / ⌐   16/20

Soft, dry, nutty, orange peel scented Amontillado from Hidalgo, with fresh acidity and tannic grip. The sort of delightfully traditional style which could restore Sherry's good name.

Over £8

PORTUGAL

Tanners Finest Vintage Character Port

££ / FB / ⌐   15/20

Sweet, chocolatey, robustly tannic Port from Churchill Graham. The fruit sweetness is highly attractive, but we found the tannins a little rustic for our taste.

THOMAS PEATLING

Head Office: Westgate House, Westgate Street, Bury St Edmunds, Suffolk IP33 1QT

Telephone: 01284 755948

Hours of opening: Monday to Saturday 9.00am to 5.00pm. Some branches have longer opening hours and are open on Sundays

Number of branches: 26

By-the-case sales: Yes

Bottle sales: Yes

Facilities and services: Free glass loan, sale or return

Cellarage: Yes. Further details supplied on request

Home delivery: Yes. Free local delivery, and £3 per single case delivery to UK mainland, free delivery for orders of two cases or more

Discounts: Yes: 5 per cent on unsplit cases

In-store tastings: Yes, every weekend in all branches. Peatlings Wine Festival is an annual tasting event with over 100 wines to taste; entrance fee is £7.50

Special offers: Monthly promotions featuring new wines, discounts on single and multi-bottle purchases

Top ten best-selling wines: Not supplied

Where some merchants are happy to put out wine lists that look as if they've been bashed out on a 1930s typewriter with a fading ribbon and a couple of duff keys, Thomas Peatling Pope has taken the designer route. The result is a stylish blend of typefaces, colours and pictures complete with the obligatory lacunae of white space.

Whether all this helps to sell wine is another matter. On occasion, we've found the list uninformative and difficult to use. Minimalism is all very well, but how does Peatlings expect its customers to spend £28.25 on a bottle of 1985 Hermitage La Chapelle if it doesn't provide *any* information about the wine (other than the fact that it's red and comes from the Rhône)?

Perhaps this is unfair, but there's a vague sense of missed opportunities in Bury St Edmunds. With 26 branches concentrated in East Anglia and a showcase shop in Farringdon, Peatlings ought to be better known.

Buyer and Master of Wine Robin Crameri has put together an idiosyncratic and occasionally daring range of wines. Choosing to bottle domaine-sourced red Burgundies from the likes of Lucien Boillot and Domaine de l'Arlot in Suffolk was an innovative way to offer fine Pinot Noir at affordable prices. And the claret range, from Cru Bourgeois level right up to the Crus Classés, is extensive and generally well-picked.

Not everything we tasted this year was as successful. The Alsace selection was overpriced, as was a rather dull Vin Santo, but there were some good new discoveries too. Hanging Rock from Australia is a super producer and Peatlings' 1993 Minervois, Cuvée des Meuliers has to be one of the best-value reds we've tasted from the Languedoc.

As we went to press, there were rumours that parent company Greene King was looking to sell Thomas Peatling. Interested suitors apparently include Thresher and Victoria Wine. There's nothing wrong with either operation, but we'd like to see Thomas Peatling remain with its current owners. Its prices are good, especially on older wines, and its selection of Ports, Burgundies, Spanish wines, German Rieslings and clarets deserves an audience beyond the boundaries of East Anglia.

White

£3–5

FRANCE

1993 Premières Côtes de Bordeaux, Côte de la Reine
££ / 6 / ½   14/20
A sweet, almond pastry, honeyed alternative to Sauternes, priced for those on their uppers.

GERMANY

1994 Rheinhessen Kabinett Halbtrocken, Saulheimer Domherr Kabinett
£ / 4 / ½   13/20
Produced in a medium-dry style and showing some grapey, floral fruit, this is a Liebfraumilch substitute for grown-ups.

ITALY

1994 Pinot Grigio, Le Veritière
££ / 2 / ½   15/20
Produced at the go-ahead Gruppo Italiano Vini in Verona, this is a well-priced, pear and peach perfumed, fruity white with attractive carbon dioxide freshness and acidity.

£5–8

FRANCE

1993 Muscat Reserve, Bennwihr
0 / 2 / ½   13/20
Coarse, slightly tart Alsace Muscat made at the Bennwihr co-operative. We're not that keen on the electric blue label either.

1993 Tokay Pinot Gris, Bennwihr
£ / 2 / ⌐   14/20

Fresh, smoky, reasonably concentrated Tokay Pinot Gris, also from the Bennwihr co-operative. Choose this in preference to the Muscat.

1993 La Mouline, Bourgogne Blanc Chardonnay
££ / 2 / ⌐   15/20

A full, sweetish, unoaked Chardonnay with ripe, buttery fruit and the crisp acidity of the 1993 vintage. A good house white Burgundy.

GERMANY

1993 Avelsbacher Altenberg Riesling, Hohe Domkirche, Mosel
££ / 4 / ⌐   15/20

A little shy on perfume at the moment, presumably due to its relative youth, but this Mosel Riesling is crisp and attractive on the palate, with green apple fruit flavours and well-integrated, honeyed sweetness. It should age nicely over the next five years.

Over £8

AUSTRALIA

1994 Hanging Rock, 'The Jim Jim', Sauvignon Blanc
££ / 2 / ⌐   16/20

From the cool Macedon mountain ranges in Victoria, this is a dry, intensely aromatic, almost New Zealand-style Sauvignon Blanc, with elderflower and gooseberry crispness and zesty fresh acidity. One of Australia's best Sauvignons. And no, we haven't a clue who or what Jim Jim is.

1994 Hanging Rock Victoria Chardonnay
££ / 2 / ⌐   16/20

Despite packing 13 per cent alcohol, this is an extremely elegant Chardonnay by the well-upholstered standards of Australia. Made by John Ellis, it's a lemony, grapefruity style with a deft touch of oak for extra complexity. Every bit as good as the Sauvignon Blanc.

FRANCE

1993 Mâcon-Viré, Domaine de Roally
£££ / 2 / ❧   17/20
Based in the village of Viré, Henri Goyard is one of the best producers in southern Burgundy, making intensely concentrated,
unfiltered Chardonnays from low-yielding vineyards. This is rich
and extremely refreshing stuff, with beautifully judged weight
and acidity.

ITALY

1987 Vin Santo Toscano di Caratello, Riccardo Falchini
£ / 6 / ❧   14/20
A golden, mature example of Tuscany's famously idiosyncratic dessert
wine style. This is a fortified (not all are) Amontillado Sherry-like white,
but with more of the sweetness of a commercial Oloroso. One for
dunking your cantuccini biscuits.

Red

£3–5

AUSTRALIA

1994 Peatlings Shiraz/Cabernet
0 / MB / ❧   13/20
A basil-scented, off-the-wall, basic Australian red, this is a curious blend
from southeastern Australia, whose slight sourness rather put us off.

FRANCE

1991 Vin de Pays des Coteaux de la Cèze
£ / FB / ❧   14/20
From Domaine Maby in the Gard region of southern France, this is a dry,
chunky, rustic red with chocolatey tannins.

1993 Syrah, Coteaux du Languedoc

£££ / FB / ➥-   15/20

In defiance of the strict *appellation* laws, which forbid the naming of the grape variety on the label, this inky, firm, blackberry fruity and slightly extracted Languedoc red is a good buy at under £4.

1993 Minervois, Cuvée des Meuliers

£££ / MB / ◗   16/20

Stunning value at £3.75, this deeply coloured, Syrah-rich Minervois shows you why the Languedoc-Roussillon is the most exciting region of France at the moment. We defy Bordeaux, the Rhône and Burgundy – not to mention the New World – to come up with anything as deliciously drinkable as this aromatic, sandalwood-spicy and blackberry fruity red at this sort of price.

1990 Château La Bourguette, Bordeaux Supérieur

0 / FB / ◗   13/20

A dry, robust, chunky claret which would fail its exams at charm school. *Supérieur* is not the word that immediately springs to mind.

SPAIN

1992 Viña Valoria Cosecha, Rioja

££ / MB / ◗   15/20

A fruitier, less oaky style than the same winery's Gran Reserva, this is a Rioja with a touch of vanilla oak and attractive orange peel and raspberry fruitiness.

£5–8

AUSTRALIA

1992 Dennis McLaren Vale Shiraz

££ / MB / ➥-   15/20

Made by Peter Dennis rather than Minnie the Minx or Desperate Dan, this *Beano* reader's wine is a pure, American oaked blend with well-harmonised alcohol, vanilla and chocolatey fruit flavours. The oak could do with a bit more time to settle.

FRANCE

1990 Château Roc-Taillade, Médoc
££ / MB / ⬤   15/20

In spite of its cheap, grubby label, this Thos Peatling-bottled claret is an extremely well-made Médoc red with full, ripe tannins and the juicy, cassis and cherry fruitiness and supple texture of the 1990 vintage. A really good 'luncheon' claret.

Over £8

FRANCE

1992 Nuits St-Georges Domaine de l'Arlot, Premier Cru
££ / MB / ⬤   16/20

Bottled in this country by Thomas Peatling to keep the price reasonable, Domaine de l'Arlot's Premier Cru Pinot Noir is smokily fragrant and full of wild strawberry fruitiness, well-judged vanilla oak and faintly rustic tannins. At just over £10, a good price for a Premier Cru red Burgundy.

1990 Château Laplagnotte-Bellevue, St-Emilion Grand Cru
£££ / MB / ➡   16/20

Chocolatey, well-oaked St-Emilion showing the supple texture and abundant fruit flavours of the 1990 vintage on the Right Bank. It's drinking extremely nicely now, but with its firm tannic structure should age well for another five years. Decently priced at under £10.

SPAIN

1985 Viña Valoria Gran Reserva Rioja
££ / MB / ⬤   16/20

Mature, brick-red Rioja made in an ultra-traditional style with delicate gamey fruitiness and dry, leafy, coconutty oak. A wine for lovers of classic Rioja.

Sparkling

Over £8

FRANCE

Champagne Brusson Père et Fils Private Cuvée
£££ / 2 / 1   15/20
An attractively youthful Champagne with some reserve wine for added
complexity, showing the strawberryish exuberance of the Pinot Noir
and Pinot Meunier grapes. A well-selected house Champagne at an
excellent price.

Fortified

Over £8

PORTUGAL

Warre's Fine Old Port
£ / FB / ⬤   15/20
This Fine Old Port began life as the 1996 Warres, but was hijacked by
Peatlings and aged in large oak casks for a further 10 years, making it an
unusual cross between a Tawny and a Vintage Port in style. The result is
a curious wine with tannins which are rather heavy for a Tawny and a
hard, spirity bite. It's also very pricey at over £25.

THE *GRAPEVINE* GUIDE TO CROSS-CHANNEL SHOPPING

'Ere we go, 'ere we go, 'ere we go – a reprise

You're standing in the not particularly busy aisle of a French hypermarket in Calais or Boulogne thinking about buying some cheese or pâté to take home. All of a sudden, from nowhere, hordes of trolley-toting bargain hunters descend like locusts on the booze department before struggling back to their transit vans, Range Rovers or more modest Minis, loaded to the gunwales with alcohol.

You can almost pinpoint the arrival time of the latest train or ferry from Folkestone or Calais. Since the Channel pipeline – sorry, Tunnel – opened, cross-Channel shopping has become an increasingly popular pastime for thirst-crazed Brits. A recent survey estimated that 1 in every 10 bottles of booze consumed in this country is now bought overseas, most of it in the Channel ports.

Have they heard, we wonder, that things are not quite as exciting as they were back on that foam-splashed day in January 1993, when a million corks popped to the tune of the Minimum Indicative Limit? New Year's Day 1993 was the starting pistol for the biggest free-for-all for the British consumer since Dale Winton's *Supermarket Sweep* TV game show.

Over the past year, however, the pound has plummeted out of the sky like a kamikaze pilot, while the French increased VAT from 18.6 per cent to 20.6 per cent at the beginning of August 1995. As Katrina Thom of The Grape Shop in Boulogne put it, 'The exchange rate was FF8.70 to the pound when we opened in 1993. Last year it was FF8, and now it's down to FF7.50.' Which all boils down to the fact that buying French wines is no longer quite such a good deal – not unless Jacques Chirac decides to devalue, that is.

When once it was a simple matter to save £1.50 by buying a bottle of wine in France, now the gap between UK and French prices is narrowing, especially on more expensive wines. Pay in sterling and you can also get stung by the varying exchange rates given by different stores. When we visited the Channel ports in August, we found the exchange rate was FF7.35 at Tesco, FF7.42 at Sainsbury's, FF7.50 at The Grape Shop and La Maison du Vin and a comparatively generous FF7.69 at Victoria Wine.

Richard Harvey of La Maison du Vin in Cherbourg and St-Malo confirms the ill-effects of the exchange rate on business, so he has absorbed the VAT increase in his prices. He still believes there are bargains to be had, but mainly on table wines in the FF15 to FF50 category and on Champagne and sparkling wines where the duty is higher.

Everyone must do his (or her) Duty

In his November budget, the Chancellor decided not to raise the duty on drink, declaring wisely that 'the increase in legitimate cross-border shopping in alcohol and tobacco, and in smuggling . . . have inevitably meant some loss of duty to the Exchequer and pressures on the British drinks industry. No Chancellor can remain unmoved in the face of this.'

So did he cut duties to bring them more closely into line with those of his European partners? Er, not exactly. In fact, in a last-minute about-turn, he raised the tax on drink a few days after the budget. The result was that the saving on duty marginally increased. At the time of going to press, UK duty is £12.64 a case excluding VAT on table wines (compared to FF2.04 in France) and £18.06 a case on Champagne, sparkling wines (FF4.92 in France) and fortified wines with between 15 and 22 per cent alcohol. That's a saving (on duty alone) of just over £1 a bottle on table wine and £1.50 on fizz, Port, Sherry, Madeira and fortified Muscats.

So the prediction by the independent consultancy, London Economics, that Britain would follow the likes of Denmark, Canada and Ireland by cutting duty rates to halt the flow of cross-border booze has not yet come to pass. The Treasury is still not convinced that lower duty rates would produce a corresponding increase in drink sales, and with it, revenue, despite the fact that the duty increases in the last budget have resulted in falling UK sales of whisky and beer.

1996 and all that

Encouraged by the success of pioneers such as EastEnders and The Grape Shop, a battalion of heavy artillery has followed in the wake of the advance guard. Sainsbury's are still in the Mammouth complex in

Calais, while Tesco and Victoria Wine have opened at the new Cité de l'Europe in 1995. The Wine Society continues to serve members who motor to Hesdin, Richard Harvey has set up a second Maison du Vin in St-Malo, and The Grape Shop in Boulogne has just set up shop in Calais.

Of the bigger players, Tesco has invested the most heavily, with a 25,000-square-foot temple of booze, the largest on the continent, called Vin Plus. Well-placed in the Cité de l'Europe, with an exit right on the car park, the brightly lit, spacious new Tesco lists over 1,000 wines, with around 250 specially selected as add-ons to the range available in the UK. Janet Lee, Tesco's wine buying controller, says that 'Tesco was losing custom in Britain as a result of cross-Channel sales. We saw Vin Plus as the best way to get it back.'

The I-Speak-Your-Weight-style machines installed in Vin Plus not only read the price of the bottle as you scan it past the screen, but then give you the sterling equivalent. A coded warning to British consumers to think twice before buying? Perhaps. Savings vary widely at Tesco, from nearly £10 on a bottle of Dom Pérignon to a mere 83 pence off a bottle of Stoneleigh New Zealand Chardonnay – less than the difference in duty.

Perhaps it's something to do with the lacklustre performance of the Shuttle, but one of the surprising things about the Cité de l'Europe is that, although ostensibly built for cross-Channel traffic, this giant America-style mall seems to be frequented more by French than British shoppers. A chance for the New World to enter the French psyche via its palates? If French shoppers suddenly start seeing the wines of Chile, Australia, Brazil and Canada as chic, as appears to be happening, who knows, there could be a revolution.

Off your trolley? – What and where to buy

If the choice of wines, beers and spirits available to the cross-Channel shopper was bewildering last year, it's even more confusing this year now that the Cité de l'Europe has opened its vast gates at the Calais entrance to the Channel Tunnel. The best savings to be made, as Richard Harvey mentioned, are on Champagne, sparkling wines and still wines between FF15 and FF50. And the lower the price of the wine, the greater the saving.

Without wishing to be too chauvinistic, the fact is that British-owned supermarkets and stores are still the best places to buy in France, although French outlets such as Leclerc, Auchan and Mammouth have some attractive deals on Grande Marque Champagnes and classed growth claret.

Most cross-Channel shoppers make for Calais. Boulogne is served by the Seacat and St-Malo and Cherbourg by longer and more expensive crossings. But that shouldn't put you off for a second. All three towns are considerably more attractive than Bootleg City and they contain at least one top-notch wine merchant.

In the most enlightened outlets, such as The Grape Shop in Boulogne and La Maison du Vin in Cherbourg and St-Malo, you can take your pick of estate wines and growers' Champagnes. You can even come across a smattering of wines from New World countries, too. Stumble into the wrong retailer, though, and you're likely to encounter considerable variation in the quality and range of wines available.

What's your limit?

The rules governing cross-Channel buying have not changed since last year. The first point to remember is that as long as you are buying wine for your own use (and that includes parties, weddings and other celebrations), you can bring as much booze into the country as the axle on your vehicle will bear.

If not for personal consumption, you are breaking the law by carrying smuggled goods. Bootleg booze (the first smugglers used to hide drink inside their boots) is anything you plan to sell to someone else without paying duty. In 1995, the owners of Death Cigarettes lost a test case designed to show that they could run a business bringing tobacco across the Channel without having to pay duty. The courts quickly nipped that one in the bud along with any plans the more enterprising members of the wine trade may have had to try the same thing with wine.

Customs can stop you while you're travelling and ask whether the wine or beer you're carrying is really for your own consumption. If you don't want them turning up at the wedding like the proverbial bad one-pence piece, carry some evidence of any impending celebration with you (a packet of party poppers is unlikely to satisfy Her Majesty's Customs officers).

The limits – or, to use the jargon, Minimum Indicative Levels – are the point at which Customs starts to ask if the goods cross the dividing line between personal and commercial. The current limits are 90 litres of table wine (of which not more than 60 may be sparkling), 20 litres of fortified wine, 110 litres of beer and 10 litres of spirits. If you want to bring back more, the burden of proving it's for your own consumption is on you.

Au revoir to all that

So this is still a good time to buy wine in France, as long as you don't get carried away. In 1995, an article appeared in a quality newspaper not a million miles from one of our own, cataloguing the brilliant wines the author had bought at a French warehouse-type operation on a day-trip to Calais. While there was nothing wrong with the wines, it turned out, on closer scrutiny, that almost all of them could have been bought more cheaply in the UK.

The French hypermarkets are still struggling to keep up. Last year we felt that the likes of Auchan and Mammouth had started to tailor their wine ranges to British palates. This year, we couldn't see any significant improvements. Not all French retailers, however, are entirely driven by price and *appellation contrôlée* wines. Shops like Perardel, Le Chais and Bar à Vins can still surprise you with their range and quality.

The day may not be too far distant when the French hypermarkets prove a match for the likes of Sainsbury's or Tesco, but until now, it's the British who have taken the initiative. Which is why we've decided to concentrate this year on what the British retailers have to offer.

SUPERMARKET AND WINE SHOP ADDRESSES (BY PORT)

Boulogne
Auchan, Route Nationale 42, 62200 St Martin lès Boulogne (21 92 06 00)
Le Chais, Rue des Deux Ponts, 62200 Boulogne (21 31 65 42)
Intermarché, 62360 Pont de Briques (21 83 28 28)
The Grape Shop, 85–87 Rue Victor Hugo, 62200 Boulogne (21 30 16 17 or 0171 924 3638 in UK); Gare Maritime, 62200 Boulogne (21 30 16 17)
Prix Gros, Boulevard Diderot, 62200 Boulogne (21 30 43 67)
Les Vins de France, 11 Rue Nationale, 62200 Boulogne (21 30 51 00)
The Wine Society, Rue Fressin, 62140 Hesdin (21 81 61 70)

Calais
Bar à Vins, 52 Place d'Armes, 62100 Calais (21 96 98 31)
Le Chais, 67 Boulevard Jacquard, 62100 Calais (21 97 47 00)
EastEnders, 110–112 Rue Mollien, 62100 Calais (20 67 81 75)
The Grape Shop, 40 Rue Phalsbourg, 62100 Calais (21 85 99 64)

Intermarché, 56 Avenue Antoine de St-Exupéry, 62100 Calais (21 34 42 44)

Mammouth, Route de Boulogne, 62100 Calais (21 34 04 44)

Marco's Calais Wine & Beer, Rue de Judé, Zone Marcel Doret, 62100 Calais (21 97 63 00 or 0181 875 1900 in UK), and Unit 3A, ZA la Français, 62231 la Coquelles (21 82 93 64)

Perardel, Zone Industrielle Marcel Doret, 190 Rue Marcel Dassault, 62100 Calais (21 97 21 22)

Pidou, Zone Industrielle Marcel Doret, 190 Rue Marcel Dassault, 62100 Calais (21 96 78 10) and Quai de la Loire, 62100 Calais (21 46 07 67)

J. Sainsbury Bières, Vins et Spiritueux, Mammouth Centre, Route de Boulogne, 62100 Calais (21 34 04 44)

Le Terroir, 29 Rue des Fontinettes, 62100 Calais (21 36 34 66)

Tesco Vin Plus, Unit 122, Cité de l'Europe, 62231 Coquelles (21 46 02 70 or 01992 632222 in UK)

Victoria Wine, Unit 179, Cité de l'Europe, 62231 Coquelles (21 82 07 32)

Cherbourg

Auchan, Centre Commercial Contentin, 50470 La Glacerie (33 44 43 44)

Continent, Quai de l'Entrepôt, 50104 Cherbourg (33 43 14 11)

Leclerc, 21 Rue des Claires, 50460 Querqueville

La Maison du Vin, 71 Avenue Carnot, 50100 Cherbourg (33 43 39 79 or 01929 480352 in UK)

Wine & Beer Company, Centre Commercial Continent, Quai de l'Entrepôt, 50100 Cherbourg (33 22 23 22)

Dieppe

Intermarché 76370 Rouxmesnil Bouteilles (35 82 57 75)

Leclerc, 76370 Etran-Martin Eglise (35 82 56 95)

LC Vins, 1 Grande Rue, 76200 Dieppe (35 84 32 41)

Mammouth, ZAC Val Druel, 76200 Dieppe (35 82 65 50)

Roscoff

Les Caves de Roscoff, Zone de Bloscon, Ateliers 7–9, 29680 Roscoff (98 61 24 10 and 0171 376 4639 in UK)

St-Malo

La Maison du Vin, 12 Rue Georges Clemenceau, St-Servan, 35300 St-Malo (99 82 69 54)

USEFUL TELEPHONE NUMBERS:
Customs and Excise Single Market Unit: 0171 620 1313
Hoverspeed: 21 46 14 14 (France); 01304 240101 (UK)
P&O Ferries: 21 46 10 10 (France); 0181 575 8555 (UK)
Brittany Ferries: 98 29 28 28 (France); 01705 827701 (UK)
Stena Sealink: 21 46 80 00 (France); 01233 647047 (UK and European head office)
Sally Line Ferries: 28 21 13 42 (France); 0171 409 2240 (UK)
Eurostar: 0181 784 1333 (UK)

THE GRAPE SHOP *** (*)

Address: Gare Maritime, 62200 Boulogne

Telephone: 00 33 21 30 16 17

Hours of opening: Monday to Friday 10.00am to 7.30pm

Also at: 85–87 Rue Victor Hugo, 62200 Boulogne

Telephone: 00 33 21 33 92 30

Hours of opening: Seven days a week 9.30am to 9.30pm

And: 40 Rue Phalsbourg, 62100 Calais

Telephone: 00 33 21 85 99 64

Hours of opening: Seven days a week 9.30am to 7.30pm

Managers: Managing director Martin Brown; general manager Katrina Thom

Payment methods: Access, Visa; sterling cheques and cash; French francs

Discounts: Quantity discounts by negotiation

In-store tastings: Yes

English spoken: Yes

Compared to the mayhem of Bootleg City, Boulogne is a walled haven of tranquillity, with considerable charm and character. There is a market in the town square and the authentic French cheeses of Philippe Olivier. L'Huitrière is an affordable restaurant dispensing fresh fish while at the Vole Hole, a tiny bar in the old village, you can slake your thirst in entertaining company with several of mine hosts' – Pam Cook and Roger Young's – Franziskaner weissbiers.

More to the point, for lovers of the grape, there's The Grape Shop. Last year we garlanded it with the *Grapevine* cross-Channel wine merchant award, and despite strong competition down the road from the new Tesco, it's still the best independent wine merchant in the Channel ports, with an unequalled range of well-chosen wines from the Old and New Worlds and friendly service.

Originally started by Englishman Martin Brown in a former car hire office in central Boulogne, the main business is now transacted a few metres from the Seacat dock in a dried-hops-festooned mini wine warehouse style operation. Although the new shop has increased the floor area tenfold, it's still not big enough to cope with the hordes. Another shop in Calais should be open just before publication of the 1996 edition of *Grapevine*.

The Grape Shop is about as far away in range and style from a French hypermarket as it's possible to get. Although around two-thirds of the 800-odd lines are French, many are wines of quality and character from individual growers, Champagnes included. It still doesn't bring in much local trade, however. The Frenchwoman browsing when we visited in August ended up buying a bottle of Australian Chardonnay.

White

Under 20FF

FRANCE

Cuvée Jean-Paul, Vin de Table Sec
£ / 3 / 1   12/20
For not much more than the price of duty, you can buy this honeyed sweet-and-sour Loire white based on the Chenin Blanc grape variety.

1994 Terret, Vin de Pays, Côtes de Thau, Jacques Lurton
£ / 3 / 1   14/20
A modern, nutty, boiled sweets style white showing the fresh acidity of the Terret grape, formerly reserved for vermouth.

1994 Domaine de Papolle, Vin de Pays Côtes de Gascogne, Peter Hawkins
£ / 3 / ↑   13/20
From Gascony-based Englishman Peter Hawkins, who also makes Armagnac, this is a sweetish, grapefruity white made from grapes which are surplus to brandy distillation requirements.

Bordeaux Sauvignon, J Lebègue
0 / 2 / ↑   10/20
Tart, unripe Bordeaux Blanc with dilute Sauvignon Blanc character just about in evidence.

HUNGARY

1994 Gyöngyös Estate Sauvignon Blanc
£ / 3 / ↑   13/20
A Hungarian attempt to create a pungent New Zealand style, which falls a little flat. There's some sweet tinned pea and gooseberry fruitiness and plenty of acidity, but it all adds up to a bit of a goulash.

20–30FF

FRANCE

1994 Domaine de Saint André, Vin de Pays des Côtes de Gascogne
£££ / 2 / ↑   15/20
Smoky, Lapsang-Souchong-tea-like aromas followed by flavours of grapefruit and honeydew melon. If that sounds like a dog's dinner, it's well worth lapping up.

1994 Château Petit Roubié, Picpoul de Pinet, Coteaux de Languedoc, Olivier Azau
££ / 2 / ↑   15/20
An unusual organic white from southern France made from the local Picpoul grape and showing ripe, waxy, honeyed fruitiness, fresh acidity and considerable complexity for a wine at around 27 francs.

1994 Touraine Sauvignon Blanc, Domaine de Marcé
££ / 2 / ▌   15/20

Crisply aromatic, fresh, nettley Sauvignon with good intensity and a green apple bite. Just the sort of thing that's worth buying from the Channel ports.

1993 Chardonnay, Vin de Pays de Gard, Auvigue
££ / 2 / ▌   14/20

Made by a producer based in the Mâconnais region of southern Burgundy, this is a super-ripe, almost tropical, unoaked Chardonnay with but a single dimension to its name.

SPAIN

1994, Chardonnay, Castillo de Montblanc, Conca de Barbera
££ / 3 / ▌   14/20

Made in Catalonia by itinerant winemaker Hugh Ryman, this fresh, lightly oaked Chardonnay with its melon and green olive characters is pleasant enough in an inoffensive, boiled sweets style.

30–50FF

FRANCE

1993 Château des Grandes Noëlles, Muscadet de Sèvre-et-Maine Sur Lie
£££ / 2 / ▌   16/20

About as good as Muscadet *sur lie* gets, this soft, peachy-fruity Melon de Bourgogne with its yeast-lees zest and prickle of refreshing carbon dioxide, is a stunner. It also has a Certificate of Excellence from the Institute of Masters of Wine, but don't let that worry you.

1991 Château du Hureau, Vatan Saumur Blanc
£££ / 2 / ▌   16/20

From Philippe and Georges Vatan, this is a rich, ripely complex, honeyed Loire Valley Chenin Blanc made in a modern style with a sheen of vanilla oak.

1993 Bourgogne Aligoté, Sylvain Dussort
££ / 2 / ⅟   15/20

Made by a Meursault-based grower, this is surprisingly concentrated for the normally tart and acidic Aligoté grape. It's rich and peachy with just the right amount of oak for added complexity.

1994 Viognier Vin de Pays d'Oc, Ryman
££ / 2 / ⅟   15/20

A smoky, oak-influenced Viognier made in the Languedoc by Englishman Hugh Ryman. There aren't many good examples of the northern Rhône's rich and aromatic white grape to be found in the Midi, but this apricoty, spicy Viognier is a good buy at 35 francs.

1993 Jurançon, Domaine de Nays-Labassère
£££ / 4 / ⅟   16/20

Made from a blend of southwestern France's Gros and Petit Manseng grapes, this is an unusual medium dry white with flavours of acacia honey and grapefruit polished by vanilla oak. Like all the best Jurançon whites, the wine is blessed with zesty, balancing acidity.

1994 Mâcon-Villages, Vieilles Vignes, Cépage Chardonnay
£ / 2 / ⅟   14/20

Minerally, liquoricey Mâcon white with a little too much austere acidity for the weight of fruit. It makes you wonder how old the *vieilles vignes* really are.

NEW ZEALAND

1994 Marlborough Sauvignon Blanc, Highfield
£ / 3 / ⅟   14/20

This has the typical gooseberry-intense aromas of Marlborough Sauvignon Blanc, but tastes a little sweet and confected. You'd be better off saving your francs for the UK, where the range of Kiwi wines is far more interesting and extensive.

SOUTH AFRICA

1993 Graham Beck Chardonnay Lone Hill
0 / 2 / ▮   13/20

Coarse, over-oaked Robertson Chardonnay which lacks richness and length of flavour. Is there a fool on Lone Hill?

50–80FF

AUSTRALIA

1993 Old Vine Semillon, Grant Burge
£ / 2 / ▮   15/20

An old-fashioned, barley-sugared Barossa Semillon, partially concealed by a forest of oak. On this evidence, the New World is not The Grape Shop's strongest suit.

FRANCE

1994 Sancerre Jean-Max Roger, Les Caillottes
£££ / 2 / ▮   17/20

Like the 1993, which is available in the UK at Davisons, this is a complex, concentrated, minerally Sancerre with a cassis-scented character, grassy flavours and mouthwatering acidity. If Sancerre was always as good as this, it wouldn't be losing out to the New World quite so dramatically. We've yet to have a bad wine from Monsieur Roger.

1994 Pouilly-Fumé Jean-Claude Châtelain
££ / 2 / ▮   16/20

On the rich side for what Dave West of EastEnders down the road in cash-and-carry city calls a Polly Foom. This is intensely fruity, honeyed and concentrated with an edge of flinty austerity.

1994 Mâcon-Fuissé, le Moulin de Pont, Auvigue, Burrier & Revel
££ / 2 / ▮   15/20

Soft, full-bodied, modern white Burgundy from the Mâconnais domaine that sounds like a firm of French solicitors, with a touch of oak and some buttery Chardonnay richness.

1993 Bourgogne Chardonnay, Mestre-Michelot

££ / 2 / ♪   15/20

A well-made, if slightly charmless, Burgundian Chardonnay from Bernard Michelot, one of the best-known growers in Meursault. There's so much charry oak here that you could almost imagine yourself in the Hunter or Barossa Valley. Well, compared with Boulogne's Gare Maritime, that wouldn't be a bad alternative.

Over 80FF

FRANCE

1994 Condrieu, La Doriane, Guigal

£££ / 2 / ⌐   18/20

Quintessence of Condrieu with a subtle array of honeysuckle, peach and apricot fruit flavours, backed up by plenty of alcohol, concentration and intensity. This barrel-fermented, single-vineyard Viognier may be expensive at 150 francs a bottle, but we guarantee that Marcel Guigal's northern Rhône white will make your day. It certainly made ours.

1990 Château La Rame, Sainte-Croix-du-Mont

££ / 8 / ♪   16/20

Marmaladey, peachy, richly textured, nougat and almond like sweet white from a small and often underrated Bordeaux *appellation*. This botrytis-affected sticky is good enough to be mistaken for a Sauternes.

Red

Under 20FF

FRANCE

Cépage Merlot Vin de Pays d'Oc, Franck & Jacques Rigal

£ / MB / ♪   13/20

Soft, grassy, slightly sweet Languedoc Merlot with a faintly astringent aftertaste made with quaffing in mind.

ITALY

1992 Carignano del Sulcis Rosso
£££ / MB / 🍷   15/20
From Santadi on the island of Sardinia, this is a very attractive
Mediterranean red with spicy, herby rosemary and thyme-like aromas
and soft, strawberry fruitiness. Infinitely superior to any of the Italian
plonk you see on the shelves of French supermarkets.

20–30FF

ARGENTINA

1992 Navarro Correas Malbec
££ / MB / 🍷   14/20
In its unprepossessing frosted bottle, this is an interesting, old-
fashioned, smoky red made from Argentina's most widely planted quality
variety, the Malbec of Cahors. The basic fruit quality is good, so with
more up-to-date winemaking techniques this winery could be a star.

FRANCE

1993 Domaine des Plantades Merlot, Vin de Pays d'Oc
££ / FB / 🍷   14/20
Chunky, robustly fruity Merlot with charry oak flavours, blackcurrant
pastille fruit and a distinctive brush of the Mediterranean *garrigue*.

1993 Haut-Poitou Heritage, Cave du Haut-Poitou
££ / LB / 🍷   14/20
A fresh, grassy, easy-drinking Loire picnic blend of Cabernet Sauvignon
and Cabernet Franc made for summer days. By the time you read this,
you'll probably be contemplating something a little more robust.

1989 Château Toudenac, Bordeaux
££ / MB / 🍷   14/20
A soft, well-made Merlot-based Bordeaux rouge, which is starting to
brown at the rim. Still, there's some fruitcake juiciness to guide you to
the end of the bottle.

1994 Domaine de Terre Megère, Vin de Pays d'Oc
££ / MB / ‡   14/20
Made by Michel Moreau, this is a plummy, spicy Languedoc red with honest, robust fruitiness at an attractive 22 franc price.

1994 Domaine de Terre Megère, Les Dolomies, Coteaux du Languedoc
£££ / FB / ‡   15/20
From the same domaine and for only 6 francs more, this is a riper, more complex red, with chocolatey Syrah and Mourvèdre-derived fruit sweetness and concentration.

1992 Château du Seuil, Coteaux d'Aix-en-Provence
££ / FB / ‡   14/20
A heady, richly alcoholic Provençal red showing the wild strawberry aromas of the Grenache grape. On the threshold of the southern Rhône in both style and location too.

1993 Côtes du Rhône, Saint-Esprit, Syrah, Delas
£ / FB / ‡   14/20
Once you've hacked your way through the oak palisade, the core of this spicy, peppery, Syrah-based red is surprisingly insubstantial. Lots of sound and fury signifying not an awful lot.

1991 Côtes du Marmandais, Les Signatures
££ / MB / ‡   14/20
Côtes du Marmandais is a little-known southwestern *appellation* which produces rustic claret taste-alikes at reasonable prices. True to form, this is a grassy, soft Bordeaux blend with a dry, tannic aftertaste.

MEXICO

1992 L A Cetto Petite Sirah
£££ / FB / ‡   16/20
Based in the Baja California peninsula, L A Cetto is the only Mexican winery we know producing interesting, good quality wines from a variety of unusual red grapes. This peppery, richly upholstered red with its dense, smoky fruitiness is every bit as good as the winery's award-winning Cabernets from the late 1980s. Brilliant value at under 30 francs.

30–50FF

AUSTRALIA

1993 Oakland Cabernet/Mataro/Grenache
££ / MB / 🍷   15/20

Made by old Barossa hand Grant Burge, this is an aromatic, well-crafted red blend with tobaccoey American oak, mint and berry fruitiness and a lift of refreshing acidity.

1993 Salisbury Cabernet Sauvignon
£ / MB / 🍷   14/20

From Victoria's Alambie winery, this red has plenty of sweet raspberry, mint and cassis fruitiness with some coarse tannins poking through on the aftertaste.

FRANCE

1992 Domaine Capion, Vin de Pays d'Oc, Fûts de Chêne
££ / MB / ➰   15/20

Domaine Capion is less well known than its immediate Languedoc neighbour, Mas de Daumas Gassac, but at their best, Philippe Salasc's attractive red wines display some of the oaky concentration of Aimé Guibert's celebrated blend. This Cabernet/Merlot blend is sweetly oaked and packed with robust blackcurrant fruit.

1991 Corbières Cuvée des Pompadour, Fûts de Chêne
££ / FB / 🍷   15/20

With its spicy, angostura bitters nose, fresh acidity and well-handled oak, this is a modern, richly fruity Corbières with sturdy tannins.

1993 Chinon, Clos d'Isoré, Jean-Maurice Raffault
££ / MB / 🍷   15/20

A solid, earthy Loire Cabernet Franc with a redcurrant tanginess and dry tannins. The wine's a little austere at the moment, but should soften nicely with a year or two in bottle.

1993 Saint Amour, Domaine des Duc
£ / MB / 🏮   14/20

As its name implies, Saint Amour is usually one of the more elegant Beaujolais crus, but this hefty alcoholic number with its southern Rhône-like headiness is a heavyweight.

1993 Domaine Brusset Cairanne, Côtes du Rhône Villages
£££ / FB / 🏮   16/20

Made by the obsessive Daniel Brusset, this is a brilliantly ambitious Côtes du Rhône Villages with robust, concentrated fruit flavours encased in polished new oak.

1991 Château de Jonqueyres, Bordeaux Supérieur
££ / MB / 🏮   15/20

Soft, modern, plumply fruity claret with plenty of vanilla oak and a stylish dinner party label made by Jean-Michel Arcaute of Château Clinet fame.

1992 Château Hanteillan, Cru Bourgeois
££ / MB / 🏮   15/20

Catherine Blasco's Cru Bourgeois property, Château Hanteillan, regularly turns out seductive, accessible clarets even in lighter vintages such as 1992. This is a perfumed, toasty/oaky claret with soft, elegant fruitiness.

1990 Château de Panigon Médoc, Cru Bourgeois
££ / MB / 🏮   15/20

Better than the rather dry 1989 also stocked by The Grape Shop, this has some of the attractive ripe fruit and flesh of the 1990 vintage. It's an old-fashioned wine with a rustic edge.

1993 Domaine Ogereau, Anjou Villages
£££ / MB / 🏮   16/20

Produced by one of the best, but surprisingly little-known, domaines in the Loire Valley, this is the grassy essence of Cabernet Franc, with masses of colour, fragrance and concentration of stylish fruit. It's a very moreish wine, evidently made from low yielding vines.

1992 Bourgogne, Edmond Cornu

££ / MB / ¶   14/20

Well-priced for a basic Bourgogne Rouge, this is an honest, strawberry fruity house red style with a faintly rustic, dry aftertaste.

1994 Côtes du Rhône, Domaine du Châtelain, Delas

£££ / FB / ¶   15/20

A structured, blackberry-like, Syrah-based Côtes du Rhône with plenty of supple textured fruit to drape around the woodwork. Well worth 3 francs more than Delas' Saint Esprit Côtes du Rhône.

1992 Guigal Côtes du Rhône

££ / FB / ¶   14/20

The style of this apparently bottomless blend veered from Syrah towards Grenache in 1992, which resulted in a more ungainly style of wine. It's still good, but no longer exceptional value.

1992 Crozes-Hermitage, Bernard Chave

£ / MB / ¶   14/20

There's always a sense, on this herbaceous, slightly medicinal Syrah, that Bernard Chave (no relation, as far as we know, to the illustrious Gérard of Hermitage renown) was fighting a rearguard action against a difficult, watery vintage.

50–80FF

FRANCE

1992 Mercurey Domaine Lorenzon

££ / MB / ¶   16/20

When French wine tasters talk of 'animal' characters in a wine, they're referring to reds like this farmyardy, chocolatey Pinot Noir. There's a sheen of spicy new oak here, too, which gives the wine much-needed sophistication. Characterful stuff, not to be pooh-poohed.

1992 Château Peyreau, St-Emilion Grand Cru
£££ / MB / ♦   16/20
Proof that the Right Bank *appellations* of Bordeaux generally produced far better wines than those of the Médoc and Graves in 1992, this is a voluptuously and highly drinkable Merlot-based claret with lashings of coffee-bean oak and good length of flavour. Well-priced at just over 50 francs.

1992 Château Les Vimières le Tronquéra, Margaux
£ / MB / ♦   14/20
Masses of sawdusty French oak can't quite disguise the leanness of fruit underneath the lattice-work. Underwined oak, as American barrel-broker Mel Knox might have put it.

1990 Château Ramage La Batisse, Cru Bourgeois
££ / MB / ➥   16/20
Still a *Grapevine* favourite, this is a supple, concentrated, well-balanced Cru Bourgeois from one of the best vintages in the last decade. The new oak is starting to soften as the wine shifts into second gear. Not quite freewheeling yet.

ITALY

1991 Rocca Rubia Carignano del Sulcis Riserva
££ / FB / ♦   15/20
We know it says Riserva on the label, but we actually preferred the purity of the unoaked 1992. Still, this herby Sardinian red, made from the Carignan grape, is a highly individual style with plenty of thyme and plum-like fruitiness.

1994 Dolcetto d'Alba, Mascarello
£££ / MB / ♦   16/20
Highly aromatic and highly rated here at *Grapevine* HQ, this is a concentrated, idiosyncratic northwestern Italian red from ultra-traditionalist and garden gnome lookalike Mauro Mascarello. It's a floral, fresh fig, cherry and raspberry-like Dolcetto with a prickle of carbon dioxide derived from ageing on its fermentation lees.

Over 80FF

FRANCE

1992 Corton-Bressandes Grand Cru, Edmond Cornu
££ / MB / ➠   17/20
A modern, oaky, Grand Cru red Burgundy with masses of vanilla
spice, structure and wild strawberry fruitiness. This is a ripe,
concentrated Pinot Noir, which comes close to justifying its 179
franc price tag.

Rosé

Under 30FF

FRANCE

1994 Château du Seuil, Coteaux d'Aix-en-Provence
££ / 2 / ▮   14/20
A grassy, soundly made rosé, which has used the technique known as
saignée (where red grape juice is bled off at the start of the fermentation
to concentrate colour) to good effect. The wine has some boiled sweets
character and a little of the blackcurrant fruitiness of the Cabernet
Sauvignon grape.

Sparkling

30–50FF

FRANCE

Vouvray Brut, Vincent Rimbault
£££ / 2 / ▮   15/20
This is a youthful, but attractively honeyed Loire fizz with freshness and
balance, which presents the acceptable face of the sometimes rather
ugly Chenin Blanc grape.

Crémant de Bourgogne, Henri Naudin-Ferrand
£££ / 2 / ¶   15/20
Another good value French fizz, this time dominated by the Pinot Noir
grape and showing lots of vibrant, toasty, Champagne-like aromas,
texture and flavours.

50–80FF

FRANCE

Champagne Brut, Michel Loriot
££ / 2 / ¶   15/20
Made entirely from the Pinot Meunier grape, this is one of The Grape
Shop's cheaper Champagnes. It's youthful, light and a little bit tart, but
good value at the equivalent of just over £10.

Over 80FF

FRANCE

Champagne Serge Mathieu, Cuvée Prestige
£££ / 2 / ↦   16/20
A fragrant Pinot Noir dominated grower's Champagne with a
mouthfilling mousse, good weight and strawberry fruit richness. It's still
on the young side, so don't be frightened to stuff a few bottles under the
stairs.

Michel Genet Grand Cru Blanc de Blancs, Chouilly
£££ / 2 / ¶   17/20
**Still priced at under 100 francs, and still one of the best bargains
in the Channel ports, this is a structured, complex, creamy
grower's Champagne made entirely from Chardonnay grown in
the Côte des Blancs to the south of Epernay.**

Champagne Brut Spécial, Georges Gardet, Chigny-lès-Roses
£££ / 2 / ¶   17/20
**A powerful, malty, Pinot Noir dominated Champagne, which
shows a surprising amount of richness and maturity for a non-**

vintage wine. Perhaps it derives its complexity and full flavour from a good dose of reserve wine. Extremely well-priced at under 100 francs.

Champagne Rosé, Michel Genet Brut, Chouilly

££ / 2 / 1   16/20

Pale pink, softly fruity Pinot-tinged blend from grower Michel Genet. The bubbles are a little coarse, but there's enough creamy fruit to make this fizz a good buy at around 100 francs.

LA MAISON DU VIN ***

Address: 71 Avenue Carnot, 50100 Cherbourg

Telephone: 00 33 33 43 39 79

Hours of opening: Monday to Saturday 9.30am to 6.30pm, Sunday 11.00am to 6.00pm (but may vary)

Manager: Andrew Gordon

Also at: 12 Rue Georges Clemenceau, St-Servin, 35400 St-Malo

Telephone: 00 33 99 82 69 54

Hours of opening: Monday to Saturday 9.00am to 6.00pm, Sunday 10.00am to 4.00pm

Manager: Rebecca Sutherland

Payment methods: Access, Visa; Eurocheques; sterling and French francs

English spoken: Yes (also Japanese in the Cherbourg shop)

In-store tastings: Yes

Richard Harvey's original La Maison du Vin, set up to cater to the yachting and Volvo set in Cherbourg, has proved so successful that the Dorset-based merchant opened another in St-Malo this year. 'We thought about Caen and Le Havre,' says Master of Wine Harvey, 'but plumped for St-Malo because it's a major tourist destination, if not necessarily a major ferry destination.'

The St-Malo store, unlike its Cherbourg equivalent (which stands opposite a neo-Stalinist breeze-block building), is in a busy street in the centre of town. The locals were curious, it transpires, when visiting builders from Bournemouth told them that the refitted shop was going to sell porno videos and sex aids.

The location inevitably attracts more local French shoppers, even without the French ticklers. 'In Cherbourg we're known as an English operation, but in St-Malo more French people come in because it feels like a shop and there's a French person behind the counter.'

As far as the wines are concerned, the formula is much the same in both shops – a well-selected range of 150-odd lines with the emphasis on France but the occasional bottle from the New World to keep the British happy. 'We have a big selection open for tasting in the shops, but I don't see the point of having a huge range of wines just for the sake of it,' adds Harvey.

Harvey buys mainly from growers in France, most of whose wines are worth trying, especially those from Châteaux Coujan, Bauduc, Richard and the Languedoc's Domaine de la Ferrandière. There's also a brilliant-value Champagne taste-alike from Limoux's Domaine de l'Aigle.

Harvey, to his credit, refuses to sell Liebfraumilch or cheap Niersteiner. In fact, he sells more red wine than white, with the majority priced between FF15 and FF50 – what Harvey calls 'the value area'. He is careful to keep his prices competitive: 'We try to offer a saving of £1 a bottle on anything that's available in the UK.' He also chose to absorb the increases in French VAT himself in order to keep his prices stable.

Despite a more difficult second year, owing to the falling pound and the decline in numbers of British holidaymakers, Harvey is upbeat. 'I'd be interested in opening another one in Calais or Boulogne,' he says. 'Hopefully, we've got a bit of a name now.' He sure has – La Maison du Vin is one of the best places to buy in the Channel ports, with knowledgeable staff and wines which represent good value for money. Now for Calais?

White

Under 20FF

FRANCE

1994 Blanc de Blancs Dry Vin de Table de France, Donatien-Bahuaud

£ / 3 / ♪   12/20

A basic, faintly honeyed blend of Chenin Blanc and Chardonnay. If you're crossing the Channel purely with the aim of saving money, this is a decent buy at around 13 francs.

1994 Domaine de Lacquy, Comte J V de Boisséon, Vin de Pays de Terroirs Landais, Sables Fauves

£ / 3 / ♪   13/20

From the sands of southwestern France's Landais region, this is a sweetish, tart Ugni Blanc based white which could easily be mistaken for a Vin de Pays des Côtes de Gascogne.

GERMANY

1994 Mosel-Saar-Ruwer Riesling Select, Josef Friedrich

£ / 5 / ♪   13/20

With its lime peel and pistachio nut aromas, this is a fruity, fragrant Mosel white which tastes more like a Müller-Thurgau than a Riesling.

20–30FF

FRANCE

1994 Château Coujan, Coteaux du Languedoc

££ / 2 / ♪   15/20

A fifty/fifty blend of the Rolle and Clairette packaged in a Bordeaux bottle, this is a rich, aniseedy Languedoc white with apricoty aromas and fresh acidity. Château Coujan was one of the pioneers of modern winemaking in the Midi.

1994 Domaine du Vieux Chai, Muscadet de Sèvre et Maine Sur Lie

£ / 1 / ≬   **14/20**

A creamy, white pepper scented Muscadet with crunchy acidity and some of the leesy prickle you expect from a *sur lie* style.

1993 Château de Beauregard, Saumur

£ / 1 / ≬   **14/20**

Made by Philippe Gourdon, this is a modern, dry, peachy Chenin Blanc with fresh fruit flavours and a tart aftertaste.

1994 Château Sercillan, Bordeaux Blanc

££ / 2 / ≬   **14/20**

A soft, waxy, Semillon-influenced white Bordeaux made in a traditional style by Alain Vironneau.

1993 Bergerac Sec, Château Richard

££ / 2 / ≬   **15/20**

A ripe, almost Alsace Pinot Blanc-like Bergerac white from English geologist Richard Doughty's southern French estate. A fat, weighty, organic style, which was deliberately picked late for extra stuffing.

1994 Château Bauduc, Les Trois Hectares, Bordeaux Sec

£££ / 2 / ≬   **16/20**

The owner this time is Welsh, not English – not that nationality has anything to do with the excellence of David Thomas' Graves-like white Bordeaux. Made almost entirely from 50-year-old Sémillon vines, this is an attractively oaked, complex style with plenty of weight and refreshing grapefruity acidity.

1994 Domaine de la Ferrandière Sauvignon Blanc, Vin de Pays d'Oc

££ / 2 / ≬   **14/20**

Well-priced Languedoc Sauvignon from an unusual domaine whose ungrafted vines are kept free of the deadly vine pest phylloxera by flooding. This is not, we're assured, a back-door form of irrigation. The result is a modern melon and grapefruit scented Sauvignon with plenty of zing.

1994 Domaine de la Ferrandière Chardonnay, Vin de Pays d'Oc
£££ / 2 / ❭   15/20
From the same domaine, this is a fat, unoaked, butter and boiled sweets
style Chardonnay with plenty of body and balancing acidity.

1992 Bergerac Sec, Richard Doughty, Château Richard
£££ / 2 / ❭   16/20
A curiosity which may not be to everyone's taste, this is a late-picked
Sémillon-based white which was left on its lees in tank to pick up extra
concentration of fruit. It's a massively rich, bread and buttered toast-like
super-ripe white, which should please the adventurous-spirited.

30–50FF

FRANCE

1993 Riesling Domaine Rieflé, Vin d'Alsace
£ / 2 / ❭   14/20
A fat, oily Alsace Riesling with lime juice and petrol notes. We found the
acidity a little out of kilter.

1993 Gewürztraminer Domaine Rieflé, Vin d'Alsace
£ / 3 / ❭   14/20
Another flabby, overalcoholic Alsace white, which has the characteristic
spiciness and lychee aromas of the Gewürztraminer grape, but burns a
little on the back palate.

Red

Under 20FF

FRANCE

La Maison Rouge, Vin de Table de France
£ / LB / ❭   12/20
The counterpart to Richard Harvey's Blanc de Blancs Dry, this is a softly
sweet, Gamay-based Loire quaffer from *négociant* Donatien Bahuaud.

1993 Domaine de la Ferrandière, Cabernet Sauvignon, Vin de Pays d'Oc

£££ / MB / ▌   15/20

The best-selling wine at La Maison du Vin, Yves Gau's intensely grassy, unoaked Cabernet Sauvignon is an attractively priced claret taste-alike from the Languedoc.

1993 Domaine de la Ferrandière, Merlot, Vin de Pays d'Oc

£££ / MB / ▌   16/20

Same producer, same domaine, different grape variety. This soft, supple, unoaked Merlot reminded us of Côtes de Castillon claret, right down to the faintly rustic, dry aftertaste. The only difference is that, at around 16 francs, this Languedoc red is half the price.

20–30FF

FRANCE

1991 La Forge, Ribonnet, Vin de Pays de la Haute-Garonne Cabernet/Merlot

££ / MB / ▌   15/20

Made in the Languedoc by Swiss producer Christian Gerber, this is an oaky, chocolatey, structured red with Bordeaux pretensions. It's well-built with good concentration and intensely flavoured, green pepper fruitiness. In this instance, the pretensions are justified.

1991 Fitou, Domaine de Roudène

£££ / FB / ▌   15/20

A powerfully aromatic, black pepper scented Fitou with the robust angostura bitters fruitiness of the best Languedoc reds.

1992 Domaine Salvat, Côtes du Roussillon

£££ / MB / ▌   15/20

Cinnamon-spicy, oaked blend of Carignan, Syrah and Grenache with smooth tobaccoey tannins, cassis and pepper fruit flavours and refreshing acidity.

1993 Château de Beauregard Saumur
£ / MB / ♪   14/20

A light, grassy Loire Valley Cabernet Franc with soft, juicy, unoaked fresh characters and palate-cleansing acidity. A good 'Déjeuner sur l'Herbe' red.

1993 Château Richard, Bergerac
£££ / MB / ♪   15/20

From Richard Doughty's organic domaine, this is a smooth, unoaked, strawberry fruity Bergerac red with malty, chocolatey undertones. Very moreish stuff.

1993 Château Bauduc, Bordeaux Supérieur
££ / MB / ♪   14/20

A robust and rather charmless red Bordeaux from Welshman David Thomas with rustic dry tannins and some redeeming flavours of coffee bean and dark chocolate.

1992 Domaine Duseigneur, Côtes du Rhône
£££ / FB / ♪   15/20

Old-fashioned, surprisingly concentrated Côtes du Rhône from a difficult vintage down south. It's a warm, Grenache-based style softened by the use of the carbonic maceration technique and rounded off with a full-bodied bite of alcohol and tannin.

30–50FF

FRANCE

1991 Château Florestan, Premières Côtes de Bordeaux
££ / MB / ♪   15/20

A plump, fleshy, Merlot-based claret with the emphasis on juicy fruit rather than oak. 1991 was a disastrously small vintage, but the wines that *were* made were surprisingly concentrated in some instances.

1994 Beaujolais Villages, Joël Rochette
£ / MB / ♪   14/20

A soft, strawberryish, alcoholic Beaujolais which finishes up rather soupy and lacking in definition. More like a straight Beaujolais than a Beaujolais Villages.

1993 Château Grava-Lacoste, Graves

££ / MB / 🍾   15/20

A grassy, well-priced, unoaked red Graves from Anne-Marie Leglise, showing plenty of robust tannin and fruit concentration.

1993 Bourgogne, Henri Prudhon

£££ / MB / 🍾   16/20

One of the best buys at La Maison du Vin, this is a lightly oaked, modern Bourgogne Rouge with plenty of red fruits flavours and solid, medium weight tannins for structure. Good, honest Pinot Noir at an equally honest price.

1992 Lirac, Domaine Duseigneur

£££ / FB / ↠   16/20

Another excellent buy at around 34 francs, this is a Provençal blend of 60 per cent Grenache topped up with Syrah and Cinsault. The spiciness of the Syrah comes through strongly on the palate to complement the rich, chunky flavours of the old vine Grenache and Cinsault. Super stuff.

Rosé

20–30FF

FRANCE

1994 Château Richard Bergerac Rosé

££ / 2 / 🍾   14/20

A modern, cherry-skin rosé, which has used the *saignée* technique to produce a concentrated, deeply coloured pink Bergerac from Cabernet Sauvignon, Cabernet Franc and Merlot grapes.

Sparkling

30–50FF

FRANCE

Crémant de Loire, Gratien & Meyer
£££ / 2 / ⟩   15/20

From a firm which is as well-known for its Champagne as its Loire fizz,
this is a creamy, youthful Chenin Blanc which has added Chardonnay
and Cabernet Franc grapes for extra flavour and finesse.

Domaine de l'Aigle Tradition, Brut Chardonnay/Pinot Noir
£££ / 2 / ⟩   16/20

With its barrel-fermented base wine, this Aude blend of Chardonnay and
one-third Pinot Noir is a rich, concentrated fizz with toasty, cool climate
crispness and a malty, savoury tang. Limoux's homage to Bollinger.

J. SAINSBURY BIÈRES, VINS ET SPIRITUEUX ** (*)

Address: Mammouth Centre, Route de Boulogne, 62100 Calais

Hours of opening: Monday to Saturday 9.00am to 8.00pm

Telephone: 010 33 21 34 04 44 (Mammouth, ask for Sainsbury's)

Manager: Christophe Delamaere

Payment methods: Access, Visa; sterling and French francs

Discounts: No, but special offers on selected wines and beers

English spoken: Yes

In-store tastings: No

The snappily named J. Sainsbury Bières, Vins et Spiritueux was the first British supermarket to set up shop on the other side of the Channel when it opened on 27 April 1994. With only 3,000 square feet of space, it's the smallest store Sainsbury's has opened since the 1930s, but it is dedicated entirely to the sales of – you guessed it – *bières, vins* and *spiritueux.*

JSBVS, if we may be so bold, is tucked away at one end of the French hypermarket Mammouth. When we visited in August, it was a rather similar story to the previous year. Loads of Brits piling it high in Mammouth, while JSVBS looked a little forlorn by comparison. It may also suffer from competition with Tesco's giant Vin Plus, as shoppers turn their backs on Calais and head for the modern Cité de l'Europe complex.

The range runs to around 280 beer, wine and spirits lines familiar to regular JS shoppers back in Britain, including a well-selected mixture of French, other European and New World wines. But in most cases, the savings hardly cover the difference in duty. As we said last year, if the venture is to prosper, JS will have to offer its British customers a little more in the way of temptation.

For details of wines available in Calais, see the main Sainsbury's entry on page 263–90.

TESCO VIN PLUS ****

Address: Unit 122, Cité de l'Europe, 62231 Coquelles

Telephone: 00 33 21 46 02 70 (01992 632222 in the UK)

Hours of opening: Monday to Saturday 9.00am to 10.00pm. Closed Sunday.

Manager: Thierry Vander Putte

Payment methods: Sterling, French francs, Eurocheques and all major credit cards.

Discounts: No

English spoken: Yes

In-store tastings: Yes, four to five wines available every day for tasting

At around 25,000 square feet of wines, beers, spirits and soft drinks, Tesco Vin Plus is the biggest off-licence in the Channel ports, and probably the most extensive in Europe. By comparison, J. Sainsbury Bières, Vins et Spiritueux looks like a phone booth.

To judge by the large number of shoppers wandering up and down its broad aisles, Vin Plus is already a success. There's certainly plenty to keep the wine lover interested. As well as the main Tesco list from the UK, there are additional wines chosen specially for the French market. In the main, according to buying controller Janet Lee, these are 'better Burgundies, clarets, Alsace whites and parcels of cheaper products'.

The total Calais range runs to more than 1,000 wines. Some of the France-only bottles are particularly outstanding – we were impressed by the 1993 JM Johnstone, Vin de Pays d'Oc Sauvignon Blanc and the 1990 Château Les Chalets Cru Bourgeois.

Prices and savings seem to vary widely, however. There's a machine in the middle of the store to tell you how much a wine would cost in

Britain, converting French francs into its increasingly pathetic sterling equivalent. In some cases – the Stoneleigh Sauvignon Blanc, for example – all this does is convince you that you'd be better off buying the wine back home.

Nevertheless, this is a very impressive operation, selling everything from Château d'Yquem to teabags and cheese. 'We sell plenty of expensive wines here,' says Janet Lee, 'even though the duty differential tends to be less over £5.' It certainly looks like a bold move. Rather than sticking a toe in the water, Tesco has dived in off the top board. The explanation? Simple. 'We were losing custom in the UK because of cross-Channel shopping,' says Lee. Setting up something like Vin Plus is a good way to win some of it back.

The following wines are a selection of bottles available exclusively at the Cité de l'Europe.

Tesco Vin Plus also stocks the entire Tesco range. See page 318–42 for further details.

White

20–30FF

FRANCE

1994 Grand Frais Bordeaux Blanc, Yvon Mau
££ / 3 / 〗   14/20
A soft, nettley, sweetish Bordeaux blend of Sauvignon and Sémillon with 10 per cent Muscadelle from the ubiquitous Yvon Mau, showing apple and pear flavours and fresh acidity.

1993 Sauvignon Blanc, J M Johnstone, Vin de Pays d'Oc
£££ / 2 / 〗   16/20
Stunning value for money at around 23 francs, this is a lees-aged Languedoc Sauvignon Blanc with richness and grapefruity complexity. It's one of the best and most refreshing Languedoc whites we've had all year.

30–50FF

FRANCE

Cuvée Océane Jurançon Sec
£££ / 2 / ♪   16/20
Made entirely from the local Pyrenean Gros Manseng grape, this is an
unusual, dry white with exotic mango aromas, good weight and crisp
lemony acidity. Well worth trying at around 30 francs, especially if
you've never come across Jurançon before.

1992 Riesling Graffenreben, Cave de Beblenheim
£££ / 2 / ♪   15/20
An aromatic, almost Muscat-like Alsace Riesling with zesty elegance and
lime-like fruitiness. It's a pleasure to find an Alsace Riesling of this
quality priced at 40 francs a bottle.

50–80FF

FRANCE

1993 Château du Seuil, Graves
£££ / 2 / ♪   17/20
Owned by a Welsh barrister who's since moved to the Graves
district of Bordeaux, this is a toasty, beautifully proportioned
white blend of Sémillon and 20 per cent Sauvignon Blanc. Oak
fermentation and stirring of the fermentation lees – known as
bâtonnage – have produced a stylish Graves. We're not sure if
Anthony Barton is thinking of suing because of the Château
Léoville Barton lookalike label, but he might meet his match in
court if he does.

1992 Riesling Schonenbourg, Grand Cru, Cave de Beblenheim
££ / 2 / ♪   16/20
A more powerful mouthful than the Graffenreben Riesling, this is a
complex, petrolly Alsace white made by Patrick le Bastard (we kid you
not), which is starting to develop some attractive bottle-aged maturity.
Good value for a Grand Cru.

1990 Gewürztraminer Sonnenglanz, Grand Cru, Cave de Beblenheim

££ / 3 / 🎄   16/20

A super-rich, concentrated rose petal and lychee style Gewürztraminer which manages to avoid the vulgarity of some overpoweringly scented Alsace whites.

1989 Riesling Vieilles Vignes, Cave de Beblenheim

£££ / 2 / 🎄   16/20

Vieilles Vignes in this case means more than 30 years old – the vines, that is, not the wine. It's a complex, minerally Riesling which has some of the kerosene notes of a mature Mosel, but the weight and body of an Alsace white. Apparently there's no truth in the rumour that Patrick is changing his name to Pierre.

Red

Under 20FF

FRANCE

Bordeaux Rouge, Chais Beaucairois

£££ / MB / 🎄   14/20

A price-fighting claret to meet the demands of the hypermarché competition from the likes of Carrefour, Mammouth and Auchan. This grassy, soft, unoaked Bordeaux Rouge stacks up rather well.

1993 Yvecourt Bordeaux Rouge

££ / 2 / 🎄   14/20

Another well-priced basic claret with soft, Merlot-based fruitiness, a nip of chewy tannin and a little more bottle age than the Chais Beaucairois.

1993 Domaine de la Perrière, Corbières

£££ / FB / 🎄   15/20

From the excellent Mont Tauch co-operative based in the boar-rich hinterland of the Languedoc, this is an angostura spice laden, sweetly ripe traditional blend of Carignan and Grenache leavened with 10 per cent Syrah for extra fruit and aromas. By the sometimes rustic standards of southern France, this is almost elegant.

30–50FF

FRANCE

1992 Château de Portets, 15 Barons, Graves
££ / MB / ♪   14/20
From a historic Gironde property, this is a chunky, farmyardy red with considerable backbone, given the relative lightness of the 1992 vintage. Good value at around 35 francs.

1993 Château Les Trois Moulins de Mazerolles, Premières Côtes de Blaye
££ / MB / ♪   14/20
An aromatic, cassis-scented claret made in a modern, lightly fruity style with good freshness and fruit.

1990 Château Les Chalets, Médoc Cru Bourgeois
£££ / MB / ♪   16/20
A funky, farmyardy claret made from old vines at Saint Christoly du Médoc, showing the ripe-fruit sweetness of the excellent 1990 vintage and plenty of firm structured tannins.

1992 La Tour de l'Impernal, Cahors, Côtes d'Olt
££ / FB / ➠   14/20
Made entirely from the region's Malbec grape at the Parnac co-operative, this is a traditional style of Cahors selected from the co-operative's best vines. Aged in new oak, it's an aromatically spicy red with the chewy tannins you'd expect.

50–80FF

FRANCE

1988 Château Fort Lignac, Haut Médoc

££ / MB / **16/20**

The second wine of Château Terrey Beaucaillou in St-Julien (we hadn't heard of it either, but we're assured it exists), this is nicely mature claret from the classically structured 1988 vintage with attractive leafy complexity and a sheen of vanilla oak. It's still on the firm side, so don't be afraid to hang on to it for another year or two.

1989 Château Moulis, Cru Bourgeois

£ / MB / **14/20**

From one of the oldest Crus Bourgeois in the Médoc, this is an extracted, foursquare claret with faintly grubby, old-fashioned oak.

1990 Château Les Grands Monteils, Pauillac

£££ / MB / **16/20**

One of the best reds we've had from *négociant* Yvon Mau, this is the second wine of Château Croizet-Bages in Pauillac. The wine's so seductively soft and ripely juicy that it reminded us more of a Right Bank claret than a Médoc.

1992 Château La Tour Léognan, Pessac-Léognan

£££ / MB / **16/20**

The second wine of Château Barbonnieux (another new one on the *Grapevine* team), this is an abundantly oaked, modern claret, which has made the most of a light vintage to produce an elegant, spicy red Bordeaux with surprisingly good length of flavour.

Sparkling

Over 80FF

FRANCE

Nicolas Feuillatte Premier Cru Brut
££ / 2 / ↑   15/20
Mature for a non-vintage Champagne, this Chouilly co-operative fizz has
plenty of rich strawberry softness and weight. Excellent value at the
equivalent of just over £10.

1986 Nicolas Feuillatte Champagne Cuvée Spéciale
£££ / 2 / ↑   17/20
**A big, powerful but finely balanced vintage Champagne with the
structure and complexity to age for a while yet. It's creamy and
richly fruity with toasty, textured, mouthfilling bubbles.**

VICTORIA WINE ****

Address: Unit 179, Cité de l'Europe, 62231 Coquelles

Telephone: 00 33 21 820 732

Hours of opening: Monday to Thursday and Sunday 10.00am to 8.00pm; Friday 10.00am to 9.00pm; Saturday 9.00am to 8.00pm

Manager: Jacqueline Brett

Payment methods: Access, Visa; sterling, French francs, Eurochqeues

Discounts: No

English spoken: Yes

In-store tastings: Yes, three to five wines available every day for tasting

We nearly had heart attacks in Calais this year. There we were in the Cité de l'Europe, clipboards in hand snooping outside Victoria Wine, when someone jumped out of the shop at us. It turned out to be someone who worked there, so desperate to meet customers that she came out into the Italian-style piazza to talk to us.

If ever a shop illustrated the fact that selling wine in France, even to British holidaymakers, is not the same as flogging it back in the UK, it is the new Victoria Wine in Calais. The shop is in essence a Victoria Wine Cellars, stuffed with the complete range available back home, but when we were there we saw almost no one come in to buy wine.

Things were sluggish to start with, according to Jacqueline Brett, but as more and more French people discover the shop, sales are improving. The store, it must be said, could be better placed, partially hidden as it is beneath a staircase. 'The French would rather come to us than Tesco round the corner,' she adds, 'because they prefer shops to supermarkets.'

Let's hope so, because Victoria Wine deserves to do well in France.

It's got enthusiastic staff, a good shop, one of the best ranges of wines in Calais and bottles open for tasting every day. All it needs is a few customers.

Victoria Wine's Calais store stocks the entire Victoria Wine Cellars range available in the UK. See page 387–413 for details. Savings vary, but prices are at least £1.50 a bottle cheaper.

THE WINE SOCIETY ***

French address: Rue Fressin, 62140 Hesdin

Telephone: 00 33 21 86 52 07

UK address: Gunnels Wood Road, Stevenage, Herts SG1 2BG

Telephone and membership enquiries: 01438 741177

Order office: 01438 740222

Hours of opening: Monday to Saturday 8.00am to 6.00pm (closed for lunch 12.30 to 1.45pm, Sundays and French public holidays)

Manager: Frédéric Picavet

Payment methods: Visa, Access; French cheques, banker's draft or French francs

Discounts: No

English spoken: Yes

In-store tastings: Yes

Although considerably more limited than that available in the UK, the Wine Society's range at its shop in the quaint French town of Hesdin, with over 100 wines and spirits to choose from, offers a good selection of the classics and the New World for any of its members to-ing and fro-ing between the UK and France.

The list is extensive enough to make bringing wine back from France, especially Champagne or sparkling wines for parties and weddings, a worthwhile proposition. More irreverent Society members, we suspect, pick up wines at Hesdin to surprise friends and perhaps even shock French winemakers as they pass through Hesdin on their way south for their holidays.

Since it opened for business on a corner of the little town's cobbled square, the Wine Society's showroom has recorded great activity, thanks to an average saving of between £12 and £15 per case. To give members the opportunity to taste a range of the Society's wines, two open evenings (contact the order office) are scheduled to take place in the Town Hall in the autumn, the latter, post-publication of *Grapevine*, on Friday 17 November 1995 from 6.30pm.

Bear in mind that to buy from the Wine Society at Hesdin, you have to be a member, which is considerably easier than being Jeremy Paxman trying to join the Garrick Club. In fact the Society is keen for as many new members as possible. All you have to do is contact them, ask for details of how to join and pay £20 for a one-off lifetime share.

Members travelling with Hoverspeed get the added benefit of discounts, and the Society provides a list of hotels in and around Hesdin.

White

20–30FF

FRANCE

1994 Le Prada, Côtes de Gascogne, Grassa
££ / 3 / 1   14/20
A full-bodied, faintly smoky Gascon white from Yves Grassa with a little bit of added sweetness to round out the grapefruity acidity.

1994 Grenache Vin de Pays de l'Hérault, Bésinet
££ / 2 / 1   14/20
A white wine with a delicate pink tinge, made at Delta Domaines near Béziers. This is soft, attractively flavoured, full-bodied and cool-fermented to get the most from the South's innocuous Grenache.

The Society's French Country White, Corbières
£ / 2 / 1   13/20
From the Languedoc and France's largest wine producer, Val d'Orbieu, this is a baked, heavy southern white with a sharpish note of acidity on the aftertaste.

The Society's Bordeaux Sauvignon, Peter Sichel
£ / 2 / ⅃   13/20
Neutral on the nose and slightly bitter and lacking in varietal character
on the palate, this is a clean, decent basic white Bordeaux from
négociant, Peter Sichel.

ITALY

1994 Cortese Alto Monferrato, Araldica
££ / 1 / ⅃   15/20
The native Cortese grape is the variety behind this distinctively Italian
white, with its angelica spice, baked apple and green olive characters
and a characteristic nip of acidity.

30–50FF

AUSTRALIA

1994 The Society's Australian Chardonnay, McLaren Vale
£££ / 2 / ⅃   16/20
Made at the McLaren Vale's outstanding winery, Wirra Wirra, this is a
fresh, citrus-fruit and peach-style Chardonnay with just the right amount
of toasty oak and refreshing acidity to bring you back for more.

FRANCE

1994 Château Bel Air, Bordeaux Blanc
£££ / 2 / ⅃   16/20
Also available on British Airways, where it's labelled as Tour de
Mirambeau, this is an equal parts blend of Sauvignon Blanc, Sémillon and
Muscadelle with minerally, unoaked fruit flavours and good grapefruity
concentration.

1994 The Society's Vin d'Alsace, Hugel
££ / 2 / ⅃   15/20
Blended by Wine Society buyer Marcel Williams at the Hugel winery,
this is an Edelzwicker-style blend of Sylvaner, Riesling, Gewürztraminer
and a touch of Muscat for extra perfume. It's a softly attractive, grapily

aromatic white with a crisp, dry finish. A good introduction to Alsace as you speed from Hesdin over the Vosges mountains towards Colmar.

1994 The Society's White Burgundy, Mâcon Villages, Dépagneux
££ / 2 / ½   15/20
A well-chosen white Burgundy, which is consistently and justly popular with Wine Society members, this is a delicately oaked, rich Mâconnais white, with its flavours and freshness enhanced by a spell on its lees in tank.

1993 Pouilly-Fumé, Bailly
££ / 2 / ½   15/20
A crisp, nettley Sauvignon Blanc with flinty, green apple aromas and appealing blackcurrant-leaf characters.

NEW ZEALAND

1994 The Society's New Zealand Sauvignon Blanc, Marlborough
£££ / 2 / ½   16/20
Made by the historic Auckland-based firm of Selaks, this is a tropical melon and mango-style Sauvignon Blanc, which is far more exotic than the elderfloral Marlborough norm. Crisp and fresh and well-balanced with the weight and intensity of flavour we've come to expect from New Zealand whites.

50–80FF

FRANCE

1994 The Society's Chablis, Moreau
££ / 2 / ½   16/20
A rich, all-tank-fermented Chablis, whose full, fat, buttery flavours reminded us of a Côte d'Or Chardonnay. Its cool climate Yonne origins are revealed by the zesty, crisply refreshing aftertaste.

1990 The Society's Gewürztraminer
££ / 3 / ½   15/20
When it comes to Gewürztraminer, the Hugel family pulls out the big

one, as the athletics commentator David Vine used to put it. We tasted this spicy wine last year and still think it's a good, weighty example of a take-it-or-leave-it grape, but needs drinking up before it goes to seed.

Red

20–30FF

AUSTRALIA

The Society's South Australian Shiraz/Cabernet
£ / MB / ▮   13/20
Lean, minty and rather obvious Aussie blend with a rasp of dry tannins. As the supply of cheaper Australian wines runs out, the quality appears to be dipping.

CHILE

The Society's Chilean Cabernet Sauvignon
£ / MB / ▮   13/20
A basic, blackcurrant pastille style red from the Carmen winery, whose whites and premium reds are considerably better than this decent if rustic red.

FRANCE

The Society's French Full Red, Peter Sichel
0 / FB / ▮   12/20
Plonky Roussillon blend with dry tannins, lots of colour and chunky chewiness. Strictly for the kitchen.

1993 Domaine de Limbardie, Vin de Pays des Coteaux de Murviel
££ / MB / ▮   14/20
From Henri Boukandara's estate in the Languedoc, this is a well-made Bordeaux-style red with fleshy, softly grassy fruit flavours, using the carbonic maceration technique for maximum suppleness.

1993 Minervois, Domaine du Moulin Rigaud
£££ / FB / ☛   16/20

Made by the La Livinière co-operative, this is a youthful, inky, richly aromatic Minervois blend of Syrah, Carignan and Grenache with freshness and elegance on the palate and flavours of black olive and thyme. One for the Mediterranean diet.

The Society's Claret, Peter Sichel
££ / MB / ♪   14/20

Considerably better than the cuvée we tasted last year, perhaps because this is largely from the 1993 vintage rather than the leaner 1992, this best-selling, green pepper scented claret is soft, juicy and well made.

1992 Cuvée de l'Arjolle, Vin de Pays des Côtes de Thongue, Teisserenc
£££ / 2 / ♪   16/20

A ripe, fleshy, attractively structured Languedoc blend of Cabernet Sauvignon and Merlot, which proves that the South of France can compete on price and quality with Bordeaux. It's a supple, grassy, almost Right Bank style, which should appeal to lovers of St-Emilion.

1989 Château Driholle, Bordeaux
££ / MB / ♪   15/20

A solid, old-fashioned, Merlot-based claret from the excellent bicentenary vintage with firm tannins and a core of ripe, fleshy, sweet blackcurrant flavours.

1992 Côtes du Rhône, Jaume
££ / MB / ♪   15/20

This is an attractive, softly spicy Grenache-based southern Rhône red produced by Claude and Nicole Jaume in the picturesque village of Vinsobres. Aromatic, rosemary-perfumed red with a surprising amount of fruit for the *'millésime du déluge'*. *Après nous* . . .

ITALY

1993 Barbera d'Asti Superiore, Araldica
££ / MB / ♪   15/20

From the excellent Araldica co-operative, this is a gamey, juicy Barbera with mouthwatering acidity and a touch of gently spicy, softening oak for balance.

1992 Chianti Rufina, Villa di Vetrice
££ / MB / ♪   15/20

From the Rufina hills above Florence, this is an old-fashioned but honestly fruity Sangiovese-based red from a winery which puts value for money before fancy labelling. It's tarry, youthful and plummy with nice fresh acidity and concentration.

SPAIN

1990 Señorio de Los Llanos Reserva, Valdepeñas
££ / MB / ♪   14/20

A leafy, dry, traditional Spanish red with tomato-skin aromas and some soft, raspberry fruitiness. Drink up.

1992 The Society's Rioja, Cosecheros Alavesas
££ / MB / ♪   15/20

Fruity, well-structured, aromatically oaked Rioja made in a modern style to bring out the red fruit flavours of the Tempranillo grape, which is the core of this savoury, coconutty red.

30–50FF

AUSTRALIA

1993 Bin 45 Cabernet Sauvignon, Lindemans
£ / MB / ♪   14/20

True to the Lindemans formula, this is softer, more velvety and blackcurranty than stablemate Penfolds' reds.

FRANCE

1993 The Society's Beaujolais Villages
£££ / MB / ♪   16/20

The best Beaujolais Villages we've tasted this year, the Wine Society's juicy, vibrant, raspberry and cherry-like Gamay from the house of Dépagneux is crunchy and delightfully drinkable.

1991 The Society's Crozes-Hermitage
££ / MB / ♪   15/20
From a vintage which was considerably better in the northern Rhône than the south, this is a fresh, aromatic, chocolatey Syrah from a co-operative which dominates production in Crozes-Hermitage.

The Society's St-Emilion, JP Mouiex
£ / MB / ♪   14/20
A dry, old-fashioned Right Bank claret with leafy tannins and some Merlot plumpness. The greenness of the 1992 vintage, on which this wine is based, shows through on the aftertaste.

50–80FF

FRANCE

1992 The Society's Châteauneuf-du-Pape, Domaine du Vieux Lazaret
£ / MB / ♪   14/20
On the light side for a Châteauneuf-du-Pape – not surprising, given the wet vintage – this is a charming, easy-drinking red which bears more resemblance to Côtes du Rhône than Châteauneuf – except on price.

Sparkling

30–50FF

AUSTRALIA

Seaview Brut
££ / 3 / ♪   15/20
A fresh, sherbety, highly drinkable Aussie fizz made from a hotch-potch of grape varieties by the sparkling wine tentacle of the giant Penfolds octopus.

Over 80FF

FRANCE

The Society's Champagne Alfred Gratien
££ / 2 / ⅛   16/20
From a Champagne house which has been slaking the thirst of Wine
Society members since 1907, this is a chocolatey, elegant Pinot-based
fizz, which is fermented in oak rather than the more commonly used
stainless steel tanks to give what the French call *le goût anglais*. No
wonder it's such a Wine Society stalwart.

WINES AVAILABLE IN THE UK ONLY

White

£3–5

ITALY

1994 Vernaccia di San Gimignano, Signano
££ / 2 / ⅛   15/20
A good example of one of Tuscany's more interesting local grapes (not
hard, mind you, when you're up against Trebbiano), this is a superfresh,
crisp, almondy white with attractive, almost quinine-like flavours and
good peachy fruit. Ditch the G & T . . .

£5–8

FRANCE

1994 Domaine de Gourgazaud Chardonnay
£ / 2 / ⅛   14/20
Designed with Oz-loving Francophiles in mind, this is an ultra-ripe,
tropical fruit salad Chardonnay with masses of smoky oak, but only one
dimension – even if it is a big one.

GERMANY

1993 The Society's Riesling, Wiltinger Klosterberg, Von Kesselstatt
£££ / 5 / ♪   16/20

Von Kesselstatt is one of the few top German estates to build a bridgehead in the UK, producing wines with great style and elegance at relatively attractive prices. This is a fresh, medium dry Riesling with typical Mosel flavours of honey, kerosene and lime zest.

SPAIN

1989 Marqués de Murrieta Blanco Reserva
££ / 1 / ►   16/20

A highly idiosyncratic Spanish white with Bourbon whisky barrel smokiness, austere acidity and tea-leafy fruit characters finishing with a Sherry-like tang. See what we mean about idiosyncratic?

Over £8

FRANCE

1992 Pernand Vergelesses, Les Caradeux, Chanson
£££ / 2 / ♪   16/20

A surprisingly high quality white Burgundy from a *négociant* which rarely makes the most exciting wines, this is an elegant, buttery, complex Chardonnay from a lesser-known *appellation* in the Côte de Beaune. Even Marcel Williams admits this is the first wine he's ever knowingly taken on from Chanson. Not quite going for a song, but almost, at just under £10.

Red

£3–5

FRANCE

1993 Château Les Palais, Corbières

££ / FB / ⌓   15/20

A Carignan-based, unoaked Corbières with a ripe, bitters-spicy aroma, employing the carbonic maceration technique to soften the more rustic characteristics of the traditional Mediterranean grape.

HUNGARY

1993 Villany Cabernet Sauvignon

££ / MB / ⌓   14/20

A minty, aromatic, almost Chilean-like Cabernet Sauvignon from the warm Villany region of southern Hungary. Jammy fruit flavours and youthful exuberance make this a good alternative to claret.

ITALY

1990 Salice Salentino Riserva

££ / FB / ⌓   15/20

A spicy, herby Mediterranean blend of Negroamaro and Malvasia Nera grapes with savoury, liquorice and bitter almond flavours and big, ripe, tarry tannins. This power-packed Puglian red gives you all the alcohol and flavour you could possibly want for under £5.

PORTUGAL

1991 Montado, Alentejo

£ / FB / ⌓   13/20

Made by the normally reliable firm of Fonseca, this is a raisiny, rustic southern Portuguese red with high acidity and robust, baked tannins.

More Indispensable Reference from Headline

DEBRETT'S GUIDE TO ENTERTAINING

CHARLES MOSLEY

The social rules governing entertaining are
no longer as clear cut and straightforward
as they once were. And, as the pattern of
modern society becomes ever more
complex, confusion as to how to deal with
any number of situations increases.
Debrett's Guide to Entertaining is the book
that will guide you smoothly and
confidently through the problems you are
likely to encounter in any social
circumstances:

*Dinner parties
*Dances and balls
*Cocktail parties
*Children's parties
*Business entertaining
*House parties
*Hosting sporting events
*Official receptions
*Entertaining royalty

NON-FICTION / REFERENCE 0 7472 4424 3

PECKISH BUT POOR

CAS CLARKE

Delicious Budget Recipes by the Author of *Grub on a Grant*

Cas Clarke's *Grub on a Grant* was hugely popular with students struggling with a single saucepan and a grant. *Peckish but Poor* is for would-be cooks who are ready to move on to more adventurous cookery and want to produce tasty meals on a still restricted budget.

The emphasis here is on easy-to-follow recipes using fresh produce with chapters giving recipes for spring, summer, autumn and winter showing how simple it is to make cheap and delicious dishes by keeping to food that is in season.

If you're short of time, money or experience, you'll find the uncomplicated, no-nonsense recipes in *Peckish but Poor* a brilliant way to build your confidence in the kitchen.

GRUB ON A GRANT
'...a useful little book for the absolute beginner.'
Prue Leith, *Guardian*
'...she reckons her recipes are foolproof, and so they are.' *Daily Telegraph*

NON-FICTION/COOKERY   0 7472 3937 1

A selection of non-fiction from Headline

THE DRACULA SYNDROME	Richard Monaco & William Burt	£5.99 ☐
DEADLY JEALOUSY	Martin Fido	£5.99 ☐
WHITE COLLAR KILLERS	Frank Jones	£4.99 ☐
THE MURDER YEARBOOK 1994	Brian Lane	£5.99 ☐
THE PLAYFAIR CRICKET ANNUAL	Bill Findall	£3.99 ☐
ROD STEWART	Stafford Hildred & Tim Ewbank	£5.99 ☐
THE JACK THE RIPPER A–Z	Paul Begg, Martin Fido & Keith Skinner	£7.99 ☐
THE *DAILY EXPRESS* HOW TO WIN ON THE HORSES	Danny Hall	£4.99 ☐
COUPLE SEXUAL AWARENESS	Barry & Emily McCarthy	£5.99 ☐
GRAPEVINE; THE COMPLETE WINEBUYERS HANDBOOK	Anthony Rose & Tim Atkins	£5.99 ☐
ROBERT LOUIS STEVENSON; DREAMS OF EXILE	Ian Bell	£7.99 ☐

All Headline books are available at your local bookshop or newsagent, or can be ordered direct from the publisher. Just tick the titles you want and fill in the form below. Prices and availability subject to change without notice.

Headline Book Publishing, Cash Sales Department, Bookpoint, 39 Milton Park, Abingdon, OXON, OX14 4TD, UK. If you have a credit card you may order by telephone – 01235 400400.

Please enclose a cheque or postal order made payable to Bookpoint Ltd to the value of the cover price and allow the following for postage and packing:

UK & BFPO: £1.00 for the first book, 50p for the second book and 30p for each additional book ordered up to a maximum charge of £3.00.
OVERSEAS & EIRE: £2.00 for the first book, £1.00 for the second book and 50p for each additional book.

Name ....

Address ....

....

....

If you would prefer to pay by credit card, please complete:
Please debit my Visa/Access/Diner's Card/American Express (delete as applicable) card no:

Signature .... Expiry Date ....